Wounded Knee II

Rolland Dewing

ISBN 0-9646780-0-4 (clothbound)
ISBN 0-9646780-1-2 (softcover)

Library of Congress
Catalog Card Number 95-92303

Cover and dust jacket designed by Larry Swanson

Printed in United States of America

 PINE HILL PRESS, INC.
Freeman, S. Dak. 57029

Contents

Introduction

Wounded Knee II is a completely revised and updated work. This new book has been edited to appeal more to the general public and includes several pictures and maps. It also contains added academic documentation and significant new sources. My approach has been to present a straight forward narrative in chronological sequence. The purpose is to provide a broad gauged, objective analysis of the 1973 occupation of Wounded Knee and of the important events preceding and following the confrontation.

Given the predisposition of many print and media accounts of the event, readers of this work should be rewarded with a more balanced perspective. My frame of reference always has been to tell the history as accurately and as completely as possible. Controversial issues are carefully documented with special emphasis on a broad spectrum of primary sources, which took years to develop. My unique advantage for this research has been my very close proximity to the Pine Ridge Reservation for the past twenty-six years. Obtaining the 25,000 page FBI file on Wounded Knee and AIM also helped secure a foundation for inquiry.

Besides a thorough analysis of the occupation from the perspective of the government, the Oglala Sioux, and AIM comprehensive studies of related incidents are included. Examples are: the 1972 murder of Raymond Yellow Thunder at Gordon, Nebraska, which ignited the first major confrontation with AIM in the region; the death of Wesley Bad Heart Bull, which precipitated the Custer riot in February, 1973; and the 1975 murders of FBI agents Ron Williams and Jack Coler on the Pine Ridge Reservation.

It is impossible to name everyone who has helped with this book in a short introduction. Most are identified in the footnotes and the bibliography. Some contributors deserve special recognition, though. Generous support from the Chadron State College Research Institute was indispensable. Invaluable assistance was rendered by Dewayne Gimeson and Jerry Ingram of the Chadron State College media center and print shop. Jerry Swanson, Agnes and Clive Gildersleeve's grandson, volunteered to illustrate the cover. My wife, Deloris, gave help and inspiration throughout the long process.

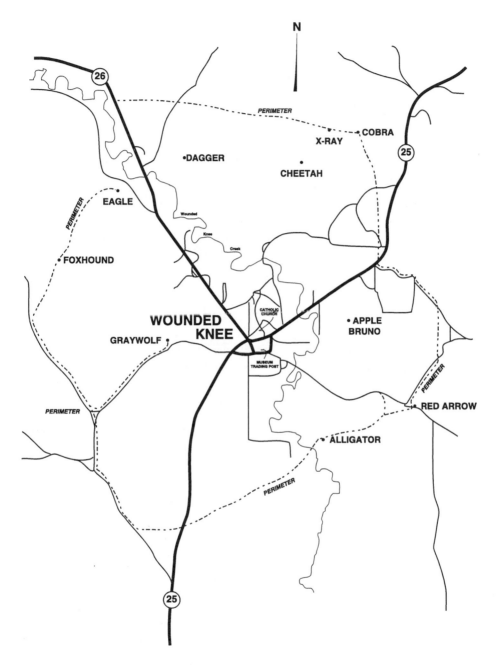

FBI map of Wounded Knee and vicinity during the height of the confrontation. Government roadblocks are located along the fourteen mile perimeter indicated by the dotted line.

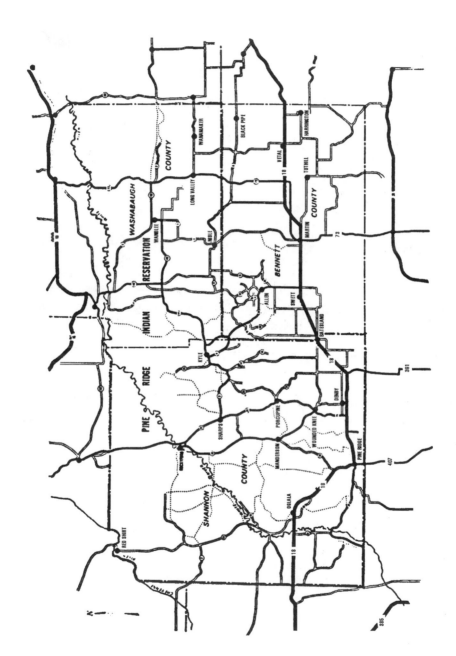

FBI map of the Pine Ridge Reservation accentuating roads.

America's Most Neglected Minority

G iven the European's superiority in technological development and their drive for material possessions, it was inevitable that the native people they encountered in the new world would be vanquished either by direct force or negotiations. In order to legitimatize the transfer of property European nations dealt with the Indians, as they called them, as independent sovereign nations—a concept not that clear to the Indians. Additionally, the Indians had no conception of "buying" and "selling" land. Because agreements made with the chiefs of one band frequently were not accepted by other bands, factionalism within tribes increased even before they were confined on reservations. The tribes could be divided on a general basis by those who cooperated with whites, known as progressives or "friendlies" and those who resisted white intrusion who were called conservatives or "hostiles." [1]

Until 1871 treaties were often used to define the relationship between Indian tribes and the United States. As the country filled up, treaties that created reservations, supplied provisions, and made at least token payments for land taken from the Indians became more expensive and the House of Representatives, which guarded its constitutional right to originate appropriation bills, balked at funding treaties ratified by the Senate only. The result was a compromise between the House and the Senate which provided that from 1871 on all government relations with Indians would be controlled by Congressional legislation instead of treaties, but treaties passed before that time were still in effect and the government continued to make agreements that were legally defined as treaties. Between 1778 and 1871 the federal government signed and ratified an estimated 371 treaties with Indian tribes. Eventually almost all of them were broken or abrogated in one way or another. [2]

Because of their western location on prairie lands that did not open for settlement until the more desirable land was occupied, serious treaty negotiations with the Teton Sioux did not begin until 1851. The Teton Dakotas are part of a gigantic linguistic family stretching from the east coast of North America to the Rocky Mountains. [3] The label Sioux was given to them by the Chippewas or Anishanabi, their neighbors and deadly enemies for over two hundred years. The Chippewas called them Nadowessi, "Snake-Like" or "Hated Enemy." French trappers made it Nadowessioux, and then merely used the last syllable.[4] Teton is derived from the word Tetonwan which means "Prairie Dwellers." As the name implies the Teton or Lakota Sioux represent the western Sioux, who migrated from southern Minnesota. The Sioux who remained near the Mississippi River, such as the Santee and Yankton are known as Dakota. The Tetons were divided into seven tribes, all of which still exist: Oglalas, Minneconjous, Brules, Blackfoot, Sans Arcs, Hunkpapas, and Two Kettles. Of the seven Teton tribes the Oglala were the most numerous and the most warlike. Oglala means scattered or divided and stems from the way they scattered out in small camps when they migrated to the plains.[5]

Considering the plains environment, the small group, the band, was most efficient in exploiting available resources. Tribal identity was an intermediate category between national and band identity; although it was very real, it was more the recognition of a common origin and kinship than of membership in a meaningful group. The Tetons had no national chiefs and no defined national council. At the tribal level there was not necessarily a sense of cooperation or any real commonality of purpose. The essential unit of social order was the band, tiyospaye. Tiyospaye means "a group of lodges" symbolizing a number of relatives who live together as a stable social group. The Oglala band usually varied from ten to twenty lodges with each lodge housing a nuclear family consisting of parents and unmarried children.

Often two or three of these tiyospaye would camp together, or very near one another, under a single chief. Each tiyospaye would defer to one as the chief of the group. Frequently the chiefs were brothers or cousins. The central institution was the band council, an informal organization consisting of all the respected males of the band. The council appointed a chief; although succession from father to son was common, it was by no means guaranteed. The chief was more of a father figure who was supposed to have the welfare of the entire group in mind. Dissenters were free to leave and join some other band or form a new one. [6]

A political murder further divided the Sioux in 1842, when Chief Bull Bear was killed by followers of a rival, Chief Smoke.[7] The Bear people became the southern element of the Oglala, and the Smoke people lived with the Brules at Spotted Tail Agency. Because of the divisiveness, it was impossible for the Sioux to present a united front when dealing with the whites.[8]

Warfare between the Chippewa and the Sioux in Minnesota increased as the Chippewa were forced constantly westward by the pressure of white settlement and superior firearms of the eastern tribes. The Chippewa obtained arms by trading with the French and English before the Sioux and were able to defeat them. The battle of Kathio about 1750 marked the end of Sioux domination in northern Minnesota. In 1827 the two tribes signed a permanent peace settlement at Fort Snelling, but a group of Sioux ambushed and killed seven Chippewa the evening of the agreement.[9] Even after Minnesota had become a territory and could boast of its modern capital, St. Paul, clashes occurred. The most memorial incident in St. Paul took place in 1852 at the corner of third and Jackson streets when a party of Chippewa ambushed a group of Sioux coming up from the river to trade in the stores of the city.[10]

As the Tetons gradually moved westward they were greatly assisted by the acquisition of horses from the Cheyenne around 1760, which they used effectively to gain control of the Black Hills area by 1775. The Tetons reached their greatest strength by 1850 when they controlled the Great Plains from the Rockies to the Missouri River and from the Platte River to the Canadian border.[11] Their domain was soon threatened, however, by the discovery of gold in California and the ensuing rush of settlers across the Oregon Trail.

Until the advance of the mining and transportation frontiers the government considered the Great Plains "One Big Reservation." Now the government felt the need to protect the westbound caravans from attack, so it was decided that specific boundaries for the various Plains tribes should be spelled out. In 1851 chiefs of the principal Plains tribes met with government officials at Fort Laramie, Wyoming, to formalize a treaty. In return for gifts, annuities, and bounties, the Indians agreed to accept carefully defined borders. The Sioux were assured the Dakota country north of the Platte River, the Mandan and Grosventres a triangle just east of the Yellowstone, the Assiniboin the region west of that river, the Crows a large area west of the Powder River, the Blackfeet the mountainous country around the headwaters of the Missouri, and the Cheyenne and Arapaho the foothills of the Colorado between the North Platte and Arkansas Rivers. There the chiefs were told they could live unmolested for all time.[12]

White encroachment prompted by new gold strikes in 1858 soon disrupted the equilibrium in Colorado. When the Arapaho and Cheyenne resisted the intrusion into their lands, the government attempted to place the two tribes on small reservations to isolate them. A bloody war erupted that did not end until 1865. Agitation for resistance against the whites among the Plains Indians was stirred up also by Santee Sioux who had fled to the west after taking part in the 1862 uprising in Minnesota led by Little Crow. It was culminated by the mass-hanging of thirty-eight Santee Sioux at Mankato, December 26, 1862.[13]

The white man's fascination with gold soon posed the threat of disruption of the Sioux lands to the north as well. By 1865 Virginia City, Bozeman, and Helena were thriving gold mining communities in Montana in need of improved transportation links with the outside world. The government proposed a new road from Ft. Laramie to Bozeman, known as the Powder River Road or Bozeman Trail.

It would run through the Big Horn country, the Sioux's favorite hunting grounds. Red Cloud, chief of the Oglalas, led the resistance which culminated with the ambush and annihilation of a force led by Captain W. J. Fetterman on December 21, 1866, near Fort Phil Kearney, Wyoming Territory. The eighty-two military deaths represented the worst setback so far in the history of the Indian wars and strengthened a popular demand that the government resolve the problem peacefully.[14]

Congress established a Peace Commission in 1867 to stop the Sioux War. It was hoped that the answer to the problem would be the establishment of smaller reservations and the assimilation of the Indians into white society by making them farmers. Two reservations were proposed. The 54,000 northern Plains Indians were assigned to the Black Hills country of Dakota Territory and the 86,000 southern Plains Indians were offered western Oklahoma in Indian Territory. Both districts would be provided with territorial governors "of unquestioned integrity and purity of character."[15]

Most of the chiefs, including, Spotted Tail and Sitting Bull signed in April and May in return for gifts; but Red Cloud stayed away on his summer hunt, indicating that he would make no agreements unless the soldiers were withdrawn from the Powder River country. Finally the government decided to abandon the Powder River Road in return for peace. Red Cloud was pleased with the offer and quickly came to terms at Fort Laramie in November, 1868.[17]

Peace was not realized. Many younger warriors and a number of minor chiefs refused to accept the treaties, denounced the leaders who negotiated them, and prepared to fight for their traditional hunting grounds. Indians who mistrusted The Great White Father soon found ample evidence to support their misgivings about peaceable surrender. The Bureau of Indian Affairs (BIA), a division of the Department of the Interior since 1849 when it was transferred from the Department of War, became a haven for party faithfuls of questionable competency and integrity. The BIA was soon a morass of corruption and inefficiency that permanently tarnished the Grant administration. The government's peace policy failed because of incompetent administration and corruption in the BIA combined with the refusal of many Indians to accept reservation life and the constant encroachment of white settlers on Indian land. Reservation agents proved so corrupt and despotic that the so-called "Quaker Policy" was initiated whereby agents were nominated by religious denominations. By 1872, most of the reservations west of the Mississippi were under the administration of Quaker, Baptist, Presbyterian, Methodist, Catholic, Dutch Reform, or Episcopal agents. Those Indians who refused to cooperate were placed under the jurisdiction of the army, which generally implied punishment.[18] Both President Grant and the Quakers agreed that besides emphasizing education and Christianization, the new peace policy should be based upon fair and upright dealings. Above all, the government should faithfully observe treaties.[19]

In spite of their religious credentials, the Indian agents appointed by the new method proved just about as ineffective as their predecessors and were phased out in 1880. Few argued that the type of Indian agent was not improved, but the agents held to an exaggerated conception of the significance of spiritual values and stressed conversion over civilization. Most missionaries shunned practical education and work in the fields.[20] Indians did not take to missionary idealism and regarded the agents as weak and ineffective, not willing to use force to maintain rules. They were also constantly incensed over the inadequate quantity and poor quality of the annuities guaranteed them. The army, charged with maintaining the tenuous peace and protecting United States citizens, regularly criticized the civilian Indian agents. On the other hand, Indian agents sometimes accused the army of responsibility for Indian outbreaks and of persecution of the Indian.[21] Colonel R. I. Dodge, Commander of the Fourth Artillery under General Crook, compared the two Federal arms to a stern but henpecked father and an indulgent mother, with a recalcitrant child (the Indian) profiting by the contention between his parents and taking advantage of their lack of harmony and coordination.[22] Cries of indignation from eastern humanitarians also caused western commanders to fight on two fronts—to carry out government policy and then defend themselves against humanitarians.[23]

By 1876, encroachment by white homesteaders, miners, hunters, and railroad builders on Indian hunting lands guaranteed to them by the 1868 Treaty created a warlike situation. Much has been made of the invasion of gold miners into the Black Hills during 1874-1875 and the consequent forced "sale" of them to the government by the Sioux. But the key source of animosity from the Indians was the apparent and increasing takeover of their lands by homesteaders who would not be moving on like the miners, and would ruin any chance the Indian may have to maintain the old ways based upon nomadic hunting. In 1868 the population of the United States was 38,200,000. In 1876, it was 46,107,000, and more importantly, a great many of them were rushing westward, following the newly built railroads and gobbling up the best land along the way. Even the failure of the Northern Pacific Railroad increased rather than decreased the problem, as the railroad stockholders disposed of the generous government land grants to private parties. Spurred by citizens's complaints and appeals from friendly tribal leaders who sought the government protection they had been guaranteed from hostiles such as Sitting Bull, who had refused to come in to a reservation, the government announced a "small reservation" policy whereby the Indians would be concentrated in a smaller area and be assimilated as farmers. Commissioner of Indian Affairs, E. P. Smith, ordered all Indians to vacate the unceded Powder River country and settle on reservations within two months in December, 1875. Crazy Horse and Sitting Bull indicated that they intended to fight, so the matter was turned over to the army, March, 1876.[24]

Except for the poor judgment of Colonel George Armstrong Custer, the plan worked out by the army proved effective. A giant pincer movement into the Powder River country was agreed upon. General George Crook led a force northward from Fort Fetterman, Wyoming. Colonel John Gibbon marched south from Fort Ellis, Montana, while General Alfred Terry, with Custer in command of the Seventh Cavalry regiment, thrust westward from Fort Abraham Lincoln, North Dakota. Custer, a Democrat, was in President Grant's doghouse for testifying against Secretary of War Belknap in a case involving fraudulent Indian trading practices and was anxious for a victory such as he had led at Washita, November 26, 1868.[25] Upon encountering the forces of Sitting Bull and Crazy Horse, Custer misread their strength; forged ahead recklessly, divided his forces; and he and his entire troup of 265 cavalry regulars were obliterated at the Little Big Horn on June 25, 1876.

This greatest victory for the Indians received tremendous publicity, partly because of the new technology in photography and communications and partly because people in the East could not imagine such a disaster during the year the country was celebrating its centennial of progress and advancement. Militarily, the same encounter would hardly have attracted press notice during the Civil War when casualties in one battle could be one-hundred times those suffered by the cavalry at the Little Big Horn, but it is worth noting that those losses represented more than one-fourth of the total military deaths of the Indian wars between 1865-1891.[26] At first the press did not accord Custer the stature that would later make him somewhat a demigod. Actually his critics were many and vocal. The New York Herald quoted an anonymous "officer of distinction" who said in part, "We all think, much as we lament Custer. . . that he sacrificed the Seventh Cavalry to ambition and wounded vanity."[27]

Custer's demise, nonetheless, only delayed the inevitable defeat of the hostiles. Crook and Terry pursued them relentlessly and did not repeat Custer's mistakes.[28] Immediately after the defeat at the Little Big Horn, General Sheridan successfully demanded that the four great Sioux agencies: Red Cloud, Spotted Tail, Cheyenne River, and Standing Rock, be turned over to the military. Agents, who frequently had been intimidated, were replaced by no-nonsense officers who treated the Sioux like prisoners.

Congress stipulated in its August 15, 1876, appropriations bill that no further appropriations for the Sioux would be forthcoming unless the Black Hills and the Bighorn countries were surrendered. The treaty of 1868 had called for the signature of three-fourths of the adult males for any change; now the government indicated that they would deal with designated chiefs only and no longer hold the great council meetings of previous years which enabled all tribesmen to participate in the traditional Sioux way.[29] Early fall of 1876 the Sioux chiefs agreed to surrender in return for $4 million and a promise of adequate provisions for the reservations.[30] Only Sitting Bull and a few loyal followers refused to quit; they fled to Canada but were not that welcome and returned to the Standing Rock Reservation in 1878. When Dr. Valentine T. McGillycuddy arrived in 1879 as the agent, there were eleven bands with as many chiefs. A year later there were thirty. McGillycuddy organized an Indian policy force and set out to assimilate the Sioux into the white culture. The traditional Sun Dance was phased out in 1884 (it has returned in the modern era).[31]

The assimilation policy extended in a number of directions. Carlisle Indian School at Carlisle, Pennsylvania, was established in 1879. Its apparent success led to a proliferation of Indian schools using Carlisle's philosophy of assimilation as a model. Control over major crimes committed on reservations also was assumed by the federal government after the acquittal of Crow Dog in the murder of Chief Spotted Tail. Crow Dog and Black Crow, Spotted Tail's son-in-law, were involved in a political plot to unseat the powerful chief when Crow Dog shot and killed him August 5, 1881. Some historians maintain that a dispute over a woman caused the murder; but George Hyde, the leading authority, insists that politics prompted the killing.[32] Murder charges were dropped against Black Crow, but Crow Dog was convicted by a white court in Deadwood, Dakota Territory, and sentenced to be hung. Crow Dog's appeal, however, was upheld by the United States Supreme Court which ruled the government did not have jurisdiction in criminal cases involving a crime committed by one Indian against another on an Indian reservation. The case helped spur Congress to pass the Seven Major Crimes Act of 1885 which made Indians on reservations subject to federal prosecution for murder, manslaughter, rape, assault with intent to kill, arson, burglary, and larceny. Another result of Spotted Tail's killing was that the government declined to name another head chief to replace him and also refused to recognize the minor chiefs.[33]

The final step in the new policy was to inculcate the principle of individualism instead of tribalism into land ownership by giving each native a farm whether he wanted it or not. Frontiersmen, who wanted land, and eastern humanitarians, who believed assimilation would resolve the West's racial problem, pressured Congress into passing the Dawes Severalty Act, February 8, 1887.[34] That significant law authorized the President to divide the lands of any tribe, giving each head of a family 160 acres, with lesser amounts to bachelors, women, and children. The plots, rather than going directly to the Indians, were to be held in trust by the government for twenty-five years, so the natives would not sell immediately. All those receiving clear title to their grants were to be made citizens of the United States. Those reservation lands remaining after the division were to be sold by the government, with profits set aside in a trust fund for Indian educational purposes.[35]

In order to create specific reservation boundaries for the various Sioux tribes and, of course, open up more land for settlement, Congress passed an act to divide up the Great Sioux Reservation into six smaller units on April 30, 1888, called the Sioux bill. This action, implemented by a commission headed by General Crook, set aside 2,809,444 acres for the Oglalas. That area was called the Pine Ridge Indian reservation. The land that was freed up was purchased at the rate of $1.50 an acre, a substantial price for the times.[36] On March 2, 1889, two days before he left office, President Grover Cleveland signed the Sioux bill into law. Many Oglalas agreed with Sitting Bull that the land should not have been sold; and as the summer progressed, poor crops, unfulfilled promises, and reduced rations increased the festering discontent.[37]

Many Sioux found an answer to their desperate plight in the teachings of a Nevada Paiute Messiah named Jack Wilson or Wovoka, "The Cutter," who promised that the old ways would return with the disappearance of the white man in the spring of 1891. Upon the death of his medicine man father, when Wovoka was only fourteen, Nevada rancher David Wilson took him into his family. But Wovoka soon became restless in a white environment and traveled to California, Oregon, and Washington where he became fascinated with the Shaker religion, whose extensive rituals and death-like trance were practiced by the Puget Sound tribes. During a serious illness in 1889, Wovoka allegedly talked with God who revealed a religion in which the white man would disappear supernaturally and the old order would be restored in 1891.

Salvation was attainable only by adherence to a code similar to the Ten Commandments and the performance of specific rituals highlighted by the Ghost Dance which made possible communion with the dead and promoted the coming of the millennium. Wovoka used several tricks to prove his power, the most notable being the demonstration that the ghost shirt could not be penetrated by a rifle bullet. Anthropologist James Mooney suggests that the ghost shirt idea may have been suggested to Wovoka by the "endowment robe" of the Mormons, a seamless garment of white muslin adorned with symbolic figures, which was worn by their initiates as the most sacred badge of their faith and was believed to make the wearer invulnerable.[38]

The first great dance was performed near Yerinton, Nevada, January 1899. The faith caught on immediately and soon disciples from tribes all over the West were spreading the new Creed. Short Bull and Kicking Bear led a delegation of eleven Sioux to Nevada and brought it back to the Sioux where it was eagerly accepted by many in the spring of 1890. As the craze spread, authorities and some Indian leaders began viewing it as another war dance and attempted to suppress it.[39] Sitting Bull, recalcitrant as ever, had established himself on the Standing Rock Reservation with about two hundred followers. He invited Kicking Bear to teach him and his followers the Ghost Dance and they became the foremost disciples of the faith, although the old chief probably never really believed in it. Some of the younger warriors went through the ritual swinging rifles and wearing ghost shirts that they believed would turn away their enemies's bullets. Other notable chiefs such as Hump, Big Foot, Little Wound, and Big Road came out for the new religion and there was increased fear and tension on all of the Sioux reservations.[40]

Considering the reputation of Sitting Bull as a trouble maker and the increasing volatility of the situation, James McLaughlin, the veteran Standing Rock agent, ordered Sitting Bull to stop the dance, and warned him that "this absurd craze" would lead to nothing positive.[41] Sitting Bull defied McLaughlin and remained at his camp on the Grand River. McLaughlin, an experienced, competent veteran of some twenty years service, knew that he could outlast the agitators with the assistance of the coming cold weather.[42]

Although Red Cloud was not as vocal, he also was solidly behind the new movement, which made the Pine Ridge Reservation the second most significant center of Ghost Dance activity. Unfortunately, white administrative leadership rested in new and uncertain hands at Pine Ridge. Harrison's 1888 victory over Cleveland signaled a patronage change of agents there. Colonel H. D. Gallagher, a Civil War veteran who was capable, well-liked and unafraid, was replaced by Daniel F. Royer, a former member of the South Dakota territorial legislature with few other credentials for the position. Royer, intimidated by the situation, soon acquired the nickname, "Young Man Afraid of Indians."[43] After several difficult confrontations Royer telegraphed the Acting Commissioner of Indian Affairs that his agency was out of control and a thousand troops were needed to restore order. By November some 3,000 troops, led by General Nelson Miles, had arrived. This force represented more than one-half of the entire enlisted force of the United States Army.[44] Many Ghost Dancers fled their reservation for the neighboring Badlands. Every move was reported by a large cadre of journalists who seemed intent upon creating excitement even where there was little.[45]

After mulling the situation over for awhile, Miles agreed with the agents that the best course would be to arrest some of the key leaders and remove them at least temporarily to a military prison. Miles wanted to maintain a moderate image, though. His career almost had been ruined when, because of his alleged mistreatment of Jefferson Davis at Fort Monroe, Virginia, after the Civil War, he had been relieved of his command of the fort.[46] McLaughlin ordered Lieutenant Henry Bull Head of the Indian police to arrest Sitting Bull. At daybreak on December 15, 1890, thirty-nine Indian police backed by a troop of cavalry attempted to make the arrest. When accosted in his cabin, Sitting Bull stalled around until his supporters gathered and a fight broke out. Both Sitting Bull and Bull Head were killed along with a dozen others.[47] About a hundred of Sitting Bull's group escaped and joined Big Foot's Minneconjou camp near Cherry Creek, also on the Standing Rock Reservation. News of Sitting Bulls death spread fear and resistance among the Ghost Dancers throughout the area.

General Miles ordered the arrest of Big Foot, who unexpectedly left the Standing Rock Reservation on the evening of December 22 in an attempt to join up with Kicking Bear and Short Bull in the Badlands. Big Foot apparently abandoned the idea because supplies were low and he was seriously ill with pneumonia, and turned his band back to Pine Ridge to surrender. Scouts located Big Foot as he neared the Pine Ridge Reservation. On December 26, General John Brooke sent out a squadron of Seventh Cavalry under Major Samuel Whitside with orders to arrest Big Foot, take away the Indian's horses, destroy whatever arms they were carrying, and hold them until he issued further orders.[48]

Big Foot, desperately ill and almost out of supplies, surrendered to Whitside near Porcupine Butte on December 28. The band, estimated at 120 warriors and 230 women and children, was taken about eight miles south to Wounded Knee Creek where camp was made. That evening Colonel James Forsyth, commanding four additional troops of the Seventh with additional artillery and a company of scouts, arrived to take command. The cavalry force now consisted of 470 men backed up by four Hotchkiss field artillery pieces. Forsyth deployed his forces in such a manner that the Indians were-completely surrounded. The four artillery pieces were set up strategically on a large knoll that overlooked the encampment.[49]

By this time the population at the small Wounded Knee trading post had been augmented with sightseers from Rushville, Gordon, and other points in Nebraska. Only three correspondents were present, nonetheless, and all three were in the village when fighting broke out.[50] No one, including Colonel Forsyth, anticipated a violent confrontation the next morning. Given the tense atmosphere that had existed for months and the recent shoot-out over the attempted arrest of Sitting Bull, however, the likelihood of violence should not have seemed that remote.

Colonel Forsyth ordered male adults and older youths to form in front of Big Foot's tent in a semi-circle for the purpose of disarmament the following morning. Forsyth instructed the captives to go by twenties to pick up their weapons and deposit them in a pile. When the first twenty returned with only two worn out guns, Forsyth ordered troops to search the camp for arms and moved a detachment of soldiers to within thirty feet of the warriors. The search, which uncovered about forty rifles of questionable value, took a good deal of time and was conducted with some harshness. Personal possessions were ripped apart and women and children treated roughly at times in part because it was evident that they were concealing weapons.[51] While the soldiers looked for weapons, a medicine man walked among the apprehensive warriors, blowing on an eagle bone whistle and urging them to fight. He told them that the soldiers were weak and powerless, and that bullets could not penetrate the sacred ghost shirts, which almost all of the Indians wore. Quite sure that more weapons were being concealed under the warrior's robes, the order was given to search them as well. Suddenly the medicine man threw a handful of dust into the air. A young Indian drew a rifle from under a blanket, waved it about, and fired at the soldiers. Other warriors threw aside their blankets and raised their weapons. Instantly the soldiers unleashed a murderous volley at pointblank range which killed perhaps fifty, including Big Foot. For the next few minutes a fearful hand-to-hand struggle ensued.[52]

Immediately the four Hotchkiss guns sent a murderous fusilage of two pound explosive shells into the tipis, killing or wounding indiscriminately. Indians who attempted to flee were mowed down by the artillery fire or by rifle fire from the inexperienced and undisciplined troops who kept up the pursuit for almost two miles. Few argue that it was nothing less than a massacre after the first flurry of fighting.[53] The government officially reported different numbers killed and wounded, ranging from as low as 128 to 300. Quite likely the total, including those killed on the field and who later died from wounds or exposure, would approximate 300.[54] Thirty-one soldiers were killed at the scene and about as many more were wounded, several of those succumbing to their wounds later.[55]

Because of an approaching storm and the possibility of a counter-attack by outraged supporters of the Ghost Dancers, Forsyth gathered his dead and wounded as well as thirty-three wounded prisoners and hurried back to Pine Ridge. All but six of the wounded prisoners were women and children. Those of the wounded Indians who were willing to accept the services of doctors were housed in the Episcopal Church. Christmas greenery was still hanging from the rafters of the church along with a crudely lettered banner hung across the chancel front above the pulpit declaring "Peace on Earth, Good Will to Men."[56]

On New Year's Day of 1891, three days after the battle, a detachment of troops accompanied by a number of civilians, war correspondents, and others went to bury the dead and pick up the few who had miraculously clung to life during the storm. Civilians under a government contract, which paid eight dollars for a twenty-four hour shift, dug a long trench that received the bodies, thrown one upon another like cordwood. It was reported that eighty-four men and boys, forty-four women, and sixteen young children were buried in the mass grave.[57] Indians later put a wire fence around the trench and smeared the posts with sacred red medicine paint. Some time later the outline of the trench was marked by a low concrete border; and a monument, inscribed with the names of forty-three of the men who were buried there, was erected on the site. "Many women and children who knew no wrong died here," it said in part.[58]

The grisly details of the battle or massacre, as it is more popularly known, flooded the media, frequently in a sensationalized manner, and loosed a torrent of criticism upon the army and the government, often based upon misinformation. Alistair Cooke, a popular British historian whom Queen Elizabeth knighted in 1973 for "his outstanding contribution over many years to Anglo-American mutual understanding," presents a typical interpretation in his best-selling book, America:

> In the autumn of 1890 near the reservation town of Pine Ridge, South Dakota, the Seventh Cavalry, the same regiment chopped up at the Little Bighorn, mustered for the kill. . . Without a parley or any attempt to establish that this horde was a band of warriors, the Seventh annihilated them, and the next day dug the bodies from the snow and buried them in a common grave. This wretched episode was known to the white man, and still is, as the "battle" of Wounded Knee.[59]

General Miles, a pompous officer who watched the torrent of criticism over the killing of innocent women and children wash his hopes for political office away, promptly made every effort to prove Colonel Forsyth had blundered at Wounded Knee on two counts: first, Forsyth was directly responsible for the unnecessary slaughter of innocents; second, his disposition of the troops had been faulty.[60] In a letter to his wife, Miles complained that a second lieutenant could have done a better job at Wounded Knee.[61] Upon Miles's recommendation, Forsyth was suspended and brought to court martial. C. W. Allen, editor of the Chadron Democrat and an eyewitness to the encounter, called Forsyth's suspension, "One of the greatest mistakes made by the War Department."[62]

A common misconception is that Forsyth was subsequently convicted of wrongdoing at Wounded Knee. In fact, the witnesses at the trial overwhelmingly supported him
and he was acquitted on all counts. They testified that Forsyth had made a supreme effort
to avoid killing women and children and had failed only because the noncombatants
were mixed with the combatants and in the heat of battle could rarely be identified as
innocents. Witnesses also maintained, with less persuasiveness, that no one anticipated
that fighting would break out, and, given situation, the troops were well placed for
disarming the Indians, if not for waging battle. In spite of persistent claims to the
contrary, it could not be proven that friendly fire had caused a single casualty to the
troops.[63] Miles made every effort to reverse the acquittal, which he maintained constituted an outright whitewash. General Schofield and Secretary Proctor disagreed with
Miles and returned Forsyth to command of his regiment.[64] In 1894 Forsyth was promoted
to brigadier general and in 1897 he became a major general. Three officers and fifteen
enlisted men received Medals of Honor for heroism at Wounded Knee.[65]

At the least the encounter itself was over-dramatized and not enough criticism was
leveled at the system that spawned the disaster.[66] Even though Forsyth was under orders
from his superiors to capture and disarm the Ghost Dancers, he still could have used more
restraint in the process. Noting that the situation was getting out of hand, why did he not
pull back and negotiate? Big Foot's band was surrounded on all sides by a vastly superior
force, and over 2,000 well equipped troops stood ready nearby. No one could anticipate
that fighting would break out, but a number of the prisoners had openly battled police
and cavalry just two weeks before during the attempted capture of Sitting Bull. In fact
the root problems that spawned the Ghost Dance, which so alarmed authorities, caused
the slaughter at Wounded Knee. The Indians were driven to a state of desperation
because of government policies which led to the loss of their traditional way of life,
confinement to reservations, broken government promises, and the inroads of hunger
and disease.[67]

As for the encounter itself, most historians have concurred with the thesis that the
first encounter at Wounded Knee was an avoidable tragedy of war.[68] Even D. Alexander
Brown, the author of the popular and influential Bury My Heart at Wounded Knee in
1970, presented a balanced interpretation in an earlier article published in American
History Illustrated. Brown concluded this 1966 article stating:

> Some journalists pictured the Wounded Knee tragedy as a
> triumph of brave soldiers over treacherous Indians; others declared it
> was a slaughter of helpless Indians by a regiment searching for
> revenge since the Little Big Horn. The truth undoubtedly lay some-
> where between these opposite points of view. Certainly it was a tragic
> accident of war.[69]

Brown's later book, of course, presented a far more one-sided viewpoint.

When South Dakota Senator James Abourezk introduced a bill in Congress in 1975
to compensate the heirs and descendants of the massacre victims $3,000 each, which
would amount to about $600,000, the United States Army produced evidence which it
claimed showed that Wounded Knee was an authentic battle. Liberals around the world

referred to the Army report as an "outrage" and a "cover-up" but Congress refused to pay.[70]

Wounded Knee did create a panic among neighboring whites that was unwarranted and led to further tragedy. This tension contributed to a rank atrocity that received little attention. About two weeks after Wounded Knee, a party of Oglalas from Pine Ridge consisting of Few Tails and his wife and One Feather and his wife and two young children were hunting under the authorization of a government pass along the Belle Fourche River. Upon breaking camp after a successful hunt, they were ambushed by six white men. Few Tails in the lead wagon was killed instantly and his wife was seriously wounded. One Feather leaped on one of his ponies and fought a courageous and successful battle to defend his family as they retreated in their wagon. In spite of proof that Few Tails was the victim of a deliberate and unprovoked murder, the perpetrators were acquitted by the local courts of Meade County, South Dakota.[71]

Wounded Knee did bring some positive results for the Sioux. Little Wound, a chief who helped establish peace, said, "We could not make our Great Father hear us until we all got out and made a big noise." On January 19, 1891, Congress pushed through legislation to make good the promises of the Crook Commission: $165,000 for improvement of education, $200,000 to the Standing Rock and Cheyenne for taking their ponies in 1876 and $100,000 for additional beef for the Sioux. The Indian appropriation for fiscal 1892 was increased to $1,100,000 for the Sioux plus $100,000 compensation to "friendly Sioux" for property destroyed by the Ghost Dancers and $6,000 to negotiate a settlement of the Pine Ridge-Rosebud boundary problems.[72]

With the allotment of specific tracts of land to each family, the change in life style on the Pine Ridge Reservation became firm but confusing. Title to the land remained with the United States. The allottee received "trust patents," which were originally intended to mature into fee simple patents in twenty-five years. The mechanics of the allotment process were complicated and its administration erratic. The Burke Act of May 8, 1906, left the trust period at twenty-five years, but the Secretary of Interior was given power to issue a patent in fee "whenever he shall be satisfied that any Indian allottee is competent and capable of managing his or her affairs. . . and thereafter be removed."[73] This act gave the Bureau of Indian Affairs the responsibility of deciding on the individual competency of each Indian applying for a patent in fee which resulted in bitter disputes. Of the Indians who received patents in 1907 and 1908, about sixty percent sold their land. Greater strictness was then enforced, and between 1909 and 1912 more than half of the 3,400 applications for fee patents were denied. In April, 1917, upon entry into World War I, the government allowed all Indians of less than one-half Indian blood complete control of their property. Sioux Indians sold their land and cattle at such an alarming rate that the policy was junked in 1921. Formal application and proof of competency were once more required.[74]

Acquisition of Indian lands by neighboring white ranchers continued at an unabated pace for the next four decades. The process had begun as early as February 28, 1891, when the government, which had determined that many of the allottees were physically incapable of utilizing their assigned lands and others were not inclined to do so, made provisions for leasing allotted lands and tribal lands under the jurisdiction of the Department of Interior. Thereafter, huge amounts of land were leased to whites for grazing, agriculture and mining. Reluctant landowners were often presented with attractive incentives to enter into lease agreements. As the situation evolved, the relationship between the landowner and the lessee became a reversal of the historical role of the landowner, who normally enjoyed the superior position in such an arrangement. Instead, on the reservation, the lessee enjoyed the major role as benefactor. Although the government intended that the "ward" would manage his own affairs through the patent fee, the intent was never realized; and a great deal of the land management process continued to be controlled by the Bureau of Indian Affairs.[75] In general the annual sale of allotments on the Pine Ridge Reservation to non-Indians averaged around 30,000 acres a year by the late 1920s and continued at that pace for the next forty years. By 1969 only 1,518,261 acres of the original 2,809,444 remained under Indian control.[76]

One of the most difficult ongoing problems that emerged from the allotment system was fractionated heirship. Few allotment recipients left wills, so the land was divided equally among the surviving heirs. Disputes were inevitable and, as the land was re-divided by ensuing generations, much of it became so fractionated that an heir might claim only an acre or two of the original allotment. Stretched over a period of time the situation has become an almost impenetrable maze for many heirs who must rely on the BIA to manage the lands, which are normally leased in a block with the fractionated owners receiving their percentage of the total rent.[77]

By the 1920s it had become apparent that the allotment system was not the answer to the Indian problem. A number of reform proposals appeared, In 1923 the newly-formed American Indian Defense Association issued a statement of general principles drawn up in collaboration with the Indian Welfare Committee of the General Federation of Women's Club. The program called for the development of Indian "group loyalties and communal responsibilities," including tribal landholding, self-government, and religious freedom, and a complete reorganization of the education, health, and irrigation services. With the aid of a grant from John D. Rockefeller, Jr. , the forty-two year old Indian Rights Association began to issue a monthly bulletin known as Indian Truth in 1924.[78] Partly as a reward for loyal service during World War I and also to eliminate questions about who qualified, on June 2, 1924, President Calvin Coolidge signed an act into law stating that "all noncitizen Indians born within the territorial limits of the United States be, and they are hereby declared to be, citizens of the United States."[79]

The publication of the Meriam report in 1928 was a turning point in the public perception of the administration of Indian affairs. In 1926 Secretary of the Interior Hubert Work asked the Institute for Government Research (a privately endowed organization subsequently called the Brookings Institution) to conduct a survey of condition among Indian tribes. Social scientist Lewis Meriam and a staff of nine experts in education, health, economics, and Indian affairs spent seven months in the field studying Indian communities throughout the United States. Their finding, published in 1928 as The Problem of Indian Administration and commonly known as the Meriam Report, focused on government ineptitude and malfeasance, particularly on the part of the Indian Service, in the areas of health, education, and land management. The report revealed startlingly high rates of illiteracy, disease, and mortality as well as extremely low per-capita incomes. Nationally, the per-capita income of fifty-five percent of reservation Indians was less than two hundred dollars per year, most of it from rent rather than wages. In South Dakota incomes varied from $86 per person annually on the Pine Ridge Reservation to $247 on the Lake Traverse, or Sisseton, Reservation. The United States Senate launched a full-scale investigation of Indian matters in 1928.[80]

President Herbert Hoover did much to improve the administration of Indian affairs during his term, but he was handicapped by the problems of the Great Depression. Hoover's good start received a strong boost with the appointment of John Collier as Commissioner of Indian Affairs by new President Franklin Roosevelt. Aggressive, fearless, and dedicated, Collier approached his job from the viewpoint of a social scientist. He enjoyed the full support of Roosevelt and Secretary of Interior, Harold Ickes.[81] Under Collier's leadership the Congress passed the Indian Reorganization Act of 1934 (Wheeler-Howard Act). Although attacked as communistic, pagan, and Bureau-bought, fifty-eight tribes representing 146,194 Indians voted for it and thirteen tribes composed of 15,213 Indians voted against it.[82]

Significant and far-reaching changes were carefully incorporated into the law whose full title summarized it well: "An Act to conserve and develop Indian lands and resources; to extend to Indians the right to form business and other organizations; to establish a credit system for Indians; to grant certain rights of home rule to Indians; to provide for vocational eduation for Indians; and for other purposes." Allotment in severalty was thus forbidden and any surplus lands were to be restored to tribal ownership. Sales of lands to and inheritance by non-Indians was drastically restricted. The Secretary of Interior was entitled to spend up to $2,000,000 a year to acquire additional land for tribal estates. Tribal constitutions were authorized to be created and ratified by the Indians themselves to give them extensive rights of political home rule. The act was not to apply to any tribe that voted against it.[83]

At Pine Ridge the Oglalas had gone through a political process that had further divided traditional and progressive elements. During the winter of 1917-1918, the new superintendent of Pine Ridge ordered the traditional chiefs's council dissolved. The sons and grandsons of former chiefs then organized themselves as the Treaty Council, also known as the Black Hills Treaty and Claims Council or the Chief's Council. The group was used as a forum for explaining BIA programs and policies. But the main purpose of the council was to pursue treaty claims against the government, especially the Sioux claim to the Black Hills.[84] The BIA attempted to revive an Oglala Tribal Council in 1926 through an election, but the Oglalas refused to support the election. A number of younger, better educated Oglalas who felt that the Treaty Council was merely a tool of the BIA organized the Council of Twenty-One, composed of representatives from each of the seven reservation districts. Their constitution was approved by the Secretary of Interior in 1928. Later an eighth district, La Creek, was added and representation was increased to five per district. This new organization immediately became a protagonist of the Treaty Council.[85] Pine Ridge Reservation accepted self-government in 1935 by the narrow margin of 1,348 for and 1,041 against.

The opposition was led by the traditional full-bloods who viewed the proposal as a further erosion of their treaty rights and a takeover of power by the more white oriented mixed-bloods.[86] Since the adoption of the Wheeler-Howard Act, tribal government at Pine Ridge has been characterized by constant disputes between the "outs" and the "ins" with changes in leadership every two years. Only once since 1935 has a tribal president

won consecutive re-election, and that was in 1974 when Dick Wilson defeated AIM
leader Russell Means a year after the second confrontation at Wounded Knee.[87]

Realizing that Pine Ridge was torn by dissent over reorganization, William O,
Roberts, the highly regarded superintendent of the Rosebud Reservation was moved to
Pine Ridge in 1936. From the outset Roberts encountered nothing but trouble. He
became engaged in a running battle with the tribal council, which was dominated by two
mixed-bloods, Frank Wilson and George Pugh. Disputes arose over the Council's
authority over hiring of employees, administration of relief funds, and leasing of
reserved lands. The bureau tended to support Roberts and urged tribal council president
Wilson to discuss the problems with the superintendant.[88] The tension eased when
Wilson resigned in 1937, but Roberts had further alienated mixed-bloods by openly
soliciting support of full-bloods to get the tribal charter ratified.[89] Roberts became the
center of more disputes in the 1940s which evolved into a series of vetoes of tribal council
acts by him and a deadlocked struggle with the tribal council by 1945. In the process
Roberts managed to alienate not only the mixed-bloods who had originally supported
reorganization, but the fullbloods and the tribal council as well. The BIA sent D'Arcy
McNickle, a Flathead Indian of the Indian Organization Commission, to investigate.
McNickle praised Roberts but suggested that he did not support the idea of self-
government for the Sioux.[90]

No doubt a part of the discontent at Pine Ridge after World War II stemmed from
severe economic stress that had returned to the reservation after over a decade of relative
prosperity. New Deal programs such as the CCC and the WPA put nearly all able bodied
men to work in the 1930s. They built roads, dams, churches, schools, and public
buildings. Almost 1,000 Oglala men and women served in the military during the war,
and jobs were quite readily available off the reservation for those who stayed behind.
When the war ended, veterans returned and the defense jobs dried up, creating
unemployment and resultant social unrest. The only real break in the bleak economic
pattern at Pine Ridge from the post World War II period to the present occurred when
the Wright and McGill fishing equipment company established a snelling facility at Pine
Ridge in 1961 with the help of government subsidies. At its high point the factory
employed some 475 workers, and the quality of work was excellent. Asiatic imports,
however, undersold Wright McGill so much that the fish-hook factory was closed in
1967.[91]

Numerous disputes stemming from the Indian Reorganization Act and previous
Indian policies as well led to the establishment of the Indian Claims Commission in
1946. Prior to that Indian tribes with grievances against the government had only one
recourse—petitions to Congress. Because obtaining enactment of special jurisdictional
acts was difficult, expensive and time consuming, and frequently the results were
unsatisfactory, Congress passed the Indian Claims Commission Act. The act created a
judicial tribunal consisting of three (later five) commissioners or judges to hear and
determine the merits of claims against the United States brought by tribes, bands and
identifiable groups of American Indians. More than six hundred claims were filed with
the commission between August 13, 1946, and Ausust 13, 1951,—the cut-off date for
filing. The majority of claims before the commission involved lands once owned by
Indians and later acquired by the United States. Judgments were awarded in 123 cases.

The commission's life was extended five times and was terminated September 30, 1978, with unfinished work transferred to the Court of Claims for completion. One of the important side benefits of the suits was the the the establishment of an "official history" of many Indian tribes of the United States, as compiled by historians, anthropologists, geographers, and other scholars employed to serve as expert witnesses in the cases.[92]

Many observers believed, however, that the true purpose of the commission was to set the state for termination of all Indian reservations in the United States. The philosophy of the government toward Indians in the 1950s was that they should be "set free" from their bondage on reservations and assimilated into the dominant society through relocation and termination.[93] The new policy resulted in six termination laws which included the timber rich Menominee Reservation in Wisconsin and the Klamath Reservation in Oregon.[94]

Termination fever was held in check by Indian interest organizations such as the National Congress of American Indians, the Indian Rights Association, and the Association of American Indian Affairs, with assistance of church groups like the National Council of Churches and liberals like Ralph Nader.[95]

The Kennedy administration junked the policy of termination and relocation in favor of helping the Indians achieve self-determination. Under Kennedy, Congress freed loan funds; the Federal Housing Authority began helping Indians build their own homes; and businesses were encouraged through subsidization of employment opportunities on the reservations.[96] Perhaps most of all Kennedy's New Frontier represented a new concern for all minority groups which fueled the civil rights revolution of the 1960s, which, of course, was led by blacks.

When Indians became militant in the late 1960s it was no accident that their strategy closely paralleled the successful black drive for civil rights which had preceeded. For over a decade after the historic Brown decision of 1954, blacks demonstrated that activism could spur action; that marches, takeovers, demonstrations—even riots—were effective in creating change through the courts and executive and legislative branches of government.[97] Television, the post-war communications phenomenom, played an enormous role in their cause as it showed first-hand accounts of oppression and brutality almost daily to millions of viewers across the land. As the Vietnam war additionally polarized the nation, breaking the law in order to change public policy became commonplace. America divided roughly along the lines of urban blue collar workers and rural conservatives who opposed these developments and the educated urban elite who tended to support them and delight in reminding their opposition of its inadequacies of thought and action in areas such as civil rights, foreign policy, and conservation.[98]

Political analysts suggested the ascendency of a New Tribalsim in American public life that challenged the "melting pot" thesis of assimilation and denied the value of the open society. Ethnic consciousness and promotion became the latest word in political fashion. A television program copied from an earlier British format called "All in the Family" featured the stress of the lower middle-class bigoted mentality in accepting the times as expressed by Archie Bunker.[99] Movies sympathetic to minorities became the vogue. As national public opinion struggled to absorb Selma, Watts, My Lai, and Watergate, Hollywood presented new versions of the Old West which portrayed the Indian favorably. Examples included Little Big Man, A Man Called Horse, Soldier Blue, and <u>Little Big Man</u>. The movie that tied the whole case together was the low-budget smash success <u>Billy Jack</u>, which featured the confrontation between the new liberalism as personified by its half-Indian hero, and the red-neck conservatives of a small western town.[100]

Reservation Indians, however, did not fit comfortably into the black civil rights movement because they felt their relationship with the government differed from the blacks, but a new militancy among younger Indians surfaced by 1961. Some five hundred Indians met at the University of Chicago that June and drew up "A Declaration of Indian Purpose."[101] The younger, more militant element at the Chicago meeting met again and formed the National Indian Youth Council (NIYC). Although critical of the recent termination and relocation policies of the BIA, their main complaints focused on the National Congress of American Indians and on tribal leadership, whom they claimed represented white society more than they did real Indians.

The NIYC borrowed terminology and tactics from black civil rights activists using terms like "Apple," "Red Power," and "Uncle Tomahawks" and instigating fish-ins in Washington State.[102] Clyde Warrior, a young Ponca from Oklahoma who had spent a summer with the militant Student Nonviolent Coordinating Committee (SNCC) in Mississippi, soon became the leading spokesman of the NIYC.[103] Warrior, who described himself as an "academic aborigine," denounced whites as racists, fascists, colonialists, and reactionaries. He also attacked white-oriented Indians as Uncle Tomahawks or Apples (red on the outside, white on the inside). Warrior is commonly credited as being "the Prophet of Red Power." His eccentric, moody and unpredictable reign ended unexpectedly in 1967 when he suddenly resigned because he felt the new Office of Economic Opportunity programs were sucking Indians into the system rather than promoting self-determination.[104] Within a year after his resignation, Warrior died unexpectedly.

President Johnson's War on Poverty encompassed Indians as well. Another special task force on the American Indian was formed. It completed its work in 1966 with the recommendation that reservations be transferred from the Department of Interior to the Department of Health, Education and Welfare (HEW) on the grounds that seventy-five percent of the reservation budget was handled by HEW. That recommendation was rejected, but Johnson, in an unprecedented special message to Congress in March, 1968, did create the National Council on Indian Opportunity (NCIO) designed to coordinate the War on Poverty programs and to be sure that Indians received their fair share of federal funds.[105] Vice President Hubert Humphrey, from Minnesota, served as chairman of the NCIO, which included six other key officials, six Indian representatives, and a small professional staff. The NCIO was not effective, however, because of the turbulent political situation and subsequent change in administrations.[106] It did meet under the leadership of Vice President Spiro Agnew in 1969, though.[107] Large amounts of funds from OEO, nevertheless, were channeled into community improvement, the training of workers, youth activities and health services for Indians. At the same time, the tribes were given legal status that gave them the power, like cities and states, to sponsor welfare and development programs funded by the government.

Most tribes bitterly opposed the Indian Civil Rights Act of 1968. It terminated the much disliked Public Law 280, which gave Washington, Nevada, and most other states the right to assume jurisdiction over Indian reservations without Indian consent. This first part of the act was accepted with enthusiasm, of course, but the second provision of the bill which made the end of Public Law 280 acceptable to the government stirred the opposition. This clause required Indian's Reservation Courts to apply United States Constitutional principles such as due process and equal protection to its proceedings, thus greatly limiting their ability to interpret the law in an arbitrary manner.[108]

Most Indians were encouraged when President Richard Nixon came to office filled with expressions of support for "the first Americans."[109] As President-elect, he appointed Indian historian Alvin M. Josephy, Jr. , to conduct a study of past and present policies in order to recommend new reforms. Basically Nixon wanted Indian control of the agencies that served them, notably the Bureau of Indian Affairs, with self-determination as the ultimate objective for both tribes and individuals. Louis Bruce, a quiet Mohawk, was named new Commissioner of Indian Affairs. Personally conservative, he surprised the staid agency by appointing militant young men to key positions. Their aggressiveness soon earned them the title, "The New Team."

On July 8, 1970, Nixon called for a sharper break with the past in dealing with "America's Most Neglected Minority."[110] The President acknowledged the "white man's frequent aggression, broken agreements, intermittent remorse and prolonged failure." During this period of oppression and brutality, the Indians were "deprived of their ancestral lands and denied the opportunity to control their own destiny." Nixon said that Justice and enlightened social policy required the nation "to break decisively with the past and to create the conditions for a new era in which the Indian future is determined by Indian acts and Indian decisions."

Finally the President acknowledged the conflict of interest existing within the federal government when it (1) exercises its trust duties as to Indian land and water interests and (2) exercises its duty to the national resource use interest. Nixon asked Congress to establish and Indian Trust Council Authority. This Authority would be independent of the Departments of Interior and Justice and would be empowered to sue. The United States would waive its immunity from suit in Authority litigation.[111]

A quiet counter revolution led by BIA directors and superintendents supported by several establishment Indians including W. W. Keeler, former chief of the Cherokee Nation and chairman of the Phillips Petroleum Company, stymied the activists.[112] Congress also failed to enact the Indian reforms sought by the President. Although BIA appropriations rose from $243 million in 1968 to over $530 million in 1973 while overall Federal expenditures climbed from $445 million to $925 million during the same period, Indian activists chafed under the paternalism of white bureaucrats and corrupt tribal governments and maintained that Nixon had betrayed his early promise of a sharp break with the past.[113]

Wallowing in self-criticism over Vietnam, the civil rights confrontations, the rape of the environment, and other transgressions, Americans seemed receptive to more criticism of their treatment of the original inhabitants. Stan Steiner, a New Yorker, compiled a series of interviews with younger, more militant Indians for radio WBAI-FM in New York. Unable to persuade his Indian interviewees to write a book about their grievances, Steiner published his interviews in a book, The New Indians, in 1968.[114] Vine Deloria, Jr. , a prominent Santee Sioux who had attended Eastern preparatory schools and held a degree in theology before becoming president of the National Congress of American Indians, answered the need for a modern book about Indians by an Indian with Custer Died for Your Sins: An Indian Manifesto in 1969. A somewhat intemperate but cleverly written indictment of the treatment of the American Indians by anthropologists, missionaries, and government officials, it became a runaway best-seller and established Deloria's position as a spokesman for the modern Indian.

Custer Died for Your Sins was topped almost immediately by the none-too-carefully written book about the traditional Indian wars, Bury My Heart at Wounded Knee: An Indian History of the American West by D. Alexander Brown, an assistant librarian at the University of Illinois who had accumulated a substantial list of publications about the early American West, including a balanced version of the 1890 Wounded Knee tragedy in American History Illustrated in 1966. Brown borrowed the key to his title from the last line of Places, a famous poem by Stephen Vincent Benet, and proceeded to present his history from that approach. First published in January 1970, it rose immediately to the top of the bestseller list and went through thirteen printings by October. Reviews from the popular press were highly favorable: The New York Times Book Review, "Extraordinary. . . A whole narrative of singular integrity;" Look "an appalling and a noble book;" Saturday Review, "It is not exaggeration to call this one of the most important contributions to the history of the frontier ever published." But professional historians were not impressed. Their verdict was summarized by Reverend Francis P. Prucha, one of the best known authorities on Indian history, in the prestigious American Historical Review in April, 1972. Prucha not only criticized the content of the book but also challenged its integrity. "That the book is thoroughly or scrupulously documented is simply not true," said Prucha. "The Indians seriously wronged as they often have been, certainly deserve something better," Prucha concluded.[115]

Regardless of the quality of scholarship, Brown's book helped bring more favorable public support for the Indian. As the grant money flowed into reservations, numerous better trained urban Indians returned to take advantage of the new opportunities. Schooled in the competitive ways of urban America, they were not ready to accept the hum-drum inefficiencies and outright dishonesties of either the tribal governments or the BIA. They also stood ready to protect tribal members from mistreatment in off-reservation towns. In this effort they were effectively assisted by the federally funded legal-aid program.[116] The reformers were joined by a number of traditionalists who wanted to do away with tribal government and go back to the treaty system in effect prior to the reorganization of 1934.[117]

Many of the off-reservation Indians became beset with Indian cultural symbols such as feathers, beads, and buckskins to a degree that extended well beyond the historical facts.[118] Indian historian Gerald Vizenor commented, "Thousands of urban educated tribal people, some adorned with pantribal vestments made of plastic and leather, are withdrawing from civilization and driving back to the reservation to live the way they have projected tribal life to be several hundred years ago."[119] Vizenor further suggested that the majority of those listening to "tribal revivalists" were white people because most reservation tribal people were too preoccupied with survival to afford the luxuries of "linguistic retreats from the present."[120] Those attitudes might well lead to conflicts with basically conservative tribal leaders, Vizenor pointed out, especially when the urban

Indians demanded immediate changes in tribal governments.[121] Undoubtedly Vizenor was referring specifically to the organization that had come to represent the militant cutting edge of Indian protest, the American Indian Movement.

Red Power

*T*he American Indian Movement was founded in Minneapolis,
Minnesota, in July, 1968, as an offshoot of a Minneapolis OEO anti-poverty
program which had been funded for over $100,000. It was designed to parallel the city's
highly successful and well-funded black organizations, especially the Black Patrol,
which was organized in 1966 to counsel groups of black youth in order to keep a lid on
potential violence. Dennis Banks, Clyde Bellecourt, and George Mitchell, all Chippewa
from Minnesota, claim to be cofounders of AIM. Mitchell and Bellecourt originally were
from the White Earth reservation and Banks came from the Leech Lake Reservation.
Banks and Bellecourt were on the staff of a Minneapolis anti poverty program called
Citizen's Community Centers (CCC) when they founded AIM. Mitchell was employed
as a social welfare worker in Minneapolis.

A well-publicized article in the March 18, 1973, <u>Detroit News</u> indicated that two
CCC board members, Matthew Eubanks, a Minneapolis Black Panther leader, and
Douglas Hall, a white American Civil Liberties Union attorney, were instrumental in
taking control of the CCC from moderates and selecting Banks and Bellecourt to head
the radical new Indian movement. Mrs. Emily Peake, also a Chippewa, and spokes-
woman of the Upper Midwest American Indian Center, which claimed to represent most
of the estimated 22,000 Indians in the area, was the source for the critical article. Hall
vigorously denied the allegation both by telephone and by letter. "I had nothing to do in
any way with the founding of AIM and with picking of leaders. . . I never functioned with
Matt Eubanks in that way. I seriously doubt that Matt would claim that it happened that
way," wrote Hall. Hall, Eubanks, and the Reverend Paul Boe of the American Lutheran
Church, also on the CCC, however, did provide advice and support after AIM was
founded.

AIM originally called themselves the Concerned Indian Americans (CIA). That was
changed quickly to avoid the obvious comparison with the Central Intelligence Agency.
Probably about fifty people were active in AIM in the beginning but recruitment was
persistent. Most members were Chippewa from several reservations in northern Minne-

sota. Other tribes, especially Sioux, were also represented. AIM stressed Pan-Indianism, meaning loyalty to race over loyalty to a specific tribe, which was best suited for the mixed group of urban Indians. Members tended to be each other's friends, relatives, or neighbors. This gave the original group a close-knit quality.[2]

The basic goals of the organization focused on the improvement of the economic and educational status of Indians. In order to achieve these goals, AIM ideology stressed that the Indian must achieve and maintain pride, as exemplified by the color red. The AIM banner portrayed a fist with the slogan "United We Are One Powerful Fist—Dignity, Pride, Unity." The official colors of red, black, and yellow stood for the non-white population of the world; and green represented the land. The organization was dedicated to strategies of demonstration, confrontation and occupation as distinguished from traditionally less militant Indian organizations. From the beginning, AIM liked to compare itself to New Left organizations like the Black Panthers.[3] As support from churches and charitable institutions increased, some members were hired as paid staff. The staff soon identified the principal enemies of Indian people as the Christian Church, the American educational system and the United States Government.[4]

The question of AIM's priorities—social service locally versus political action at home and away—was hotly debated, with the latter finally prevailing. AIM's two local long-term projects, both patterned after black creations, were the Indian Patrol and the AIM Survival Schools.[5] The Indian Patrol operated regularly on Friday and Saturday nights during the fall of 1968, patrolling East Franklin Avenue, the area of greatest Indian concentration in Minneapolis. Some ten or twenty people, many of whom were non-Indian, patrolled on a typical weekend evening, using citizens band radios to coordinate their activities. Many bought red jackets with "Indian Patrol" sewn in large letters on the back, which afforded them a high degree of visibility and a sense of organizational unity. They monitored the police, not only for blatant use of unnecessary force, but also for more subtle forms of mistreatment, such as the use of insulting language. Indians who appeared to have too much to drink or requested help for one reason or another were offered assistance.

The experience provided an excellent proving ground for young AIM leaders.[6] Some leaders had trouble containing their new-found prosperity, though. According to Vizenor, "The issue was police harassment—which is still a good issue—but the method of trailing police cars in expensive convertibles became an extravagant parody."[7] The convertible issue brought out an enduring and at times vexing problem of internal control within the organization that has never been resolved.

AIM established its first Survival School in Minneapolis in January, 1971, funded by the OEO. By fall, 1972, they had four in operation. The schools provided Indian teachers and emphasized Indian culture and racial pride. On the second anniversary of AIM, Banks said, "We must commit ourselves to changing the social pattern in which we have been forced to live. . . the government and churches have demoralized, dehumanized, massacred, robbed, raped, promised, made treaty after treaty, and lied to us. . . we must now destroy this political machine that man has built to prevent us from self-determination."[8] Banks continued, ". . . we must, ourselves, build machines that will prevent this—not a political type machine—but a machine built on beliefs, self-determination, freedom from oppression, and on the difference between what is morally right and wrong as opposed to what is legal and illegal."[9] Critics insisted that the schools were operated as a vehicle to attract federal funding and promote politically correct thinking. The teachers, it was alleged, were chosen more by their race and political inclinations that by their academic qualifications with a resultant lack of student academic progress in basic skills. Certainly AIM was eager to communicate its newly-developed racial pride to other Indians and also to non-Indians. The schools represented a natural avenue of dissemination.[10]

Critics of AIM's militant posture abounded among both white and Indian spokesmen. Although the concept of Pan-Tribalism caught on fairly well among more heterogeneous urban Indians, it never had much appeal to reservation Indians who have always been especially conscious of their tribal heritage. Opposition to AIM emanated especially from those tribal Indians who were socially and economically tied to the existing system and therefore viewed AIM as an urban threat to their established order.[11] AIM never has gained control of a reservation for that reason.

Vine Deloria, Jr. warned in <u>Custer Died for Your Sins</u>, "There is added danger to urban Indians from their involvement with the militants of other minority groups, particularly the black power movements." Deloria further suggested that it made a great deal of difference what kind of philosophy provided the basis of militancy. He urged that urban Indians first make sure that they had full support of the urban community before following the path of the black militants because otherwise they, too, would have to resort to violence as a means of taking up their demands. "Simply to invite violence upon oneself for the sake of temporary concessions seems ridiculous and stupid," Deloria concluded.[12]

Possibly some of Deloria's apprehension stemmed from the success AIM was enjoying in competing with a myriad of Indian organizations for financial support from various church groups, institutions, liberal organizations and individuals, plus the government. Church support of black militants readily transferred to AIM. Deloria commented, "They believed deeply in the militant version of black power as violent confrontations, and grants were made to organizations within the respective minority groups that they were sure would produce the desired confrontations."[13]

Although at best only a rough estimate of AIM's funding is available, a figure of around $400,000 from church groups from 1968 through 1973 is usually quoted. The American Lutheran Church donated the most from among the church groups. It donated an officially reported $110,181.73 from 1968 through 1972.[14] Other known figures for church donations include $40,000 from the Roman Catholic Church in September, 1971, and $10,000 from the Episcopal Church by 1972.[15] Additional substantial church donations came from the National Council of Churches, the United Methodist Church, the Presbyterian Church, and the Church of Jesus Christ of the Latter Day Saints.

Paul Boe, from a prominent Norwegian family in Minnesota, provided the impetus for Lutheran involvement with AIM. As Executive Director of the Division of Social Services of the American Lutheran Church, Boe decided by 1968 that the time for real movement in the area of Indian social and economic betterment had come. Boe supported AIM from its inception in Minneapolis as the most effective vehicle for change available.[16] His personal support for and allocation of church funds to AIM provoked a storm of protest from Lutherans all over the country, but especially in the Midwest.[17]

What AIM received in grants from the federal government remains even more difficult to ascertain with any certainty. More than likely it exceeded the amount contributed by churches because a good deal of the church contributions qualified for federal matching grants.[18] At the time of the 1973 Wounded Knee occupation the Detroit News estimated that AIM had received $400,000 in federal grants; however, much of that was earmarked for specific programs such as Survival Schools and community centers.[19] Moreover, a substantial portion, perhaps half, of the leading AIM members and sympathizers held positions in social welfare agencies financed primarily by the federal government.[20] AIM kept no known records of any of its financial transactions. It is known, however, that OEO began phasing out its Minneapolis anti-poverty program as early as 1970 because of its dissatisfaction with the lack of accountability, misappropriation of funds, and bad publicity. In fairness one must recognize that the Nixon administration was in the process of phasing out the entire national program for the same reasons, but Minneapolis OEO seemed worse than most. OEO reported that $25 million had been spent in Minneapolis in seven years, ninety percent to Blacks and Indians, with little measurable achievement.[21]

Daniel Moynihan, a noted critic of OEO, commented, "With militancy the mark of merit is increasingly measured in terms of the ability to be sufficiently outrageous to obtain press and television coverage—or so one is forced to conclude from the behavior of those involved—more and more the antipoverty program came to be associated with the kind of bad manners and arrogance that are among the mark of the rich rather than the poor. . . ."[22] By the late 1960s, AIM was well on its way to becoming a symbolic confrontation group that fit Moynihan's description.

Driven by substantial financial support and increasing publicity, AIM established chapters in Cleveland, Denver, Milwaukee, Chicago, San Francisco, and other urban centers that had attracted a substantial Indian population. AIM was especially strong in Los Angeles and San Francisco. Russell Means, an Oglala Sioux from the San Francisco area, was chosen to head the second AIM chapter, which was established in Cleveland, Ohio. Vernon Bellecourt, Clyde's older brother, headed the active Denver chapter. A number of reservations formed AIM chapters as well. For example, Robert Ecoffey, whose son, Robert, would later be a captain in the BIA police force and is presently acting BIA superintendent, briefly headed the AIM group on the Pine Ridge Reservation. It did not last long, however, apparently because of disagreement with the national leadership.23

AIM's central headquarters were located on the first floor of an old red brick building on East Franklin Avenue in St. Paul. The windows on the upper two floors were boarded over. The main office contained old furniture and a generous amount of pegboard holding publicity literature and Indian art. A prominently placed desk placard showed an enlarged nickel coin with the statement, "The only Indian America ever cared about."[24]

By any measure the AIM leaders presented a striking image. As a group they were a virile, handsome return to the days of Crazy Horse and Geronimo. They wore their hair long and frequently dressed in traditional Indian garb, which included plenty of jewelry and feathers. Complaints against white society were recited in strident tones with total confidence. One of their appeals stemmed from their personal backgrounds which had, in a number of cases, included prison sentences that had introduced them to police brutality and harassment first hand. These were not ivory-tower intellectuals, but street-toughened men of the world. Young Indians found them especially appealing. Banks, Means, and the Bellecourt brothers emerged as the dominant leaders, with Banks generally recognized as the natural leader. AIM soon developed a reputation, however, for its internal bickering, jealousies, and power struggles.[25]

Banks, an erect, stoic, Chippewa whose profile bears a strong resemblance to the Indian profile on old United States five cent coins, claims that he made his commitment to an American Indian Movement while serving nine months in solitary confinement in the maximum security prison at Stillwater, Minnesota, for violating parole.[26] Categorized as a "habitual criminal," he served a year in 1964 for burglary and did another six months shortly thereafter for forging a government check. Banks was born April 12, 1930, into a family of six at Walker, on the Leech Lake Reservation in northern Minnesota. Banks's brother, Mark, has gained some stature as a Hollywood bit actor, "Johnny West." At age five, Banks was bused about four hundred miles to the Pipestone Indian School where he stayed nine years. He attended schools in North Dakota and South Dakota for the next two years; returned to Leech Lake where he continued in school for six months before joining the United States Air Force in 1953, serving in Japan and Korea. Banks was a recruiter for the Honeywell Corporation in 1968 when he asked for a leave of absence plus financial support to organize a new Indian movement with two other Chippewas, George Mitchell and Clyde Bellecourt. Honeywell terminated Banks's leave and their financial support when they learned of AIM's radical posture.[27] By 1971 Banks had eleven children by two marriages. Since then he has had three more children by his third wife, Kamook, a young Oglala whom he married just before the Wounded knee takeover. Presently, they, too, are separated.

Clyde Bellecourt and his brother Vernon grew up in a family of twelve children on the White Earth Reservation in Minnesota. Eleven of the twelve served terms either in reform school or prison. Clyde, born May 8, 1936, was sent to Red Wing Training School for three years at age eleven. He returned twice for parole violations. When he was freed again, a condition of his release was that he could not return to the White Earth Reservation. His parents then moved to Minneapolis. In 1953 he was sent to the St. Cloud Reformatory for slugging a sixty-four-year-old man. After that he was in an all-Indian burglary ring until he was caught and sent back to St. Cloud for three years. Eight months after his release he was returned to prison on the same charge. During his last stay, Clyde obtained his high school equivalent diploma and also received a license as a steam plant engineer by working in the prison's heating plant and taking courses. His leadership skills were polished by a Dale Carnegie course in public speaking. At Stillwater prison Clyde met Eddie Benton Banai, a fellow Indian prisoner from Wisconsin who had organized a group to study Indian religion and culture, which Bellecourt joined. Benton later became the Saint Paul director of AIM and "founder" of the Little Red School House. Clyde was working for the Northern States Power Company, which had nine dams on Indian reservations, when he was elected first national director of AIM in 1968. He took a paid leave of absence from NSPC and never returned to it.28

Vernon Bellecourt, born October 17, 1931, dropped out of school in the eighth grade. He drifted into the Minneapolis ghetto and at age nineteen was sentenced to the St. Cloud Reformatory for robbing a tavern. While in prison he studied barbering and ingratiated himself with prison authorities with his excellent haircutting. After thirty-six months, Vernon was released and became one of the better known hair stylists in Minneapolis. He moved to Denver ostensibly to enter a new career in commercial real estate sales but soon began working full-time as the director of AIM's active Denver chapter. Articulate and urbane despite his limited educational background, Vernon Bellecourt frequently served as AIM's public spokesman.[29]

Russell Means founded the second AIM chapter at Cleveland. He was recruited by Dennis Banks at an AIM meeting in San Francisco in 1969. Banks invited him to the convention of the National Council of Churches in Detroit. From there Means went to Cleveland where, in addition to his AIM organizing activities, he directed the Indian community center and served as a part-time dance instructor.[30] One of four brothers, Means was born on the Pine Ridge Reservation on November 10, 1939. His father was recruited for work in the naval shipyards in San Francisco during World War II, as were a number of other Sioux. Means spent his infancy on the reservation, mainly with his grandparents, then joined his parents at a Vallejo, California, housing project at age six. He was baptized and confirmed in the Catholic Church and was active in the Boy Scouts. Tall and well-built, Means had considerable promise as an athlete, but dropped out of San Leandro High School, becoming a drifter, a heroin addict, and then an alcoholic.[31] After several arrests, but no felony convictions, and a year on skid row in Los Angeles, Means controlled his drinking and began attending colleges intending to become an accountant. After enrolling in four different colleges he obtained senior standing at Cleveland State College in Cleveland, Ohio, but never graduated.[32] Those who remember his return trips to the Pine Ridge Reservation before his AIM days recall Means as a meticulous dresser who was greatly concerned about his personal appearance. Means was working for the tribal council on the Rosebud Reservation when he met Banks in San Francisco. During his stint on the Rosebud Reservation, Means also became closely acquainted with William Janklow, a young legal aid attorney, who would later become governor of South Dakota and an avowed enemy of AIM.

At Cleveland Means soon demonstrated a genius for staging well-publicized demonstrations. He led the capture of the Mayflower II on Thanksgiving Day, 1970; took part in the brief occupation of Mount Rushmore in June, 1971; and helped lead an unsuccessful attempt to take over the central BIA office in Washington, D. C., the same year.[33] Means left Cleveland to return to Pine Ridge shortly after filing a multi-million dollar lawsuit against the Cleveland Indian baseball team because Chief Wahoo, their symbol, was "racist, degrading, and demeaning to the American Indian."[34] Although Banks and Means frequently were regarded as a team during AIM's peak years, actually they never were very congenial in age, personality or philosophy.

Another Indian organization, the American Indians United, organized on the West Coast about the same time as AIM, came up with the coup that some commentators characterized as "the red man's Selma."[35] Alcatraz Island in San Francisco Bay, the home of the famous federal prison which had been abandoned by the government for several years, provided the stage. After several aborted attempts about eighty Indians seized it on November 19, 1969, maintaining that a treaty with the government allowed Indians to occupy abandoned federal territory. They announced their intention of converting it into a Native American Cultural Center. Although the government did not agree with this interpretation, it was decided that nothing that significant could be gained and a great deal could be lost in an attempt to physically remove the occupiers, about half of whom were women and children.

During its eighteen month span, the Alcatraz takeover spawned a torrent of media publicity, featuring a number of plays on history. The original leader, Richard Oakes, a muscular twenty-seven-year-old Mohawk, offered the government $24 in glass beads for the Island and suggested the formation of a Bureau of Caucasian Affairs for the white caretakers who remained on Alcatraz.[36] John Trudell, twenty-three, a Santee Sioux, and a four-year navy veteran, eventually assumed leadership. Trudell organized a radio program called "Radio Free Alcatraz," which regularly broadcast from Berkeley on the Public Pacifica Network.[37] Most of the media remained sympathetic to the occupiers and cautioned against government use of force. In less than a week after the occupation, for example, the New York Times carried a story citing two instances: Jolo Island in the Philippines, where six hundred men, women, and children died in an attack led by Generals Wood and Bliss in 1913; and Wounded Knee, where indiscriminate killing of women and children had also occurred because of government harshness.[38]

Although the occupiers clung tenaciously to their perch on the island, maintaining that they would fight to their death if need be, they were torn by internal dissent and personal tragedy. Indians from the San Francisco area deeply resented Indians from outside the state who usurped authority. Oakes's eight year old daughter fell to her death down a three story stairwell on January 8, 1970. Oakes suspected foul play but eyewitnesses insisted that it was an accident. Oakes was accused of mishandling the considerable amount of donations that were attracted by the takeover, and resigned in disgust. The insolent behavior of the "Alcatraz Security Force," an elite group who dressed in special jackets and headquartered in their own "training room," further disrupted morale. As the occupation dragged on, both water and food grew increasingly scarce, but a small force managed to continue its vigil in spite of all adversities until United States Marshals peacefully removed the remaining fifteen some eighteen months after the original takeover.[39] Although the Indians did not succeed in obtaining permanent possession of Alcatraz or other major immediate concessions from the government, their action spurred the government into pouring money into urban Indian programs which in turn stimulated increased militancy.

Success at Alcatraz sparked a series of takeovers and takeover attempts by Indian activists around the country. Most of them did not last for an extended period. Examples of property temporarily seized during the Alcatraz occupation period include: an abandoned United States Coast Guard station at Milwaukee; an abandoned Nike missile site on Lake Michigan; the Twin Cities Naval Air Station at Minneapolis; Fort Lawton, a former army base near Seattle; the Sheep Mountain, North Dakota, gunnery range. An attempt to take over Ellis Island in March, 1970, was stymied when an outboard motor on a boat launched from Jersey City failed.

AIM carried out its first sustained takeover in late July, 1970, at a Lutheran Church-Indian relations meeting on the campus of Augustana College at Sioux Falls, South Dakota. That summer a group of three-hundred people, nearly two-hundred of whom were Indian, held the second annual meeting co-sponsored by LUCHIP (LutheranChurch and Indian People) with LCUSA (Lutheran Church in the USA). The AIM delegation, headed by Dennis Banks, only consisted of about forty representatives; but they took over the meeting and demanded $750,000 from the American Lutheran Church immediately. "If you lift up your goddamn eyes from the Bible, you'll see what's happening to our people and help us," said one AIM member.[40] When the AIM demands were not approved, the AIM delegation locked itself in Bergsaker Hall, their dormitory, and announced that they were there to stay until their demands were met. College officials decide that the quarrel was not with Augustana, but with the church, and requested a peaceful settlement. That was accomplished and by Wednesday night the approximately twenty remaining Indians left.[41] Among the unfulfilled AIM demands was a request for a National Council of Churches Indian Board that must be seventy-five percent Indian. Clyde Bellecourt also claimed one billion dollars in damages had been inflicted by the church against Indians in three categories:

> 250 million for violations of the Ten Commandments 450 million for alienation of ecumenical affections 300 million for punitive damages[42]

In the perspective of AIM's demands, the $45,000 that the American Lutheran Church granted them in 1971 was relatively minute.

Encouraged by financial support and favorable publicity, AIM expanded its membership and its militant activities swiftly. Dennis Banks and several other AIM leaders disrupted a government sponsored conference on urban Indian problems at the plush Airlie House at Warrenton, Virginia, in December, 1970. Airlie House is a privately operated meeting center often leased by the government for conferences. The Indians got into a dispute with management over the closing of the house bar, and vandalized the center stealing cash, liquor, and food. Total losses were estimated at $25,000, but the government chose not to prosecute.[43]

Russell Means led about sixty Indians in an invasion of the BIA's Washington office on September 22, 1971. They attempted to place a citizen's arrest on Wilma Victor, an educator who had been chosen as Interior Secretary Rogers Morton's special assistant on Indian affairs, and John Crow, Deputy BIA Commissioner. Means characterized Victor as a dictatorial sadist because of her controversial role as headmistress of the Intermountain Boarding School near Brigham City, Utah. Crow, an acknowledged enemy of AIM, was accused of subverting President Nixon's policy of Indian self-determination. The activists were promptly arrested and twenty-six of them were jailed, but they were released quickly and sent home at government expense. BIA Commissioner Louis R. Bruce, once ridiculed by AIM as "Bruce the Goose," apologized to AIM.[44]

Immediately after the BIA encounter, AIM organized on a national basis in October. By now there were over sixty AIM chapters spread across the United States, and the need for a more unified approach had become evident. Originally AIM had provided almost total autonomy for local chapters, which seemed to fit the Indian cultural heritage; but now coordination of funding requests, policy statements and philosophy was badly needed. Numerous AIM groups gathered at Camp Owendigo, an Episcopal summer camp on Carver Lake near Minneapolis, in mid-October to re-mold AIM into a national body with a group of national directors. AIM adopted articles of incorporation and a set of bylaws giving each chapter two votes on the national board. Means was elected national coordinator, Banks was named interim executive director, and national head-quarters remained in Minneapolis. Means and others emphasized that AIM, among other things, was a spiritual movement which would continue to practice Indian religion. Means also spoke for a committee that insisted that the bylaws should provide for the ouster of board members who abused drugs or alcohol while on AIM business. AIM leadership, he said, "must set an example" to help combat the stereotype of the drinking Indian.[45]

Jim West, a consultant for the Inter-religious Foundation for Community Organizations (IFCO), also came to the convention to discuss past and future support of AIM. IFCO was designed to channel funds from various church denominations into social action projects. IFCO gave $10,000 to the Minneapolis AIM in 1971, West reported. The Campaign for Human Development, a Catholic fund, gave another $40,000, he added. West also indicated he told AIM leaders that more money might be available when the national group organized fully. "This is exactly the kind of thing that IFCO is here for," he said.

Later in 1971 AIM met at Reno, Nevada, to unite urban and reservation groups. What had here-to-fore been mostly a Midwestern urban organization was now extended to the focal point of Indian concern—the reservation. Full-bloods, especially, tended to take AIM leaders seriously when they talked about treaties because they had generally boycotted tribal governments set up under the Indian Reorganization Act of 1934 on the basis that they represented a violation of treaty rights.[47] Ironically, almost all of the AIM leaders were mixed-bloods.

Certainly not all reservation Indians supported AIM. They distrusted its left-wing orientation and many did not regard it as an organization appropriate to reservation Indians and their needs. To a number of reservation Indians AIM appeared to be associated with the anti-war protesters who were regarded as unpatriotic. AIM seemed to belong to the hippie fringe element and express an urban flippancy alien to traditional Indian values. AIM, consequently, always encountered difficulty establishing its credibility as an organization which could serve reservations as well as urban areas.[48] Although many Indians disagreed with AIM's militant tactics, most supported the purpose of the movement and respected the energy and dedication the AIM people gave to expressing grievances and changing conditions of life for them.[49]

Raymond Yellow Thunder's unfortunate death at Gordon, Nebraska, triggered the first large-scale AIM intervention in a reservation matter and it proved a smashing success. Yellow Thunder was a fifty-one-year-old Sioux from Porcupine on the Pine Ridge Reservation, who was found dead in a panel truck in a used car lot on Sunday, February 20, 1972, by several boys who were playing in the area. Sheridan County Attorney Mike Smith was called from a pick-up basketball game to view the body, which did not appear badly injured. When the autopsy revealed death from a cerebral hemotoma, Smith began an official inquiry because he was investigating a case involving an Indian who had been stripped from the waist down and shoved into the local American Legion Hall on February 12. Yellow Thunder was identified by those who were there as the Indian involved in the Legion incident.

Investigation reveals that the perpetrators of the act had discussed the incident at a truck stop the same evening it had occurred. When news of the death spread, an eyewitness who had observed the incident in the Legion parking lot stepped forward. Smith filed a manslaughter and false imprisonment complaint on February 22 against five people, all living in Longmont, Colorado, at the time. They included brothers Leslie, 28, and Melvin, 26, Hare, former Gordon area residents; Robert Bayliss, 28, a former Gordon auto mechanic; Bernard J. Lutter, 23; and Jeanette Thompson. Thompson was Leslie Hare's girlfriend and was not directly involved, so charges were dropped against her. Lutter, a slightly built carpenter, whom Smith described as "obviously not being the same type as his companions," agreed to plead guilty to false imprisonment in exchange for dropping of the manslaughter charges. Lutter proved to be the key witness for the prosecution of the Hares and Bayliss.[50]

Lutter testified that the group had been coyote hunting the afternoon of February 12 and got together in a Gordon bar that evening. Sometime after 10:00 p.m. , they rode around and picked up a case of beer. The talk turned to "busting an Indian," a practice that the Hares allegedly had pursued on previous occasions. When they spotted one on Main Street, Leslie Hare got out and yelled at him and shoved him, but the Indian walked away with no further incident. When they located him again in the cab of a pickup truck, they roughed him up and took his pants off and threw him in the trunk of Bayliss's car.

The Hare brothers had been removed from the premises of the Gordon American Legion Club several weeks before by manager Bernard Sandage for failure to comply with club rules for guests, and they wanted to embarrass him.[51] So, after driving around for awhile, the group stopped at the Legion and agreed to throw Yellow Thunder into the club through a side door. At about 12:00 midnight, Melvin Hare and Lutter shoved Yellow Thunder into the crowded club and slammed the door shut. Marvin Wheeler, a club member, and Sandage immediately came to the aid of Yellow Thunder, who held one hand over his face and pulled down his shirt with the other while quickly exiting the building through the door he had just entered. Few people in the club saw the incident, which took place in an estimated thirty seconds.[52]

Yellow Thunder refused further assistance and walked back toward the center of Gordon alone. Yellow Thunder's attackers reencountered him a few blocks from the Legion Club and loaded him into Bayliss's car again, drove to a laundromat, where the put his clothes back on and released him. Later the group openly talked about the incident at the Seger Oil all-night truck stop. All five returned to Colorado the next morning.[53]

Yellow Thunder had suffered the head injury sometime during the course of events but was still capable of self-control. Smith admits that the injury may not have been a direct result of a blow, but it seemed to be more consistent with a severe bump that he may have received while riding around over railroad tracks and rough roads in the trunk of the car. Sheridan County deputy sheriff John Paul testified that Yellow Thunder voluntarily came to the jail shortly after midnight with bruises and scratches about his right cheek. He asked to sleep there, not an uncommon practice for Yellow Thunder, who had done it many times before and was readily recognized by Paul. Paul testified that he already knew about the Legion incident and Yellow Thunder told him that he was the one who had been pushed inside by "four white boys" whom he did not know.[54]

Yellow Thunder left the Gordon jail at about 7:00 a.m. "with a staggering gait."[55] George Ghost Dog saw Yellow Thunder the same day inside a pickup truck cab at the car lot. He told Ghost Dog that "white guys beat me up." Ghost Dog noted that he had a fat lip and some blood on his face and asked him if he was all right. Yellow Thunder said, "Yes." Ghost Dog saw him lying down in the truck several days later but thought Yellow Thunder was asleep and did not disturb him.

Some eight days after the incident, the body was found and turned over to pathologist W. O. Brown of Scottsbluff, Nebraska. He found the corpse had several bruises and lacerations about the head, right side and right leg. An internal examination showed no skull fracture but did reveal a subdural hematoma, which covered the entire right side of the brain. Death was described as being caused "mechanically" by the subdural hematoma. Brown suggested that the process could take hours, days or even weeks. He also reported signs of bronchial pneumonia and pulmonary edema in Yellow Thunder.[56] Brown claimed there was no doubt about the immediate cause of death—it was the subdural hematoma caused by a wound on the forehead that was "externally rather inconspicuous, but inside it spread." He estimated time of death as Thursday, February 17.[57] Brown said "some instrument" other than a fist caused the forehead wound.

Justice moved as swiftly as one might expect, at least after Yellow Thunder was found dead. On February 25, the five involved in the incident appeared in the Sheridan County Court House for a preliminary hearing on two charges: (1) false imprisonment and (2) manslaughter. Four of the men were so charged and released on $6,250 bond each. Regional and national media picked up the story immediately. Rumors circulated that Yellow Thunder had been forced to dance Indian style to the delight of the crowd at the Legion Club; that he had been mutilated, burned with lighted cigarettes, and castrated by his attackers.[58] AIM congregated at Omaha where they chartered two Greyhound buses for the four-hundred mile trip to Pine Ridge and Gordon for protest rallies.

Jo Matula, wife of the Gordon Jack and Jill grocery store owner, encountered Russell Means on a Gordon street with an upside down American flag draped around him. She expressed dismay that the symbol of American patriotism should be so badly treated. Means said, "Lady an upside down flag is used as a signal by the navy when a ship is in distress. Our people are in distress. I will wear this flag upside down as long as my people are in distress." The upside down flag had been adopted as the AIM symbol, and an Indian wearing it in that manner was featured in the Life magazine story on the incident at Gordon.[59]

Reporters and television crews from around the world converged on the little Sand Hills community of 2,500. The town, whose main claim to fame prior to this was that it served as a backdrop for many of Mari Sandoz's works because her father, "Old Jules," had homesteaded nearby, was subjected to intense scrutiny and pressure. Gordon's leadership handled the situation with moderation and skill that impressed many reporters. Negotiations began when Severt Young Bear, a massive 6'3" 250-pound AIM leader from Porcupine, who was Yellow Thunder's nephew, arranged a large rally at Billy Mills Hall at Pine Ridge. More than five-hundred people attended. Mike Smith and Nebraska State Patrol Investigator Max Ibach, were there to face a stream of charges and accusations from AIM leaders.

The next day, an AIM group estimated at about three hundred took over the Gordon Community Hall after securing food and camping privileges from the town. They set up an "Indian Grand Jury" to hear complaints.[60] Demands included: justice in the Yellow Thunder killing, and a complete examination of Gordon's relationship with Native Americans including police policies, medical practices, education, schooling, housing, treatment in the local newspaper, and job discrimination.

There were a number of Gordon area residents who wanted to physically oust AIM from the Community Center, but Smith, who had been flown to Lincoln for a special meeting with Governor J. J. Exon concerning the crisis, preserved order by insisting on negotiations. He indicated that the negotiations with Means and Banks were indeed quite amicable under the circumstances. The AIM leaders needed a symbolic victory before leaving, and Smith worked out an offer that they accepted. Gordon agreed to form a Human Relations Board to investigate Indian grievances and to exhume Yellow Thunder's body, which was buried at Porcupine, so it could be examined for evidence of mutilation in front of AIM leaders. When the body was re-examined in front of numerous witnesses including Smith, AIM leaders and the press, no mutilation was revealed.

Ultimately, the Hare brothers and Bayliss were convicted by jury trial and received one to six year sentences for manslaughter. Reacting to the national attention, the Gordon Journal editorialized, "People of the Gordon community had a good and painful look last week at 'big city' reporters of every media in action. They saw and heard the truth distorted beyond all belief."[61] Governor Exon declared shortly after the trials that the facts of the case and the court proceedings "leave no doubt that some Indians at least are very badly treated in the state."[62]

Popular misinterpretations of the Yellow Thunder killings abound. Vine Deloria claimed, "Gordon officials had done nothing about the incident until the American Indian Movement called nearly a thousand Indians into the town as a protest." Clyde Bellecourt asserted on a Pacifica Library Tape, "They pushed this Indian out there and they made him dance naked Indian style to the applause of the whites." The European version was even more sensationalized, Pierrette Desy, a French AIM fund raiser, wrote in the March 1974 Paris based La Gueule Ouberte, "After being locked up in the boot of a car belonging to two whites for two days, he was then castrated and beaten to death. The murderers were arrested, accused of manslaughter and set free."

The most damaging misinterpretation is in Peter Matthiessen's popular In the Spirit of Crazy Horse:

> In February 1972, an Oglala from Pine Ridge named Raymond
> Yellow Thunder was severely beaten for the fun of it by two white
> brothers named Hare, then stripped from the waist down and paraded
> before a patriotic gathering at an American Legion dance in Gordon,
> Nebraska; the merry crowd was invited to join the Hares in kicking the
> Indian, after which the brothers stuffed him into a car trunk, where he

perished. When his body was found, the Hares were arrested, then released without bail while awaiting trial for second-degree manslaughter; even this charge might have been dismissed had not Raymond Yellow Thunder's family, in the absence of meaningful interest or help from local authorities or the FBI, made the decision to call AIM.[63]

Alvin M. Josephy, Jr., former editor of American Heritage magazine and past president of the National Council of the Institute of the American West, also deceives in Now that the Buffalo's Gone:

> In February 1972, when nothing was done to punish the tormentors and murderers of Raymond Yellow Thunder, Means and Banks led some 1,300 angry Indians, mostly Sioux from Pine Ridge and Rosebud, into the town of Gordon, occupying it for three days and threatening town and state officials if they failed to carry out justice. To the relief of the frightened townspeople, two whites were finally jailed in connection with the crime, a policeman was suspended, and the local authorities were persuaded to promise to end discrimination against Indians.[64]

Immediately following their success at Gordon, AIM leaders held a ten-day session on the Pine Ridge Reservation to celebrate their victory and plan for the future. Tribal chairman Gerald One Feather had been defeated by Dick Wilson and was about to go out of office, so he did not interfere with the AIM visit. On the way from Gordon, a large group stopped off at the Wounded Knee Trading Post and called out owners Jim Czywczynski and Clive Gildersleeve for a dressing down because of complaints of mistreatment that had been brought up during the "Grand Jury" hearings. The specific incident that Means, Banks, and the Bellecourts alluded to as an example of brutality involved the shaking up of a youth of about fourteen. Allegedly Czywczynski abused the boy after he had mocked his wife and cursed him when he ejected him from the store. The boy was shaken up but not injured.[65] While AIM was denouncing the store owners, a number in the crowd chanted "burn, burn, burn." [66] Others took an estimated $50,000 worth of artifacts out of the neighboring Wounded Knee museum, also owned by Gildersleeve and Czywczynski. When Wilson heard of the incident, he vowed that AIM would never be allowed to hold another meeting on Pine Ridge while he was in charge.

If the venture to Gordon and Pine Ridge proved to be an unqualified success for AIM, its first official venture onto a reservation created a near disaster. AIM held their national convention at Cass Lake on Banks's Leech Lake Reservation in Minnesota, May 10-16, 1972. The Leech Lake Chippewas were trying to enforce a federal court ruling that White men had to buy tribal fishing licenses. AIM moved in with guns to back them up. Leech Lake Indians informed AIM that they were not needed and asked them to leave. Some AIM members voted to leave and others voted to stay in defiance of the tribe. The ensuing argument almost turned into a gunfight.[67] "Many militants stated then that they had come to Cass Lake to die for tribal people. The issue was won through the courts, and suicide was not necessary," commented Gerald Vizenor in the Minneapolis Tribune.[68]

AIM hurried back to Alliance, Nebraska, for the trial of the Hare brothers in late May. A change of venue had been granted, so the trial had been shifted some sixty miles south to the cattle and railroad town of Alliance. An advance party of AIM arrived in Alliance on May 23. City leaders were contacted and asked for accommodations one thousand to five thousand people. The mayor and city manager agreed to give them a camping area, but did not accede to give money or free food. Other demands such as the closure of liquor outlets during the trial and the formation of a human relations board were also agreed upon. The free food request was taken to the Alliance Ministerial Association which reportedly turned it down. Later it was learned that individual ministers did agree to help.[69]

Less than two-hundred AIM supporters showed up. They attempted to hold a grand jury similar to the one in Gordon but canceled it. Clyde Bellecourt was given permission to address the high school graduation assembly at the local football stadium. His appearance was incident free. Because would-be jurors took most of the 104 seats at the courthouse the morning of the first day of jury selection, nearly one hundred Indians were turned away. Banks, who was being advised by a member of the Justice Department's Community Relations Service, protested. He was informed by District Judge Robert Moran that when the jury was impaneled seats would be available on a first-come, first-served basis. Banks then addressed the crowd and declared that the courtroom was barred to Indians. He exclaimed that the town and the judge were racist and that the court would allow the Hare brothers to go free. "Instead of sitting in the courtroom for nine hours a day and doing nothing, we can now expose Nebraska as the number one racist state in the country," said Banks.[70]

As the jury selection process got under way that afternoon, the Indians held a powwow on the courthouse lawn. The sound of drumbeats and chants drifted up through the open windows of the non-air-conditioned courthouse that afternoon. And they did throughout the trial. Smith conducted a vigorous, well-planned prosecution. At 8:55 p.m. on May 26, the jury returned a guilty verdict. AIM sang a war chant while Clyde Bellecourt rushed up to shake Judge Moran's hand. Banks addressed the group with a fateful promise, "We of the American Indian Movement are here to tell you that the struggle still lies ahead and we are starting to battle this struggle tonight."[71]

South Dakota would be the ultimate focus of that struggle. Nature provided Banks an opportunity to become involved in Indian affairs in Rapid City, the leading city in Western South Dakota. On June 9, 1972, a terrific rainstorm broke a dam near Rapid City, resulting in a massive, deadly flood. Because many of the city's three thousand or so Indians lived in low-lying areas, they bore a disproportionate brunt of the damage. Although AIM sit-ins had occurred at Mount Rushmore in 1970 and 1971, Banks made his first official appearance in Rapid City after the flood. He helped with a coalition of Indian people to coordinate various relief projects. They also monitored state and federal aid to insure that the Indians would receive and equitable share. Bank's efforts, however, were not entirely welcomed by local Indians, who maintained that he and his followers attempted to dominate the locals and dictate policy to them. AIM's attempt to take advantage of the situation by issuing unilateral press releases and appeals for money proved especially irritating. Finally, under heavy criticism, Banks and AIM left.[72]

AIM appeared to be on the decline. Its leaders realized that something impressive on a national scale like Alcatraz was needed to restore momentum. All sixty-seven chapters of AIM met to map strategy at the Sun Dance ceremonies at Crow Dog's Paradise on the Rosebud Reservation in July, 1972. There it was decided that all of the activists of all tribes would gather and prepare a peaceful march on Washington, D. C., that fall. This endeavor was named the Trail of Broken Treaties. Final planning for the demonstration was completed in Denver in September. Caravans were to begin on the West Coast from Seattle and San Francisco, pick up supporters as they traveled east, and arrive in Washington during the final week of the 1972 presidential race between Nixon and George McGovern.[73]

The shooting death of Alcatraz leader Richard Oakes near Santa Clara, California, on September 20, sparked AIM's interest. Michael Morgan, director of a YMCA youth camp, had quarreled with Oakes several times during the preceding week. Morgan maintained that the shooting occurred when Oakes suddenly appeared from behind a clump of bushes and threatened him. The charge was set at involuntary manslaughter and bail was set at $5,000. Indian witnesses insisted that Oakes was unarmed and that the charge would have been murder if the situation had been reversed. Ultimately Morgan was acquitted.[74]

Trail of Broken Treaties caravans set forth from Seattle and San Francisco in October. They stopped at every reservation within convenient driving distance. Funding came primarily from churches, especially the Episcopal diocese of Seattle. Early leadership was spearheaded by Hank Adams, head of the Survival of American Indians group, and Robert Burnette, former tribal chairman of the Rosebud Reservation. Although not as many Indians joined the caravan as anticipated, quite a few agreed to participate. Besides political motives, they were lured by the offer of free transportation and food plus an opportunity for adventure. In response to the government's later charge that the Trail of Broken Treaties was primarily an urban movement, AIM could respond that over eighty percent of the group were residents of reservations and many of them were older people, women, and children.[75] Undoubtedly, nevertheless, a huge majority of reservation Indians were innocent pawns in a political game.

When the caravan laid over in Minneapolis-St. Paul for several days, AIM militants took charge and reworked the original more moderate fifteen point proposal, which was mainly the work of Hank Adams. AIM substituted a list of twenty demands which they felt summarized for the government a reform program they could accept.[76] Basically, AIM demanded that all Indians on reservations be governed by treaty relations. This would define one basic status for all Indian people, which could be easily understood by Indians and which could not be whittled away by the actions of the different states and governmental bodies. During their stay in Minneapolis AIM took over the area BIA office for two hours.[77]

The caravan pulled into Washington November 1, 1972, and was directed to St. Stephen's Episcopal Church. AIM immediately condemned the accommodations and staged a brief protest march on the White House. From there they proceeded to the BIA building, overpowered the guards, and occupied it. At first it appeared as if the confrontation would be peacefully negotiated. AIM leaders, however, sensing that their demands were not being taken seriously and also that they had created a media event of the magnitude they wanted, barricaded the building the evening of November 2 and refused to depart. As far as can be determined, the takeover was not planned beforehand but rather was a spontaneous and opportunistic reaction to the climate of the moment.[78]

A lengthy series of highly publicized negotiations followed. The Nixon administration treaded softly with the election forthcoming but did not capitulate to any of AIM's substantive demands. During the siege, Vernon Bellecourt and Means were the most visible leaders, serving as spokesmen for the protesters and handling inquiries from the news media. Inside the building, Banks and Clyde Bellecourt were involved in security and other internal aspects of the occupation. Friction among AIM leaders was constant and well reported. Several of the weapon carrying guards wore red berets signifying membership in the AIM security patrol.[79] On November 9, under a promise of limited amnesty that no criminal charges would be filed for events which happened during the occupation and $66,500 travel money, the Indians agreed to leave. Later, Frank Carlucci, an Office of Management and Budget official, directly responsible to President Nixon, told a House Interior Subcommittee that ten cents per mile and $6 per day in travel funds were allocated for the 1,200 Indians that the protesters claimed were present. In response to complaints that AIM leaders pocketed most of the money, Carlucci allowed that, "We could not follow the actual dollars past the first level of disbursement. Nor could we insist on travel vouchers. . ."[80]

The government viewed the payment of travel money and the granting of limited amnesty as a not unreasonable policy under the circumstances. There would be no prosecution for the seizure of the building, but amnesty did not apply to acts of destruction to the building and its contents or to theft. Officials opined that the government would have to provide the food, shelter, and travel home to many of the stranded anyway. Some urgency for settlement existed because a militant minority of AIM wanted to burn the building, thereby creating a "funeral pyre" that would produce martyrs and dramatize the Indian cause.[81] No one has charged with any wrongdoing in the incident, in spite of an estimated $2,000,000 damages to the building and theft of over a ton of documents, a number of art treasures and other items. Many observed that AIM was permitted to demand rights without demonstrating responsibility. The three top BIA officials, however, were relieved.

George Mitchell, the man who had actually drawn up the AIM charter and who was in charge of a six man AIM office in Washington, quit in disgust. In an interview with the Washington Evening Star Mitchell said he knew that AIM leaders were in possession of treaties and documents stolen from the BIA, but he did not know who had them or where they were. He indicated that the organization had a number of full-time staffers on salary, including the Bellecourt brothers and Banks. Mitchell claimed that AIM had about 4,500 members in sixty-seven chapters in the United States and two in Canada. Commenting on the survival schools for Indian children, now established in Cleveland, Milwaukee, Minneapolis, and on the West Coast, Mitchell said, "The curriculum is about eighty percent 'true Indian history' and about twenty percent 'the three Rs.'"[82] He was disgusted with the way the leaders divided up the travel money and at the ego tripping that had characterized the entire Trail of Broken Treaties operation.

The New
Indian Wars

*T*ribal chairman Dick Wilson also was disturbed over the events in Washington. The day after the BIA takeover ended the Oglala Sioux Tribal Council passed resolution 72 - 55 which said in part "... the sovereign dignity of the Oglala Sioux Tribe be upheld and protected against any threats or the intent of destructive action on the part of the American Indian Movement on this Pine Ridge Reservation." The resolution pledged full support to Dick Wilson in any decision or action he might take to protect "the property, interest, and dignity of the Oglala Sioux Tribe." It also prohibited AIM from using any tribal buildings for a victory dance related to their "recent and unjustifiable actions in Washington, D. C."[1]

Wilson said that Russell Means had telephoned Toby Eagle Bull, the tribal secretary, 'indicating that AIM wanted to hold a victory dance at Billy Mills Hall in Pine Ridge. When he was turned down, Means told Eagle Bull' "get your pigs together because we are going to take Billy Mills Hall and use it."[2] Consequently the Pine Ridge BIA Agency provided funds to hire about forty men to stand guard over 'the BIA offices, Billy Mills Hall, and the tribal offices. This group was branded as Wilson's "Goon Squad" by Hobart Keith, one of Wilson's opponents.[3]

Means arrived on the reservation on November 20. He was arrested by BIA police officers before he could address the Oglala Sioux Landowners Association which was meeting at Pine Ridge. Means insisted that he was a member of the organization and his rights as a member of the tribe were being trampled. After being held for six hours he was released on $75 bond.[4] Accompanied by former tribal vice president David Long, who had been suspended by Wilson that day for his AIM activities, Means went to Rapid City where they called a press conference to denounce the arrest as a violation of constitutional rights to freedom of speech, religion, and assembly. Long charged Wilson was influencing the council in a violent way to keep people quiet."[5]

The Oglala Sioux Tribal Council voted 11 to 2 to express confidence in Wilson on December 12. At the same time, in a conciliatory gesture, Long was reinstated as vice president.[6] Means and AIM stood ready to challenge Wilson's authority on the troubled Pine Ridge Reservation anyway.

After reputedly having been turned down for residency by the Navajos, Means had returned to Pine Ridge in 1972 after the Yellow Thunder incident. He established himself in Porcupine, an outlying village about eight miles north of Wounded Knee, and operated a food cooperative. Most of the residents in that area of the reservation were fullbloods who opposed Wilson. Means indicated that he intended to go back to the traditional ways of his people and made it clear that he intended to become tribal council president as soon as possible. Gerald One Feather, a traditionalist in spite of his Master's degree, had just been defeated by Wilson in a bitter struggle for re-election. Wilson, a pugnacious mixed-blood plumber from Pine Ridge, had the dubious distinction of being the first tribal council president not fluent in Lakota. He made it clear that he favored economic progress through cooperation with the government over preservation of traditional culture. Although jealousy and infighting in Oglala tribal government represents the ordinary rather than the extraordinary, the dispute between Wilson and the traditionalists was more heated than usual.7 Vine Deloria commented on Sioux politics in Custer Died for your Sins, "Each election on a Sioux reservation is generally a fight to the finish. A ten-vote margin of some 1,500 votes cast is a landslide victory in Sioux country. . . the tendency is always present to slug it out at a moment's notice."8 Wilson's direct, no-nonsense style complemented by his stocky, crew-cut appearance aggravated the situation. Most white administrators and many Oglalas were impressed with Wilson, nonetheless, because he could be relied upon to act efficiently and carry out his promises.9

Pine Ridge contained all the ingredients for a political explosion in 1972. Although it is the second largest reservation in area in the United States, its 15,000 people were mostly unemployed and impoverished. The normal rate of unemployment hovered at over fifty percent and it was not uncommon in bad times to see it go up to over seventy percent. Income per capita usually rates lowest in the nation. Very few communications such as a regular newspaper or reservation radio station existed.

All of the barometers of living standards such as life expectancy, income, disease rate, suicide rate, housing, and social values were appalling. The average age at Pine Ridge is incredibly young compared to national averages. In 1969, the median age was only 16.7 years compared to 28. 8 years for the white population nationwide. Over fifty-three percent of the reservation population were under eighteen.10 The breakdown of ethnic groups also revealed wide differences: mixed-blood males (66%), mixed-blood females (57%), full-blood males (44%), and full-blood females (28%).11

Loyalty to the government during the combined crises of Vietnam and Watergate was not what one might suspect of the Oglala. The proportion of men who have served in the armed forces is high, and most of the veterans maintain their loyalty to the military. The most prestigious and active organizations on the reservation are the American Legion and the Veterans of Foreign Wars. On patriotic holidays, there are community celebrations; and many houses, especially full-blood homes in rural areas, display an American flag.12 The Oglala's quarrel with the government was not so much involved in foreign policy as it was over treaty rights and the BIA. It was not difficult, therefore, to find individuals on the reservation eager to throw Wilson out of office.

Because AIM was barred from Pine Ridge, an alternative group, the Oglala Civil Rights Organization (OSCRO), was formed by reservation Indians who opposed

Wilson. At least on the surface the backbone of the organization consisted of politically inexperienced middle-aged women like Gladys Bissonette, Helen Moves Camp, and Louis Beane. Pedro Bissonette, Gladys's nephew, served as the liaison between AIM and OSCRO. Gladys Bissonette had campaigned for Wilson in 1972 and was rewarded with a position at the newly constructed old people's home. She claimed Wilson fired her when she revealed financial irregularities in the administration of the home.[13]

Another group sympathetic to AIM was the Oglala Sioux Landowners Association, headed by Gerald One Feather. They wanted to break up the unit leasing policy of the BIA so they could combine their individual allotments into a community grazing unit in the traditional way.[14] Yet another group that supported AIM was the Inter-District Council. This group, dominated by full-bloods from the outlying districts, sought to give the people of the local districts political autonomy through a new constitution. All eight of the tribal districts were represented in this group.15 The existing bureaucracy, of course, firmly opposed all of these ideas for change.

After Nixon turned down their twenty point demand, AIM embarked on a Campaign for Human Rights in Rapid City and the surrounding area while they waited to see if Wilson could be toppled. Tension mounted on the reservation as Wilson and his forces stepped up their efforts to maintain control. Talks between AIM and Rapid City officials, however, appeared to be making such progress that the Rapid City Journal, which seldom editorialized on anything concerning Indians, reasoned, "It is far easier for light to be shed on a subject at a conference table than through tear gas at a violent confrontation." Soon a Rapid City American Indian Civil Rights Working Committee was organized to work with city officials for better race relations.

Means had not done as well at Scottsbluff, Nebraska, which lies about two-hundred miles south of Rapid City. There discussion was abandoned in favor of confrontations, violence and arrests. Means and a contingent of followers had responded to an invitation for AIM representation from a Chicano group called the New Congress of Community Development. The intention was to discuss an informal alliance to deal with mutual problems. A $30,000 grant from the United Methodist Church Commission on Race and Religion in combination with the National Board of Missions provided the money.[16] The grant was made November 5, 1972, without consultation with the Nebraska Bishop, district superintendent or local ministers or church bodies. The Council of Ministers of the neighboring Gering United Methodist Church said it did not favor the grant and urged members to express their feelings to national officials of the Board of Missions. The Gering Ministers voted not to take up the Human Relations Day offering of January 28.[17]

Shortly before noon on Sunday, January 14, 1973, the group of Indians and Chicanos began a series of protests. About eighty appeared at the local police station and attempted to present a list of complaints focused on police brutality. The police refused to talk to them and told them to come back during business hours without the crowd.

Monday evening firemen were called to the Scottsbluff Junior High School where a gasoline-filled coke bottle had been thrown into the woodshop. The blaze was quickly extinguished with minor damage. Later the same evening police stopped a Volkswagen van driven by Leroy Casados for a routine check. They spotted the butt-end of a pistol in the luggage. Further investigation revealed three pistols, a large knife, and what appeared to be molotov cocktail supplies—a five gallon can of gas and assorted rags.

Casados, John Two Birds Arbuckle, Carter Camp, Stan Holder and Alonzo Victor were arrested at the scene. Several hours later Means and Edgar Bear Runner, also from Porcupine, were arrested at a local motel and charged with everything from intoxication, disorderly conduct, resisting arrest, to carrying concealed weapons. Concerning the weapons charge, Means contended that a loaded gun had been tossed into his jail cell and he was told to "make a break for it."[18] Means added, "The frontier mentality of people in this area makes the Ku Klux Klan look like a Girl Scout troop." The Scottsbluff daily newspaper replied, "Anyone who gives the illusion of having a following and who puts out enough applications can find a grant somewhere." It commended local law enforcement for a "tremendous job" and responded to the racism charge with "the shoe fits and we'll wear it."[19]

Apparently United States District Judge Warren K Urbom of Lincoln, Nebraska, thought the shoe fit too well. On January 24, as a result of a class action suit filed by AIM, Urbom issued a temporary restraining order against local city and county officials. The order restrained them from denying minority group's civil rights. It specifically allowed visits to those in jail, especially by out-of-state attorneys.[20] Ultimately all charges against the activists were dropped because of illegal search and seizure procedures.[21]

Means's racist charges appeared to be further substantiated when AIM member Wesley Bad Heart Bull, 22, was stabbed to death. The incident happened in the little town of Buffalo Gap, South Dakota, on January 21. Without a doubt racial tensions heightened by the on-going encounter at Scottsbluff played a role—almost to the extent that one might suspect a planned strategy. But no direct connection can be documented.

Darld Schmitz, a white service station operator from Custer and the self-admitted killer, was booked for second degree manslaughter and released on $5,000 bond. AIM spokesmen protested the death of yet another Indian at the hands of a white man and insisted that the charge should have been first degree murder. Schmitz appeared before Judge George Brady, who set the preliminary hearing for the manslaughter charge for February 26 and continued the $5,000 bond. AIM designated the town named after the leader of the Seventh Cavalry as the focal point for an Indian Rights Day to be held there February 6. Their rallying cry was Crazy Horse's famous advice to his warriors at the Little Big Horn, February 6 would be "a good day to die." All Indians in America were urged to gather at Custer "for their final hour."[22]

Unlike the Yellow Thunder case, where there was little doubt that a crime was committed, the Bad Heart Bull killing involved far more complex circumstances. The tragic similarities were that both cases involved alcohol, racial antagonism, and individuals engaging in antisocial behavior. Bad Heart Bull grew up in Hot Springs, South Dakota. School officials described him as a "big, good looking kid, but difficult to control, especially when he was drinking." He was known to possess a nasty temperament and had a tendency to attack with fists, chains, or whatever might be available. Bad heart Bull had accumulated a record of nineteen arrests including assault, disturbing the peace, and public intoxication.[23] At the time of the Buffalo Gap incident, authorities were looking for him in connection with the brutal beating of Mike Borland in Hot Springs. The attack took place at the home of Bad Heart Bull's friend, Eddie Clifford, when they got into an argument over a bottle of wine belonging to Borland. Allegedly Borland was attacked from behind when he was leaving. Injuries included a fractured nose, broken bones in the face, a torn wind pipe, and bruises on his chest and shoulders.[24] Bad Heart Bull also had an altercation with Chris Bernard, manager of the Hot Springs Pizza Pub, and another couple at the bar the night before his fatal confrontation with Schmitz.[25]

Schmitz's trail to the dance at Buffalo Gap was a twisted one, too. An air force veteran, married for about six years and the father of three, he had acquired something of a reputation as a barroom fighter, but he had no record of serious crime.[26] On January 19, Schmitz's wife delivered her third child at Rapid City. The next day Schmitz and a friend, Alvin Wheeler, Jr. , drove to Rapid City. After visiting Schmitz's wife and Wheeler's mother they proceeded to a bar, then drove to another in Hot Springs. There they picked up two women and went to Buffalo Gap. During the course of the evening at Bill's Bar, the foursome consumed five or six more drinks each.[27]

Bad Heart Bull, Eddie Clifford and a female companion arrived at the bar about 12:30 a.m. Apparently they had been in a running dispute with a group of seven young men, who arrived at about the same time. After a brief argument they shook hands, and the seven youths entered the bar. Bad Heart Bull was turned away, so he stood in the gravel street in front of the bar rattling an eighteen inch chain at departing customers. Nothing happened until the bar closed at 2:00 a.m. Jim Geary, an employee of Bernard's, sometimes called by his high school wrestling nickname "Mad Dog," took exception to something Bad Heart Bull said and challenged him. It proved an almost fatal mistake for "Mad Dog" because Bad Heart Bull soon connected with the chain, knocked him unconscious and continued the beating.

Schmitz's date knew Bad Heart Bull. As her party was leaving, she observed the assault and got out of her car." I got out of the car and went to grab Wesley as I knew I could stop him but every time I tried to do that, someone pulled me away," she said.[28] When it appeared as if Bad Heart Bull was threatening her, Schmitz intervened. Schmitz, a rather short, husky individual, claimed he ducked Bad Heart Bull's swinging chain a couple of times while pulling out an ordinary pocket knife. He then grabbed Bad Heart Bull by the shirt and stabbed him in the middle of the chest. Bad Heart Bull went down but got up immediately, holding his chest and saying, "I've been stabbed." Clifford attempted to accost Schmitz with a half empty whiskey bottle, but was stopped by the bar owner and a deputy sheriff. Schmitz saw blood on his knife but left the scene immediately.[29]

Bad Heart Bull kept threatening people with the chain until it was taken from him. He soon collapsed and was hurried toward the hospital at Hot Springs. After about seven miles the car ran out of oil and the engine burned out near a truck stop called Maverick. The men in the car carrying Geary to the hospital picked up Bad Heart Bull and delivered them both to the Hot Springs hospital.

Schmitz's knife had just penetrated the aorta of Bad Heart Bull's heart, and the delays caused so much loss of blood that he died on the way. Geary was taken to the veteran's hospital at Hot Springs where he was treated for severe injuries. He stayed a full month.[30]

Local law enforcement officials immediately began an investigation of the death. One of the girls with Schmitz was located, and it was determined from her that Schmitz had done the stabbing. That morning Schmitz was arrested in Custer. He readily admitted the stabbing and surrendered the knife involved. He was questioned at the sheriff's office and released on $5,000.00 bond. His court appearance was scheduled for January 22.

After taking statements from numerous witnesses and participants, veteran Custer County Attorney Hobart Gates questioned whether any criminal charge that would result in a conviction could be leveled. Gates reasoned that it certainly was not murder because it was not premeditated with malice of forethought." The only homicide that I could use legitimately in my belief was second degree manslaughter and I was quite sure at the time that we would have a difficult time convicting Darld Schmitz of that and this was certainly proven at the trial," said Gates.   Judge Brady released Schmitz with a continuation of bond and set preliminary hearing for February 26.[32]

Light charges in the death of yet another Indian at the hands of a white man caused Banks and Means to issue furious protests. Indians were urged to gather at Custer on February 6 for a day of reckoning. Means called Sheriff Peppin to set a conference about the Bad Heart Bull case at 9:00 a.m., February 6, at the old Custer County Courthouse.

Custer authorities were well aware of the difficulties with AIM at Gordon, Scottsbluff and Washington, D. C. They contacted law enforcement leaders in Gordon and Scottsbluff for advice, and in each instance a show of force was recommended. South Dakota had never had an officially described riot in its history, so they were not sure what to do. Governor Richard Kneip and the United States Justice Department officials told Custer officials to "play it cool" when they indicated they planned to have forty or fifty officers lined up in front of the courthouse.[33]

Custer officials reassured the citizenry of their confidence in controlling the situation as early as February 1. A front page notice in the Custer Chronicle said:

> The City Council, County Commissioners and your local law enforcement officers are aware of the impending commitment of the American Indian Movement (AIM) to have their National Day of Indian Rights Assembly in Custer on the 6th day of February.
> All the necessary implementation of plans to handle any situation which may arise are being made. Also, outside sources of assistance have been contacted and are available. We, therefore, urge that all business and functions continue as usual until further notification.[34]

February 5 about sixty Custer civic leaders met at the City Hall to discuss necessary preparations for the protest. Publicly they indicated they did not anticipate any trouble, but they made a number of preparations just in case. Mayor Gene Reese asked Kneip to make National Guard assistance available, and they were placed on alert. According to Reese, nineteen highway patrolmen, four DCI (Criminal Investigators from the United States Justice Department) and three FBI were at Custer the morning of February 6. In addition, the Forest Service had offered personnel and equipment if needed. All public buildings and power facilities were under twenty-four hour surveillance. All bars in Custer and the city off-sale liquor stores were ordered closed on February 6.[36] The editor and publisher of the Custer Chronicle, Mrs. Jessie Sundstrom, was informed that she would not be allowed at the meeting.[37]

During the February 5 meeting Jack Paulton, an alleged member of the John Birch Society, showed a film, Anarchy-USA. This ninety minute release of the John Birch attempted to link the civil rights movement with Communist success in China, Algeria, and Cuba. Some national observers highlighted this as a reflection of Custer's mentality. Custer leaders, however, were not impressed with the film. "It did not fit this situation whatsoever, and most people, I'd say half the people, were bored with the picture and left," said Gates.[38]

By noon of February 6, nothing had happened at Custer. Many began to doubt that AIM would even make an appearance on that snowy day. Only the presence of an unidentified camera crew across the street from the courthouse gave any indication that something unusual might be in the offing. When reporters questioned their presence, they replied that they were planning "footage for a movie of the 'Billy Jack' type."[39] Diane Orr, of KUTV in Salt Lake City, reportedly a close friend of Banks, headed the group. At the time Banks claimed Salt Lake City as home, so KUTV's involvement hold some merit.[40]

A caravan of about two-hundred people arrived in front of the courthouse about 1:20 p.m. AIM had stopped on the way from Rapid City to burn a chuck wagon, a symbol of the pioneer tradition, in front of a restaurant in Hill City. They were told that only four negotiators would be allowed into the building at once but were assured that as many as wanted wanted could disscuss the matter as long as there were no more than four in the courthouse at once. Banks, Means, Utah state AIM director David Hill, and William Salome, a public relations man, also from Salt Lake City, went in first. Sheriff Ernie Peppin and Deputy Bill Rice were positioned on the front porch. Special agent Bernie Christiansen manned the door, and about nine riot equipped state patrolmen were concealed inside the courthouse with about ten others parked inconspicuously on nearby side streets.[41]

Gates began by assuring the delegation that the Bad Heart Bull Case would be prosecuted to the fullest extent possible. Banks and Means then controlled the discussion which lasted about thirty minutes. Banks did most of the talking. He insisted that the whole affair was a farce and an Indian would be charged with first-degree murder under the same circumstances. Banks further charged that even if Schmitz were convicted on the token charge, he would be free in ninety days. Moreover, Banks wanted to know why there was a warrant out for Bad Heart Bull's arrest when he was the victim, not the perpetrator. Gates explained that the warrant was for a different incident that had taken place in Hot Springs, January 2.[42] Within a few minutes the Indians on the steps and porches became restless and threatened to break down the front door. Means left the conference to talk to the group. When he returned he brought Leonard Crow Dog and Carter Camp, who replaced the two from Utah. Means indicated that leaders of the outside group planned to break the door down in forty minutes.[43]

Banks and Means shouted Gates down when he attempted to explain why the charges against Schmitz were not murder. Banks indicated he had taken enough run-arounds. It seemed to him that the situation never changed; from Sand Creek to Wounded Knee, to Gordon, to Cass Lake and now at Custer, Indians seemed always to be victimized by white men. Soon rocks started flying through windows into Gates's office.

The crowd pushed Peppin and Rice aside and rushed into the courthouse. One Indian shouted, "Let's take all these mothers prisoners of war!"[44]

A ten-minute brawl ensued. A radiator was ripped from the courthouse wall and windows as well as doors were broken. A fire truck was brought out to disperse the crowd, but the high pressure hose was frozen, so only a dribble came forth. The crowd threw rocks, sticks and bottle at the fire truck, forcing the crew to back it away. Tear gas was thrown into the courthouse and into the crowd to disperse it. The Indians broke into a service station across the street and commandeered gasoline. They poured about thirty gallons of it on the courthouse and set it on fire.[45] The fire became so intense that it forced Gates to exit the building by jumping out the back window of the auditor's office. Banks left by jumping out of the windows in the Sheriff's office.

As the riot continued on Custer's snowy streets, considerable property damage was done, but almost incredibly no one was killed or even permanently injured." We were not totally unprepared, but we were not expecting what happened," said Mayor Reese.[47] The courthouse fire was soon extinguished, but the nearby chamber of commerce building, a log cabin-like structure, burned to the ground.[48] Two police cars were vandalized and burned, and the service station received about $1,000 in damages. One Indian woman ran from behind the burning chamber of commerce building with her clothing on fire . Indian people and the highway patrol came to her rescue and put the fire out before she was seriously injured.[49] A number of Indians were hit on the head and were bleeding badly. When they were taken to the hospital for treatment, some refused to remove their bloody clothes because they wanted to retain them as evidence of police brutality.[50] Eleven police were injured severely enough to see a doctor, and twenty-seven Indians were arrested—among them Banks, Means, and Sarah Bad Heart Bull, Wesley's mother.[51] National media coverage was enormous.

Ample measures were taken to prevent any reoccurrence of violence. The South Dakota National Guard was placed on standby alert. Law enforcement personnel from all ovor South Dakota and Eastern Wyoming converged on Custer. Custer citizens openly carried rifles and pistols, while the town rested uneasily under near-martial law for the rest of the week.[52] AIM aired requests in Colorado, Kansas, Idaho, Nebraska, and Wyoming for 7,000 reinforcemonts. Eddie Benton, Executive Director of the Saint Paul, Minnesota, AIM, said several caravans planned to leave for Custer to protest "the war being waged against our people."[53] Banks promised he would return to Custer on Friday and, "For every rifle on the street pointed at an Indian, I'm going to have ten rifles aimed at a white man."[54] Caravans of AIM cars were turned back on highway 385 from the north and highway 16A from the east on Thursday. Other than a mysterious plane flight over Custer on Friday, nothing happened. But Banks did announce from Rapid City that he would ask the Sixth District Crime Commission to withhold law enforcement assistance act funds from Custer and Fall River Counties because funds were being used "to carry on racist programs that block Indian initiative."[55]

February 8, Gates and Mayor Barnett of Rapid City met with Means, Banks, and Ramon Roubideaux, the only Indian attorney in the area, to discuss the Schmitz matter. Means suggested that Roubideaux could assist Gates in prosecuting Means for charges stemming from the Custer riot. Gates declined on the ground of conflict of interest, but accepted Means suggestion that Roubideaux help prosecute Schmitz. It was agreed that the Custer County Commissioners would pay Roubideaux up to $2,000 to assist in the investigation and for assistance at the preliminary hearing and the trial.[56] It was agreed also that the charge against Schmitz would be changed if new evidence turned up before the February 26 hearing.57

Roubideaux is an enrolled member of the Brule tribe. He won the Air Medal with oak leaf cluster and three battle stars as an air force lieutenant in World War II. After the war he served as a part-time assistant to Congressman Clifford Case, while attending George Washington Law School where he graduated in 1950. He lost a close race for South Dakota Attorney General in 1970.

Roubideaux did not show up for the preliminary hearing nor did he present evidence to change the charge against Schmitz. He protested that his investigation was not totally completed. "You took action to have this case tried before we have had a chance to complete the report of our investigation. . . ." charged Roubideaux.[58] Gates, however, had written Roubideaux a letter on March 23, 1973, telling him, "Darld Schmitz will be arraigned in Circuit Court at 10:00 a.m. on March 30 in Custer at which time a date for trial will be announced."[59] In a subsequent interview Roubideaux conceded that the manslaughter charge probably was appropriate, but he maintained that Schmitz should have been convicted. Roubideaux claimed that Bad Heart Bull was drunk and at the mercy of the group of white toughs who goaded him into the fight. He insists that Schmitz bragged that he was "going to get an Indian" when he left the bar.[60]

Schmitz's trial lasted just three days and the not guilty verdict surprised few. Both the prosecution and the defense agreed upon the general background for the killing as has been described. According to the state, however, Schmitz and his companions deliberately got out of their car to engage in the fight. The prosecution maintained that Schmitz drew his knife and opened it immediately, which made him guilty of manslaughter. The state presented a number of witnesses who presented quite different versions of the incident, according to Schmitz.[61] On several occasions, the defense proved that the prosecution's witnesses were not even present when the fight occurred. Janie Atkinson, Schmitz's companion that night, served as the star witness for the defense and supported Schmitz's version.[62] Only South Dakota news media took any interest in the trial.

The Bad Heart Bull case represents one of the more intriguing case studies of modern mass-media news coverage. Large or small, South Dakota newspapers register numerous protests about the lack of objectivity of the out-of-state news media during the entire AIM-government confrontation. The Bennett County Booster of Martin edltorialized:

> Nothing can shake a person's deepseated convictions about a free press in a democratic government more than an invasion by a horde of national and international news media reporters. . .
>
> It's not the articles that have been written and publicized that are so objectional. It's the failing of those people to provide their readers and viewers with anything more than some 'pre-conceived notion' of what their own narrow political views dictate.[65]

If the truth was not buried at Wounded Knee, it might well have been buried at Custer as far as the out-of-state mass media was concerned. The <u>Custer Chronicle</u> and the South Dakota dailies reported just about all of the basic information in the case, but virtually none of it received space elsewhere.

Outside observers might respond that the lack of coverage of the acquittal was because it represented just one more example of separate-but-equal justice for Indians in South Dakota. Although the charge may well have held up for a number of prior cases, it was simply not true for this case.

One might assume that the media would descend upon Buffalo Gap en masse to find out what really happened on January 21; but only Terry Divine, an Associated Press writer, filed a story. His account, which proved essentially accurate as documented by the court proceedings, was filed on or about February 10. The <u>Aberdeen American News</u> carried it in full on its front page, February 11, but it claims the distinction of being the only paper in the country to do so. The only news concerning the Buffalo Gap incident in the <u>New York Times</u> at the time of the Divine story concerned the protest riot in Rapid City over the arrest of the demonstrators in Custer.[66]

Lack of thorough media coverage allowed gross distortions of the Buffalo Gap incident to circulate. Speaking to a college audience, an AIM leader said, "On January 28, 1973, a young man named Wesley Bad Heart Bull was set upon by four whites in Buffalo Gap, South Dakota. . . fifteen miles off the Pine Ridge Reservation. He was stabbed a total of twenty-seven times in broad daylight. He was tied to a bumper of a car and drug down the main street, fifty to sixty people witnessing it."[67] If nothing else, this type of blatant misrepresentation illustrates the service that a free and objective press can perform in a democratic society and what follows when it neglects to do so. Since the rough outline of what happened at Buffalo Gap was readily available to journalists and the trial took place during the Wounded Knee occupation, it might be assumed that the story did not receive coverage because the information was not what journalists and their editors were seeking. Favorable treatment by the news media keyed AIM's early successes.

After AIM had mobilized for Scottsbluff and Custer, they had no intention of easing pressure for change in the Black Hills area. AIM called for a meeting of the Rapid City Racial Conciliation Committee for the evening of February 7. About 150 AIM members led by Dennis Banks and Russell Means met with the committee. Supported by cheering and drum beats from his followers, Banks again dominated. He complained that of the 5,000 arrested in Rapid City in 1972, 3,500 were Indian. The Rapid City school system was assailed for racist practices. Numerous other economic and social complaints alleging Indian mistreatment were aired. Youthful Mayor Donald Barnett appeared to become unglued by the threatening situation and radioed out that he seemed to be a hostage. But Banks managed to control his followers and Barnett delivered a credible speech. He said that he understood Indian problems in Rapid City and was determined to help resolve them.[68]

Violence erupted in Rapid City Friday night, February 9, in spite of Barnett's conciliatory tone. Even though AIM had declared Rapid City a "demilitarized zone" Indians ransacked three taverns and ran through the streets breaking windows to protest the Custer arrests and the mistreatment of Indians in Rapid City. Forty Indians were arrested. Rapid City officials met with Banks the next afternoon. Banks announced that AIM had set a moratorium on all violent activities in the Black Hills. To help ease tensions, Banks said AIM had imposed a curfew for all AIM people.[69] AIM stopped the curfew and "cease fire" in the Black Hills Monday afternoon because of "city council attempts to intimidate AIM." "They have asked us to work within their system, but they have systematically denied us the opportunity," charged Banks.[70]

Banks led over two-hundred Indians to Sturgis, South Dakota, the same day to protest a $25,000 bond for an Indian charged in the death of an elderly woman. AIM complained that compared to Schmitz, the bond was unreasonable. Preparations for defense of the county seat town of 5,000 were elaborate. Schools, liquor stores, bars, and most service stations and businesses were closed. The Sturgis armory held two units of the l09th National Guard. Cordons of state patrol and deputized volunteers blocked vehicular access to the courthouse. The inside of the courthouse was loaded with law enforcement officers, bringing the total to about 150 men plus the two national guard units. Plywood coverings had been placed over the glass doors and windows in the courthouse.

Five handpicked AIM representatives were allowed to enter the courthouse. When Circuit Court Judge Clarence Cooper set bail bond at $15,000, AIM leaders hurried to the court railing to ask why the bond had been set so high. Cooper told them it was lower than the $50,000 bond set for a white man recently charged with raping an Indian woman. His explanation was accepted, and the AIM caravan left peacefully with horns honking. "Custer obviously was not prepared. Sturgis was. And it paid off," said the local newspaper.[71]

AIM also requested that Hot Springs, South Dakota, officials meet with them on Thursday, February 15, to hear Indian grievances in that community. Four basic charges were leveled: Indians were being unfairly arrested, Indians were being confined and held against their own wishes in the Veteran's Administration hospital, the bars were too rough on Indians and employment discrimination was rampant.

Hot Springs officials agreed to hold a conference at the Fall River County Courthouse. It rests against a steep embankment and is served by narrow, hilly streets, making it easy to defend. Hot Springs was turned into an armed fortress that surpassed Sturgis. An estimated seventy highway patrolmen were brought in to assist the regular local law enforcement officials who had also deputized fifty local citizens. Additionally, the local National Guard unit stood combat ready inside Case Auditorium.[72] Stores were closed and parked vehicles were removed from the streets. Two or three helmeted deputies were stationed behind every lower window and door in the courthouse. Fifteen or sixteen highway patrol cars parked at least four abreast along the street in front of the courthouse. A contingent of men with rifles were stationed on the roof of a service station across the street. More armed men were positioned on the high ground above the courthouse and in a neighboring hotel.[73]

When the twenty-four car AIM caravan arrived carrying about 150 persons, many of whom were women and children, the atmosphere grew electric. Eyewitnesses said they had never seen such a potentially volcanic situation.74 Many of the Indians wore blankets that obviously concealed clubs and other items. When one young man reached back inside his car, apparently to get something, the loud click of safeties being released on rifles stopped him. The winds of Wounded Knee 1890 seemed to be blowing. But no attempt was made to search or harass the visitors who were content to sing and beat a few drums while Banks parlayed. His most significant proposal, which was never implemented, was for a human relations board to be funded for $15,000 by the churches of Hot Springs or by local taxes. The caravan immediately returned to Rapid City where a big powwow was scheduled that weekend concerning the situation on the Pine Ridge Reservation.

In the meantime Ramon Roubideaux filed a $1.8 million damage suit as a class action against a number of Black Hills area county and city officials, charging them with harassment and intimidation of Indians. He also sought a temporary restraining order against them. Federal Judge Fred Nichol denied the temporary restraining order but scheduled a hearing for March 12 to consider the charges.[75]

Relative quiet had prevailed at Pine Ridge until the confrontation at Custer. At that time the Rapid City Police Department and other law enforcement agencies informed authorities at Pine Ridge that they had information that AIM was coming to the reservation in force. When three pro-AIM tribal council members—Hobart Keith, Birgil Kills Straight, and Richard Little-commenced impeachment action against Wilson of February 9, Wilson requested and obtained a court order from the Oglala Sioux tribal court requesting United States Marshalls and other Federal officers.[76] The charges against Wilson included nepotism, misuse of tribal funds, failure to hold meetings, operating without a budget, and false arrest.

That same day, in response to a request from BIA Superintendent Lyman, the chief of the United States Marshals in South Dakota and a deputy United States Marshal from North Dakota were sent to Pine Ridge to make a report. That same day the Special Operations Group (SOG) of the United States Marshals was placed on telephone alert. Thirty special officers, trained in riot control and experienced in civil rights confrontation were sent to Pine Ridge immediately.[77]

Citing "road and weather conditions," Wilson postponed his own impeachment hearing that was scheduled for February 14. AIM leaders reported that they received the invitation to come to the assistance of the OSCRO on the Pine Ridge Reservation the weekend of February 17 and 18. Pedro Bissonette issued the invitation. Informed sources indicate that Bissonette was the actual central figure of the OSCRO, which had been formed shortly after the November 1972 banishment of AIM from Pine Ridge.[78] Veteran Pine Ridge police officer Fred Two Bulls insisted that OSCRO was a "fraud." Two Bulls suggested that there were stories circulating at the time that lots of outside money was made available to militant leaders who pocketed much of it.[79]

In response to Bissonette's request, AIM voted to support OSCRO with intervention if necessary. Clyde Bellecourt stated at a press conference that AIM sould support all Indians upon request. He also urged all AIM chapters and other concerned American Indians to converge on Rapid City immediately.[80] Leaders of OSCRO demonstrated against the presence of United States Marshals at Pine Ridge.

Rapid City police evicted AIM leaders from the Imperial 400 Motel the evening of February 21. AIM had rented twenty-two rooms and run up an unpaid $2,500 bill. Among the several weapons confiscated were a shotgun, a .357 magnum pistol, and one ruger automatic pistol. Those in the motel moved to the Catholic-supported Mother Butler Indian School for the remainder of their stay in Rapid City. When police cordoned off that building and attempted to evict them, the priests in charge protected their lodgers, who subsequently damaged the building severely before leaving.[81]

By February 22, Wilson was forced to face the impeachment charges brought against him for the fourth time in eleven months. AIM leaders were hoping that this would set the stage for allowing them to enter the Pine Ridge Reservation to assist in a peaceful takeover. More than three hundred convened at Billy Mills Hall. Wilson delayed the start of the meeting by broadcasting Anarchy-USA via closed circuit television. After that the Council proceeded to vote for an impeachment trial on Wilson. In a surprise move, Wilson waived the available twenty-day waiting period so the trial could be held the next day. Wilson's accusers claimed they did not have time to document their charges and that the trial was totally controlled by Wilson and the BIA. Whatever the circumstances, the five councilmen who supported impeachment soon saw their cause was hopeless and walked out. Impeachment charges were dropped by a 14-0 vote with one abstaining.[82] Wilson and his family remained in the BIA building under police protection. The disgruntled losers called for a meeting at the community hall at Calico, a reservation village a few miles north of Pine Ridge.

A series of meetings held over four consecutive nights followed. On Sunday, February 25, the OSCRO claimed its decision to go to Wounded Knee was made with unanimous consent of participating chiefs, medicine men, and headmen. Among the names listed were: Chief Red Cloud, Chief Iron Cloud, Chief Fools Crow, Chief Bad Cob, and Chief Kills Enemy. Pete Catches was identified as the medicine man.[83] Vine Deloria said, "Perhaps the most important aspect of the Wounded Knee protest was the fact that the holy men of the tribe and the traditional chiefs all supported the AIM activists and younger people on the issues that were being raised."[84] A great deal of evidence exists to refute this important and widely publicized claim.

At least three of the eight listed—Edgar Red Cloud, Everette Catches, and Peter Catches—said they did not give consent to have their names used. Red Cloud, a spiritual leader and a direct descendant of Chief Red Cloud, said that AIM leaders invited him and several other older Indians to a meeting at Calico where he was asked what he thought concerning the problems of the American Indian at Pine Ridge. Red Cloud answered, "If you take a bundle of sticks and try to break them it would be very difficult. One stick from the bundle is easily broken." Red Cloud reported he was not contacted any further at the meeting, and at the end of the meeting he returned to his home and had no further contact with AIM. Red Cloud said he did not authorize the use of his name on the list of demands presented to Department of Justice Officers on February 28.[85]

Other Oglala traditional leaders denied involvement, too. Everette Catches and his son Peter both denied that they were consulted regarding the demands. Nor did they give written consent to have their names used . They claimed to be active in the Oglala Civil Rights Organization, however, and strongly supported Pedro Bissonette, its vice president. Peter Catches, who is considered a Medicine Man by the Oglala, travelled to Wounded Knee on February 28 upon the request of the FBI and BIA officials to "communicate with AIM leaders" to convince them to withdraw. Catches found AIM leaders unwilling to listen to any proposals he made. He seriously doubted whether the messages set forth by the Justice Department to AIM leaders were actually presented to the entire group in Wounded Knee.[86]

Other medicine men who did not support AIM before, during, or after Wounded Knee included: Charlie Hard Heart (Number 4 District, near Oglala); Dawson No Horse, Frank Fools Crow's understudy, now deceased (from Wakpamani Lake near Pine Ridge); and Robert Steed (Rosebud Reservation). One should not imply that they were all vocally opposed to AIM; they merely did not offer support.[87] A number of other traditional leaders supported Red Cloud's position.[88]

Vernon Bellecourt announced in Rapid City that an AIM caravan would leave Rapid City Sunday afternoon in response to requests from the people of Pine Ridge. Means had told television reporter Jim Likens of local station KDUH, Hay Spings, to be at Wounded Knee Sunday "if he wanted to be in on the biggest news story of his life." Likens showed up but Means did not—at least not until two days later.[89] AIM continued to congregate at Calico for strategy meetings. On Sunday evening, United States Marshals responded to reports that the Calico meeting center contained a large cache of illegal weapons by staging a surprise search. The Marshals found none. On Monday most of those already at Calico attended the funeral of Ben Black Elk, son of the famous chief Black Elk. Ben claimed that his role as a subject for tourist pictures at Mount Rushmore made him the most photographed Indian in the world.

While returning from Black Elk's funeral, Means got into a scrape with Wilson's BIA police in front of the Sioux Nation grocery store in Pine Ridge but was not seriously injured. Means played an active role in the intense discussion of strategy at Calico later in the day. Supposedly the debate was over whether to take the BIA building in Pine Ridge or to occupy historic Wounded Knee. Quite likely the decision came relatively easily because the entire force of eighty Federal Marshals was defending Pine Ridge, and no law enforcement personnel were at Wounded Knee.[90] Thirteen carloads of Indians departed the Mother Butler Center at noon Monday, headed for Calico. Banks had tactfully stayed away from Pine Ridge until Monday evening when he and about a dozen others drove down from the Cheyenne River Reservation. Diane Orr served as Banks's chauffeur.[91]

At approximately 7:15 p.m., the AIM caravan drove by the heavily fortified BIA building, approached the four-way stop in the center of Pine Ridge, and proceeded east toward Wounded Knee. FBI agents followed a late model U-Haul rental van which had been reported to be stolen. After filling up with gas in Pine Ridge, the van proceeded with the caravan on Highway 18.

The agents observed the main body of the motorcade within the village of Wounded Knee at about 8:00 p.m. They heard shots a few minutes later and observed several cars from the caravan returning toward them. At that time the agents returned to Pine Ridge to request assistance.[92] At approximately 8:30 p.m. , two BIA policemen drove their squad car into Wounded Knee. When they reached a point about fifty yards from the Wounded Knee Trading Post, they observed numerous vehicles parked in that area. At that point they heard two blasts from what sounded like a shotgun. Although not certain whether the fire was intended for them, they immediately left the area.[93] The FBI and Federal Marshals hastily established roadblocks on the four roads leading into Wounded Knee.

Considering the flow of information available to law enforcement authorities, one might be tempted to question their tactics during the days preceeding the seventy-one day takeover. Ultimately it cost an estimated seven million dollars directly and an incalculable amount in indirect costs, including two dead and one permanently paralyzed. Why was there no preparation against a takeover at Wounded Knee? It seemed like a logical place for a confrontation based on its international notoriety, its vulnerability, and its ease of defense. Surely the objective of the caravan could not have been that carefully concealed considering the large number of clergy, community relations workers, informants and the like who were at the Calico meetings and accompanied the caravan to Wounded Knee.

Answers to these questions are complex and not always convincing. Part of the reason for the lack of decisive action before the takeover can be found in the nature of the federal bureaucracy. Three different agencies—the FBI, the Federal Marshals Service, and the BIA shared responsibility. Everyone feared making a mistake, so the best strategy fequently appeared to be that of taking no action unless forced to do so. Law enforcement leaders, moreover, had become more cautious after Kent State, Attica, Chicago, Miami, etc. , and they were encouraged by the results restraint had brought at Alcatraz and the Washington BIA building. J. Edgar Hoover, the legendary FBI director, had passed away the previous May, creating a scramble for his position, which could well be decided adversely if an individual prone to resort to violence too readily was identified. Acting Director L. Patrick Gray wanted the job on a permanent basis and preferred moderation if at all possible. If an attempt was made to stop any of the AIM caravans, there was a strong chance that the heavily armed group would resist and women and children would be involved. Killing women and children under any circumstances would result in disastrous publicity for the government. Although federal leaders admitted that Wounded Knee would be a good target for an AIM demonstration, they suggested that numerous other sites with great historic significance to Indians, such as Mount Rushmore, were readily available and it was just impossible to fortify them all. Perhaps, too, the fact that almost everything at Wounded Knee except the post office was private property influenced the government's decision not to fortify it.

Return to
Wounded Knee

Walter Fisk, bureau chief with the United States News Service, was an invited observer at the AIM takeover. He released his story in an exclusive interview with the Rapid City Journal. Fisk described it as "a commando raid in the accurate sense, well organized and lightning fast, and executed in almost total darkness." He kept his tape recorder running during the Calico Center meeting, during the caravan trip to Wounded Knee, and inside the Catholic church where he observed defense preparations being made by the Indians. There, Fisk interviewed Russell Means. The sound of sporadic gunfire could be heard on Fisk's tapes as the caravan neared the church, along with shouts such as, "What are you shooting at?" "We've got the whole Wounded Knee Valley here; we have secured it and we are definitely going to hold it until death do us part," Means told Fisk.[1]

Given their military skills, their equipment, and the physical features of the territory occupied, the militants were able to establish an effective defensive perimeter. The village of Wounded Knee proper rests in an island formed by the confluence of four roads leading in from Manderson, Porcupine, Denby, and Pine Ridge. Both the government and the defenders established roadblocks on each of these routes. The unpaved road southeast to Denby passes over Wounded Knee Creek into open ranching country. AIM placed two bunkers, Denby and Lil California, on either side of it by the creek. Almost a mile away on the Denby road, the Marshals manned Red Arrow bunker with roadblock three set up in front of it. Big Foot Trail passes over Wounded Knee Creek into the low-lying hills to the east and leads to Porcupine. AIM placed Little Big Horn bunker just to the west of the creek there. Federal roadblock four was originally established a good two miles up the road, but by late April it was moved to within five hundred yards of Little Big Horn. Manderson Road begins from the Big Foot Trail almost exactly at the heart of the 1890 massacre site and winds in a northeasterly direction through the new cluster housing project, which is located about a mile from the old village of Wounded Knee. Last Stand bunker was established just north of the housing project and was countered by federal roadblock five about a mile away on Manderson Road. Star roadblock, the main center of negotiations activity during the occupation, was established just ahead of the road that veers off Big Foot Trail and leads into the old village of Wounded Knee from the west. Federal roadblock one stood almost two miles south on the Big Foot Trail. Additionally, both sides established three or four other fortified positions to solidify their respective perimeters. The AIM perimeter was only about three miles, but the federal perimeter stretched to an estimated seventeen miles. The area in between the two perimeters was commonly referred to as the DMZ or Demilitarized Zone, a term first used by AIM leaders.

"Downtown" Wounded Knee consisted of about ten buildings where the occupiers ate, slept and held meetings. The newly remodeled trading post and post office and the highly regarded museum sat side by side on the north side of the street. Across the street to the south were four private homes and several trailer houses. About two hundred yards east the home of Reverend and Mrs. Orville Lansbury sat next to their round Tipi Church of God. Less than half mile north of the village, on the fairly steep hill that served as the site for Forsyth's Hotchkiss rifles in 1890, stood the white Roman Catholic church just in front of the mass grave of the 1890 victims. A small Episcopal church was located on a downhill slant about two hundred yards due south of the Catholic church. AIM placed Hawk Eye bunker just in front of it on the south side. The Catholic church provided a commanding overview of Wounded Knee valley because of its elevation and because the surrounding hills and level areas contained virtually no vegetation of any size. The heavy cover of trees and brush along the creek beds, on the other hand, afforded natural avenues of ingress and egress for the occupiers, especially at night. "We got written up for maintaining a loose perimeter," said Kent Frizzell, "but there was no way that we could patrol seventeen miles effectively with the number of personnel we had." He also indicated that the perimeter was kept loose during the early going in part by design to prevent violent confrontation.[2]

The task of the defenders was made considerably easier by the availability of materials and equipment of the R and S Construction Company of Rapid City. R and S was working under a government contract with the Oglala Sioux Tribal Housing Project. The list of equipment included: one #301 John Deere loader, one #550 John Deere tractor, one front-end loader, two mortar mixers and wheelbarrows, two house trailers, and various tools. Supplies included 25,602 concrete blocks, 680 sacks of masonry cement, 30 tons of sand, 21,000 feet of construction lumber and various other items. Additionally, the proprietors of the trading post had a Jacobson Trench Digger, five house trailers, and two dump trucks.[3]

The Wounded Knee Trading Post and Museum were established by Clive Gildersleeve and his father about 1930. On March 27, 1934, President Franklin Roosevelt granted forty acres of land including and surrounding the business to Clive and his father. After his father's death, Clive and his vivacious Chippewa wife, Agnes, maintained the enterprise. They were well accepted on the reservation. In 1968, the Gildersleeves sold majority stock in their business to Jim and Jan Czywczynski, who formed the Sioux Corporation with Jim as manager. The Czywczynskis had not gained the acceptance enjoyed by the Gildersleeves for several reasons. Their newness, of course, worked against them. They were stricter on credit and accused of charging higher prices.

Furthermore, they were ambitious to capitalize on the historical site, which did not set well with the Sioux. A group called the Wounded Knee Memorial Association proposed erecting a Grecian-style marble memorial with a Kennedy-like "Eternal Flame" that would become "America's first privately owned national park." One of the incorporators included Clive Gildersleeve's brother-in-law, Wilbur A. Riegert, a former career servant with the BIA, who was considered an authority on Indian lore and history. His specialty was the development of the Wounded Knee Museum. Riegert and Agnes Gildersleeve were related to the Bellecourts.

When the AIM caravan arrived and began the takeover, the residents were helpless. With the Czywczynskis away at a basketball game, the average age of the adults remaining in the village was over seventy-five. At 7:40 p.m., the desk clerk of the Pine Ridge Police Department received a call from Agnes Gildersleeve indicating there were two vans full of Indians parked in front of her store apparently about to break into it. The clerk immediately called for police assistance for the Gildersleeves. Before the call from Mrs. Gildersleeve, an unidentified person had called the same clerk from Scottsbluff, Nebraska, saying his newspaper had been called by the Sioux Falls press alerting them that they had been informed by the Omaha World Herald that Aaron DeSersa, editor of the Shannon County News, had informed them that something would happen at Wounded Knee that evening. The Scottsbluff paper requested information but the clerk said she had none to release.[4]

When the Indians arrived in front of the Gildersleeve home, which was right across the street from the trading post, they started shooting out street lights. The Gildersleeves and Agnes's sister, Mrs. Amelia M. Clark, got down on the floor in fear. Mrs. Gildersleeve made her way to the telephone and called Pine Ridge for the BIA Police, the FBI, the Federal Marshals, and the Fire Department. At about 11:00 p.m., Russell Means led a group to their door. "Just what exactly do you think you are doing here?" asked Mrs. Gildersleeve. Means responded that they were there, "Because we couldn't get into Pine Ridge; it was too well fortified." They were told to consider themselves hostages "from here on out."[5] Two armed guards were placed in the Gildersleeve house. The Gildersleeves spent that night and the following day in the kitchen, sleeping and eating there. Wilbur Riegert, 82, confined to a wheelchair with a heart condition; his daughter, Jean Fritze; her husband, Guy; and her twelve year old daughter, Adrian, were crowded into the Gildersleeve home. Dennis Banks took over Mrs. Mary Pike's home and Means took over Riegert's trailer house.

The Fritzes, who lived next door, also had hidden on the floor when the shooting commenced. They observed food from the trading post being loaded into a U-Haul van and a pickup truck and then being taken to the Catholic Church. Mrs. Fritze also called the Pine Ridge Police, who assured her that help was on the way. After about two hours, five armed men entered the Fritze residence. They took a 30-30 rifle and a .22 pistol and told them either to move in with the Gildersleeves or vice-versa. Ultimately the Gildersleeves were also joined by Bill Cole and Mary Pike.

Reverend Orville Lansbury was trying to get over the flu, so he had retired early. About 8:00 p.m., the couple heard a lot of shooting at the trading post and hid in their basement for about an hour. Then they put on coats and hid in a gully at the lower edge of their property for about an hour until it got too cold. Upon returning to their house, they heard Mrs. Gildersleeve calling for help and they tried to call for help, too. That seemed fruitless, so they sneaked their car out of the garage and drove, with their lights out all the way, to safety.[6]

Guy Fritze claimed that he personally observed and overheard Banks, Means, Bellecourt and others use the telephone at Wounded Knee Trading Post to call various unknown parties and ask them to travel to Wounded Knee. He heard them request additional weapons, foodstuffs, medical supplies, and other equipment. They also urged people to stage protest demonstrations in support of the takeover and attempted to solicit additional people who would be willing to travel to Wounded Knee. Fritze opined AIM would be better controlled by Banks, Clyde Bellecourt, or Carter Camp rather than Means because of Means's volatile nature.[7]

Reverend Paul Manhart, Jesuit Pastor of the Wounded Knee Catholic Church, was returning to Wounded Knee on February 27 the same time AIM was taking over the village. When he observed numerous cars at Wounded Knee, Manhart drove to the back of the church and parked. He had spent much of the last two years finishing a dictionary of the Lakota language, which had been planned and started by the late Eugene Buechel.[8] He removed the manuscript for the dictionary from the church and took it to the custodian's home for safekeeping. Then the priest returned to the shadows of the front steps of the church. When people approached him, he asked if he could help them. Someone came through the front door of the church from the inside, so Manhart entered to find out what was happening. He encountered Russell Means in the back and asked him if he knew the church was a sacred place. Means replied, "We've heard too much of that stuff get him out of the way." Manhart was taken to the basement, searched, relieved of a one-dollar bill, and tied up. After about thirty minutes, he was taken upstairs where he could be seen, and his hands were untied. The occupiers powwowed until 3:00 a.m. Next morning Manhart was removed by car to the Gildersleeves where he remained under guard until Thursday afternoon. He then accompanied John Terronez, of the Community Relations Service, to the roadblock on Wounded Knee Road where another CRS worker took him to Pine Ridge. Manhart was free to come and go until his final departure from Wounded Knee on March 8.[9]

Manhart told authorities that he counted between 100 to 125 AIM males in Wounded Knee plus about forty women and forty children. He estimated that they had around fifty rifles and twenty shotguns and about one third of them had handguns.[10] He saw little or no drinking, but he thought there was plenty of evidence of marijuana. It appeared to Manhart as if the two factions on Pine Ridge that wanted Wilson out, the Interdistrict Council and the OSCRO, seemed to be using AIM and vice versa. He thought AIM and the Civil Rights group were in control.[12]

AIM leader Carter Camp, of Ponca City, Oklahoma, called the Rapid City Journal on February 28 to report that the hostages had not been hurt and were in no danger "unless the police come in here and try to annihilate us." Camp said the demonstrators had vowed "to die if necessary unless their demands are met." He said, "The church sits on high ground and gives a commanding view of the area. We have the means and the weapons to hold it." He added, "It is symbolic that we have seized Wounded Knee and there is a definite threat that another massacre could occur here. We are not going to give in without a fight."[13]

In addition to holding hostages to insure temporary safety from attack, most of the AIM leaders believed their personal security was dependent upon plentiful news coverage. For over a decade minority groups from the left, center, and right had relied on the press to air their grievances. AIM leaders had established reputations as masters in dealing with the media, and they took every precaution to insure coverage of this their most daring venture. Newspaper, television, and radio services, as indicated earlier, were advised by an AIM official to send reporters and photographers to Wounded Knee to witness something "very important."[14] As the AIM caravan was pulling into Wounded Knee, Aaron DeSersa, an AIM member and publisher of a local newspaper, telephoned the news services and the television networks about the occupation. Press cards were distributed and every courtesy extended to official media personnel. After the roads were blockaded and newsmen were prohibited, DeSersa and his son Byron led three television crews and several other newsmen into Wounded Knee through back canyons and trails.[15] Press coverage was so good that on the day after the takeover NBC showed a film of AIM ransacking the Wounded Knee Trading Post. NBC credited the film to KUTV, Salt Lake City, which led Phil Hogen, assistant to conservative South Dakota Congressmen James Abdnor, to call KUTV to object. KUTV replied that KUTV news reporter Diane Orr had been on the scene, both at Custer and Wounded Knee, to put together a story centering around Dennis Banks, who at that time called Salt Lake City home.[16]

Not only did television devote an abundance of prime time to the Wounded Knee confrontation, but so did almost every major newspaper throughout the world. When one reads the newspaper coverage or examines the television scripts concerning the occupation, almost every facet of it is thoroughly examined. Newspapers did a much better job.[17] AIM leaders later insisted that the media had betrayed them by not showing the real issues at stake. "We tried hard to educate the press inside Wounded Knee about the meaning of the takeover," said Dennis Banks. "I told the newsmen, 'We don't care if you totally condemn AIM, but please convey the real reasons why we're here.' We held briefings everyday so the TV people wouldn't just take pictures of the weapons and the bunkers. But a great deal of TV's coverage went to the battle action anyway," lamented Banks.[18]

Press involvement in political confrontations had become a sore point with law enforcement officials. They especially resented what they considered to be unfair coverage slanted against them, particularly by network television.[19] The issue surfaced immediately at Wounded Knee when SAC Joseph Trimbach banned all television representatives from the area as soon as the federal blockades were formalized. His FBI superior in Washington, R. E. Gebhardt, agreed that television representatives should not be permitted into Wounded Knee or within the road blocks but advised that they should not be removed from the general area.[20]

The next afternoon, CBS executive Bill Small called Jack Herington of FBI Press Services to complain that CBS personnel at Wounded Knee were being prevented from covering the story. Small asked when the FBI had acquired the authority to prevent coverage of a news story. Herington replied, somewhat illogically, that no one was preventing CBS from coverage of a news story; but since the FBI was the law enforcement agency responsible, they had the right to keep the area cleared for the safety of people involved, including newsmen, and there had been sporadic firing of weapons by the Indians. Small asserted that the safety of his people was their own responsibility and not that of the FBI. When L. Patrick Gray received the report, he underlined the last statement and noted, "They can foul up hijacking, too!" Apparently Gray was referring to an earlier fiasco involving an FBI attempt to stop the hijacking of a passenger plane.[21]

Herington's memorandum went on to indicate, "I replied that he was wrong; that we had the investigative jurisdiction on an Indian reservation, and if one of his people was shot, it very definitely was our responsibility and it was also our responsibility under the circumstances to take the action necessary to prevent one of his people from being killed or seriously injured." Here, Gray penned on the message, "Very good answer!" Small was not as impressed. He objected that he had never known of a law enforcement agency interfering with the press in this manner, where no state of martial law had been declared, and wanted to know who had the ultimate authority in the matter. Herington replied that, since the FBI was a part of the Department of Justice, the ultimate authority would lie with the Attorney General. Small said, "O. K. , I will take it up to the Department," and hung up. At the bottom of Herington's much-initialed memorandum, Gray scrawled, "Very good, Jack, stay with them."[22]

Evidently Small and his colleagues pursued the issue beyond the office of the Attorney General. Also on March 1, former FBI Special Agent Harold Leinbaugh, who was then working for the White House, telephoned Gallagher and indicated that the White House "was getting all kinds of pressure from the media because they were being barred from Wounded Knee." Leinbaugh asked if something could be done about the situation. Gallagher responded that the FBI had nothing to do with the banning of the media and that all pertinent information about the situation was available through press reports. Leinbaugh, too, indicated that he would probably pursue the matter further by calling the Department of Justice.[23]

Technically the FBI had not banned the media because that policy was set by Ralph Erickson, who represented the Department of Justice and was in charge of the overall operation by February 28. Erickson enjoyed a reputation as a no-nonsense type who could be relied upon to resolve the most difficult situations. His credentials were impeccable, at least to the white establishment he represented. Erickson was the rifle-shooting champion of Western New York as well as a star forward on the high school basketball team. He was also voted most popular boy in his class. At Cornell University, he was a varsity basketball player and an excellent student. Erickson graduated from Harvard Law in 1955 and went to Los Angeles to build a successful law career. In spite of his formidable background, Wounded Knee proved unresolvable for him. Erickson was only one of many highly qualified officials who would just as soon forget their service on the Pine Ridge Reservation during this period.

The media ban did not stop coverage of events within the village to any great extent, though. A number of media representatives had entered with the caravan and several others had sneaked in via the many concealed trails that traversed the area.[24] Those reporters who attempted to enter through the roadblocks were turned back in no uncertain terms. Ed Sykes, editor of <u>Western Outlook</u>, Ogallala, Nebraska, complained that guns were pointed at reporters and they were abruptly turned away when they approached government roadblocks.[25]

Conflict among the various law enforcement entities dealing with the Wounded Knee crisis was inevitable, given the number of jurisdictions and the political complexity of the case. Most Indian reservations, including Pine Ridge, lie under the jurisdiction of the federal government which administers them through the Department of Interior's Bureau of Indian Affairs. Reservation police forces can be either under tribal control or be under the authority of the BIA. At Pine Ridge, the Indian police force was under the BIA, a fact often misrepresented by the media and by AIM, who portrayed them as Dick Wilson's private goon squad. Crimes of a serious nature such as murder, rape, kidnapping, and arson come under the auspices of the FBI, in spite of its somewhat tarnished image at that time, still regarded as the elite investigative branch of the Department of Justice.[26]

Gray had been Assistant and Deputy Attorney General, but he had had no FBI experience prior to his appointment as Acting Director in mid-1972. Gray wanted to be Director badly and was fairly popular with the more progressive elements in the organization. In an agency noted for its almost fanatical stress on conservative conformity, Gray allowed longer hair, colored shirts, and encouraged women and minorities to join. During the process he quietly moved Hoover people out of positions of authority and campaigned for full-time Director status. Gray, the son of a St. Louis railroad man, won a scholarship to Rice Institute and went from there to the United States Naval Academy. After serving as a submarine commander during World War II, he went to George Washington Law School and became a legal officer, retiring as a captain. Gray helped in Nixon's 1960 presidential campaign and remained close to him. Ironically, perhaps, the Senate hearings on Nixon's recommendation that Gray become Director of the FBI began February 27, 1973.[27]

The Federal Marshals Service also serves the Justice Department. They differ in responsibility from the FBI in that they are less of an investigative body and more of an enforcement agency. Marshals execute duties such as transporting federal prisoners, picking up federal property, delivering warrants, and executing orders of federal courts. As is true at all levels of law enforcement, a considerable amount of jealousy, distrust, and competition exists between the FBI and the Marshals. Especially in the days of J. Edgar Hoover, the FBI considered the Marshals as distinct inferiors. "High school graduates" represents one of several debasing terms used by the FBI in private conversation to describe Marshals. Each state also has a United States Attorney to assist the Justice Department. William Clayton held this position in South Dakota in 1973. Additionally, during the civil rights confrontations of the previous decade, the Justice Department established a Community Relations Service (CRS) to serve as a liason between minority groups and the law enforcement agencies at all levels. It is supposed to "help communities resolve disputes based on race, color, and national origin." CRS representatives tend to be more liberal and prone to support the positions of their clients, frequently to the dismay of other established law enforcement agencies. John A Terronez headed the several CRS representatives at Pine Ridge and Wounded Knee during the occupation. Although only a handful were present at any one time, they were rotated in and out so rapidly that a total of forty served at Pine Ridge during the crisis.

In times of extreme duress, the Department of Justice can request assistance from regular military forces or the National Guard. Both the FBI and the Marshals quickly agreed that the military should be called in to resolve the stand off at Wounded Knee and so requested. But the decision rested with the White House, which must regard political as well as law enforcement implications. They wanted no part of a recreation of the 1890 disaster, especially after Kent State, Chicago, and Attica. Military equipment and military advisors, however, were present most of the time. This military presence played an important role in the subsequent trial of Russell Means and Dennis Banks for the takeover. Section 1385 of volume 18 of the United States Code states, "Whoever, except in cases and under circumstances expressly authorized by the Constitution or Act of Congress, willfully uses any part of the Army or the Air Force as a posse comitatas or otherwise to execute the laws shall be fined not more than $10,000 or imprisoned not more than two years or both."[28]

Erickson, Special Assistant to the Attorney General, arrived at Pine Ridge on February 28 as the ranking Department of Justice official on the scene. He was accompanied by Wayne Colburn, Director of the United States Marshals Service. He cooperated with William Clayton, who had established an informal headquarters at Pine Ridge. Erickson met with Justice Department personnel at Pine Ridge and established a chain of command for the three enforcement agencies there—Marshals, FBI, and BIA police. Erickson instructed all personnel to use restraint in the use of deadly force. He told them the primary immediate concern of the department was the release of hostages; another lesser concern was the arrest of lawbreakers.[29]

When it became clear to law enforcement officials that the roadblocks were not effective, Erickson called a meeting with the heads of the various law enforcement agencies. They forwarded three recommendations to Washington:

1. Maintain the present position. This was the least desirable in view of the fact the Indians have more fire power than the law enforcement officers on the scene.
2. Completely withdraw from the area. Erickson opposed it because Indians might cause another confrontation and kill innocent citizens.
3. Call out the National Guard.

Erickson strongly recommended the third policy and gained the unanimous support of everyone at the meeting, so it was sent to the Attorney General.[30] Erickson explored through Clayton the availability of the South Dakota National Guard. After considering the matter, Governor Richard Kneip advised Erickson on March 2 that he had turned down the request because the encounter was on federal jurisdiction territory.[31]

Erickson immediately called Attorney General Kleindienst concerning Kneip's decision and indicated he intended to request the Army, preferably paratroopers, to clear out the Indians. SAC Trimbach and Colburn met with Colonel Volney Warner, Chief of Staff of the 82nd Airborne, at Ellsworth Air Force Base near Rapid City to brief him. Warner called his report to the Pentagon with an understanding that a decision concerning the use of troops would be made after considering the report.[32]

The federal plan involved the use of the military to put down civil disturbances and was known since its 1968 origin as "Garden Plot." It had begun on February 12 when the Attorney General sent a sixty-five man force of Marshals belonging to the Special Operations Group (SOG) especially trained to quell domestic disturbances. Most were combat veterans skilled in the use of a wide variety of weapons and equipment supposedly reserved for the military. "These men are highly disciplined and motivated and we have to be careful how we handle them on an operation like this," said group leader William Whitworth. "When you turn these boys loose, it's like turning a dog on a cat—there ain't no getting them back," boasted Whitworth.[33]

Under Garden Plot, the 82nd would be the primary unit sent to the Wounded Knee area if needed. Warner was in the midst of preparing contingency plans for the deployment of the 82nd to Sudan, where two United States diplomats had just been assassinated. When Warner was ordered to prepare for a quick trip to analyze a situation, he assumed it was Africa. Instead, Warner was instructed to go to Wounded Knee, maintain a low profile, and not wear uniforms or engage in any confrontations or kill anyone.[34]

When Warner met with Colburn and Trimbach, they requested that he urge the use of federal troops. After inspecting the situation, however, Warner concluded that the government was dealing with "an embarrassment rather than an insurrection" and recommended denial of the request on March 3. "The name of the game is not to kill or injure the Indians. An Army involvement resulting in loss of life and injury would reflect badly on the Army, time is not of the essence. The object of the exercise is not to create martyrs," said Warner. Warner's counter-proposal was to increase the size of the FBI and Marshals forces and give them military supplies. He assured them that the 82nd Airborne would back them. During the seventy-one day confrontation, the Army did supply unlimited ammunition, fifteen APCs, 1,100 parachute flares, twenty sniper rifles, gas masks, bullet proof vests, c-rations, helmets, aerial reconnaissance planes, and more. To implement the strategy of waiting the Indians out in a form of house arrest, Warner ordered authorities to shoot to wound, not to kill, if they had to shoot.[36]

After the confrontation ended, former White House aide John Ehrlichman recounted his version of the Wounded Knee policies in a private, handwritten letter to actor Marlon Brando, a well-known AIM supporter. "Fred Buzhardt, general counsel for the Defense Department, sent an observer to Wounded Knee at one point—a professional soldier. He came back with very strong criticism of the way the Marshals were handling it," wrote Ehrlichman.[37] Throughout most of the Wounded Knee crisis, Ehrlichman confided, President Nixon was "holed up" at Camp David and left the decisions up to a second-string aide, Ken Cole. "Cole knew he had authority to act. The problem was one Nixon didn't know any more about than the staff people handling it, but Cole's orders were to avoid bloodshed and try to negotiate a peaceful result," said Ehrlichman.[38]

Ehrlichman described Colburn as the super-hawk and villain. According to him, Colburn authorized the Marshals to return fire at Wounded Knee. On a given night thousands of rounds would be fired, with little effect. Colburn reported to his superiors at Justice, "The firing was necessary because Indian fire 'pinned down' federal people, who then had to be extricated with counter-fire." When columnist Jack Anderson questioned Colburn about his actions, Colburn acknowledged that he had urged police action. He said he was "proud of my people" who never opened fire, he swore, unless they were fired upon.[39]

SAC Trimbach found his task formidable from the beginning, Colburn being not the least of his troubles. Within the FBI the term SAC has a prestige akin to that of captain of a ship or head football coach. Only so many SAC slots are available, and they are keenly pursued by young agents who relish the idea of being the leading FBI man in the area assigned. Salary and benefit considerations also appeal, as does the opportunity to make an impression upon superiors by adroitly handling a difficult situation. Trimbach, already in his 40s, had taken his first SAC assignment in Minneapolis just two weeks before the Wounded Knee occupation. He arrived in Minneapolis February 12 and on the next day was sent to Rapid City to head a federal antiriot investigation of the Custer confrontation. One of the assignments for his task force was to predict AIM's next move. They erroneously singled out the BIA headquarters in Pine Ridge.[40] Given the known volatility existing in the Minneapolis region, one wonders if J. Edgar Hoover would have selected a rookie SAC of no particular distinction for Minneapolis from his large pool of experienced agents.

Trimbach assumed he was in charge of the law enforcement aspect at Wounded Knee. But he was working with the chief of the entire United States Marshals Service, who did not attain the post by a lack of assertiveness. This was the first time such a large combined force of FBI and Marshals had had to work together so closely in a siege-like operation. It was made necessary because neither group had the manpower to handle the situation alone. Colburn was the former chief of the San Diego Police Department who had been elevated to his federal post because of his connections with Nixon political supporters. As Chief, Colburn had direct access to Sneed and Kleindienst and was not above utilizing that leverage, even with the Justice Department representatives in charge of the negotiations.[41]

The first difference occurred when the two met with Colonel Warner at Ellsworth. Only one half hour after the meeting started, Trimbach advised his FBI superior, Gebhardt, that "Chief Marshal Wayne Colburn had interfered with FBI operations and was beginning to cause some confusion relative to the United States military intervention." Trimbach requested immediate assistance from the Department of Justice to control Colburn's activity.[42] Deputy Attorney General Charles Ablard was contacted concerning the Colburn matter. He suggested that Ralph Erickson should resolve the dispute. Immediately Trimbach advised that he and Colburn had completely resolved their differences. Trimbach maintained that Colburn did not understand who had basic responsibility but now accepted the fact that the FBI was planning the operation. It was agreed that the FBI would maintain all contacts with the Army and the Marshals would assist the FBI manning the roadblocks in the vicinity of Wounded Knee.[43]

Another problem Trimbach faced with less success concerned the use of "deadly and non-deadly forces" as outlined by Erickson on March 4 to all law enforcement personnel at Wounded Knee. The statement Gebhardt especially objected to involved "in the application of deadly force: aim to wound, rather than kill." Gebhardt was told that the instructions were recommended and drawn up by Colonel Warner. Gebhardt talked to his superior, Mark Felt, and they both agreed that the FBI should not be bound by such instructions. When Gebhardt discussed the matter with Gray, Gray contacted Erickson who indicated everyone had approved the instructions. As a result, Gray felt the FBI would "have to live with it."[44]

AIM made their demands clear from the beginning. The night of the takeover, they delivered a long list to Trimbach through John Terronez of CRS, who was at Wounded Knee when AIM seized it. The list of demands included:

> I. Senator William Fulbright convene the Senate Foreign Relations Committee immediately for hearings on treaties made with American Indian Nations and ratified by the Congress of the United States.
>
> II. Senator Edward Kennedy convene the Senate Sub-Committee on Administrative practices and procedures for immediate, full-scale investigations and exposure of the Bureau of Indian Affairs and the Department of the Interior from the agency reservation office, to the area offices, to the central office in Washington, D.C.
>
> III. Senator James Abourezk convene the Senate Sub-Committee on Indian Affairs for a complete investigation of all Sioux Reservations in South Dakota.

The people AIM would negotiate with were: Mr. Erhlichman of the White House; Senators Abourezk, Kennedy, and Fulbright—or their top aides; the Commissioner of the BIA, and the Secretary of Interior. AIM proclaimed, "The only two options open to the United States of America are: 1. They wipe out the old people, women, children, and men, by shooting and attack us. 2. They negotiate our demands."[45] AIM closed their request by spuriously indicating they had "asked for and received complete direction and support of medicine men and chiefs of the Oglala Nation: Frank Fools Crow, Peter Catches, Ellis Chips, Edgar Red Cloud, Jake Kills Enemy, Morris Wounded, Luke Weasel Bear, Severt Young Bear, and Everette Catches."[46]

These were matters primarily for the Department of Interior's consideration since the Federal Government had stopped negotiating treaties with Native Americans more than a century ago. Ablard contacted the Interior Department on February 28 to request that they send someone to negotiate with the Indians, because the FBI had indicated correctly that it was not Trimbach's role to negotiate political matters with groups the FBI was investigating for criminal charges. Interior officials told Ablard that they would not negotiate because the Indians were armed and holding hostages.[47] When Senator Abourezk arrived at Ellsworth on his way to Wounded Knee on March 1, he charged that Interior officials had not been doing much about the takeover and the holding of hostages. "I called officials in the Interior Department last night and asked if they would come out and join us," said Abourezk; "they said they would absolutely not negotiate as long as any property or persons were being held. I think that perhaps with the lives of people in the balance we can't take that attitude."[48] Abourezk was quoted on the same day as saying he would go anywhere to negotiate, "But I am not willing to discuss substantive matters of legislation in a situation where a single group is seeking commitments on legislation under the threat of physical violence to innocent victims if that group's viewpoint is not accepted."[49]

Trimbach began negotiations the next morning with a call to the Gildersleeve residence and asked to speak to the persons in charge. He was connected with Carter

Camp, who identified himself as AIM Security Chief. Trimbach arranged a meeting with Camp at the AIM roadblock on Wounded Knee Road in the interest of avoiding bloodshed. At the morning meeting Trimbach requested that the rifle fire cease Camp responded that AIM wanted assurance that law enforcement personnel would not advance from their present positions. Trimbach said he could not make such an assurance, but he would be sure to inform AIM before an advancement was made.[50]

Early in the afternoon, Trimbach returned and spoke with Pedro Bissonette. Bissonette said it would be necessary to summon the traditional people listed as advisors in their original statement. He also indicated one of the elderly hostages was in need of medication. When Trimbach came back with the medicine, Russell Means took it and presented him with the requested list of hostages. Means referred to the hostages as "prisoners of war." When it was suggested that the FBI should leave the area, Trimbach said there was "no way" that would happen and Means's only hope was to surrender. Means became extremely angry and Trimbach left the negotiating site.[51]

On the morning of March 1, Erickson asked Trimbach to arrange a meeting place for Senators McGovern and Abourezk and the Indians. Trimbach returned to the roadblock and told Means that the Senators had arrived; and he was there to arrange a meeting place if, in fact, the Senators were willing to meet with them. Trimbach suggested a location two miles north of Wounded Knee, but no meeting could be held until the hostages were released. Means then brought three hostages with him to the roadblock to meet Trimbach. They said they were free to come and go as they pleased, but they did not choose to leave. Means indicated the other eight were free also, but none of them wished to leave, either.[52]

Subsequently, Senators McGovern and Abourezk and the aides to Senators Kennedy and Mansfield were driven to the roadblock where they learned there were no hostages. During the negotiations at the Riegert home, the Senators assured the Indians that BIA officials Lyman and Babby were already due to be transferred away from the area. The Senators also indicated that the demands for meetings of Congressional committees to hold hearings on problems relating to Indians would be met.[53]

An evening meeting followed in a tipi set up in front of the Catholic church almost exactly in the center of the 1890 massacre site. No media representation was allowed during the four-hour meeting, which ended at midnight. At the press conference the next morning, McGovern called for a full-scale investigation of the BIA and new legislation to meet the needs of Indian people. He said the function of the BIA should be changed so that it did not have "so much voice" in policy on the reservation. Instead, it should serve as an institution providing technical advice and funding assistance for the Indian population. McGovern said he understood the frustration of Indians who had been going through governmental channels for years, only to have their letters and petitions ignored. He also cited the need for employment on reservations to help solve existing problems, suggesting that a possible solution might be to institute a public works program similar to the CCC of the 1930's. McGovern indicated that most of the conference was consumed by listening to a long list of things Indians felt were legitimate grievances. The Senate group promised protesters that every effort would be made to get them a fair hearing on the matters they were concerned about. "We urged very strongly that, as soon as possible, they get together with the federal law enforcement officials here with the Department of Justice and work out an end to the armed confrontation that is going on, and they indicated they were interested in doing that," said McGovern. "The suggestion was that, working with the Community Relations Service of the Department and its officials who are here, a meeting be set up as soon as possible for the purpose of putting an end to the armed truce," McGovern concluded.[54] Following the press conference the Senators met with BIA Superintendent Lyman and Dick Wilson at BIA headquarters and discussed grievances presented by AIM.

As the Senate delegation issued press releases and suggestions for ending the confrontation, an incident occurred that would typify the seventy-one days of negotiations. Jim Czywczynski informed Erickson via the FBI that Mrs. Gildersleeve had called him to advise that she and her family were being held in their home under guard. She reportedly said, "I may not have been a hostage yesterday, but I certainly am now." At 1:00 p.m., however, Mrs. Gildersleeve was brought to a roadblock with Paul Boe and Stanley Holder where she informed Erickson that "She wanted to retract the statement that she had made this morning," she added, "We want to stay here because we live here." Further interrogation by Erickson led to no response except repetition of the statement, "I want to retract the statement I made this morning." When asked whether she could speak for the other hostages she responded that she could speak only for the four members of her family.[55] The Gildersleeves were hoping for a quick settlement and had been told they were free to do what they wanted the previous day. But they were placed under armed guard as soon as the Senate delegation left and were afraid their considerable property holdings would be completely destroyed if they did not cooperate. They were also upset with Lyman for "hogging the law" and at the federal forces for setting up their perimeter so far from the village, which they felt, made it ineffective.[56]

When the representatives from the CRS met with AIM on March 2, they were told that the occupiers were unwilling to negotiate without legal assistance. Lawyers from the Native American Rights Fund arrived the next day, apparently under the leadership of Roy Haber. Erickson met with them and explained the government position, which did not include amnesty. That led to objections by the lawyers against a mass arrest. The lawyers entered Wounded Knee around noon on March 3 and exited late the same day. They reported to Erickson that there were no hostages, that the AIM people were invited in by the residents of Wounded Knee who had signed a petition to that effect, and that they had no specific suggestions as to how the confrontation might be ended. The attorneys returned to Wounded Knee that same evening. Six newsmen selected from the press pool, Dr. Paul Boe and Bishop James Armstrong of the National Council of Churches, and the Czywczynskis were also allowed to enter.[57]

Ramon Roubideaux had contacted Jim Czywczynski on the morning of March 3 to discuss possible property settlement concerning damages done in Wounded Knee. Czywczynski and his wife, Jan, met Roubideaux at 2:00 p.m. at Pine Ridge. They, along with Carroll Swan and John Echo Hawk of the South Dakota Legal Aide Office, and unknown female reporter, drove to Wounded Knee. Czywczynski was asked to make an estimate of the damages to his property by a group including Reverend Wesley Hunter, Executive Director of the South Dakota Association of Christian Churches; Dr. Boe and Reverend John P. Adams, representing the National Council of Churches; and the AIM group. When Czywczynski estimated a high figure, by his own judgment, of $1,025,000, the group did not "bat an eye." When asked how much it would cost to buy the corporation outright, Czywczynski said he would sell for $2,500,000 with thirty percent down and guaranteed payment or cash. In response to another question he said he would not continue to run the corporation.[58] Several weeks later Boe announced that a world-wide appeal for $2,500,000 would be launched when the confrontation ended to buy the trading post and other property at Wounded Knee for the Indians of the area and to erect a memorial there. That never eventuated.

AIM actively solicited support from other tribes, antiwar groups, civil rights organizations, religious groups, and other organizations throughout the confrontation.[59] This was accomplished by telephone directly from Wounded Knee and by AIM personal appearances around the country. Vernon Bellecourt, one of the few well-known AIM leaders not at Wounded Knee at the beginning, served as the movement's main spokesman on the outside during the early going. On February 27, he was at Dartmouth College on a fund-raising tour. He proceeded to New York City to redouble his efforts for a legal defense fund to protect the people at Wounded Knee. While in New York, Bellecourt had an interview with Penthouse magazine editor Richard Ballard. Penthouse carried a seven page article concerning Indian grievances accompanied by a full-page close-up of the braided, necklaced AIM leader, who was described as "the symbol of the most militant Indian group since Geronimo."

Bellecourt also led a group of Indians to the United Nations headquarters in New York where he asked for United Nations observers at Wounded Knee. He also requested a seat in the United Nations for his group, so they could air grievances about United States tyranny.[60] His requests were not honored. Bellecourt and his cohorts, nonetheless, enjoyed considerable success raising money and support, especially on college campuses.

Possibly AIM's greatest coup came when William Kunstler, the famous defense attorney from New York City, accepted their invitation to come to Wounded Knee. He arrived on March 4. Without Kunstler, the by then legendary "Legal Wagon Master" of the New Left, AIM's fate might have been much different. An honors graduate of Yale College and Columbia University Law School and former Army major who won the Bronze Star in World War II, Kunstler had won a fearsome reputation as a defender of liberal clients. Kunstler started defending activism in the 1961 Freedom Rides cases, appearing in courtrooms in Albany, Georgia; Birmingham, Alabama; Danville, Virginia; and St. Augustine, Florida. Clients included Martin Luther King, Stokely Carmichael, H. Rap Brown, and Adam Clayton Powell. Kunstler was one of the team of lawyers who won a new trial for Jack Ruby and had served as a pallbearer at his funeral. H. Rap Brown was married in Kunstler's home in 1969. While defending Bobby Seale, Kunstler took a weekend trip to Paris to talk to the North Vietnamese representatives and claimed to have received their agreement to release long-sought information on the identity of United States prisoners of war. Perhaps his greatest notoriety sprang from his emotional defense of the Chicago Seven, the group of radicals charged with riot and assault in an attempt to break up the 1968 Democratic convention. Fellow attorneys claim that his weakness is lack of preparation and his strength is in cases where eloquence is important.[61]

Mark Lane, a New Yorker whose background was similar to Kunstler's, was also invited to Wounded Knee from his home at Mountain Home, Idaho, by representatives of the Vietnam Veterans Against the War (VVAW), who had had several of their leaders arrested at Wounded Knee. Lane graduated from Brooklyn Law School in 1951 and served as New York State Assemblyman from East Harlem and Yorkville, 1960-62. He had earned the distinction of being the first legislator arrested on a Freedom Ride in 1961 and was write-in vice presidential candidate in Dick Gregory's presidential campaign in 1968.[62] Lane was retained by Lee Harvey Oswald's mother to represent her son's interests in the Kennedy assassination inquiry. When the Warren Commission came to the conclusion that Oswald was the sole assassin, Lane gained national prominence through his book, Rush to Judgment, which disputed the Commission's report. Lane also had defended civil rights activists in the South and was an outstanding critic of United States involvement in the Vietnam War. Lane was extremely unpopular among government representatives at Wounded Knee and later lost much of his credibility with his own clients. Several years later, he barely escaped the mass suicide in Guyana where he had been serving as a legal consultant for cult leader, Jim Jones. These two legal luminaries attracted a flock of young, liberal attorneys to assist them during the Wounded Knee occupation and the ensuing trials. When the outstate attorneys were not at Wounded Knee, they were usually at a command post established in Rapid City.

Besides enjoying outstanding legal assistance, the occupiers received a steady flow of personnel and material goods from outside sources. Support for the Indians at Wounded Knee was widespread and crossed social and political boundaries. But most of the direct support in the form of personnel and weapons came from what the government liked to call "the radical fringe." Probably the three most radical organizations who had direct representation at Wounded Knee were the VVAW, the Black Panthers, and the Venceremos. The latter was a Marxist, Maoist organization with most of its strength in the Bay area of California, which was the place of origin of the Black Panthers as well. The Venceremos gained some notoriety for sending young people to Cuba annually to study and work to learn about the Cuban revolution first hand. Their publicly stated goal was to build a United Front against the imperialist United States leading to the overthrow of the United States government by force. The VVAW was an antiwar organization organized in 1967 with headquarters in New York City. Its published objective was to demand an immediate cessation of fighting and the withdrawal of all American troops from Indochina.[63] Two other groups that were active sympathizers and supporters of AIM on the Pine Ridge Reservation were Volunteers In Action For America (VISTA) and the Year of Action Program (ACTION) sponsored by the University of Colorado. Both were supported by federal grants.

On the nearby Rosebud Reservation, a flurry of activity accompanied the occupation of Wounded Knee. Crow Dog's Paradise was the center of support for Wounded Knee, with trucks, pickups, and carloads of people moving in and out at all hours of the day and night. Armed guards patrolled the fence lines near the highway. Members of the occupying force commonly rotated out to Crow Dog's Paradise for a shower, some clean clothes, and a rest. The government's barricade around the hamlet did not effectively contain the militants who knew all of the fifteen mile perimeter.[64] Staging for entry and departure into Wounded Knee usually occurred from the home of AIM leader Severt Young Bear, located near Porcupine. Other homes in the area were used, too.

Young Bear, a nephew of Raymond Yellow Thunder, was the elected AIM leader for the Porcupine District. The use of his home, located southeast of the Porcupine store, for infiltration in and out of Wounded Knee was common knowledge to most people in the area, including law enforcement officials. People who wanted to go to Wounded

Knee had to obtain permission from Young Bear. They were then directed to a secret route used to sneak in and out of the village.[65] On March 4, Lloyd Goldstedt, Acting Principal of the BIA school at Porcupine, saw approximately five out-of-state cars parked in the vicinity of Young Bear's home. Richard Tomahawk told Goldstedt that he and a lot of others were going to re-enter Wounded Knee on horseback via Birdhead Creek.[66] A rancher reported to the FBI that he observed Dennis Banks and one other Indian ride on horseback into the property of Severt Young Bear. He later saw Banks leaving Young Bear's in a car. On the night of March 7, he observed about twenty-four males, apparently carrying shoulder weapons, in and about the Young Bear residence. The rancher said for the last week or two he had observed a great many cars with out-of-state license plates or no license plates entering and leaving the place.[67]

Reverend Sam Rouillard, Presbyterian minister at Porcupine, advised the FBI that Severt Young Bear told him four hundred cars of AIM sympathizers were on their way to Wounded Knee in response to Russell Means's call for support. Young Bear said these were hard-core members of AIM or sympathizers. Rouillard indicated there were a large number of AIM sympathizers living around the general area of Wounded Knee. He also believed the AIM people who had recently arrived were a great danger to the cease-fire because they had no communication or poor communication with the leadership inside Wounded Knee. He further suggested that the newcomers might provoke a fight by attempting to enter Wounded Knee; or if a firefight should break out, it might encourage a massive attack on federal agents from the outside.[68]

Other homes in the Porcupine area also assisted AIM. Orville Schwarting, owner of the Guest Ranch, Porcupine, told the FBI that Rudy Bissonette, Pedro's older brother, told him during the week of March 7-14, he had seen AIM people passing rifles from one automobile to another at Emily Yellow Thunder's house. Emily was the elderly mother of Raymond Yellow Thunder. Bissonette claimed AIM also was using a house belonging to Douglas Horse, two houses past Young Bear's, for meetings and for supplying AIM.

On March 9, a reliable FBI informant attended a local meeting of AIM at Porcupine. He observed a member of the Black Panther Party from Los Angeles, numerous Chicanos and a good number of ACTION and VISTA workers. The informant said that ACTION workers were using government cars, pickups, and station wagons to assist in moving people and supplies in and out of the vicinity of Wounded Knee. They were also acting as guides into and out of Wounded Knee during the night. The informant indicated many newcomers were hostile towards Russell Means and Dennis Banks because they were discussing an agreement with the government. Recent arrivals felt their time had been wasted if the Indians were going to settle their differences over the bargaining table so quickly.[69]

On March 10, Severt Young Bear surrendered himself to the FBI. He was charged with violating Title 18, Section 231 (a) (3), U.S. Code, interfering with and impeding a federal officer, the most common charge filed by the government during the confrontation. Young Bear was incarcerated in Rapid City on $20,000 (l0%) cash bond. His attorneys forced the bond lower to $1,000 and gained his release on March 13.[70]

Not everyone who got to Wounded Knee appreciated the opportunity. Young Christopher Calvin Bald Eagle exited Wounded Knee early. He, along with several younger companions, drove to his aunt's trailer house at Wounded Knee on February 27 to take part in the action. When they got to Wounded Knee, "a little mean guy" (probably Pedro Bissonette) who drove a nice looking blue Cadillac took their car, saying they needed it for patrol. Bald Eagle said the "little mean guy" was a "squad leader" and had a high-powered rifle. This leader and others drove around at night with a spotlight and shot at anything that did not give the proper blinking light signal. The youth complained that the "big guys" would not let them do anything once they got there. On March 2, they asked for their car back, but were refused and told they would be shot if they attempted to leave. They hid in their car that afternoon and drove out that night.[71]

AIM security was directed by Vietnam veterans Carter Camp and Stan Holder. They possessed proven skill in the tactics necessary to defend a perimeter, such as deployment of bunkers and weapons and coordination of communications and patrol work. Both were originally from Oklahoma, although Camp had spent a good deal of time in the Los Angeles area. Camp held the title of Director of Security, but much of the military responsibility rested on young Holder who had served two combat tours in Vietnam. Holder was especially well-schooled in counter-insurgency warfare and noted for possessing an unusually even temper that gave him an uncanny ability to stay calm in a crisis.[72] He scheduled around-the-clock guard duty, monitored the numerous sources of intelligence information, and designed the physical defense of Wounded Knee. Holder and Camp could draw on the experience and skills of a number of other experienced combat veterans, many of whom belonged to the VVAW. Means attributes special recognition to the VVAW representatives for setting up a communications system which proved tremendously valuable in a number of emergencies.[73] Communications were monitored with citizens band radios through a command post at the trading post.

AIM presented a fairly formidable defensive perimeter. Immediately after the occupation, nine bunkers were constructed along with a number of ditches and foxholes. They were manned constantly by the best men available and equipped with the best weapons in their armory. Although government forces constantly overestimated the Indians's firepower, they did possess high-powered rifles, shotguns, handguns, and dynamite. They fused the dynamite so it could be thrown at oncoming attack vehicles or would blow up fortifications on a delayed basis. AIM also put together a good quantity of molotov cocktails, using pop bottles and fuel taken from the trading post. By far the most highly publicized weapon the Indians had at Wounded Knee was a Russian built AK-47 automatic rifle that had been smuggled back from Vietnam.

It was pictured in newspapers and magazines throughout the country and created a furor among those with an interest in gun control. Members of the National Rifle Association protested that it was an illegal weapon. Guards reported to the trading post for duty and, when relieved, slept either in the store or in the Catholic church. AIM set a 6:00 p.m. curfew for all persons in Wounded Knee. Everyone except AIM members was to be in the church at that time.[74]

Others carried out specific assignments to maintain stability and survival of the occupying force. Banks and Means served as spokesmen and information officers. Women and older children manned the community kitchens and took care of other domestic duties. Noncombatant males helped with construction and maintenance. Also, two medicine men, Leonard Crow Dog and Wallace Black Elk, were primarily responsible for religious leadership at Wounded Knee. Black Elk was the grandson of the original Black Elk of Neihardt's noted book, <u>Black Elk Speaks</u>. Crow Dog's great grandfather was the one who killed Spotted Tail. Leonard Crow Dog's father, Henry, chose to keep Leonard out of white-controlled schools so he could grow up in a traditional environment.

Government forces on the scene amounted to about 230 men with very adequate backup personnel and equipment. Included in the government arsenal were seventeen armored personnel carriers at the roadblocks and airplanes and helicopters from nearby Ellsworth Air Base. The eight roadblocks were manned by an almost evenly divided force of 116 FBI and just over 100 Marshals. This represented the largest group of Marshals and FBI ever to work together on one case over an extended period of time. Around 25-30 BIA officers also lent assistance. All eight roadblocks were manned during the day and seven were manned at night. Each roadblock had at least one APC along with several other government vehicles for assistance. Other law enforcement vehicles and personnel were used for roving assignments.[75] Trimbach complained from the beginning that FBI were being used as Infantrymen in a military role. He suggested to his superiors that the military was best equipped to handle the tactical situations by using tear gas, special weapons, and aircraft. On March 4, Felt recommended that Herbert E. Hoxie, SAC Milwaukee, and SAC Wilburn K. DeBruler, Oklahoma City, report to Wounded Knee to lend experienced support to Trimbach. Gray indicated that he sympahized with Trimbach and agreed that the operation should be considered a military one, but that, "until such time as the jurisdiction is such matters is given to the military, the FBI had to assume the role due to its jurisdiction."[76]

To further assess the defenses at Wounded Knee, the FBI managed to infiltrate an undercover agent under the guise of being an electrical repairman. The agent reported that he was under close surveillance from heavily armed Indians throughout his visit. He was able, however, to bring back valuable intelligence data that indicated that the Indians were capable of defending their position and seemed to have no intention to leave.[77] Ordered to take no chances, Erickson accepted the idea that a negotiated settlement represented the only acceptable policy until he was informed differently.

If AIM had their supporters, federal forces also had theirs. They included local ranchers and anti-AIM Indians, who were willing to help. Erickson, though, was not eager to accept allies, other than United States military forces.

Tribal Chairman Wilson maintained he had as many as eight hundred supporters who could get the job done against AIM unilaterally, but was dissuaded from doing so by Erickson. Wilson pledged his support for all means necessary to end the takeover, including the use of federal troops. On March 2, Trimbach met with William Leavitt, head of the ranchers's Protective Association, whose membership of about one hundred ranchers was up in arms because the Indians at Wounded Knee had slaughtered three and rustled thirteen head of cattle. Leavitt warned they would give the government twenty-four hours, and if action was not taken, they would take it upon themselves to clear out the Indians. Trimbach had heard that some of the ranchers intended to go into the area on the morning of March 3. He told Leavitt that, should any of the ranchers attempt to enter Wounded Knee, they would be arrested for interference with officers in performance of duty.[78]

AIM appeared in no hurry to pull out. They presented authorities with a resolution signed by Wounded Knee residents asking the government "to cease and desist from firing upon our guest members of the AIM and members of the news media who are here at our invitation..." Sixty-seven of the signees listed themselves as "residents;" twenty-four listed themselves as "Wounded Knee."[79] The activists had clearly spelled out their demands to the Senate representatives and to the mass media. They indicated they did not plan to leave until they were satisfied. The demand that the federal force steadfastly refused to honor was that which called for suspension of tribal government and its president. The government, especially the Interior Department, viewed that proposal as a threat to the whole reservation structure as it existed throughout the country. Many observers had trouble accepting the AIM logic, which, on the one hand, stressed self-determination and independence for the Indian and on the other called for the government to assist them in overthrowing a duly elected tribal government.[80]

Erickson formulated a proposal to end the affair that he forwarded to Wounded Knee on March 4. Reportedly it was approved by Attorney General Kleindienst. It proposed:

1. Commencing 8:00 a.m., March 5, 1973, all nonresident Indians will be permitted to leave Wounded Knee providing the following conditions are met:

a. The departing person must identify himself except in the case of women and children.
b. No weapons can be carried by the departees, not even to the roadblock.
c. Should the Indian own the weapon and want it back, he should identify it, leave it behind, and, of course, it will bo returned to him later.
d. At this time, no arrests will be made providing the departee is orderly. The matter will be presented to a Federal Grand Jury later.

2. All wishing to leave have to do so by 6:00 p.m., 3/5/73.

3. As soon as the nonresidents have left, and there is no indication of violence, the Federal guard force will dissolve and the Indians will be permitted to come and go as they please.

4. The FBI would be allowed to search the departing Indians for weapons, loot and contraband; and they should only be allowed to leave through Roadblock 1.[81]

AIM spent most of March 5 discussing the proposal. That evening Banks and Means ceremoniously burned it at a meeting in the Catholic church. They expanded their demands to include an agreement that any federal hearings must be held at Wounded Knee and that the Department of Interior schedule new tribal elections after suspending Dick Wilson and his government. They also requested that federal Marshals remain on the reservation to protect them from reprisals from Wilson's people. The government's original offer was extended twenty-four hours until 6:00 p.m., March 6. No one left. Trimbach informed his superiors that it was his personal opinion that none of the Indians were in a hurry to move out.[83]

Wilson was not pleased with the government offer, either. He told the press, "I was not consulted in this offer of amnesty to any of them knuckleheads out there and I'm just completely upset about it."[84] Wilson was especially perturbed by the role of Ralph Erickson and the Justice Department, "We asked the United States Marshals, not the Justice Department. If I knew they were coming, I may not have asked for the Marshals. I think the Marshals are doing a terrific job. I am upset with the entire Washington staff of the Justice Department."[85]

Governor Kneip also felt the tribal council was being neglected. "There seems to be too much discussion with the American Indian Movement leaders, leaving out South Dakota Indians who should be a part of the discussion," Kneip told the press. "I'd like the discussion to be calm," he said, "but I am disturbed that the people of the state, the elected tribal chairman and council members are not included."[86]

Negotiations during the day of March 6 focused around AIM's demand that Wilson be removed and the tribal government be suspended. The government negotiators insisted that there was no legal way to comply with those requests even if they were so inclined. AIM negotiators showed up at the evening meeting with their weapons. After the meeting broke up, there was a considerable amount of shooting but no injuries for either side. Roy Haber, who had been the Chief AIM attorney, left Wounded Knee and was replaced by Ramon Roubideaux. Charles Ablard, Associate Deputy Attorney General, came to replace Harlington Wood, Jr., as Erickson's deputy.[87]

March 7 featured a flurry of events throughout the day. They began at 4:45 a.m., when a red, white, and blue single engine plane circled Wounded Knee and then landed on the roadway in front of the church. It was met by a van and several automobiles. Supplies were unloaded, and the plane departed in about twenty minutes.[88] Bruno Torres, a photographer employed by United Press International, got a picture of the plane in flight that included its aircraft identification number. Torres turned his picture over to the FBI, who tracked down the organizers of the flight before the day ended.[89]

The perpetrator of the flight was Dr. Dwain Cummings, an osteopathic surgeon from Stanwood, Michigan, who was raised on the Sisseton Indian Reservation in South Dakota. His hospital used to be the county poor farm and was surrounded by pasture land. Cummings purchased this land and brought in a herd of buffalo. His work with buffalo was so successful that he had become known as "The Buffalo Doctor." When he learned the Indians needed food and supplies at Wounded Knee, Cummings agreed to organize a flight to assist them. Local Indians and white sympathizers helped him acquire the relief cargo.

Cummings hired Paul R. Davids for $300 to fly the cargo to Wounded Knee. Davids, who operated a flying school at Grand Haven, Michigan, had been featured in the Muskegon newspaper about eighteen months earlier for his role as a pilot in South America, carrying contraband from one country to another.[90] He agreed to make the flight if foodstuffs only were carried. Davids reported that there were fifty pound sacks of dried milo, about two hundred pounds of pinto beans, a quantity of flour, several five gallon Cans of soy bean oil, toilet paper, and two cartons of cigarettes. The total weight of the cargo was around five hundred pounds. By 5:45 a.m., March 8, Cummings was taken from his residence under arrest by the FBI. He was charged with obstruction of justice but plead guilty to flying an overloaded plane and reckless flying and paid a $1,000 fine.[91]

Later, on the morning of March 7, Mrs. William Leavitt told FBI agents that her husband had lost several cows since the Indians had taken over Wounded Knee and he was currently at the village attempting to recover his cattle. Leavitt and his friends did not fare well. He, along with Charles and Kevin Sasse of nearby Batesland, rode horseback to a point just south of Wounded Knee along Wounded Knee Creek, where they spotted three of their missing bulls across the creek from them. When they attempted to cross the creek to retrieve the bulls, they were confronted by four heavily armed Indians. Leavitt said two of the younger Indians were going to let them round up the cattle, but an older Indian with long gray hair, a tough face, and a headband approached and told them, "You are not going to get those bulls. You are going to get your asses out of here or get your head blown off." Three other young Indians, all armed with high powered rifles, appeared during the meeting.[92] During the later trial of Banks and Means in St. Paul, their attorneys claimed Leavitt was plotting with his group to drop explosives on the demonstrators at Wounded Knee.[93]

Obviously frustrated by his failure to bring about a settlement, Erickson announced on March 7 that he had reached the conclusion that further negotiations would be useless. He suggested the situation might improve if he and the United States Attorneys from North and South Dakota left the scene. "Every effort was made to meet their requests reasonably," said Erickson. "But," he added, "every time a settlement seemed near the AIM group would come up with an additional demand, or change a demand which had already been accepted by both sides to make it unacceptable to us."[94] Erickson released a statement indicating there was nothing more the Justice Department could do or offer and, in his opinion, the matter was now in the hands of the Interior Department, particularly the Bureau of Indian Affairs.[95]

Before leaving, Erickson sent word to the AIM leaders through Ramon Roubideaux that negotiations were still possible if desired and that no attack was presently planned. Erickson indicated that the offer to depart without arrest, which first had been made on March 4, would expire at 6:00 p.m. , March 8. He described the situation as very grave and urged the occupiers "to send the women and children, both resident and nonresident, out of Wounded Knee before darkness falls tomorrow."[96] Erickson also announced that a Federal Grand Jury would convene in Sioux Falls on March 12 to investigate the possible commission of federal crimes on the reservation." We're confident that the government is going to move against us at six o'clock tomorrow night," claimed Banks. He issued a national call for assistance for "the Second Battle of Wounded Knee."[97] Thirty-eight children and four women drove out of Wounded Knee in two groups the evening of March 7. Erickson later denied that his statement represented a final warning, "This was not an ultimatum," he said, "it was simply the withdrawal of an offer which had been repeatedly extended in an effort to avoid bloodshed."[98] Charles Ablard remained at Pine Ridge as the senior Justice Department official.

Most of the remainder of the residents of Wounded Knee who were originally hostages also departed on March 7 and 8. Clive Gildersleeve left with Father Manhart the morning of March 7 but returned to stay overnight. Jean Fritze and Wilbur Riegert exited the evening of March 7 with Jean's son, David Fritze, a student at the South

Dakota School of Mines. Riegert, David's grandfather, was taken to the Rushville Community Hospital immediately. The remainder of the group, including the Gildersleeves and Mrs. Clark, left the next day.

While in Wounded Knee, David Fritze attended a meeting at the Wounded Knee Trading Post where about two hundred occupiers were advised to reject the government peace offer. Means told the audience there were over two hundred Canadian Indians waiting at Porcupine ready to enter Wounded Knee. Means said anyone could leave Wounded Knee if they wanted to "but for some of us it is our time to die."[99] The Reverend Ralph Abernathy, head of the Southern Christian Leadership Council, appeared at the meeting and assured, "Indians have won a great vicory already."[100] Abernathy described the Indians's plight as similar to the American Negro. He suggested the BIA should be called MIA—"Missing in Action." [101] Possibly the well circulated picture of a tall Indian standing alongside Abernathy with an AK-47 held at ready attracted more attention than did the distinguished black leader.[102]

The morning of March 8, a high level meeting was held in the office of Deputy Attorney General Sneed, former dean of the Duke University Law School. Erickson; Harlington Wood, Assistant Attorney General, Civil Rights Division; William Tyson of the Criminal Division; Inspectors Richard Gallagher and John Gordon of the FBI; and representatives of the Department of Interior and BIA were in attendance. Erickson reviewed the developments at Wounded Knee and described the current situation as "quite grave." He said the situation had alternately improved and deteriorated throughout the past week. It appeared that an agreement was about to be reached on March 4; but when the Indians demanded an immediate audience with a ranking official of the Department of the Interior, Interior would not agree to meet until after the occupiers gave up. Erickson said Dick Wllson was a problem. "He is very affable and agrees to keep his hands off and then turns around and incites the situation," reported Erickson.[103]

The group considered what should be done at 6:00 p.m., March 8, if the Indians did not leave Wounded Knee. It was agreed that the Department of Justice would issue a press release saying the United States Government's offer was withdrawn. Any non-resident that now left Wounded Knee would be subject to immediate arrest, and the evidence concerning this matter was to be presented to a grand jury. Interior and Justice representatives bared their bureaucratic claws as well. Interior representatives requested that the press release be handled by the President. Justice suggested that Interior should build up the police force of the BIA in the event trouble broke out in other parts of the country. Then it could be handled immediately prior to developing into a state of siege, as had been the case at Wounded Knee. Erickson additionally insisted that a statement be made that he had been fully briefing the Department of the Interior officials in Washington concerning conditions at Wounded Knee.[104]

On March 8, Trimbach filed a wiretap request for the Wounded Knee trading post with the United States District Court. Trimbach justified his request by saying, ". . . which telephone is now being used by Dennis Banks, Russell Means, Clyde Bellecourt, and others, as yet unknown, who are presently occupying and controlling the village of Wounded Knee, South Dakota, and are committing other acts in violation of Sections 231 (a) (3), 371, 1201, and 2101, Title 18, United States Code."[105] Use of the wiretap proved a key defense issue in the later trial of Means and Banks.

The tribal government acted on that day,too. Their attorney entered a petition into the tribal court petitioning that the court issue an "order of eviction" to all nonmembers of the Oglala Sioux tribe and to all participants presently occupying the Wounded Knee area. The petition was based on the grounds that such occupants were trespassers and that participants had "declared war" on the United States government without authorization of the Oglala Sioux tribe. The tribal government also sent a message to the residents of Wounded Knee advising them to leave before 6:00 p.m. , March 8, or be subject to arrest. AIM refused to allow distributors of this message to enter Wounded Knee.[106]

Whether or not AIM's plight was as desperate as they made it appear, AIM enjoyed huge success in stirring up support throughout the country from a variety of concerned individuals and groups. Demonstrations, speeches, telegrams, letters, editorials, and the like urging the government to use restraint blossomed forth from an imposing number of sources. In New York City on March 7, 150 people demonstrated for AIM at the Federal Plaza. The next day, 150 Indians marched in Tuscon. Passamoquoddy Indians blocked parts of Highway 190 in Maine. In Los Angeles, Indians and other minorities planned to storm and hold the Justice Department building. In North Carolina, a band of Tuscaroras rode through the streets of a small town smashing windows in protest.[107] At Kent State, five hundred students demonstrated, as did students on a number of other campuses. The White House was deluged with telegrams sympathetic to AIM. In New York, the Reverend Robin Moss, United Church of Christ, said the federal authorities's ultimatum "presages bloodshed and loss of life." Sister Margaret Traxler, executive director of the National Catholic Conference for interracial justice, said in Chicago, "We as a nation are already heavily responsible for our brother's blood crying to us from the ground."[108] Kunstler told the press he hoped there would not be another Attica. About twenty Indians demonstrated in front of the BIA headquarters at Pine Ridge. Their focus was Dick Wilson Nellie Red Owl blamed Wilson for BIA stoppage of services. She did not claim to support AIM and waved an American flag while saying, "I am Oglala Sioux. That's all I am." Others carried signs, including one that said "Yankee Go Home."[109]

Besides the threat of violence and demonstrations at selected sites around the country if the confrontation was ended by force, authorities at the scene were almost certain they would be attacked from the rear. Father Charles Leute, the Catholic Priest of Porcupine, thought such a possibility was strong. Reverend Rouillard of Porcupine indicated Indians reportedly were grouping west of Pine Ridge and east of Porcupine for a possible counter-attack.[110] It was also reported that the Denver VVAW and AIM were working on an air drop. State police and FBI in the surrounding region were alerted to detain suspicious individuals. Nebraska State Police additionally were ordered to establish roadblocks on the boundaries of the Pine Ridge Reservation to stop AIM supporters from entering.[111] As one example of the blockades Mrs. Ramona Bennett, Puyallup tribal councilwoman, said nine carloads of supporters including two from Washington State were turned back by authorities.[112]

Senator James Abourezk, appearing on NBC television's "Today Show" from Washington, D. C. , said he was informed by his aides that an agreement had been reached. "I was informed last night by my people out there that some form of agreement had been reached between the Indians and the government," said Abourezk. "I understand the announcement will be made today (March 8). If everything works out we'll see not only a ceasefire but an agreement."[113] Congressman James Abnor advised the FBI that he had received information that Frank Fools Crow, Chief Medicine Man of the Oglala Sioux, was proceeding with the Oglala Sioux ritual symbolic of going into battle at Wounded Knee.[114]

Just how close the protestors were to annihilation remains a matter of conjecture. Given the records of government planning, which were not available to the Indians, one would conclude that an attack definitely had not been authorized, nor would it have been condoned. Most of the media representatives became convinced that AIM played the federal threat to the hilt for promotional effect. Newsweek's Mary Alice Kellog sneaked into Wounded Knee early and stayed during the second week. She reported that the repeated ultimatums and reports of a truce made for a low note of comedy that made the showdown at Wounded Knee resemble guerilla theater more than guerilla warfare. Kellog concluded, though, that the grievances behind the posturing were real enough.[115]

As the deadline for evacuation drew near, the Indian warriors commenced traditional religious ceremonies signifying the possibility of death. Seven leaders, some naked and some stripped to their shorts, began by entering a sweat lodge covered by an orange carpet and a purple blanket, to receive clarity of mind and body. About 150 warriors formed a semicircle and watched as the tribal fathers emerged from the steaming lodge. Leonard Crow Dog struck up a chant in the Lakota language. As each warrior passed by, he blessed him and painted a slash or a circle of red powder under the left eye. Each warrior proceeded into a white tipi, making a holy sign over the bleached skull of a buffalo head.[116]

Beginning at 5:20 p.m., a one-hour-and-ten-minute firefight broke out near roadblock three. During the course of the intensive firing, two Indians were hit by gunfire. The AIM attorney in Wounded Knee called out and requested that the CRS send in an ambulance to bring out the two wounded Indians. Floyd Condon, Cheyenne River Sioux, was shot in the hand. Milo Goings, Oglala Sioux, was hit in the leg. Both were hit from a range of about three hundred yards and were not seriously wounded. Webster Poor Bear was also injured when he fell from a pickup truck and suffered a broken kneecap as an Air Force jet dropped down on Wounded Knee to take aerial photographs. None of the injured Indians would leave Wounded Knee.[117]

Fighting was dramatically interrupted when a blue Cadillac roared up to the AIM staging area. Dennis Banks got out to announce that both sides had agreed to a ceasefire proposed by the National Council of Churches. "There were shouts of joy as the sun set behind a ridge spotted with the silhouettes of jagged pines," related a Time reporter on the scene.[118] To prevent infractions against the truce, thirty-four observers from the National Council of Churches, clearly identified by their white armbands with the NCC logo, took up positions around Wounded Knee. Two Indian lawyers dashed back and forth in the Cadillac between the BIA office in Pine Ridge and the AIM fortress with fresh proposals. The point of contention was the Justice Department's intention to arrest any protestors leaving the village and confiscate their weapons as evidence. The Justice Department maintained the roadblocks around the area at full alert to carry out the threat.[119]

Much of the credit for coordinating the truce effort belonged to Methodist Minister John Adams, representing the NCC. Adams, a World War II bomber pilot who had been a German Prisoner of War, brought extensive experience in the area of nonviolent civil rights confrontation and negotiation. He had first joined Father James E. Groppi in demands for fair and equal opportunity in Milwaukee. After that, the black civil rights movement occupied most of his time. Adams was at Gary, Jackson, Memphis, the Poor People's Campaign in Washington, D. C. , and had also served as a peacemaker at Kent State, Jackson State, and the national Republican convention at Miami Beach in 1972. As a staff member of the National Board of Church and Society of the United Methodist Church, his primary assignment was conflict resolution and crisis intervention. The main objective was to support nonviolent strategies of social protest by helping to identify specific grievances and offering options for action through opening lines of communication and response. Adams, a Caucasion, had served Methodist congregations since 1948. He was asked by Bishop Armstrong to go to Wounded Knee to replace Reverend Boe.[120] Unfortunately, Adams had no experience working with reservation Indians, and was constantly frustrated by their divisivenese. Though Bishop Armstrong liked to picture the NCC role as that of a neutral arbiter, no one close to Adams during the Wounded Knee crisis doubted that his sympathies were with AIM.[121] Unlike Boe, Adams did not stay at Wounded Knee, thinking he would be more effective working from the outside.[122]

Reverend and Mrs. George Pierce invited the NCC representatives to stay in the rectory of the Episcopal Church in Pine Ridge. These two buildings headquartered NCC activities for the next three weeks. Most of the consultation with the government occurred during the day, and meetings with AIM usually took place at night. Bishop Armstrong monitored developments from Aberdeen, South Dakota, as did NCC officials in New York and Washington, D. C. The effectiveness of the communications network is illustrated by the Indian request to Adams for a visit with civil rights leader Ralph Abernathy. Within forty-eight hours, Abernathy was conferring with the occupants of Wounded Knee at the site. With the help of Father Pierce and Sister Margaret Hawk, who knew the resident families in Wounded Knee, NCC officials transported food and other supplies into the occupied area. The food, which was furnished by the NCC, was inspected by a United States Marshal, packed in NCC vehicles in his presence, and escorted into Wounded Knee by CRS representatives. During their two-week presence at Pine Ridge, the NCC estimates they contributed around $7,500 in food and supplies. They have since adamantly maintained that their help only went to needy families and none benefitted AIM.[123]

By March 7, when violent confrontation appeared imminent, Adams proposed a fifteen-point ceasefire under NCC auspices to go into effect before the March 8 deadline. Bishop Armstrong flew to Wounded Knee to meet with AIM leaders, who accepted the proposal as did the Justice Department. Agreement seemed to be at hand on March 9. Justice Department spokesmen announced at the morning press briefing that negotiations, based on the NCC proposal, had resulted in an agreement in principle and that the only problem left was the manner and time nonresidents would leave Wounded Knee. Ablard and Roubideaux negotiated a formula under which the occupiers would come out and identify themselves but not be subject to arrest. Federal forces would be withdrawn, and a high official of the Department of Interior would go to the reservation to hear grievances the day following the departure of the protestors. When Ablard agreed to a Monday departure date for nonresidents, instead of Sunday which he had requested originally, it appeared as though the confrontation would end.[124]

AIM, however, was not willing to accept a set date of departure, especially that soon. Instead they counterproposed that they would depart only after they had met with the district chiefs on the reservation to plan the meeting with Interior officials. Roubideaux, who was about to be upstaged by Kunstler and his legal colleagues, refused to appear before the press and make any statement of agreement. By the end of the day, sporadic gunfire underlined the point that no settlement had been reached. At noon on March 9, Kunstler, accompanied by Chicago 7 defendant David Dellinger, Bill Matheson, Ted Glick, and Barbie Kinzie, sought entrance to Wounded Knee. Ablard advised them they could not enter per request of the NCC. Kunstler and his party tried again at 3:15 and were again denied. At 7:25 p.m., Kunstler and Matheson were allowed to enter Wounded Knee. Kunstler remained there throughout the weekend.[125]

Because the roadblocks had not been effective and since they seemed to serve as a symbolic focus for resistance, Erickson, Colburn, and Sneed agreed to propose on March 10 that they be removed. This break in negotiations may have been dictated by officials high in the Nixon administration. Robert Finch, former member of Nixon's cabinet, had been in touch with attorneys for the Indians for several days.[126] This new strategy was discussed with Oglala tribal leaders who supported it. Colburn also met with Stan Holder of AIM to see what AIM would do if the government withdrew. Holder promised that his people would withdraw from their fortifications and would permit free movement into and out of Wounded Knee. Trimbach, however, assured Holder that the FBI would continue its investigation and that, sooner or later, he and all of his associates would be arrested.[126] The order to remove the roadblocks then was issued by Sneed upon the authority of the Attorney General. It was transmitted through Director Colburn to the United States Marshals and other law enforcement officers on the scene.[127]

Amid a general air of celebration the withdrawal began about 2:00 p.m. Sunday. The APCs were withdrawn, but government surveillance was maintained from automobiles parked several miles from the village. The leaders of the occupation began a victory celebration and promised they were going to stay in Wounded Knee to deal with conditions on the Pine Ridge Reservation. They began filing past the mass grave monument. Then someone noticed smoke coming from the trading post. Dennis Banks led a bucket brigade to save the building.[128] About 4:30 p.m., two FBI agents approached Wounded Knee in a car to see if the occupiers had withdrawn. They appeared not to have done so. At that point, Interior Department officials announced they would not deal with AIM until all arms were turned in and Wounded Knee was vacated. Time reported, "In a state of confusion since the firing of several BIA officials and the illness of Secretary Rogers Morton, who is being treated for prostate cancer, Interior had reacted to the entire Wounded Knee affair with stubbornness."[129] Marvin Franklin, former chairman of the Iowa Indian Nation, the Acting Director, was quoted by Time as saying he would rather quit than talk with AIM leaders. "This is strictly a law enforcement problem, a Justice Department matter," he maintained, "How can you deal with criminals? How can you handle revolutionaries?" asked Franklin.[130]

No doubt Franklin had taken the cue from his ailing superior, Secretary Rogers C. B. Morton, who had released a press statement Saturday from Menlo Park, California, where he was undergoing treatment for his long and troublesome illness, vowing the government would not bow to threats by militant Indians but would "continue to provide a ladder of federal programs and opportunities on which the Indian can climb out of the bottom of the social barrel." "Nothing will be gained by promoting a national guilt complex over past mistakes, and nothing is gained by blackmail," Morton said in his first public pronouncement since AIM took over Wounded Knee. "They believe the pursuit of their criminal methods," he said, "and they do not represent a constituted group with whom the government can contract or can serve." Morton went on to explain that programs and services of the BIA are by law directed only to federally recognized tribes and groups for which the government has a specific trusts responsibility originating from treaty agreements, and AIM did not fall into that responsibility.131

In spite of Morton's criticisms, the government's move to withdraw to implement a peaceful conciliation at Wounded Knee generally was well supported by national media, although a number of newspapers in the area agreed with Morton. Time commented "In fact the Justice Department has done the sensible thing. The wonder was not why its agents had suddenly withdrawn, but why they had not been ordered to do so earlier, to defuse a dangerous situation."[132] The Lincoln Journal, Nebraska's most liberal paper, suggested editorially as early as March 6, "Surely the time has come to make peace at Wounded Knee. . . prolonged confronation will only risk tragedy. The Indians could honorably withdraw at this point knowing they have accomplished a great deal. It is a cause with a great deal of justice in it." The usually conservative Yakima (Washington) Herald Republic, located near one of the country's large Indian reservations, provided sympathetic coverage throughout the conflict. It carried an editorial, "Uncle Toma-hawk?" on March 10, "The Plains incident is an outgrowth both of internal tribal feuding and a national movement, and to this point the government appears to have acted with restraint and common sense." The Denver Post, which would later toughen its stance, expressed willingness to put up with the situation as it developed but a bit of impatience to get the incident settled, "So far, although what some of the AIM people did at Wounded Knee—especially looting the trading post—was clearly illegal, no one has been arrested for it and no blood has been shed. While AIM people are thus ahead of the game, we strongly suggest they return from the area. They have already succeeded in dramatizing Indian grievances—of which there are many." The Post showed no sympathy for AIM's demand that the government oust Richard Wilson." That proposal strikes us as wholly inconsistent with Indian demands for autonomy, and strange in general."[133]

Not unexpectedly, conservative criticism surfaced as well. Columnist Don Oakly, of the Newspaper Enterprise Association (NEA), wrote, "No one alive today had anything to do with the injustices done the red man in the settlement of this continent, anymore than anyone alive today had anything to do with the sin of slavery against the black man. Nothing that has gone before can be recalled or undone."[134] The Omaha World Herald, Nebraska's largest metropolitan daily, long noted for its hostility to the confrontation politics of the era, had sent a reporter to the scene but, by March 10, had seen enough to convince it that AIM was not sincere. The World Herald ran an editorial, "Bury the Nonsense at Wounded Knee," on March 10. It said in part, "Wounded Knee supposedly has 'dramatized' the plight of Indians. What it has dramatized most visibly is that the real concerns of real Indians are being obscured and distorted as the nation's attention is focused on the preposterous posturings of the handful of lawless publicity seekers." Many of the smaller newspapers in Nebraska reprinted this editorial.

If AIM planned to stay at Wounded Knee, it was acceptable to SAC Trimbach. He fully intended, however, to continue investigating what he was convinced were serious violations of the law at Wounded Knee and to arrest those responsible. This approach soon ended the truce—and Trimbach's stay at Pine Ridge. An Indian informant, who had ridden a horse into Wounded Knee several times before, told authorities he entered Wounded the evening of March 10. He witnessed a white man being struck in the face by an Indian and then taken to a log structure that served as a jail. He heard Dennis Banks address the group and advise them he was not leaving. Banks urged the group not to leave because they would be arrested one by one. He assured the group that food was being brought in from another area. The informant saw rifle pits leading from Wounded Knee to Highway 18, which he thought were manned twenty-four hours a day. He also reported AIM had requested that more people come to Wounded Knee.

Trimbach attempted to enter Wounded Knee with SAC DeBruler early March 11. They were met at the AIM roadblock by four armed Indians. Trimbach identified himself as FBI and said he had special work to do at Wounded Knee. Saying they were holding up the progress of the FBI's investigation, Trimbach asked if he would be shot if he drove through the roadblock. An Indian replied they would stop them from entering. After about ten minutes, the agents left.[135]

Four United States postal inspectors approached Wounded Knee on the Manderson road the same day. They also were stopped at a roadblock by three Indians. The inspectors explained their purpose was to investigate possible postal violations and to ascertain what equipment would be needed to restore postal services. An Indian left the roadblock and returned shortly. The postal inspectors were then taken into Wounded Knee at gunpoint. They were relieved of three government pistols, one personal pistol, their credentials, and wallets. Next they were bound to chairs with ropes.

After about a half hour, the inspectors were joined by two ranchers, Charles Merrill and Louis P. Hansen. They said they had heard the roads through Wounded Knee were open and decided to save time by going that way. When they were stopped at the Wounded Knee roadblock about 9:OO a.m., they were taken to the museum in Wounded Knee where they, too, were tied to chairs with ropes. After Merritt and Hansen were bound, the Indians read a list list of approximately forty ranchers in the Pine Ridge area whom they would burn out if any harm came to the Indians. Merrill believed the person who made the statement was Carter Camp because someone had said to get Carter Camp, and he arrived shortly thereafter. While they were being taken to the museum, Merrill told his captors that his grandfather owned the bar in Scenic. An Indian said that was where Indian girls were being raped and that Merrill was one of those responsible. After they were tied up, an Indian female came into the room and started calling them pigs and said Merrill was a "rapo." Milo Goings, who had been shot in the leg during the March 9 firefight, hit Merrill in the face with his hand. Goings chambered a round in his rifle, pointed it at Merrill's leg and said, "I ought to shoot you in the leg like you shot me." Bernardo Escamilla, a Mexican from Scottsbluff, also threatened Merrill with his own rifle. The Indians had taken three guns from Merrill and Hansen: a Beretta Model 948, a Winchester rifle, and a pistol—all loaded. When Trimbach heard nothing from the postal inspectors, he threatened that federal forces were going to go in and get them. All six of the hostages were taken by truck to the highway and allowed to leave in their own vehicles at about 11:30 a.m.[136] While this incident was underway, the press took many pictures of it, which made front pages around the world.[137] AIM leaders were quoted as saying the three postal inspectors were federal agents participating in an attempt by the FBI to discredit AIM. "I don't think they came down here to protect no mailboxes," said Banks.[138] Unfortunately for the Indians involved, they were indeed postal inspectors as later court proceedings would bear out.

The incident that finalized the end of the truce involved the much visible U-Haul van. Two FBI agents spotted it about seven miles north of Wounded Knee near Manderson the afternoon of March 11. Since the van had been reported as stolen, the agents relayed their information to the Command Post at Pine Ridge. They were ordered to stop the van. The agents were backed up by another nearby FBI vehicle and three BIA police cars. As the agents approached the van, it headed South toward Wounded Knee. The FBI turned on their siren, but the Indians ignored it. When the government vehicle pulled alongside the van, a gun was sighted in an open window of the van, and reports that sounded like gunfire were heard. The agents thought they saw a round hit the pavement in front of them. Agent Curtis Fitzgerald of Chicago attempted to shoot back with his M-16 rifle, but the rifle misfired. Fitzgerald was hit in the left hand and right forearm by gunfire from the van, causing him to drop the rifle on the pavement. Knowing the firepower of an M-16 at close range, perhaps it was best that it jammed. Fitzgerald, seriously wounded, nevertheless, got off six rounds from his revolver, firing left handed from the car window. He could not reload because he was bleeding profusely. Agent McGee, the driver, fired six shots from his .357 magnum, radioed that they had been hit, reloaded, and continued to pursue, firing an additional six rounds into the rear of the van through the windshield of the FBI car. By that time the van had reached the perimeter of Wounded Knee and pursuit ended. Fitzgerald suffered a superficial gunshot wound in his left hand, but his right hand and wrist were punctured, tearing the radial artery.[139] The Indians in the van told about the same story as the FBI, but insisted Fitzgerald fired first.

Since Trimbach had been at the scene of the shooting incident, Hoxie and Colburn met with Stanley Holder within the Wounded Knee perimeter to discuss the deteriorating situation. Holder immediately apologized for the Fitzgerald incident and reported he had taken disciplinary action against the two individuals involved, including taking their van away. He conceded that they were outside the perimeter where they should not have been. Holder was told that AIM was not living up to the agreement which authorized Wounded Knee to be an open city. He replied that conditions had changed—there had been harassment from the Wilson faction and the ranchers. Hoxie insisted that the FBI maintained the authority and responsibility to investigate the takeover of Wounded Knee, which meant they must have access. Another meeting was scheduled for the next morning.[140]

That evening, Trimbach sent Gray a message urging prompt action. "The situation at Wounded Knee is such that AIM can now obtain supplies including weapons and ammunition without restrictions as there are no roadblocks;" he reported. Trimbach indicated there were at least three hundred persons at Wounded Knee, most of whom were armed, and they had terrorized ranchers and others and shown a willingness to shoot at law enforcement officials. The four SACs on the scene unanimously urged that the United Army put down the insurrection immediately by first employing tear gas dropped by helicopter and then overrunning their positions with APCs. Trimbach warned that if the army did not come in the safety of the agents was in jeopardy.[141]

The Attorney General held a meeting with Gray and Erickson the morning of March 12 to reconsider the ill-fated plan to abandon the roadblocks. Kleindeinst decided to reinstate the roadblocks, but in a position further back out of rifle range from Wounded Knee. He repeated that the instructions relative to the use of deadly and non-deadly force as set forth by Erickson on March 4 were still in effect. Trimbach was instructed to obtain affidavits from the two agents involved in the van incident "hitting on the point as to who shot first," since the Indians claimed the agents shot first. Gray instructed Felt and Gebhardt that Trimbach would be relieved by SAC Roy Moore, "because of the extensive pressure and tension he had been under in the past two weeks and the need for supervision in the Minneapolis office and the grand jury presentation growing out of Wounded Knee." When Gebhardt advised Trimbach of his release, Trimbach "became rather upset and insisted upon discussing the matter with Mr. Gray. . ." Felt added a footnote to Gebhardt's message in heavy ink, "Trimbach and Hoxie leaving as soon as their replacements arrive."[142] Erickson also issued instructions that the FBI would back away from vigorous investigation at Wounded Knee and concentrate on intelligence gathering. Public information officers from the Justice Department were replaced by spokesmen from the Department of Interior at Pine Ridge.[143] These significant changes followed instructions from Kleindeinst that (1) "the FBI should cut back on its efforts to obtain evidence; ease off investigative efforts substantially, even to the point of not making efforts at this time to obtain evidence as we have in the past, and (2) the FBI should concentrate on intelligence work." Gebhardt instructed DeBruler, "The safety of one Agent was not worth a thousand dirty militant bedraggled Indians."[144]

That the Justice Department leadership was displeased about the failure to resolve the crisis and with the violent confrontations of March 11 seems self-evident. AIM leadership seemed especially unhappy with Trimbach. It stemmed from Trimbach's perception of his role as an enforcer of the law rather than an referee of political issues. Trimbach held that criminal suspects were to be investigated and arrested with maximum efficiency. In retrospect, one could argue that a softer approach by Trimbach may have achieved a permanent settlement when the roadblocks were pulled out. But the Indians had not achieved their stated goals, and they had to be achieved through Interior—not Justice. At least at that point in time, AIM seemed content to stay put. Specifically, strategies such as refusal to allow free entry into Wounded Knee, the "arrest" of the four postal inspectors and the two ranchers, and informant information that the occupiers had no intention of submitting to arrest, negated the idea that a peaceful resolution was near on March 11. Trimbach in his first SAC assignment and no doubt anxious to establish a reputation, more than likely was as much a victim of circumstances as anything. Certainly, the judgment of his superiors in placing him in a known center of controversy should be questioned. FBI insiders say Trimbach's conduct at Wounded Knee plus his substandard performance at the ensuing trial at St. Paul blighted his chance of advancement. He was transferred to Memphis, Tennessee, in 1975 and retired in 1979.

Just how abrasive the federal forces were and how willing they were to fire the first shot remains controversial. Threatened by the possibility of an attack from the rear, with reports of huge numbers of AIM allies departing for Wounded Knee from various parts of the country, they understandably were not hospitable to outside visitors and were anxious to end their tedious and sometimes dangerous mission. Whether they stayed within the framework of their legal prerogatives remains in doubt. A <u>Newsweek</u> story, for example, claimed law enforcement officials sabotaged reporters's cars that were parked near roadblocks by breaking glass and slashing tires.[145] No further damage happened after the story appeared.[146] Olthel Pearson, an Indian studies instructor at Porterville College near the Tule Indian Reservation in California, claimed he and his two travelling companions, Craig Camp, brother of Carter Camp, and Ken Tiger, were abused by federal authorities when they were apprehended near Wounded Knee. Pearson and his companions arrived at Porcupine on March 8 "to find out first hand what was going on." Pearson was told on March 9 that a negotiated settlement had taken place, so they left Porcupine for Wounded Knee. On the way they were detained by United States Marshals, who took them to Pine Ridge in handcuffs when weapons were found in their vehicle. Pearson charged that he was not allowed to contact a lawyer, not booked, not arrested, but placed in a cell with five bunks along with fourteen other persons. When he was interviewed, Pearson alleged an FBI agent grabbed him by the shoulder and flung him at a chair. "From that time on I was cursed, verbally abused and I felt as though I was being both insulted and assaulted," he said. He further asserted that after they were transported to Rapid City, they were fed for the second time since their Friday arrest. The meal was a plate of beans and three cookies. They were released on Sunday. This story was carried on the front page of the <u>Fresno Bee</u> under the headline "'Nightmare' Federals Capture Valley Teacher at Wounded Knee."[146]

Anyone with the vaguest knowledge of criminal justice problems realizes that charges of harassment, brutality, and police malfeasance while under arrest are commonplace and always difficult to refute. Whether or not the Pearson story was embellished to appeal to a sympathetic public is a valid question. The <u>Bee's</u> decision to carry it on its front page, however, demonstrated the public relations problem federal officials faced and the necessity to protect themselves from such criticism if at all possible. That was the role SAC Trimbach and others, as well, did not seem to fully comprehend at Wounded Knee.

Tourists at the commemorative marker of the Massacre at Wounded Knee.

The Shooting Star Casino and Lodge owned by the White Earth Reservation in Minnesota. Many of the customers are Canadian.

The chimney of the museum is only prominent remainder of the central cluster of buildings at Wounded Knee.

The foundation of the burned out Catholic church with the Wounded Knee cemetery and the new church in the background.

The Longhorn saloon at Scenic, South Dakota, where Martin Montileaux was murdered in 1975. The sign used to say "No Indians Allowed."

Wesley Bad Heart Bull was fatally stabbed on the street in front of this bar in Buffalo Gap, South Dakota. His death precipitated the Custer riot of February 1973.

Russell Means addresses a college audience, fall 1993.

(Photo courtesy of Con Marshall, Chadron State College Information Office)

Lawrence "Buddy" La Monte's grave is located beside the 1890 mass burial site and monument which is in the immediate background.

Agnes and Clive Gildersleeve
early in their Marriage.
(Photo courtesy of grandson, Larry Swanson)

An Impasse
Upon An Impasse

*R*oy E. Moore, Trimbach's replacement, was one of the best known SACs in FBI history and only a year away from retirement. To have been with Moore on one of his many "specials" is considered a badge of honor by most agents.[1] Moore was known as a take-charge type who believed not everything had to be done by the book. As early as 1961, Moore was Chief Inspector of the Bureau and considered a sure candidate for an assistant directorship. An argument with the autocratic Hoover over a conflict between two agents in Oklahoma City got him demoted. Among several important civil rights cases Moore was assigned in the 1960s was the Freedom Rider murders in Philadelphia, Mississippi. He was responsible for opening the new FBI office in Jackson, Mississippi, after the incident.[2]

At Wounded Knee, Moore promptly withdrew from the negotiations spotlight. He told Gebhardt on March 14 that negotiations with the defendants and dealing with the press should be left to the Justice Department. Moore insisted that as an investigative and arresting organization that may have to testify before a grand jury and in court proceedings, the FBI's effectiveness could be limited by negotiating with the Indians and dealing with the press.[3] From that point on the FBI neither negotiated grievances nor handled press relations. A Sioux Falls Grand Jury authorized arrest warrants for Banks Means, Camp, Bissonette, and Clyde Bellecourt for their roles in the takeover of private property at Wounded Knee.

Several strategies had been employed to improve AIM's position. Former tribal chairman Gerald One Feather led a movement to upset the governing body and oust Wilson. The strategy was to convince at least seven of the twenty-member tribal council to resign, making it impossible for a quorum. If this could be accomplished, One Feather's group thought Wilson would be forced to resign.[4] Six of the eight district chairmen did resign, but Wilson refused to be flushed out and continued to control the tribal government with BIA backing. Wilson's opponents next began to plan a petition drive to force a new tribal election. The attempt to purchase the land and buildings from the private Wounded Knee Trading Corporation had not materialized either. Ralph Abernathy suggested that a $10 million trust fund be established to purchase Wounded Knee and handle other financial obligations. At one time in early March, Carter Camp claimed AIM had a $2.5 million option to buy. When reporters contacted the legal owner's attorney, he indicated that no one had attempted to buy Wounded Knee.[5]

The matter of legal ownership was taken care of, at least in the occupier's minds, by simply issuing a Declaration of Independence on March 11. It proclaimed the Wounded Knee area the new Independent Oglala Sioux Nation (ION). They announced after an all-day meeting that the Oglala chiefs led by Frank Fools Crow had requested the OSCRO and AIM to form a provisional government which could speak for the new nation to the outside world.[6] The ION announced that the Treaty of 1868 would be the basis for all further negotiations. The first nation the ION called upon for support and recognition was the Iroquois, who were invited to send emissaries.[7] Means had warned the four postal inspectors and two ranchers as they departed, "Any spies who violate our borders will be subject to international law and will face a firing squad." Means issued a call for 300,000 persons to be in Wounded Knee by Easter Sunday, April 22.[8] As substantiation of their sovereign status, the ION began issuing ninety-day visas to "foreign visitors."

The formation of the ION rested upon flimsy legal grounds at best. A long line of Supreme Court decisions, beginning with Cherokee Nation v. Georgia in 1831, denied Indian nations complete independence. This decision and others have consistently ruled that Indian tribes possess inherent sovereignty but only to the extent that the sovereignty has not been specifically taken away from them. Indian tribes may be described as domestic dependent nations. Consequently, they do not have the authority to declare independence from the United States. The Supreme Court in Williams v. Lee (1959) said, "Through conquest and treaties they were induced to give up complete independence and the right to go to war in exchange for federal protection, aid, and grants of land."[9]

Within the village, AIM was having increasing difficulty controlling the polyglot group which included Chicanos, Blacks, Caucasians, and Indians. The militants appeared more and more to the press as a disparate collection of urban outsiders, "rucksack revolutionaries," rather than a band of dissatisfied Oglala Sioux from the Pine Ridge Reservation. Means revised his call for 300,000 volunteers and AIM leaders placed careful restrictions on those allowed into the village. Those prohibited included "freaks, lazies, pot smokers, and drinkers."[10] A number of hangers-on fitting the above categories were expelled and, although many people of assorted backgrounds flocked to the area, only a handful were allowed to enter. On March 12, to contradict statements made by the Justice Department and Richard Wilson to the effect that most of the inhabitants of Wounded Knee were white radicals, the "provisional government" released a census which revealed 183 Oglalas, 189 other Indians, and only thirty-four non Indians. Many of the Oglalas, however, had come in when the government roadblocks were removed and would not remain at Wounded Knee for any length of time.

One of those ordered out of Wounded Knee on March 12 was a man who identified himself as Iona Andronov, a staffer for a weekly Soviet magazine, New Times. Andronov was taken from the village because he did not have the identification papers required of newsmen.[12] If the John Birch magazine American Opinion is accurate,

Andronov held no bad feelings. It included a picture of the cover of the March 1973, New Times described as "A Soviet Weekly of World Affairs." The headline story was "South Dakota U.S.A." and was illustrated by a close-up of Porcupine resident Edgar Bear Runner grasping a rifle in front of the negotiations tipi. In the New Times of January 3, 1974, Andronov wrote about his encounter with Means at the trial at St. Paul: "Russell Means was surrounded by lawyers and guards when I met him at the courtroom door. He put his arm around my shoulder and said, 'Hello, Russian. It's good you are here again.'"[13]

In addition to tightening its control of personnel within Wounded Knee, the ION leaders increased their efforts to beef up defensive capacity. Several Indians from Wounded Knee arrived in Los Angeles on March 13 to purchase guns, ammunition, and explosives. They contacted an Indian group known as Red Wind, which had been established for several years to rehabilitate Indian alcoholics. Red Wind occupied buildings owned by a religious cult in Box Canyon, Simi Valley, California, in the hills just north of Hollywood. The Asian Movement for Military Outreach (AMMO), a group organized in the summer of 1971 by people of Japanese descent to support anti Vietnam War activities, was contacted. Five members of AMMO went to separate sporting goods stores and purchased 5,000 rounds of assorted ammunition and delivered them to Red Wind.[14] Groups sympathetic to the AIM cause throughout the country also proclaimed their support for the ION.[15]

Assistant Attorney General Harlington Wood replaced Ablard on March 13. Direct negotiations were again initiated with AIM in cooperation with John Adams. Adams's story is that Wood called him when he arrived at Pine Ridge and asked him to take a message to AIM leaders saying he wanted to talk to them as soon as possible. Adams said he carried the message and AIM replied they would talk, but only in Wounded Knee. Against the advice of the FBI and the Marshals, Wood agreed to the AIM demand. Adams claims there was a level of communication between ION leadership and wood "that was really superb."[16] Means was not as completely captivated by Wood. "This guy seems to be, he's one of them guys that can really trick you. Pat you on the back and at the same time he's getting his knife ready," said Means. "That is the kind of negotiator we're dealing with now. The other ones, we knew where they were at; they were just out and out hicks. This guy is a sneaky pimp," Means concluded.[17]

Wood discussed the following with ION: 1. No movement on the Indians by the government, Medical attention at Wounded Knee, 3. AIM's desire to meet with representatives of the U. S. Department of the Interior, 4. No excessive bail for Indians, and 5. AIM's repeated request for removal of Richard Wilson as tribal president.[18] The negotiations seemed to be so satisfactory that Wood left immediately for Washington, D. C. , to confer with Department of Justice and Department of interior officials. His proposed plan provided for the Secretary of the Interior and other top Interior officials to meet with AIM leaders to discuss grievances.

Wood's optimism was soon to be chilled, almost as much as the South Dakota prairies which were hit by a severe blizzard the afternoon he completed his negotiations at Wounded Knee. The storm increased during the night to a full-scale blizzard with winds up to sixty knots piling drifts up to eight feet high. Traffic was paralyzed. In spite of adverse conditions, or possibly because of them, about thirty AIM vehicles set up a roadblock on the road to Porcupine on the morning of the fourteenth, but it was abandoned before law enforcement officials arrived.[19]

SAC Moore's arrival was delayed until the fourteenth. When he got there, Moore wasted no time making his assessment of the situation. If the Indians expected a softer deal from the new SAC, they were to be disappointed. That afternoon, Moore reported that a consensus of federal law enforcement there agreed that the ultimate solution would necessitate a military operation. He gave notice that the FBI planned to arrest Indians "coming and going."[20] Moore proposed that the confrontation should be ended the weekend of March 17-18 by direct attack if necessary. Moore suggested that a force of twelve armed APCs with ten men in each could take the compound if the attack were preceded by a gas attack from helicopters.[21] When he was informed that Assistant Attorney General Henry Petersen believed that the wiretap request was based largely on information obtained from illegal monitoring of a party line and, therefore, had not approved it, Moore said he "deeply resented" anyone claiming that there had been party line monitoring: this claim had absolutely no basis in fact; Title III wiretap was obtained exclusively from interviews. Moore maintained he did not see a great need for a wiretap anyway.[22]

The new SAC demonstrated that he meant business on Friday, March 16, when two of his agents got their vehicles stuck near the pro-AIM community of Porcupine. They were confronted by hostile Indians, believed to be the ones who had set up the impromptu roadblock. Moore immediately organized three squads of agents in three armored personnel carriers and approached Porcupine from three directions on the main roads. this force surrounded approximately forty Indians and took them to the Porcupine Community Center, where a grand total of ninety-seven people, mostly Indian, were identified. An agreement was reached to allow foodstuffs in their possession into Wounded Knee. After that was done, they were to depart the reservation peacefully. When the cars returned after delivering the foodstuffs, those who had been told to leave indicated they had consulted counsel and they felt the agreement was illegal. The government then modified its stand and allowed all enrolled members of the Oglala Sioux to stay, but others would be arrested if they did not leave. Those who could not prove tribal membership were escorted out by BIA police.[23]

Eviction of non-tribal members had been legalized on March 16 when reservation superintendent Stanley Lyman approved the order passed March 14 by the Pine Ridge Tribal Council. It said in part, "all members of the National Council of Churches and all non-members of the Oglala Sioux Tribe who are not residents of the Pine Ridge Reservation are hereby ordered to leave the Pine Ridge Reservation immediately."[24] The order charged that members of the National Council of Churches refused to meet with the Executive Committee of the Oglala Sioux Tribe to determine if they could stay. Wilson was especially perturbed with the NCC because they had expanded delivery of supplies to Wounded Knee in spite of a government ban. Both Wilson and the government were increasingly convinced the NCC was openly pro-AIM, rather than a neutral peacemaker, a view that was not without merit.[25] Wilson claimed the NCC was also Communist-oriented. He maintained he "believed in the Good Lord, but not the clowns who carry His message."[26]

When the eviction notice was served at the Episcopal Church in Pine Ridge where about a dozen NCC members were staying, they maintained they would not leave because the church belonged to the Episcopal Church of South Dakota and they had been advised by their attorneys to stay.[27] Wood, who had returned from Washington, requested Adams to reduce the number of NCC workers but specifically asked Adams to stay. Twenty-five NCC members left. Finally under pressure from the BIA, Wood asked all persons working with the NCC except Adams, to leave. That provoked Wilson to say, "The Reverend John Adams is the most arrogant son of a bitch I ever met." At a press conference the next morning, Adams replied, "I am an ordained son of a bitch."[28]

Wood proceeded to set up negotiations in the Tipi Chapel of the Church of God— a fairly new tipi-like structure, which had been the Lansbury's church. Permission to use the chapel was granted by the home missions office of the national headquarters of the Church of God in Anderson, Indiana. In order to continue negotiations, however, Wood determined that Adams must leave the reservation, which he did on March 23. Adams took a temporary home in nearby Rushville, Nebraska, but claimed he was forced to leave because of pressure from local businessmen and the chief of police. For the duration of the crisis, Adams operated from a trailer park in Chadron, Nebraska. A second NCC base was opened in Rapid City in a small house trailer parked in the back yard of the United Methodist district superintendent, Preston Brown.

Reverend John Paul Hantla, pastor of the United Methodist Church, Sioux City, Iowa, indicated that a considerable difference of opinion existed among clergymen on the scene at Wounded Knee. He had been invited to go to Wounded Knee as a representative of the United Methodist Church by Paul Moore, District Superintendent of the United Methodist Church, Sioux City, Iowa. Moore told Hantla that AIM wanted some clergymen to be there when they surrendered to avoid a possible massacre. Bishop James Thomas of Des Moines opposed the idea. But Chet Guinn, Pastor of the United Methodist Church of Perry, Iowa, and a member of the liberal United Methodist Board of Christian Concern, contacted Preston Brown, and, without the knowledge or approval of Bishop Thomas, made arrangements for himself and three other Methodist ministers to travel to Wounded Knee on March 16.

Hantla called Bishop Thomas on March 12, and told him he was opposed to AIM and would not be a representative of his church. Thomas then asked Hantla to travel to Wounded Knee as his personal deputy and Hantla accepted, leaving the same day. On his way, Hantla called Means's mother, Mrs. Theodora Means, at Fremont, Nebraska. She had been working at Midland College in Fremont, since January as Director of Talent Search, a minority program funded by HEW.[29] Mrs. Means told Hantla to tell Russell that she loved him and was praying for him and that his wife was moving from Arizona to Fremont to stay with her until the Wounded Knee confrontation was over.[30] When Hantla got to Wounded Knee, he gave Means the message from his mother. Means was appreciative but seemed extremely nervous all of the time by Hantla's judgment. Some of the representatives of the National Council of Churches told him that violence, such as Wounded Knee, was sometimes necessary to bring about change. A confidant told Hantla that the Indians planned to make a last-ditch stand if necessary at the Catholic Church. Women and unarmed children would be placed inside, and all male Indians in the village would surround the church and fight. Hantla believed AIM leaders expected a pitched battle.[31]

Just after the NCC expulsion from Pine Ridge, attorney William B. Quigley of Valentine, Nebraska, filed his second suit against AIM in the United States District Court at Sioux Falls. The first, on March 8, was a $2 million suit against AIM only for damages incurred during the BIA headquarters takeover in Washington, D. C., the second, for $3.2 million, was expanded to include not only AIM but also its officers and the NCC, "and John Adams, personally and as an officer of said National Council of Churches." Quigley's charges received a good deal of favorable attention in the surrounding area.[32]

When the events of March 10-11 resulted in the formation of the ION instead of the expected settlement, the chorus of opposition to the activities swelled. Freshman Congressman Abdnor, whose district included Wounded Knee, released a two page statement that condemned AIM and called on federal officials to employ "whatever force and technology is necessary" to evict the insurgents.[33]

Abdnor attacked AIM on March 14 in a house speech which gained commendations from ten of his conservative colleagues. Abdnor said, "I wonder if we could have ever kept any President or elected official in office over a month with tactics of a similar kind?" He suggested that if the Oglala Sioux really wanted to change tribal presidents, a petition should be circulated to obtain the necessary one-third approval of voting members of the tribe for a new election. [34]

Comments from his colleagues included: "The situation at Wounded Knee is a national disgrace," Philip Crane, Illinois; "They (Indians) do not want them (AIM) in our state," Conlon, Arizona; "Stop the terrorism," Gross, Iowa; "We have not received adequate and full reporting on the issue in some of the news media," Rousselot, California; "A clergyman said he had been told clergy were actively smuggling arms to the insurgents," Hudnut, Indiana; "It (AIM) is clearly a small minority of radicals trying to accomplish by violent confrontation what they have failed to accomplish by working democratically through the tribes," Shoup, Montana; "Their revolution hurts the efforts of Indian tribes everywhere that are trying to solve Indian problems and grievances," Melchor, Montana.[35] Senator McGovern said, "The law must be enforced" and called for the arrest of those indicted by the Sioux Falls Grand Jury.[36] Also, on March 14, a Rapid City Grand Jury returned a list of thirty-one more sealed indictments against AIM leaders.

With the crisis dragging on, many began to question the Nixon administration's devotion to "law and order," a position that had won many votes for him in both of his successful campaigns. Typically, each arm of the government hastened to place the blame on other branches. Predictably, the executive branch blamed the Indian discontent on the Democratic-controlled Congress because it did not pass the legislation Nixon had requested that was designed to allow the tribes more self-determination and economic autonomy. In turn, Congressional spokesmen charged that Interior Department officials wasted too much time before submitting the needed legislative bills for consideration.[37]

At the local level Wilson and his tribal council officers were becoming even more restive. They signed a letter addressed to Marvin Franklin and "Wood Harrington" on March 19 calling for immediate resolution of the problem. The letter said in part, "We can no longer condone the attitude of the Department of Justice or the fact that they do not want to tarnish their image in the eyes of the American public by using necessary force in bringing the Wounded Knee situation to an end."[38] The Rapid City Journal continued the constant refrain of South Dakota newspapers that all the trouble emanated from Washington, D. C. "There are no instant answers to the problems as complex and historically tangled as have been dramatized at Wounded Knee. The point is, these solutions must come in Washington, not Wounded Knee," it said.[39]

Prospects for a settlement improved when Secretary of the Interior Morton announced he would fly to Pierre, South Dakota, on March 17. There he would be willing to meet with the Indians from Wounded Knee.[40] If this was not possible, he said he could go to Wounded Knee. Later the same day, Morton changed his mind. He issued a statement calling the insurgents "renegades" and "adventurers" and accused them of preferring violent, publicity-generating confrontations to sincere negotiations. "Some of their leaders are struck with self-righteousness," Morton said. He termed the militants's actions "criminal operations" and said they should be dealt with accordingly.[41]

In Morton's stead, Marvin Franklin, Assistant to the Secretary for Indian Affairs, accompanied Wood back to Pine Ridge with a detailed proposal to end the confrontation. Phase one of the offer suggested a meeting by AIM leaders with Department of Interior officials to discuss grievances. An official of the Civil Rights division of the Department of Justice was to be present at sessions to consider any grievances related to civil rights. Phase two concerned the laying down of weapons and their collection by federal authorities. It also detailed the process of identification and processing of all nonresidents and residents and the provision for arrest of those with warrants out for them. Phase three contained miscellaneous provisions, including the right of federal agents to remain a reasonable time on the reservation after the settlement. Wood told the FBI that it was his final offer and, if it was not accepted, he would return to Washington and not participate further in negotiations, as Erickson had done.[42]

Wood presented the overture to Dennis Banks on March 17 at the main roadblock. He termed it the government's best offer, but stressed it was not an ultimatum. The proposal called for a meeting in Sioux Falls between AIM and Franklin. After the meeting began, but before discussions would begin, the persons remaining in Wounded Knee would submit peacefully to arrest if warrants were out for them. In an exchange of gunfire that evening, one AIM supporter described as Rocky Madrid, Chicano medic, suffered a superficial wound in the stomach.[44]

Wood, Assistant Attorney General Richard Hellstern, and Wayne Colburn entered Wounded Knee, March 18. They met with Means, Banks, Camp, and Clyde Bellecourt to discuss the proposal. AIM objected to each point of the offer and reiterated their complaints against Wilson, the Department of Interior, and so on. The scene was witnessed by a number of spectators and news media representatives. Wood suggested that if AIM's grievances were submitted in writing, two Department of Justice officials and two representatives of AIM would discuss them and the government's recommendation on the following day. AIM agreed. Chief Marshal Colburn, who was sizing up AIM's defensive capacity during the discussion, told the FBI he thought the previous estimates of weapons, personnel, and fortifications had been overestimated.

Colburn's appraisal turned out to be quite accurate after the occupation ended. FBI reports that the Indians had firepower such as rocket launchers and machine guns never could be substantiated, and it was proven that AIM had constructed several wooden dummies to mislead the government. Of course, AIM scoffed at media reports that they had such high-powered weapons in Wounded Knee. They did have enough firepower, nevertheless, to discourage an outright attack, such as law enforcement officials had urged from the beginning. It was clearly established that they had a number of high-powered rifles, including semiautomatic AK-47s, plus assorted shotguns, revolvers, and .22 rifles. They also had a plentiful supply of dynamite and molotov cocktails. Given the wide defensive perimeter, the quality of the fortifications and personnel, and the effectiveness of the communications system, the FBI estimated a casualty rate of ten percent, at least for the invaders, could be expected.[45] How many women and children along with the male defenders would be killed or wounded never was seriously estimated. That spector simply was not acceptable to government elected leaders and the public. It meant that negotiations must continue.

March 19, Wood offered several compromises he hoped would lead to at least a general agreement. Marvin Franklin agreed to meet with valid members of the Oglala Sioux tribe, not AIM, to discuss grievances involving the Interior Department. Community Relations Representatives would be allowed to enter and depart Wounded Knee freely. Also, bail for Severt Young Bear, who had been arrested previously and held on $20,000 bail, would be reduced to $5,000. The government would request the Red Cross to render immediate assistance to the local residents of Wounded Knee when an agreement was finalized. AIM presented a lengthy counter-proposal based upon the 1868 Treaty. They insisted the 1868 Treaty assigned the responsibility for forming agreements and restoring peace with the President. One of the stronger statements in the offer said, "We will deal with the President now as the Treaty prescribes—or we shall defend ourselves against his outlaw nation!"

The official delegation of the Iroquois, a tribe noted for their expertise in international law and their defense of tribal sovereignty, arrived for a four-day visit on March 19. They were led by three tribal chiefs from New York: William Lazore, Harry Jacobs, Jr., and Oren Lyons. Their first act was to read a statement of support for "their brothers at Wounded Knee."[46] The FBI seemed confused about the intention of the Iroquois visitors. Their files read, "Three tribal chiefs from New York. . . are entering Wounded Knee in an effort to convince AIM leadership to surrender."[47] When the Iroquois walked out of Wounded Knee on March 23, they were greeted by black activist Angela Davis. Davis and the Iroquois were promptly escorted off the reservation by Wilson's police.[48]

Also on March 19, superintendent Stanley Lyman received a petition bearing 1,400 signatures of reservation residents. It requested a referendum to determine when to dissolve the existing form of government and establish a new system based upon the 1868 Treaty. "This is what they should have been doing all along," said Dick Wilson.[49] The petition drive was led by Gerald One Feather, who appealed principally to the traditionalists in the outlying districts.[50] Barbara Means, Russell's cousin, informed authorities that Russell was ready to surrender if the petition was accepted as legal. She indicated Means intended to hold out until April 2, the date which would represent the fifteen day deadline for Wilson to contest the petition. Barbara disclosed that her group, called Better Government, intended to hold a series of meetings between Sunday, March 25, and Wednesday, March 28, to explain the provisions of the petition and to enlist support for it.[51]

Wood departed for Springfield, Illinois, on March 20 to visit his seriously ill father. He planned to proceed from Illinois to Washington, D. C., the next day and return to Pine Ridge on March 22. Richard Hellstern remained in charge for the Justice Department at

Pine Ridge. Wood instructed that the official policy of restraint would stay in effect during his absence. Any change in roadblock position by Marshals or FBI had to be cleared beforehand with the Justice Department, and AIM leaders had to he advised ahead of time through the CRS before any change could be made.[52]

After three weeks of siege with relatively lenient ingress and egress policies, federal forces began to tighten the noose. The press again was prohibited and their surveillance ability was intensified with a system of flares and spotlights combined with more sophisticated night weaponry. AIM supplies were beginning to run short. Indians were observed slaughtering cows behind a church on March 20 and unsuccessfully attempting to round up others. Because they suspected that AIM was siphoning gas out of visitors's tanks, authorities announced as of March 20 that a comparison of odometer reading against fuel consumption would be made on all visitors's cars to Wounded Knee.[53]

The all-out effort to drum up support for the protesters, mainly through left-leaning antiwar and civil rights organizations, continued to enjoy success. The FBI identified twenty-one different groups sponsoring and participating in demonstrations throughout the United States for AIM. They included: Students for a Democratic Society, Socialist Workers Party, Workers World Party, Youth Against War and Fascism, Young Socialist Alliance, Vietnam Veterans Against the War, Black Panther Party, Venceremos Organization, Progressive Labor Party, Republic of New Africa, National Committee for Defense of Political Prisoners, United States Committee to Aid the National Liberation Front, Medical Aid for Indochina, The Red Collective, The Black Workers Medical Committee for Human rights, Pittsburgh Peace and Freedom Center, and Committee for Asian American Action.[54]

Support from the Bay area of California continued to be especially strong. About two hundred people held a "United People for Wounded Knee" demonstration on the plaza of the federal office building at San Francisco on March 20. Robert Wesley King, introduced as a medic recently returned from Wounded Knee, spoke. King said, "A state of war exists in the United States today and if the United States government attacks at Wounded Knee, a civil war should exist in this country." Attempts were made to collect money from passersby to aid Wounded Knee.[55] Five members of the Venceremos held a press conference on March 22 to describe their experiences at Wounded Knee and solicit support at their headquarters in Palo Alto. King, Daniel Friedman, Tom Pillsbury, Marck Sapir and Jesse James Young related they had gone to Wounded Knee for nine days as a medical team and had started a hospital there.[56] The March 23 edition of the Berkeley Barb, an underground newspaper, contained several articles urging radical groups in the Bay area to support the Indians at Wounded Knee. The theme of the articles was that Wounded Knee would serve as a rallying point for radical groups in lieu of the Vietnam War.[57] Another piece urging support for Wounded Knee appeared in the Sonoma County Bugle, published in Santa Rosa, California. It stressed the need for medical supplies, indicating that lack of power and heat and the inadequate diet had created many respiratory illnesses. The report suggested that medical supplies could be sent to the Community Action Church, in care of George Gibbons, Rapid City, South Dakota.[58] The United Council of Churches purchased and delivered eleven portable restrooms to Wounded Knee on March 20.[59]

Another mass-media coup for AIM came March 21 when the entire Dick Cavett television show was devoted to Wounded Knee and the Indian grievances involved.

Vernon Bellecourt, Robert Burnette, Richard Two Bulls, Charles Kills Enemy, Vernon Quinn, Charles Trimble, and Frank Fools Crow and his interpreter, Matthew King, attempted to explain the situation and interpret their concerns over broken treaties. Charles Trimble was invited to represent the Wilson faction, even though Wilson was willing to participate. The show managed to get across some basic Indian concerns, but its impact was far from devastating—tending to be dull and repetitive, and surprisingly lacking in depth of understanding and interpretation of tribal politics. The posturing of Fools Crow as a legitimate hereditary chief of the Oglala Sioux certainly did not set well with many Oglalas, for example. Cavett, obviously out of his element, gamely attempted to lend some direction to the meandering monologues. The night before his appearance on the Cavett program, Burnette told an audience at the State University of New York at Binghamton that at least ninety places around the country "will get hit" if the Indian takeover at Wounded Knee ended in violence.[60]

Appeals for support for the ION in the form of an actual march on the federal roadblocks were issued throughout the nation. At a news conference at the University of New Mexico, officials of the Kiva Club, an Indian student organization, asked those who sympathized with the Indians at Wounded Knee to travel to Rosebud, South Dakota, to participate in a peaceful march against the federal roadblocks around Wounded Knee. They said calls were going out to members of minority groups all over the nation for this march.[61] The request got some response. Richard Schwaiger, an elected city commissioner in Grand Rapids, Michigan, announced he planned to fly to Wounded Knee with Chester Eagleman, President of the Grand Rapids Intertribal Council.[62]

Pembroke, North Carolina, a town consisting of almost all Cherokees, produced the most turbulent demonstration of support for the march. Vernon Bellecourt arrived there March 23 to initiate a caravan to Wounded Knee. Bellecourt and his followers wanted to use the Prospect School for a meeting place but their request was denied. Instead, they met in front of the school, where Bellecourt urged the assemblage to follow him to Wounded Knee. When the group of around two hundred built a huge bonfire, Robeson County Sheriff's deputies attempted to disperse them. They refused and threw empty bottles at the deputies. Thirty-five were arrested for disorderly conduct, including Bellecourt. He said he did not mind being arrested as long as he could make bail, because he had an important meeting to attend in New York City.[63]

Not many Wounded Knee supporters made it through to the Pine Ridge area. Authorities monitored movements of known activists with the intention of stopping them long before they could get to Wounded Knee. This practice was soon stopped because of its questionable legality. Arrests were made as far away as Oregon and Nevada. The charge was violation of the federal antiriot law, frequently referred to as the "Rap Brown" law. Sixteen persons were arrested near Las Vegas, Nevada. They had a van, a truck, and a station wagon loaded with supplies for Wounded Knee from Los Angeles. Sammy Davis, Jr., put up the $5,900 bond to free the twelve Indians who were detained.[64] Sheriff Manke arrested seven white males, aged 19-24, and one white female, age 16, at an Edgemont, South Dakota, motel room after their conversations about going to Wounded Knee were reported. The group had four rifles, two shotguns, one pistol, two crossbows with arrows, three knives, assorted shells and bullets, gas masks, face paint, and marijuana. Three of the group were from Fayetteville, North Carolina. They had met the others at Denver, where they obtained the supplies and food.[65]

One group of twelve vehicles with fifty-nine persons from Kansas drove into Crow Dog's Paradise on March 18. There they joined about two hundred people, almost half of whom were evicted from the Porcupine Community Hall several days before. The FBI established new roadblocks at Martin, South Dakota, to stop and arrest militants if necessary. Crow Dog's Paradise was placed under discreet surveillance.[66] SAC Evans and other law enforcement officials met with four AIM members and other spokesmen. Ted Standing Cloud and Jim Burnette did almost all the talking. They said they were in a holding pattern awaiting developments at Wounded Knee and would take no action unless an Indian was killed at Wounded Knee. Then they would start may Wounded Knees in other places including Rosebud.[67]

To counteract the mounting number of arrests and what they considered to be an illegal siege, AIM formed a "Wounded Knee Legal Defense/Offense Committee." Ramon Roubideaux, Beverly Axelrod, and Mark Lane made the announcement. The committee planned to headquarter in Rapid City with a branch office at Pine Ridge and an annex at Wounded Knee to be manned by Axelrod. Altogether, a total of twelve attorneys, headlined by Kunstler and Lane, were identified as members of WKLDOC. Roubideaux announced that the committee would attempt to raise funds on a nationwide basis and would initiate action in Federal District Court seeking a temporary restraining order against the Department of Justice, United States Marshals Service, the FBI, and others concerned. WKLDOC also sought punitive damages against the United States government and individuals who had deprived Wounded Knee residents of their civil rights. Roubideaux asserted that the committee regarded the government action as genocide and claimed all those arrested had been detained illegally. The committee further stated it was prepared "to launch a massive legal assault against the federal government, its hired guns operating with armed personnel carriers and helicopters, and its other agents until South Dakota begins to look more like America and less like war-torn Southeast Asia." Following the press conference, Roubideaux and Axelrod requested permission to enter Wounded Knee. It was denied by the Justice Department.[68]

About an hour later, Roubideaux appeared at road-block one requesting entry to Wounded Knee. An agreed-upon search of his vehicle revealed a loaded .38 caliber revolver in his glove compartment. The officers at the roadblock called Hellstern in Pine Ridge, who authorized Roubideaux's arrest. When he was being taken to Pine Ridge, Roubideaux said, "Well that's the end of any thought of negotiations, you're going to have to kill everyone of them now."[69] To be sure his decision was the correct one, Hellstern called Clayton at Sioux Falls. Clayton advised that he knew Roubideaux had a weapons permit. The angry Roubideaux was released immediately and allowed to enter Wounded Knee.[70]

During the early morning hours of March 23, about 2,000 rounds of fire were exchanged, mainly in the area of roadblocks two, three, and four. No injuries were reported in spite of the heavy gunfire. Roadblock observers reported that nine armed Indians on horseback herded twenty-eight cattle into Wounded Knee. As further evidence of AIM determination to take a hard line, Means and Banks advised CRS representatives they were banned from Wounded Knee. They added they would no longer negotiate with Harlington Wood or any other government representative except one from the White House, preferably President Nixon or Henry Kissinger. Wood announced the same day he was no longer dealing with AIM, but he implied that negotiations would continue.[71]

With Justice Department authorization the roadblocks were moved up about an hour after Wood's announcement. After notifying AIM about the change, roadblock seven was moved forward three hundred yards, roadblock six was advanced two hundred yards, and BIA police established two new roadblocks between roadblocks five and six and roadblocks five and four. If the government showed no sign of backing away, neither did AIM. An ABC news crew, leaving Wounded Knee the afternoon of the 23rd, reported that Means told them they might want to return Saturday night, March 24, or Sunday morning, March 25, because something of interest to them would happen. Means also advised CRS representatives that AIM intended to have groups come in with supplies on Sunday.[72]

WKLDOC filed a complaint against the government Saturday asking for an order permitting free movement of six attorneys with food and medicine. Free movement of residents into and out of Wounded Knee was requested, too. Peaceful demonstrations of support throughout the country peaked on Saturday.[73] The proposed Sunday march from Rosebud to Wounded Knee, however, did not materialize because of poor response to the AIM appeal for supporters and the unrelenting attitude of the government.

To enhance the negotiating process, AIM requested that Hank Adams, the Washington fishing rights leader, be brought in, as a go-between. Adams had built a reputation as an able and ethical negotiator. He had spent his early years on the Fort Peck Reservation in northeastern Montana. When his mother married a Quinault from the Olympic Peninsula in Washington State they moved to Taholah, on the Peninsula, where he spent his teenage years. A self-styled lawyer, Adams played a crucial role in the litigation involving Indian fishing rights in Washington State and had been instrumental in organizing the Trail of Broken Treaties.

Adams arrived on Saturday night and was briefed by Harlington Wood. After the meeting, however, he was escorted off the reservation by BIA police in compliance with the recently approved tribal order banning outsiders.[74] Although he was thrown off the reservation several times more by tribal authorities, Adams proved instrumental in eventually obtaining a resolution of the confrontation, according to Vine Deloria, Jr. In an article entitled "The Most Important Indian," Deloria said, "Yet without his constant and quiet work behind the scenes, Wounded Knee might well have been a repeat of the earlier massacre. The ironic aspect of Hank's career is that he has shunned the spectacular dress and rhetoric of the militant who is familiar to the general public and thus has been consistently overlooked in the rush to identify important Indian figures."[75] Government negotiator Kent Frizzell was not nearly as impressed with Adams.[76]

Sometime during the early morning hours of March 25, Means and Banks left Wounded Knee. Rumor circulated that their leadership had been rejected by the many dissatisfied OSCRO there because the reservation group was ready to settle. The hardcore AIM members and their white attorneys reportedly insisted on continuing indefinitely. Undoubtedly, a great deal of infighting among various factions and personalities took place throughout the siege.[77] Also, it was well known that the situation regarding food, fuel, ammunition, and other needed supplies was growing desperate. In a press conference the day before, Banks remarked that the takeover could not continue past its supply of resources and everything hinged on March 25.

Much to the relief of the ION and the consternation of their adversaries, Federal Judge Andrew Bogue granted the temporary restraining order against BIA Superintendent Stanley Lyman, Secretary of Interior Rogers Morton, Assistant Attorney General Harlington Wood, and Attorney General Richard Kleindienst on March 25. It required that the defendants immediately instruct "all United States Marshals, Federal Agents, Sheriff's personnel, police officers, and all law enforcement personnel and persons carrying out law enforcement functions of any kind or nature in and around the Pine Ridge Reservation" to allow six lawyers, each with a carload of food, to come into Wounded Knee each day from March 26 through March 31.[78] Bogue advised the permanent residents of Wounded Knee that it was only a temporary order. Arrangements should be made by permanent residents to leave Wounded Knee on or before March 31 "and thus protect themselves from any harm or inconvenience until the blockade is lifted."[79]

Six attorneys confronted Kent Frizzell in the BIA building in Pine Ridge the evening of March 25. They complained they had been kept waiting an unreasonable amount of time and charged harassment because they were being prevented from delivering supplies which they had in their possession to Wounded Knee. The delay involved allowing Federal Marshals to inspect them first. Since no Marshals were around, Frizzell said he would do it himself if necessary. He also insisted it was too dangerous to go in because weapons fire was being exchanged. Mark Lane insisted that the attorneys had been listening over a walkie-talkie located in the BIA building at Pine Ridge, and they heard no reports of firing. When Frizzell took exception to the inference that he was lying, Lane maintained he had proof that the FBI had initiated firing in some instances. Frizzell, a direct-spoken man, bluntly suggested that Lane come forth with his evidence, which Lane promised he would do but not at that moment. The six attorneys in three automobiles were then allowed to proceed to the roadblocks.[80]

In addition to being upset by Judge Bogue's action, Wilson and his supporters were outraged by the death of tribal council member Leo Wilcox, often described as Wilson's right-hand man. Wilcox had been found burned to death in his car near Scenic, South Dakota, the night of March 25. He was burned so badly that his feet and hands had been completely destroyed, and he had to be identified from dental charts.[81] Word spread around the reservation that Wilcox's car had been firebombed by AIM. Wilcox assuredly had provoked them with his consistent and outspoken criticism of Means and AIM. He had appeared on KOBH, Hot Springs on March 24 and said, "Russell Means is trying to be a second Crazy Horse. The only part that fits him is the crazy part. He is a genuine second Fidel Castro."[82] Wilcox had attended an Oglala Sioux tribal meeting on the 24th and was in Rapid City on the 25th with another member of the tribal council. Both claimed they were threatened by AIM. Around 7:00 p.m. , Wilcox, who had been drinking heavily, had his car pulled out of the mud by Joe Montileaux and Alvin Cuney. At about 7:30 p.m. , Wilcox purchased five gallons of gas for his vehicle at Scenic. Wilcox headed south from Scenic toward the Pine Ridge Reservation but never reached his destination.[83] State investigators determined that Leo Wilcox died accidentally from asphyxiation because his fuel line, which had been heavily caked with mud when he was stuck near Scenic, broke; and the car burned as a result.[84] His family and a number of supporters doubt that Wilcox perished accidentally.[85]

For Wilson and his supporters, Bogue's decision, coupled with the death of Leo Wilcox, represented a mandate for action by the duly constituted tribal government. Wilson circulated an open letter on March 26 calling for support to drive out the invaders. It read in part:

Fellow Oglalas and Fellow Patriots:

> The time has come for all good citizens of the Pine Ridge Reservation to lay aside their petty differences and squabbles and unite. . . What has happened at Wounded Knee is all part of a long-range plan of the Communist Party. . . When the Federal Government has yielded, conceded, appeased and just short of surrender, we will march into Wounded Knee and kill Tokas (Indian outside enemies), wasicus (whites), hasapas (blacks), and spiolos (Mexicans).[86]

On the authority of the Oglala Sioux Tribal Council, armed Indians set up a roadblock about one-half mile from Highway 18 on Big Foot Trail behind federal roadblock one. No one other than U. S. Marshals Service and FBI would be allowed through. Specifically, they would not permit AIM attorneys to transport food and supplies into Wounded Knee.[87] Several sources indicate the Marshals held a big party joined by Wilson at Rushville the night the tribal government threw up the blockade.[88] For the remainder of the confrontation, Wilson's forces would intermittently set up roadblocks. No federal force was used against them, but they were threatened with arrest on a number of occasions. Indians on the blockades reported at times FBI agents, as individuals, would quietly leave boxes of shotgun shells or rifle cartridges, even though the FBI officially remained opposed.[89] Wilson's roadblock proved especially irritating to the WKLDOC because the Indians maintained that Bogue's order did not supercede the orders of the Pine Ridge Tribal Council in regard to unauthorized outsiders.

Judge Bogue's restraining order also prompted a strong reaction from Justice Department representatives. Assistant Director Felt urged Gray to concur with the unanimous recommendation of the FBI agents assigned to Wounded Knee that they be withdrawn from the roadblocks by the close of business on March 27. Felt said, ". . . the situation at Wounded Knee has deteriorated beyond our control." He estimated the cost to the FBI at around $600,000 and grumbled that agents on roadblock duty were performing duties normally associated with GS 3, 4, and 5 personnel."[90]

Felt's proposal followed a rejection of the sixth request by the FBI to the Justice Department to employ the military or other personnel to forcibly end the takeover. On March 25, Trimbach suggested to Gray that FBI personnel using APCs and gas could end the occupation with "likelihood of possible injury to Bureau personnel minimal." Trimbach said the plan had been presented to Harlington Wood, who sent it along to the Justice Department, but no answer had been received. Trimbach described the possibilities for a negotiated agreement as weak because the occupiers were not under much pressure to settle and AIM wanted to delay as long as possible in order to collect maximum donations and other support.[91] "Current roadblocks cannot prevent all entrance and exit from Wounded Knee due to the extended perimeter," said Trimbach. He also indicated AIM was using a phone paid for by the government to solicit help; that utilities had been restored; public health and medical services were available from the government and others; and free access through the roadblocks was available to religious representatives, social workers, news media representatives, attorneys, and others.

Trimbach brought out the Communist theme, too, claiming, "two of these attorneys, Axelrod and Tilson, can be documented either as Communist Party members or sympathizers."[92] The remaining national press was told to leave Wounded Knee proper. Local papers were told all information about the Wounded Knee situation would come from the Department of Justice Information Center in Washington, D. C.[93]

March 26 proved hectic for both sides. It began with the establishment of Wilson's tribal roadblock and the removal of the remainder of the press from Wounded Knee village. Heavy firing from both groups was capped by the shooting of Marshal Lloyd Grimm. That evening, Banks and Means again slipped out of Wounded Knee to the Rosebud Reservation. Their motive apparently was to seek assistance at Crow Dog's Paradise, some eighty miles away, where several hundred Indian people were stockpiling food and training a security force to back up Wounded Knee in case of a federal attack.[94] Another possible motive for their leaving involved the chance that leaders of the OSCRO, considering the Wilson roadblock and the shooting of Grimm, had had enough and were ready to settle, but the AIM leadership was not.

Grimm was hit in the right chest at about 5:25 p.m., apparently from a bunker about three hundred yards away. Deputy Chief of Marshals William Hall had invited the newly arrived Frizzell to take a helicopter ride over Wounded Knee for reconnaissance purposes. Marshal Grimm, who had not left BIA headquarters during his stay, said, "Hey how about letting me go along?" As the flight was ending, Hall asked Frizzell if he would like to see a Marshal's bunker. They landed on the far side of the hill and walked up to the bunker where the Marshals had pulled two APCs together in a V-shape. The bunker sat in front of the APCs. Frizzell stood on top of the sandbags to survey Wounded Knee. He observed a peaceful scene where a steer was being barbecued and the evening change of guards was taking place. "All of a sudden all hell broke loose from the new guard," Frizzell reported. The group ran down the backside of the hill to the helicopter, but the pilot said he did not want to risk a takeoff under such heavy fire. So they ran back up the hill toward the bunker with Grimm on the far right about eight feet from Frizzell. Grimm came up above the rise of the hill and was dropped immediately. Everybody thought he was dead, but the helicopter took off immediately with him in spite of the fire.

Frizzell and Hall spent the next two hours crouched behind an APC while some two or three thousand rounds of fire were exchanged. Frizzell said he had no doubt that the angry Marshals were shooting to kill someone, but miraculously, and a tribute to the AIM bunkers, no one else was hit. Frizzell maintained the AIM bunkers were better constructed than those of the government.[95]

The bullet that hit Grimm went down and took an unusual turn around the rib cage and came out the base of the spine. He was first flown to the Pine Ridge Hospital and later to the Fitzsimmons Army Medical Center in Denver for five hours of surgery. Grimm, who had retired as an Air Force Lieutenant Colonel before joining the Marshals, remains paralyzed from the waist down. He was especially well known in Nebraska, having played end on the 1936-38 Nebraska football teams.[96]

The AIM version of the shooting claimed "the vigilantes" (Wilson's group) probably shot him because the direction of the fire made it virtually impossible for the Wounded Knee defenders to do the deed.[97] SAC Moore insisted that if his recommendation to move roadblocks five and six forward had been approved instead of rescinded by Joseph Sneed (on the advise of Colburn), Grimm would not have been shot because better observation and protection would have been available. Sensing the temptation to revenge Grimm's shooting, Gray instructed Moore to insure tight control and good discipline of agents.[98]

March 27 proved equally eventful. It began with a heavy firefight that led to a ceasefire negotiated by the CRS about noon. A four-place Cessna landed at Wounded Knee at 12:41 p.m. and disgorged several three-by-five cardboard containers thought to contain weapons and ammunition.[99] In response to a government request to remove all tribal roadblocks, Dick Wilson agreed to remove all but the roadblock outside government roadblock one. When Judge Bogue rescinded the court order allowing six carloads of food to move through the government lines each day, AIM attorneys promptly announced an appeal for a stay to the Court of Appeals of the Eighth Circuit.[100] Actor Marlon Brando also sent an "Indian Maiden" to pick up his Oscar for his role in Godfather. And reports were circulated that AIM had lost control inside Wounded Knee and peace would be negotiated shortly with the OSCRO group, most likely at a meeting scheduled for Rapid City the following day.

Senator James Abourezk was so confident that meaningful negotiations were going to take place that he again announced to the press that the confrontation was about to end.[101] Aaron DeSersa had told him that the OSCRO, led by DeSersa, Vernon Long, Francis White Wolf, and Hildegarde Catches All, had taken over negotiations.[102] Pedro Bissonette and Leonard Crow Dog also seemed to be leaders of this group of about one hundred who offered to surrender in exchange for new tribal elections, an investigation of tribal accounts, and a government guarantee that they could leave unharmed.[103]

Kent Frizzell announced that a confrontation occurred just before midnight on the 27th when Means and Banks returned and challenged the OSCRO for power. According to Frizzell, Means and Banks claimed Bissonette's group had no right to negotiate with the government regarding a cease-fire. "It began as a heated discussion and then they pointed guns at each other," said Frizzell, "then the AIM guards came down from the bunkers and joined with Banks and Means and they were back in firm control."[104] The next day, Means and Banks denied that a confrontation had occurred. They brought television tapes of Pedro Bissonette proclaiming his loyalty to AIM to the conference with Abourezk, Frizzell, and Franklin. Journalists who watched the tapes suggested that the usually buoyant Bissonette acted like a man with a gun at his back.[105] Given the known reliability of the government informants, Frizzell's story should be believed. Negotiations were called off.

Ramon Roubideaux had been quoted in the local media as saying, "This could have been terminated earlier if not for the shenanigans of AIM, but AIM is out of it now. . . ."[106] Later Roubideaux rejected DeSersa's assertion that the OSCRO group had taken over. "This talk about separate negotiations has been a comedy of errors," he said. Roubideaux suggested DeSersa apparently believed that Banks and Means had left and he was interested in resuming negotiations without AIM.[107] A group of six AIM lawyers, including Mark Lane, entered Wounded Knee the 28th. When they left, Lane said no dispute existed, and an "Oglala Council" with Bissonette at its head had been formed by the occupiers to handle negotiations.[108]

One of the most sensational maneuvers in support of Wounded Knee happened at the annual Academy Awards banquet. Brando sent "Sacheen Littlefeather" to decline his Oscar for Godfather. She said, "He regretfully cannot accept the award because of the treatment of the American Indian in motion pictures and television and television reruns and because of the recent happenings at Wounded Knee."[109] After a fairly lengthy and not well received oration on Indian Grievances, she was virtually dragged off the stage. Predictably Brando's stratagem was panned by conservative critics. The Columbus (Nebraska) Telegram said, "Big John (Wayne) was on the stage Tuesday night but, unfortunately, he appeared with only seconds to go."[110] Sacheen, who introduced herself as an Apache, was identified as an aspiring part-Philippino actress named Marie Cruz, and a Hollywood neighbor of Godfather director Francis Coppola. Her most significant achievement prior to substituting for Brando had been her selection as "Miss Vampire of 1970" in a national contest to promote the television series Dark Shadows.[111] Several months after her Oscar performance she posed for Playboy as "Sacheen." In a 1979 Playboy interview Brando fondly recalled the Indian maiden who represented him in 1973. The day after the academy awards turndown, ironically, a group of Italian Americans protested that Brando's portrayal of Italians was worse than his criticism of the Indian's treatment by Hollywood.[112]

After a month of unproductive rhetoric and violence much of the media began to question the authenticity of AIM's motives and methods. Many newsmen on the scene began to accept the idea they had been duped. Conservative newspapers such as the Omaha World Herald, Chicago Sun-Times, Washington Evening Star-News, Birmingham News, and Detroit News led the attack. The March 18 story in the Detroit News concerning the origin and funding of AIM received wide circulation. In addition to tracing AIM's roots to the Black Panthers, the story said AIM had received over $400,000 in federal funds since its founding. Moreover, a large percentage of AIM members were employees in social welfare agencies funded by the government. The role of church support in founding and maintaining AIM and the Wounded Knee occupation was detailed in the March 14 Omaha World Herald.

R. W. "Red" Fenwick, the only journalist cited for service to American Indians by the National Congress of American Indians, came to Pine Ridge and expressed dismay in his popular Denver Post column "Riding the Range." "As the armed invasion of the Oglala Sioux Indian Reservation neared the end of its first full month Saturday, it became increasingly clear that the United States government has allowed itself to be maneuvered into an almost impossible situation," wrote Fenwick. "Thus far, the invaders, consisting primarily of three hundred or more young city Indians led by the generals of the American Indian Movement, have carried out a military coup which would strike envy in the heart of any North Vietnam commander," added Fenwick.[113] Even the New York Times began to doubt AIM's equity, "If AIM wins, policies of forty years standing will be imperiled."[114]

Probably most damaging to the AIM image were two articles appearing simultaneously in the nation's two leading news magazines, Time and Newsweek. Both questioned the sincerity of the Indians involved in the takeover. Time wondered out loud in its Press section whether the media were not providing much of AIM's momentum.[115] Newsweek described the confrontation as "a mouse-that-roared confrontation with moments of pure farce and days of talky heroics, laid on by the Indians for the white man's media and their own instamatics."[116] By the end of the month Means conceded that the media was exhibiting unfriendly traits. But he maintained that treaty rights alone were the reason for his presence at Wounded Knee. "They're laughing it off in Time and

Newsweek, and the editors in New York and what have you. . . We're tired of being treated that way. . . I'm going to die fighting for my treaty rights period," said Means.[117]

Not all of the media were that hostile, however, and Means and his followers still enjoyed enormous popular support. Max Lerner, author of America as a Civilization, wrote a syndicated column called "Wrong Road Leads to Wounded Knee," that appeared March 19. Lerner maintained that American policy toward the Indian followed the rough policy toward the Indian followed the rough policy enunciated by Andrew Jackson over the kind approach preferred by Thomas Jefferson. "No cosmetic words can gloss over the fact that the European whites settling in the East pushing even farther West to the Pacific took the land away from the Indians by fraud and force," wrote Lerner. He concluded, "Wounded Knee comes sadly just at the point when many young whites are questioning the aggressive acquisitive values of their own culture and turning to the gentler Indian values and to the historic road not taken."[118] At the same time as the Time and Newsweek articles questioning Wounded Knee, the Lincoln (Nebraska) Journal asked in "Forked Tongue?"

How much has the United States invested in keeping its word to the American Indian?

Not much, in the Indian's view.

Let us have law and order, say those who disapprove of the Indian protesters.

What could be more lawful than solemn treaties entered into by our government?

What could be more orderly than thoughtful practical interpretation and implementation of those treaties?[119]

The New York Times expressed what seemed to be the mainstream of public opinion in mid March: "Yet no official in his right mind can want to employ the armed might of this country to subdue a tiny band of men engaged in a symbolic war in a nation that has, in fact, broken its treaties with them, decimated their people and reduced their entire race to a wretched remnant. Sooner or later, the braves will weary of this unheroic 'house arrest.' "[120]

An editorial by C. I. Sulzberger in the Lincoln (Nebraska) Star, "AIM and Pan Indianism," struck to the heart of the matter. "Only in the last two years have reservation Indians joined or at least supported, their urban brothers in the Pan-Indian movement," said Sulzberger. "We must question whether AIM can pose (as it has) as the sanctioned spokesman and representative of all Native American tribes. . . While we agree that Indian demands that their suppression be ended and their grievances be resolved, we believe that AIM might only stifle the legitimate Pan-Indian effort," he concluded.[121]

"The braves" were greatly encouraged in their determination to hang tough by a mid-March Harris Poll which indicated ninety-three percent of the population of the United States had heard of Wounded Knee, fifty-one percent sympathized with the ongoing takeover; twenty-one percent sympathized with the federal government; and twenty-eight percent were not sure. In the East, the most sympathetic area, sixty-two percent agreed that the Indians had been mistreated throughout history.[122]

Church support for AIM on the national level, at least, continued firm. An impressive "Native American mass" sponsored by the Episcopal Church was held March 26 at the famous Cathedral of St. John the Divine in New York City. Some 4,000 people, perhaps half of them Indian, gathered to observe the special day. "May your cause be heard by all the people in America," said the very reverend James Morton, dean of the cathedral, who escorted the Indians through the main doors of the huge building. The reverend Vine Deloria, Sr. , called for a government peace mission to Wounded Knee, rather than Marshals. Officials of St. John the Divine had housed seven chiefs who came to plea their case to the United Nations. A variety of religious organizations donated money to bring other Indians to the church.[123] Miami University in Ohio coordinated an effort in Ohio, Kentucky and Indiana to collect food, funds, and medical supplies for Wounded Knee.[124] The Friends central office in Richmond, Indiana, also assisted. Almost 2,000 members of the Young Women's Christian Association marched in San Diego. A motion calling for the march instead of lunch was approved by acclamation at their national convention site.[125]

Church members back in South Dakota were not appreciative of such support. When the leaders of the Episcopal Church of South Dakota passed a resolution calling for a careful study of Indian treaties and improvement of Indian education, they were flooded with opposition." I am heartsick over the number of letters and telephone calls I have received full of hate and vindictiveness telling me how wrongly the Episcopal Church has acted," said Bishop Walker Jones of South Dakota.[126]

On March 27, the Church Council of the Rapid City Trinity Lutheran Church voted unanimously to condemn the recent acts of AIM in the Black Hills community.[127] Reverend Boe visited Rapid City the next week to review the complaints. Boe explained that the 1972 grant to AIM was a small part of the $500,000 granted to Indians. He added that he didn't think AIM wanted to be violent and that violence could achieve nothing.[128]

Sturgis was one of the vehement centers of opposition to the NCC, prompting Bishop Armstrong, who had served in the South during the height of civil rights agitation, to write, "The irrational intolerance, uninformed racism and vigilante mind-act, common in the rural South during those days, is present on our doorstep."[129] Armstrong's views were supported when Valentine attorney William Quigley announced the formation of a new group called Action for Security and Liberty on March 28. Quigley hoped to attract millions to his organization which seemed to be a thinly disguised vigilante group.[130]

As the stalemate at Wounded Knee continued, the various governmental agencies responsible for settling the issue became increasingly uneasy with one another. Special counsel to the President on Minority affairs, Leonard Garment, held a White House press conference on March 28 to clarify the executive branch's role. Garment said the short-range objective was to "indict and prosecute the lawbreakers." Then the government could "get into the business of correcting whatever real deficiencies there are in the BIA tribal circuit out at the Pine Ridge Reservation and at other reservations." The low profile of the White House in the Wounded Knee confrontation was deliberate, as it had been in the area of civil rights generally, Garment maintained. The administration view was that more could be accomplished by quiet, back-of-the-scenes persistence than bold, rhetorical crusades.[131] Nixon spokesmen placed a large measure of blame for the Wounded Knee episode on Congress. "On July 8, 1970, the President sent a special message to the Congress proposed an entirely new and progressive set of policies for Indian people," said Garment. "If Congress had enacted this legislation, the principal grievances among Indian people, which have given rise to such tensions as broke out at

Wounded Knee, would be well on their way to being effectively handled," he added. Asked about AIM demands for new treaties, Garment responded, "We are not America of 1867 or 1769—we are America today. We celebrate, and in fact encourage, cultural pluralism, but we are one nation, under one Constitution." The administration proposed $25,000,000 be allocated to the BIA in the form of block grants to strengthen Indian tribal governments.[132]

At Pine Ridge government agencies were more contentious. The FBI was especially distressed because they believed they were in charge at the scene as authorized by jurisdictional prerogative. Instead, they were used to man roadblocks and perform other infantry type duties while Colonel Volney Warner, Chief of Staff, 82nd Airborne Division, the Army military advisor on the scene, dictated policy such as the fiercely resented directive to shoot to wound and only if provoked. FBI officials were particularly upset with a proposed battle plan that Warner drew up in late March and did not bother to share with them. On March 28, SAC Moore advised his supervisor, John Gordon, that Warner had dictated the battle plan over the telephone to the office of Deputy Attorney General Joseph Sneed. The plan specified the use of FBI Agents and U. S. Marshals equipped with military equipment. When Gordon tried to obtain a copy, it was not available. Gordon then telephoned Associate Deputy Attorney General Charles Ablard and asked for the plan. Ablard claimed he did not know whether he had a copy but would send one if it could be found and Sneed authorized it. The next morning, Gordon contacted Ablard again and was told the battle plan was at the Pentagon, and no information could be released. Later in the day Moore reported he had been informed by Marshal Wayne Colburn the plan had been definitely turned down by the Attorney General because the Attorney General did not want another Kent State. "I feel that we should have been given a copy at FBI level," Felt initialed on the report.[133]

The protesters were also still resolving differences and experiencing internal unrest. The New York Times editorialized on March 30, "Off-reservation Indians, both physically and culturally more white than native, try to apply current techniques to redress Indian grievances." The Times seemed to have heard of Warner's proposal: "The worst possible course for the Federal Government would be to resort to naked force. At least a hundred of those who seized the village are now eager to give up," it claimed. "The Marshals may in the end have a hard time preventing the Sioux from fighting each other," the Times concluded.

Across from the editorial a letter from Dick Wilson responded to Vine Deloria, Jr.'s earlier letter to the Times charging that the occupation was in response to Wilson's brutal police state. Wilson said, "The issue at Pine Ridge is whether we are going to be run by self-appointed saviors with guns."[134] Aaron DeSersa, "national communications director" of AIM, announced he had been suspended. The publisher of the Shannon County News said he would have nothing further to do with AIM.[136]

Now that it was clear the government had no intention of removing Wilson, AIM shifted its negotiations away from him toward demands for civil rights violations investigations. AIM also wanted to negotiate new treaties with the government if possible, but they knew that was most unlikely, given Leonard Garment's stance on the subject. They had a number of old treaties they wanted to reconsider, too. Although the government was not keen for that proposal either, it represented a much more plausible and potentially productive course. Dennis Ickes, Civil Rights Division of the Justice

Department, was sent into Wounded Knee on March 29 to investigate allegations of civil rights violations. Ickes reported there were about thirty to forty civil rights complaints, primarily against BIA officers. All of the complaints concerned events that occurred prior to the takeover of Wounded Knee.[137] After considerable discussion Frizzell agreed to negotiate directly with the ION and to include a discussion of the 1868 Treaty.

Two FBI agents, who had no prior contact with Wounded Knee, accompanied by Barbara Means and Justice Department representatives Carlton Stoiber and Dennis Ickes, attempted to meet with AIM leaders March 30 to discuss possible violations of civil rights and other allegations. AIM postponed the meeting. Possibly the reason for the cancellation was that Judge Mathis, Court of Appeals, St. Louis, refused to stay the modified restraining order of Federal Judge Bogue. Next day, the same group met at an AIM roadblock with Dennis Banks, Clyde Bellecourt, Pedro Bissonette, Ellen Moves Camp, Francis Mesteth, and Douglas Hall, an AIM attorney from Minneapolis. The list of allegations was presented and discussed and the government representatives promised to investigate them.

Another group of four government officials, headed by Frizzell, met in a tipi inside the "DMZ" with Russell Means, Wallace Black Elk, Ramon Roubideaux and twenty-four other Indians. Frizzell was convinced the government had been too restrictive in the number of Indian negotiators, and the AIM representatives were not taking back accurate reports. He opened the meeting up to as many representatives whom the occupiers wished to send and made it a point to cultivate Pedro Bissonette, whom he felt best represented the local Oglala.

From the beginning Frizzell insisted there were two non-negotiable items: reparations for the local property owners and amnesty. One dispute involved food and supplies coming into Wounded Knee. Frizzell offered to set up a dining tent so anyone in Wounded Knee could obtain food. Anyone coming to the tent, however, would have to submit to a search and would be arrested if there was a warrant for his arrest. The occupiers said they were not that hungry. Frizzell's only concession was that milk and baby food would be allowed through the roadblocks.

Roubideaux suggested that the key to a resolution would be the return to a tribal form of government and the restoration of the Fort Laramie Treaty of 1868. Frizzell replied both of those matters were dependent upon Congress and the courts. Other demands included: A firm guarantee of a thirty to sixty-day moratorium on arrest actions against persons Oglala Sioux and otherwise, invited and granted permission to join in the defense of Wounded Knee. . . ," That Oglala Sioux and others assisting in the defense at Wounded Knee not be denied permission to remain in Wounded Knee; Action be taken upon criminal complaints and criminal violations reported to authorities; All receipts and expenditures of the Oglala Sioux tribal council be investigated and audited and those results be made available generally to tribal members; Under the authority of the Sioux Treaty and the "Indian Bill of Rights" of 1868, the Justice Department should protect the rights of all Oglala Sioux against unlawful abuses by "tribal governing authority." If trials should occur concerning any matters arising out of Wounded Knee, the United States would hold all trials outside of North and South Dakota; services such as medical services, communications and phone service remain in force and on the agenda; administrative, congressional and executive actions to deal with all matters of concern to Oglala Sioux Indians must proceed at the earliest possible time.[138]

Roubideaux promised that, would agreement be reached on the ten points, the occupation force inside Wounded Knee would halt the takeover and proceed to the courts. By the end of the three-hour session on April 1, Frizzell indicated general agreement had been reached on more than half of the demands. One point of alarm for the protesters was that both Wilson roadblocks had been allocated an APC.[139]

On April 2 the New York Times ran an article entitled "Wounded Knee is Slipping Back Into a Sleepy Routine." It said, "At the roadblock on the Big Foot Trail, the main road to Wounded Knee, Mr. Wilson's men appear to occupy much of their time pitching horseshoes by an old Army truck or firing random shots across the prairie." The piece said only a handful of reporters remained.[140] Those who were directly acquainted with Wilson's roadblock held it in healthy respect, nonetheless, and indicated unauthorized personnel were arrested quickly and firmly.[141]

Two FBI agents accompanied by Barbara Means went into Wounded Knee on April 3 to collect documents concerning abuse of Indian rights. They were instructed to bring a jeep, camera and film, and tape recorder and tapes. The two agents were met by Pedro Bissonette and Reed Bad Cob and guided to the home of Edith Wounded Horse. There they were presented documents for a proposed settlement which they agreed to forward to the Justice and Interior Departments. Fifteen Wounded Knee residents attended. Most of the complaints were directed at the Czywczynskis and involved abuse of Indian mail and credit. Florine Hollow Horn charged that they made loans of up to $10 at an interest rate of $2.25 per week. She also charged Wilson with voting fraud in the 1972 election. Mrs. Edward White Dress charged that Jim Czywczynski grabbed her stepson Ross Red Feather by the throat and choked him so hard his throat was bruised for several days. (This incident had been the focus of AIM's first visit to Wounded Knee.) LeRoy Pumpkin Seed presented a signed statement that charged BIA officer Francis Two Bulls with police brutality, claiming Two Bulls had struck him unnecessarily.[142]

As an agreement neared, political pressure against the occupation mounted. Senator Dewey Bartlett of Oklahoma claimed, "AIM's victory at Wounded Knee would be another loss for the American Indian." Senator Jesse Helms of North Carolina entered the police records of the principal leaders in the Congressional Record. Helms contended that the idea of a nation making treaties with its citizens was absurd. He insisted that the confrontation was entirely contrived "to exploit the feelings of the Indian people on the one hand and the propensity of the press to wallow in sympathy with anyone who asserts a so-called 'grievance' against the United States Government."[144] The Office of Economic opportunity cut off funding for both the AIM Survival School and the Red School House in Minneapolis. They were both to receive $20,000.[145] Meanwhile, the Connecticut General Assembly issued a proclamation urging Congress to take immediate steps to resolve the Wounded Knee crisis.[146]

Government forces maintained tight surveillance of the Wounded Knee area and apprehended a number of would-be infiltrators. A five-man camera crew from CBS was arrested as it attempted to sneak into the area. They were escorted to their chartered Lear jet and informed that no more CBS representatives would be allowed on the reservation.[147] On April 5, after an agreement seemed to be reached, three Red Cross trucks from Minneapolis were let into Wounded Knee. Robert Bender, the Red Cross field representative in Minneapolis, complained to the FBI that armed Indians siphoned almost all of the gasoline out of the trucks.[148]

Frizzell sensed that the split that reportedly had occurred in the AIM camp just before the bargaining began had not been repaired. He reported to the FBI that Roubideaux and Hank Adams were honestly seeking a settlement while attorneys Mark Lane and Kenneth Tilsen favored further disruption. FBI sources reported an apparent schism between Dennis Banks and Russell Means. Ellen Moves Camp, Gladys Janis, and Delilah Bean appeared to favor Banks while Pedro Bissonette and the majority leaned toward Means. Stan Holder, AIM head of security, remained uncommitted to either faction.[149] Carter Camp and Means had a glaring personality clash, so Camp opposed Means on general principles.

Hank Adams, writing as the National Director of the Survival of American Indians, to Lloyd Meeds, Chairman of the House Subcommittee on Indian Affairs, substantiated Frizzell's assessment of Lane and Tilsen. Adams said, "Personally, I became greatly distressed that some lawyers involved with the Wounded Knee matter seemed to be more staunchly opposed to any peaceful settlement than any Indian people involved—and appeared to actively pursue continuation of the occupation despite the possibilities of tragic consequences." Adams said that one lawyer publicly supported "recognized leaders" in virtually all of their decisions, except those that might lead to settlement, but privately attempted to discredit the Indian leaders as being only interested in their own appearances before the news media. Adams also charged that much of the non-Indian support for Wounded Knee was based upon continued confrontation regardless of the circumstances or consequences. Support was offered to any Indians who would serve as their "surrogate revolutionaries." Their interest was confined to obtaining guns and increasing firepower rather than obtaining justice for Indian people, claimed Adams.[150] Columnist Jack Anderson substantiated Adams's claim when he reported he had obtained access to the government's daily crisis reports, which were intended for official use only. They indicated Mark Lane and Beverly Axelrod, two militant outside attorneys, poisoned AIM against the Justice Department mediators. According to Anderson, the field memos indicated Federal mediators had shown surprising sympathy for the Indians.[151]

Notwithstanding political and legal pressures, outside advice, and internal bickering, Means, the Oglala, remained the official head negotiator. He demanded that a Presidential Treaty Commission be formed, rather than merely creating a commission to study the need for a Treaty Commission. In order to establish this agency, the Wounded Knee negotiators proposed that a preliminary meeting with the White House take place before the evacuation. Frizzell responded that he did not think the government would entertain any visitors as long as somebody had a gun pointed at the head of the United States.

AIM negotiators then proposed a stand down of arms supervised by the Marshals while the meeting with the White House occurred. Although Frizzell never fully accepted them, he essentially agreed to settle on the basis of AIM's ten-point proposal, except for the site of the preliminary meeting. The ION accepted Washington as the site for the preliminary meeting. It was agreed that, after the White House meeting with Russell Means, Chief Tom Bad Cob, and Crow Dog, talks between Wayne Colburn and AIM would follow concerning the resolution of the arms situation.

Frizzell returned to the white tipi April 5 to "smoke the pipe." He told the group, "I pray to my Father in heaven, as you do to your Great Spirit, that the agreement we are about to sign is not full of empty words and that the promises will be fulfilled." Banks smoked the pipe but refused to join others in signing the agreement.[152] The accord called for Russell Means to submit to arrest at the main roadblock, where he would be taken into custody and transported to Rapid City for arraignment. The federal version of the plan was that AIM leaders agreed to lay down their arms on Saturday morning, April 7, as soon as the meetings in Washington got underway. After the lay down, those for whom arrest warrants were outstanding would be apprehended with no amnesty. The Washington meetings were to discuss the creation of a Presidential Commission to look into the reexamination of the 1868 Treaty. The government also agreed to pursue the major requests and grievances outlined in AIM's April 3 proposal concerning the governance of Pine Ridge and the audit of tribal council funds.

Lack of harmony among AIM leaders, which had been evident throughout the negotiations, surfaced at Portland State University on April 5. There Vernon Bellecourt told an audience that the occupation would continue despite newspaper reports that a settlement had been reached. On April 6, Bellecourt affirmed that the Wounded Knee occupation would continue until Russell Means confirmed that a treaty with firm and binding commitments had been signed by the government. Bellecourt added he would be in Albuquerque, New Mexico, on April 7, to address the Brotherhood Awareness Conference where prominent leaders of black, chicano, white liberal, and Vietnam veteran organizations would be forming a political coalition.[153]

After the accord was reached, Means surrendered and was flown to Rapid City where he was released under $25,000 bond supplied by Stanford Adelstein, a wealthy Rapid City businessman. One condition of Means's bail was that he was not allowed to reenter Wounded Knee. Roubideaux considered the bond very excessive and announced that efforts would be made to get it reduced and to also secure the release of additional AIM leaders on reduced bond. The high bail rate may well have helped stiffen resistance among those remaining at Wounded Knee. Some seventy-seven were under indictment for federal charges, and there simply was not that amount of money available for bond. On Friday Means and his party, consisting of Roubideaux, Hank Adams, Tom Bad Cob, and Leonard Crow Dog, flew from Denver to Washington. Their first scheduled stop in Washington was the National Center for Disputes Settlement.

AIM called for a meeting with Marshal Colburn the same day, April 6, to work out the details of dispossession. Colburn, who had not taken part in the negotiations, replied that there was no need for a meeting because he planned to take over the village the next morning as had been already established in the agreement. According to his interpretation, at the time the conference began in Washington, at 9:00 a.m. , Means would call his security man, Stanley Holder, at Wounded Knee, and, at that point, the ION would begin laying down arms, exiting the bunkers, and submitting to arrests, crime scene searches, and interviews.[154] Those remaining in Wounded Knee told Frizzell that that was not their interpretation of the agreement. Only upon satisfactory completion of the meetings would they surrender. Frizzell instructed that no one or anything would be allowed through the roadblocks until further notice. Two hours later, however, four attorneys were permitted through the roadblocks.

When he arrived at Washington, Means announced that final settlement may not be at hand. "The federal government has duped the press and the world again," Means said. Frizzell immediately contacted Means and his group and insisted that he was assured by them that dispossession the following morning remained the agreement.[155] Frizzell and Assistant Attorney General Stanley Pottinger then held a lengthy meeting that concluded with no further accommodation. AIM leaders were told that no discussion at the White House level would transpire until federal officials were allowed into Wounded Knee. Also, Means and Roubideaux must confirm to the Justice Department that the surrender would begin when the meetings in Washington began. Leadership in Wounded Knee said they were not bound by the views of Means.[156] Pedro Bissonette, leader of the OSCRO, apparently was now totally removed from a meaningful role. He released a letter to the Department of Justice, the FBI, the United States Marshals, and the BIA on April 6, saying he declined to be interviewed or questioned in any way by any authority regarding any matter at that time. He instructed that all future communication with him was to be directed through one of his attorneys.[157] Bissonette was out on bond for hitting and seriously injuring a police officer with his car while attempting to flee from arrest in an earlier incident.

President Nixon officially withdrew his recommendation for L. Patrick Gray on April 7. Officials at Wounded Knee came up as frustrated as the acting FBI head. Colburn and Pottinger proposed that the bunkers and roadblocks on both sides come down simultaneously. AIM refused this offer when government officials refused to undertake the operation without weapons. Hellstern met with Means in Washington the same day. Hellstern said Means acknowledged that dispossession was to take place as soon as the Washington meeting began. Means was supposed to have called Wounded Knee to advise of this accord. On April 8, however, Means reversed his position, announcing on television that he would not tell the people at Wounded Knee to lay down their arms until after his meeting with White House representatives had produced meaningful results. The government refused to meet with Means until a disarmament agreement had been settled, so the deadlock continued. Frizzell said the April 5 offer was clear to the Indians, to the public, and to the government, and he would stand by the agreement "until hell freezes over." There is a suspicion that the embattled Nixon administration did not mind the prolongation of the crisis out in South Dakota, because it was tying down a good deal of the FBI and diverting at least some attention away from the rapidly expanding Watergate scandal. If the government was in no hurry to settle, certainly the militants saw no great advantage in quitting under the terms offered.

Hearings on Wounded Knee and the Trail of Broken Treaties began in the House of Representatives Indian subcommittee on April 9. Toby Eagle Bull, secretary of the Oglala Sioux tribal council, appeared as the first witness. Eagle Bull complained that Pine Ridge had been invaded by outsiders, but the heart of the matter was the sixty percent unemployment rate. When Means testified, Chairman James Haley, a Florida Democrat, described the AIM leaders as "hoodlums, goons, and gutter rats."[158] Means kept his poise and insisted that AIM had not violated a law "of anybody we were at peace with." Others who testified included Ralph Erickson, Charles Ablard, and Richard Hellstern. In the Senate, Abe Ribicoff presented a resolution adopted by the general assembly of the state of Connecticut. It stated the people of Connecticut were increasingly disturbed by the deteriorating situation at Wounded Knee and urged the United States Congress to take prompt action to investigate the claims of AIM and restore peace.

Means also was the featured speaker at a meeting sponsored by the Wounded Knee Defense Committee in Washington the same day. The session was chaired by Lorella

Langberg, a former activist in the Black Panther Party. Means discussed the general situation at Wounded Knee, saying that the press was not accurate and he planned to return to Wounded Knee the next day.[159] AIM presented Frizzell with a counter-proposal on Monday. It focused on a vision of Leonard Crow Dog that pictured the Indians's weapons placed in a tipi with a peace pipe across the door. AIM proposed that their arms be placed in such a tipi in Wounded Knee as the resolution of the disarmament question.[160] Other provisions of the AIM proposal included: the government would move its perimeter back to its original location; a meeting in Washington would begin three days later to begin implementation of the terms of the April 5 agreement; and six passenger carloads of food should immediately be allowed into Wounded Knee along with other supplies and services. The government rejected the offer on the grounds that the dispossession procedure was inadequate. Late April 9, Frizzell advised other government agencies he could not obtain a negotiable agreement and was returning to Washington, April 11. The next morning AIM took down the negotiating tipi as an apparent signal bargaining was ended. "For weeks I have been hearing about a Trail of Broken Treaties," said Frizzell, "now I have a better understanding of that phrase because it has happened to me."

Stanley Pottinger, who became the ranking Justice Department official, described the situation as "An Impasse Upon An Impasse." Means and his group went to New York City April 10 to the Center for Constitutional Rights which was formed by as group of lawyers headed by William Kunstler. There, Means blamed the breakdown in negotiations on the government's insistence that the Indians must surrender their arms before bargaining could begin. "We bent over backwards and acceded to the government's demands that no guns were to be pointed at any federal officials while talks were going on," said Means. Kunstler announced that his group would represent Means. Although Means had originally planned to stay overnight, he unexpectedly changed his schedule and returned to Washington.

Pottinger and Colburn attempted further discussions at Wounded Knee but got nowhere. On April 11, AIM rejected another government offer that would accept putting "legal" weapons in a tipi. Only after that would the government forces pull back, and Wounded Knee occupants facing arrest would be taken into custody. The new overture acknowledged the preliminary meeting in Washington was cancelled and called for AIM to submit an agenda for later treaty talks. AIM flatly rejected the government's offer.

Many reasons have been advanced to explain the failure of the April 15 accord. The obvious fault in the agreement was its failure to specifically spell out the details of arms dispossession. Faced with numerous criminal indictments, the occupiers were in no great hurry to surrender, especially after they learned of Means's bail arrangements. More than likely there just was not enough money available to free all of those under indictment. In the meantime, Means, Banks, the Bellecourts and others were in the national spotlight and could effectively raise support. Having already occupied the village for six weeks, there was little reason to expect a dramatic change in federal policy that would lead to a direct military-type attack. The advantages of waiting unequivocally outweighed those of settling on the government's terms, which offered no substantial concessions.[161]

Reaching
An Accord

*H*olding on at Wounded Knee seemed like a good idea at the time, but, in retrospect, it may have been a tactical error. From that point on, the weight of public opinion turned against them. Newsweek wondered on April 9 whether the Indians still were sincere in their stated goals or if their main purpose now was merely to continue the confrontation.[1] After the collapse of the Washington meeting, television and newspaper coverage dwindled. What used to be front-page news now was relegated to small stories in the middle sections. Senator McGovern gave up on negotiating as a solution and announced that the dispute was now a matter of law enforcement.[2]

SAC Moore clearly had had enough of the maneuvering, too. Stung by the Watergate revelations, FBI morale and image were in a shambles. At Wounded Knee, they were forced to man roadblocks like soldiers while other cases, including Watergate, went unattended. Moore recommended to the Justice Department that nonfatal gas, tear and sickening or a combination, be spread from the air and from the ground with the escape routes for the occupiers left open. As the protesters were forced out, they would be arrested at the federal blockades. Moore suggested that, if that proposal was not implemented, all law enforcement activities should be turned over to the BIA police. Frizzell and Colburn concurred with Moore, but his proposal was turned down at higher levels. Gerald Gereau, a member of the professional staff of the Senate Insular Affairs Committee, claimed that leaflets warning about the possible use of tear gas had been dropped on Wounded Knee.[3] Again, the government implemented a practice of encouraging restraint by its officials on the scene by changing leadership. SACs Moore and Loetterle were rotated on April 12 by still Acting Director Gray, who ordered that all agent personnel at Wounded Knee were to be rotated at a maximum of every two weeks.

By April 13, the Justice Department surmised that the situation had been stabilized enough so that the FBI and the Marshals could return to functioning in their traditional roles. The Marshals were authorized to assume command of all protective and containment activities while the FBI would return to handling all investigative duties. Marshals were placed in charge of all roadblocks except roadblock one, which was to be maintained by the FBI as the sole government processing and interviewing site for persons entering or leaving the Wounded Knee area.[4] To prepare for a possible use of force, the Department of Justice also approved a plan to borrow necessary equipment from the military and located it at Fort Carson, Colorado.[5]

When it became clear to the public that no settlement was imminent, local citizens, led by William Quigley, began intensive organization of Quigley's Action for Security and Liberty Organization. By mid-April his movement peaked. The FBI estimated that "about 800 citizens were in attendance" at the meeting held in Gordon. Local newspapers more realistically set the figure around 350.[6] Quigley told the Gordon audience, "They (AIM) began to get funds from the United States, and large sums of money from gullible bleeding heart groups. And we are told a larger amount of money from more dangerous and sinister sources." The speaker received a standing ovation when he charged that AIM did not represent one-half of one percent of the Indian people.[7]

Crawford, Nebraska, also held a meeting attended by about one hundred on April 9. Possible civil defense steps to be taken in case of a large militant group moving in on Crawford or nearby Fort Robinson were discussed. On the weekend of April 7-8, Governor J. J. Exon had ordered a practice run to Crawford of a special force of state troopers and other law enforcement officials especially organized to deal with Indian unrest. "The weekend so-called 'test run' by the troopers, game commission and sheriff's personnel shows that they are ready, able, and willing to handle the situation," said the Crawford Tribune. "They are the group that should handle any further problems that might arise with militant Indians that might try to make trouble at Fort Robinson or Crawford," the editorial concluded.[8] Sheridan County Mike Smith also took a dim view of what appeared to smack distinctly of an Old West vigilante movement. Smith issued a public statement indicating that authorized law enforcement agencies, including FBI, Federal Marshals, and state and local personnel, were perfectly capable of handling whatever situation might develop.[9] Discouraged by government officials from taking a more active role, the Quigley group never got directly involved in the crisis and soon disbanded after it ended. Quigley personally refunded the membership dues.[10]

On April 11, reverend Timothy Willert of Vermillion, state chairperson of the South Dakota Civil Liberties Union, expressed concern about the civil rights of AIM and its supporters. He announced that the state organization had made Indian civil rights one of its highest priorities. Willert said his group was especially concerned about "spurious arrests and excessive bail."[11]

Saying he could be more valuable to the occupation on the outside than inside, Clyde Bellecourt submitted to arrest on April 12. He surrendered under custody of Paul Boe and was taken to Rapid City where he was released on $25,000 bond under Boe's custody. Bellecourt could now join the cadre of AIM leaders drawing generous fees on the lecture circuit to raise money for others under indictment. Means and Bellecourt appeared in U. S. District Court in Pierre on April 16 and pled not guilty to ten identical charges. If found guilty, they faced a maximum of eighty-five years in prison and $96,000 in fines. Saying the South Dakota mentality toward Indians "made the Ku Klux Klan look like Girl Scouts," the pair asked for a change of venue. Conditions of release for the two included forty-eight hour notification to the court if they wanted to leave South Dakota, and keeping away from Wounded Knee.[12] Stanley Holder also surrendered on April 16, leaving the ION under the leadership of Banks and Camp. Internal friction between the national leadership of AIM and their advisors increased daily, according to inside reports.[13]

Meanwhile, a peaceful demonstration by local Indians presented a petition requesting the government to negotiate with reservation Oglala Sioux representatives regarding the corruption of Richard Wilson. The group, led by Hildegarde Catches, Louis Bad Wound, Delores Swift Bird, Geraldine Janis, and Barbara Means, promised that the occupation of Wounded Knee would end if the complaints were acted upon.[14] On April 16, Stanley Pottinger, trying to break the deadlock, barred all attorneys from Wounded Knee with the exception of Roubideaux, who was having his own problems getting along with AIM leaders. "I've dealt with some big ego problems in my day, but this AIM bunch is the limit," said Roubideaux. He indicated Banks was the best and most tractable of the lot.[15]

Another impasse proved too much for some of the residents of Wounded Knee, who had not supported the takeover and had departed when it happened. Those opposed were individuals who held positions within the existing framework of the Wilson administration. Following a meeting on April 12 between Justice Department attorneys and the dissatisfied Wilson supporters from Wounded Knee, the refugees established yet another roadblock on Big Foot Trail. They denied ingress to Wounded Knee to everyone they suspected of bringing in supplies for AIM, including CRS personnel. The only exceptions were Marshals, FBI, and Sioux tribal authorities. The Wounded Knee residents, furthermore, asked the government for $100 a day since February 27 for each of their houses and said they would allow the government three weeks (until May 4) before taking action themselves.[16] Several days later, Ramon Roubideaux showed reporters a petition signed by thirty-five Wounded Knee families saying that the dissident roadblock group did not represent them. The Justice Department considered issuing a restraining order against the new blockade, but did not because of the potentially explosive situation.

To circumvent the new roadblock, Mark Lane and four others were helicoptered in with medical supplies, toilet paper, and sanitary napkins. Authorities demonstrated a new hard line when they allowed only one hundred of the five hundred sanitary napkins in. saying they could be used as fuses for molotov cocktails. The remainder were held by the FBI until the supply taken in was exhausted.[17] AIM was reduced to reliance upon backpacked supplies, carried in at night. Although a number of backpackers were apprehended and arrested, many got through. On April 16, fourteen, the largest number yet, got through.[18]

The Wounded Knee Legal Defense/Offense Committee filed two suits with U. S. District Judge Bogue on April 16 on behalf of the OSCRO and "other individuals" on the reservation. Their first suit asked for a temporary injunction against the federal government for food and supplies, indicating that the Wounded Knee occupants were "near starving." The suit said, "In effect, it has arrested, punished and imprisoned the entire population without due process." The second suit sought a temporary injunction against the activities of Dick Wilson and his supporters. One count charged Wilson with organizing an armed force to "terrorize, harass, intimidate, assault, threaten and maintain surveillance upon those who opposed his administration or supported AIM." The second count charged Wilson with denying constitutionally guaranteed civil rights. Bogue denied both motions. The WKLDOC announced they would appeal. Richard Hellstern claimed there was an adequate food supply at Wounded Knee. "It is not the government's policy to starve them out. And it also is not the government's policy to let them live normal lives," said Hellstern.[19]

At daybreak on April 17, three light airplanes dramatically flew over Wounded Knee and parachuted supplies into the village. Each of the parachuted bundles contained a printed message which said, "The delivery of these packages of food to the courageous people in Wounded Knee is being carried out by a large number of Americans who have worked and continue to work to end American aggression in Indochina. Wounded Knee shows us that the just struggles cannot be stopped by any President or policy."[20] One man was fatally shot in the head and another in the hand when bitter fighting erupted after the supplies were dropped. The exchange of gunfire, which consumed an estimated 4,000 rounds of ammunition, started at 6:00 a.m. and did not stop until 4:00 p.m. The FBI helicopter, "Snoopy II," was called to assist. It received fire from the ground, provoked according to AIM, because the helicopter fired first. Held, of course, firmly denied the charge. At 7:44 a.m. , Snoopy II confirmed that an Indian had been shot in the vicinity of roadblock six.[21]

The AIM version of the first death at Wounded Knee was that Frank Clearwater, who had just hiked in the day before with his pregnant wife, Morningstar, was resting in the Episcopal church when the shooting started. When he rose up, he was hit in the back of the head. The bullet entered behind the ear on one side and exited behind the ear on the other side. The FBI said their records showed Clearwater was shot in an open field. He was removed to Rapid City with virtually no chance of survival. AIM first identified the victim as Matthew High Pine from Pine Ridge; then Frank Still Water, a Cherokee from Oklahoma; finally, Frank Clearwater, an Apache from Cherokee, North Carolina. When the FBI received a negative identification report from Oklahoma City, they sent the victim's prints to Washington. Positive identification returned April 23, 1973, said, "Frank J. Clear, FBI #4-483-139."

With the help of reporter Tom Oliphant of the Boston Globe, who reported from Sioux City that he had been in one of the planes, the FBI quickly unraveled the story of the three-plane airlift. The trail led to Robert Talbot, professor in the Department of Aviation, City College of Chicago. Talbot said he had made arrangements for the rental of two Piper Cherokee 6 aircraft by a former flight student of his from Boston whom he refused to identify and a man whose first name was Tom. Talbot arranged for three of his aviation students to act as copilots. Two thousand pounds of food were taken into his house and packed into ten parcels weighing two hundred pounds each. Regular parachutes, purchased from a war surplus store, were cut and resewn into cargo parachutes. The third Cherokee was rented at Midway by William Wright, who flew it to Wounded Knee via Omaha, Huron, and Rapid City, meeting the others at Huron, South Dakota.[22]

William Zimmerman, a former student at the University of Chicago and former Kennedy worker who had moved to the radical left in politics, organized the airlift. He was working at the Medical Aid for Indochina office in Boston when approached by the AIM legal defense office about leading an airlift for Wounded Knee.[23] The pilots were arrested for three separate federal felonies, each one punishable by up to five years in a federal penitentiary and a $10,000 fine. Oliphant was also charged, but his were dropped.

The Justice Department dismissed all other charges on February 27, 1975, the second anniversary of the Wounded Knee takeover.[24]

The Attorney General was so concerned about the gunfire and wounding that he instructed Pottinger to supply an "honest evaluation" of what happened to cause gunfire. Stan Holder, who had just surrendered, was granted a forty-eight hour temporary release and flown back to Wounded Knee in an effort to effect a ceasefire. Holder was instructed to return himself to custody by 1:30 p.m. , April 19. To increase security, a number of M-79 grenade launchers were supplied to all government roadblocks on April 18. They were to fire tear gas or smoke projectiles only if roadblock positions were fired upon first. The FBI training center at Quantico, Virginia, also forwarded 150 gas masks.

Pottinger and Colburn entered Wounded Knee April 18 to talk with Holder. Holder's hearing date was moved up to April 23, instead of April 19, so he could stay at Wounded Knee to help keep things under control.[25] Russell Means also received a federal offer to return to Wounded Knee, but he refused because he was on a speaking tour.[26]

Thirty-five people, mostly Oglala women and children who had been involved in the April 16 demonstration at Pine Ridge, tested the government's stricter policy by approaching roadblock five and demanding entry into Wounded Knee on April 18. When they were refused, the group attempted to walk right by the roadblock. Eleven of them made it. Twenty-two men, women and children were detained by the Marshals but the Justice Department declined to prosecute. They remained subject to BIA police rules, however, and those who were not residents of Pine Ridge Reservation, including attorney Fran Olsen, were evicted.

Pottinger, who had just announced that the Marshals would not take rifle fire without returning it, was recalled on April 20. Hard-liner Richard Hellstern replaced him. On his departure Pottinger said, "I am concerned that the option I represent—to negotiate a settlement not involving force—has come to an end. The United States is in control of the situation but not in control of the people."[27] He warned, "If we come to the conclusion that the civil negotiations processes are exhausted, it becomes a police question."[28] Colburn reenforced speculation that the government might be ready to end the confrontation through direct action. He had been called back to Washington to confer with Justice Department officials. Although his Washington superiors conceded that it was becoming apparent that the government would eventually be forced to "a law enforcement solution," they insisted upon further attempts at negotiation.

The restraining factor remained the almost certain knowledge that fatalities would result from any attempt at forcible entry. Colburn returned to Pine Ridge on April 19 and reported that, while he had authority to put in place equipment and supplies needed to carry out an attack on Wounded Knee, he would have to await further orders from Washington before executing the plan.[29] With federal authorization, Colburn moved roadblock five three hundred yards forward on April 21.

Worried about the possibility of mass support for Wounded Knee materializing on the upcoming weekend, the Justice Department announced on April 19 that persons traveling with the intent to aid or abet the takeover would be subject to five years in prison and a $10,000 fine. Gray's top assistant, Felt, sent him a memo the same day indicating the FBI might be placed "in an untenable position" by the Justice Department instructions if they arrested persons far away from Wounded Knee. "Because of the very nature of this situation we necessarily are operating on probable cause that is extremely vulnerable to challenge," Felt commented. He said Portland agents already faced a $125,000 civil suit based on arrests under those exact circumstances.[30]

AIM maintained a vigorous attack upon the press, whom it claimed was prejudiced against them and was setting the stage for an attack at Wounded Knee.[31] On April 21, Ted Means charged that there was a conspiracy between the press and the federal government to annihilate the Indians at Wounded Knee. "The two are working overtime at gearing the public for this atrocious act by producing nothing but one-sided, slanted news coverage," said Means.[32] Russell Means issued the same charges at the Tulsa airport. He accused the Oklahoma press of being racist and guilty of false reporting. Means said, "The same frontier mentality exists in Oklahoma as in South Dakota. The White Man's treatment of the Indians in Oklahoma makes the Ku Klux Klan look like a bunch of Boy Scouts." Means further asserted that Indians planned to take over all of Western South Dakota beginning at the east bank of the Missouri River.[33] Based upon Means's threat, the Sioux Falls Argus Leader ran an editorial calling for the revocation of his bond.[34]

Mass support for Wounded Knee did not materialize on Easter Sunday. It was confirmed, however, that a protest march was underway from the Rosebud Reservation and would begin marching for Wounded Knee Monday, arriving next Saturday. The highlight of Easter Sunday at Wounded Knee was the "crucifixion" on a wooden cross of a mannequin dressed like a Marshal. The figure was beaten and kicked for about six hours in full view of the village and the Marshals, who thought, based upon scrutiny through field glasses, that it was a human being.[35] Later, authorities confirmed that the figure was only a mannequin.

Hellstern sent a memo to Attorney General Kleindienst and Deputy Attorney General Sneed on Sunday indicating that he "felt most strongly that negotiations would not end the problem." Hellstern listed five reasons why settlement through negotiations would not work: the government had nothing to offer that would be acceptable; Dennis Banks, now in control, did not want a settlement; the non-AIM people could not agree with one another; agreements could not be implemented because of distrust of the government; and occupants were resolved to stay until the government employed force. Hellstern recommended police action was due because Wounded Knee currently was weak—he estimated eighty-five whites and eighty-five Indians, consisting of few residents; problems with vigilantes were increasing; problems could increase with the end of college; the public was now ready to accept police action; and there was very little press coverage at that time.[36]

Although the turnout was disappointing, the group who had assembled at Crow Dog's Paradise decided to go ahead with the march to Wounded Knee, hoping to pick up momentum along the one hundred mile route. Based upon arrest records and pictures of the demonstrators, a substantial number were individuals who had been shuttling in and out of Wounded Knee for the past several weeks. The organizer of the march appeared to be an unidentified black driving a car with Minnesota plates. Also in the entourage were ten to fifteen other cars and a large van carrying supplies.[37] A half dozen persons carrying a long strip of canvas with "Liberty and Justice for All" written on it led the way. They were stopped Wednesday, near Martin, South Dakota, by BIA police backed up by the FBI and U. S. Marshals. They were read the tribal order that the Pine Ridge Reservation was closed to the demonstrators. On the advice of Vernon Bellecourt, who was acting as their spokesman, they agreed to return to the Rosebud Reservation.[38] Late that evening, forty-six were arrested attempting to join AIM at Wounded Knee.[39] Among those arrested were Anna Mae and Nogeeshik Aquash, who both falsely maintained they had never been to Wounded Knee. Pictures of their April 12 wedding at the Wounded Knee Trading Post had been highly publicized.[40]

Never cordial, relations between the FBI, the U. S. Marshals, and Wilson's BIA police reached the breaking point in a dispute over the Indian roadblock on Big Foot Trail on April 23. The incident began when CRS agents complained to Colburn that they were being harassed at the Sioux roadblock. According to the CRS, the Indians were confiscating legitimate items they were attempting to take to Wounded Knee and also turning back CRS personnel. Determined to rectify the situation. Colburn and two of his deputies went out to the roadblock that evening. According to Colburn, the discussion became so "belligerent and rough we decided to file assault charges against them." Eight Indians were taken at gunpoint, placed in a van, and driven to Rapid City where they were arraigned for assaulting and impeding federal officers.

The two FBI agents, who were cooperating with the Indians at the roadblock to protect evidence seized by the Indians, had been away pursuing a van during the confrontation. They returned in time to witness the arrests. When they asked Colburn what was happening, he told them to guard the Indians. The agents replied they were not aware of any arrest orders, but they would back up the Marshals and cooperate. Colburn said it was not important that the agents were aware of the arrests and told them they should proceed to the rear of the arrest area or get off the roadblock. One of the agents advised Colburn that they were assigned there as an interview team and were under direct command of the SAC at Pine Ridge and could not evacuate their position until so instructed by the SAC. Colburn replied that the FBI operation at the Indians's roadblock meant about as much to him as "piss falling from the sky." The Chief Marshal further asserted, "I am in charge of the CRS, FBI, and U. S. Marshals." Suggesting that a man of his position should command a little respect, Colburn proceeded to tear down the roadblock.[41] Later that evening, an angry Richard Wilson sent a message to local radio and television stations calling for all able-bodied Oglala Sioux to report to reservation headquarters with their rifles. Wilson complained that his Indian roadblock had been smashed by federal agents, and eight Indians had been arrested. He vowed he would restore the roadblock the next morning.[42]

Early next morning, United Press International carried a dispatch quoting Hellstern that it would be impossible for the Sioux to re-establish their roadblock because the FBI had taken total control of the road down to U. S. 18. Hellstern told SAC Held the FBI would be charged with the responsibility for preventing the Sioux from re-establishing their roadblock because not enough Marshals were available. Felt told SAC Held "unless he heard to the contrary from me or Mr. Gray" he was not to take any action involving physical force. Felt also indicated the FBI had no responsibility for containment or protection.[43] At about 1:30 a.m., six to eight Indians in four automobiles had reestablished the roadblock at the same site. They were disbursed by FBI agents, but the Indians promised they would return with three hundred Indians—take over—and not allow anyone to enter Wounded Knee except FBI personnel. The agents thereupon returned to their command post at roadblock one.

Twelve carloads of armed Indians arrived at the U. S. Marshal's roadblock later that morning to confront Hellstern, Colburn, and his Marshals. The Indians were told no unauthorized roadblock would be allowed and they should leave. As the discussion continued, Richard Wilson and about eighty Indians including women and children arrived. In FBI terminology, "A volatile situation was at hand." SAC Richard Held and another senior FBI agent proceeded to the scene immediately by helicopter. Held told Wilson that word had come from Washington that the tribal council could re-establish the roadblock. Wilson later said he understood that CRS employees would leave and the eight Indians who were arrested the night before would be released. Hellstern held an afternoon press conference to deny Wilson's assumptions.[44] Held had called Felt and advised that the negotiations broke down when neither side would compromise. The Indians, according to Held, were on their way to establish their roadblock and the Marshals were on their way in APCs to break it up. Held thought the situation was mainly a "head butting contest" between the Oglala Sioux on one side and the Marshals Service and CRS people on the other side. He said the Indians were still being held in jail. Held doubted that, if the roadblock were re-established, Marshals or CRS would be allowed through. Held said access to Wounded Knee was no problem since other roads and even helicopters were available.[45]

With neither side willing to back away, Held called Felt once more and reported that twenty-six carloads of Indians were waiting to move into position. He suggested that the situation could be controlled if Colburn was recalled to Washington and the CRS ordered out. Felt talked to Gray, who advised he would recommend that action to Deputy Attorney General Sneed. Gray quickly got back to Felt and told him Sneed said it would be impossible to remove Colburn. Gray ordered Felt to tell Held to take over from the Marshals, take every possible measure to control the situation, and at the same time avoid a confrontation.[46]

Late that afternoon a confrontation did occur when Frizzell and Colburn were challenged by Wilson's men near the newly re-established roadblock. Wilson told reporters they came within an inch of shooting Frizzell and Colburn.[47] Frizzell had just flown in to the Pine Ridge airport and was met by Colburn late that afternoon. When they got into the car, a radio message from CRS indicated there was a problem with Wilson's roadblock on Big Foot Trail. Frizzell said, "Let's stop by." But Colburn, who quite likely had had his fill of roadblock encounters, wanted to go eat. Upon Frizzell's further insistence they drove out to Wilson's roadblock. Just before they got there, they were stopped by two cars full of Wilson supporters. One approached Frizzell's side of the car with a shotgun and ordered him to roll the window down. Irritated, Frizzell snapped that the Indian could roll it down himself. The Indian leveled his shotgun and ordered Frizzell to get out of the car or he would be a dead man. As Frizzell was complying, Colburn grabbed his automatic rifle from under the front seat and exited the car via the driver's side, leveled his weapon on the Indian, and indicated he would be a dead man if he shot Frizzell. Both sides backed off at this juncture.[48]

Hellstern announced the next day that CRS personnel would not be allowed into Wounded Knee, at least on a temporary basis. Marvin Franklin hurried back to Pine Ridge to mediate the "tempest in a teapot." After two days of meetings among government officials and tribal council leaders, Wilson agreed to take down the tribal council roadblock and to allow CRS representatives into Wounded Knee. The government consented to give the tribal leaders a voice in the situation and to provide them with a daily briefing. Also, the FBI and U. S. Marshals promised to train tribal council supporters for police duties around the area.[49]

When Frank "Clearwater" died on April 25, AIM requested that the burial be held at Wounded Knee. Hellstern refused because the FBI investigation had revealed the dead man was really a Caucasian named Frank Clear. Wilson opposed the burial of an outsider at Wounded Knee even more and released the complete FBI report on Clear to the press to substantiate his position. It said that Defense Department records identified the man as Frank J. Clear, 47, a Caucasian of Irish descent, born in Virginia. Clear was inducted into the United States Army in 1943, and was tried by general court martial for misbehavior before the enemy and running from his company in the face of the enemy during combat operations in Italy in 1944. Clear was given a dishonorable discharge, forfeited all pay and allowances and was sentenced to ten years of hard labor. The sentence was remitted to an other-than-honorable discharge after Clear had been confined until his release in 1946.[50] AIM continued to insist "Clearwater" was an Apache. Crow Dog even sent out a tape-recorded message inviting Indian people to come to Wounded Knee "for the burial of their Apache brother." Clyde Bellecourt promised AIM would file suit against the government over Clear's death.[51] Ultimately, Clearwater was buried on Crow Dog's property on the Rosebud Reservation.

AIM leaders sent a message from Wounded Knee that they were in mourning for Clearwater, and no negotiations could be held for four days. Vernon Bellecourt flew to Des Moines, Iowa, on April 26, where he spoke before a group of fifteen representatives of various church groups that had paid for his trip. Bellecourt told that AIM "under no circumstances" would negotiate any more with the Justice Department. "The Department of Justice is only interested in law and order and not the issues of Indian rights, poverty or needs," he claimed. The only way Wounded Knee could be negotiated was through "a representative of the White House and the President of the United States and not the Department of Justice."[52]

Neither the Interior Department nor the White House offered any concessions significant enough to resolve the conflict. Both the government forces and AIM built up their weaponry and dug in for what promised to be the final firefight. Colburn had drawn up a battle plan involving the use of Marshals and the Army to overrun Wounded Knee using tear and sickening gas in combination with helicopters and armored vehicles. This plan, very similar to the Army's earlier proposal, was still awaiting White House approval when the FBI heard about it. "It is inconceivable that the FBI, which is the foremost law enforcement agency, would not be given a copy of a plan of operation in which it is both directly and indirectly involved," complained Assistant Director Bates.[53] Aware that an armed showdown was imminent, AIM sent out a desperate call to all its fund raisers to obtain arms, ammunition, and explosives because their supply was dangerously low. Federal forces brought in new personnel generously supplied with armament and backed up by the Army and Air Force. "If the government finally does have to crush the occupation by force, it will not be as unpopular a move in the eyes of fair-minded people as it might have been regarded earlier," said the Denver Post.[54]

Both sides accused the other of aggression and firing indiscriminately. AIM alleged that either the federal forces or the BIA police fired at Wounded Knee to provoke fire so they could open up their own counter fire. Some AIM witnesses also suggested the

BIA forces fired at the federal lines to provoke fire.[55] Local ranchers, too, were accused of firing indiscriminately to provoke shooting. One Marshal, however, complained to the press, "We can't even fire back when we are fired upon until we call our superior officer."[56] Weighing the amount of firepower trained on Wounded Knee, even the most critical observer would have to admit that the government effectively contained the number of casualties.

By the afternoon of April 26, the most intense firefight of the siege was underway. Federal estimates place the number of rifle-rounds fired by them at around 6,500. AIM shot an estimated 2,800 rounds during the twenty-four hour battle. For the first time the government employed gas, lobbing about eighteen gas grenades. Held received authority to move roadblock one forward five hundred yards on the 27th. Held wanted to move it 1,300 yards closer "for better protection of Agents manning this roadblock." Because of heavy fighting, roadblock one could not be advanced on the 27th.[57]

Carter Camp contacted the federal command post at 2:30 p.m. and asked for a ceasefire because "we have a dead warrior and an injured warrior." A ceasefire, which would be maintained until the final settlement, was immediately ordered. CRS personnel brought out the dead warrior, who was identified as Lawrence Dean "Buddy" Lamont, 32, a resident of the Pine Ridge Reservation. Lamont was an Army veteran who had served a tour of duty in Germany during the Kennedy administration.[58] Oglala Sioux tribal secretary Lloyd Eagle Bull was his brother-in-law. His sister, Lou Beane, was a leader in the OSCRO and was at Wounded Knee when he was shot. Other relatives there included Buddy's niece Darlene Nichols, who identified herself as Banks's wife, Kamook. Lamont's mother, Agnes, was a teacher's aide at the Pine Ridge Community School. Her mother had been present at the 1890 Wounded Knee encounter as a young girl and had survived. But several other of her close relatives had perished then. Lamont was not an AIM member, but he and his mother had offered Means a place to stay when Means returned from the BIA takeover in Washington.[59]

As do many other interpretations of the events at Wounded Knee, the versions of Lamont's death vary prodigiously. Burnette and Koster say, "A heavy burst of machine gun fire slammed Buddy Lamont into the ground as he emerged coughing and choking from the gas being lobbed into his bunker."[60] Zimmerman wrote, ". . . killed as he knelt beside a bunker, a bullet slammed into him from behind. It passed through his heart, emerged from his chest, and shattered the stock of his rifle."[61] Akwesasne Notes said, ". . . he was not armed at the time. Witnesses said that he was shot in the back by BIA police."[62] Pathologist W. O. Brown performed an autopsy on Lamont on April 28. Brown reported the cause of death was a bullet which entered the left front chest, severed the dorsal aorta, and lodged in the right portion of the back. The spent bullet was recovered and forwarded to the FBI laboratory. No information about it has been released. Testifying in a Wounded Knee trial at Lincoln, Nebraska, Buddy York, an FBI sharpshooter, said he was almost certainly the one who shot Lamont. He said he was one of three agents using the type of weapon and ammunition that slew Lamont. York testified that he had been told to "shoot to kill" although official government policy was still "shoot to wound."[63] The second death at Wounded Knee marked the end of armed resistance and initiated negotiations that finally achieved a settlement.

Lamont's death, somewhat paradoxically, barely found its way into the news. Most newspapers buried the story in their middle pages. The Lincoln Journal, for example, carried a very short story on its second page. One of the front page stories in the same edition was datelined Argentina and headed "Two-Headed Baby Boy Dies."[64]

Lamont's demise also was overshadowed by the resignation of L. Patrick Gray as Acting Director of the FBI on the same day. Gray admitted he had destroyed documents connected with the Watergate case, an act that totally discredited him. Lowell Weicker, his friend from Connecticut, said Gray destroyed sensitive political documents taken from the White House safe of Watergate conspirator E. Howard Hunt after the previous summer's bugging raid on the Democrats. Weicker said Gray told him he acted on orders of presidential aides John W. Dean III and John D. Ehrlichman, both of whom would be sacked on April 30.[65] Informed sources have later suggested that Gray was "Deep Throat" in the Watergate drama.

As was true for Watergate conspirators, the net around AIM was drawn tighter on April 27. At Deadwood, South Dakota, Judge Bogue revoked Russell Means's $25,000 bond and issued a bench warrant for his arrest because Stanford Adelstein's written approval for the bond to cover charges filed in a second arraignment had not been filed with Bogue as required. The arrest warrant stemmed from Means's failure to appear. Mark Lane insisted that Means could not get a plane to Rapid City. Bogue said he could.[66] Means was arrested outside Los Angeles AIM headquarters on April 27 in a vehicle driven by newsman Joseph Alletto. Just before his arrest, Means had told a news conference, "Wounded Knee cannot be resolved in a peaceful manner in the event of my arrest." Alletto's role confused authorities because he was the one who claimed he had been held prisoner by Means and others at Wounded Knee and had reported to authorities that Means asked him to take care of press inquiries. At the press conference, Alletto thought Means was afraid of his own people and was extremely nervous. Charges against Alletto were later dropped "inasmuch as source on 4/27 was not burnable."[67] In other words, the FBI declined to reveal their informant. Means was taken to Sioux Falls where bond was set at $125,000 by U. S. District Judge Fred J. Nichol. Bissonette was arrested the same day in Rapid City.[68]

Means was indicted at Sioux Falls the next week also for conspiring to illegally transport arms to Wounded Knee and to cross state lines with intent to incite a riot. The indictment came from Federal District Court in Phoenix, Arizona. Others indicted were: Herbert Powless, Milwaukee; Eugene Heavy Runner, Jr., Browning, Montana; Stan Holder, Lawton, Oklahoma; and Ronald Petite, Rapid City. The indictment charged the five with conspiring from April 11 to April 25 to transport an unspecified quantity of firearms from Phoenix to Wounded Knee, knowing they were being used to further a civil disorder.[69]

Other AIM leaders continued to seek support around the country with some success. Vernon Bellecourt spoke at the University of Colorado and Colorado State on April 27. He urged those who attended to join a convoy headed for the Rosebud Reservation with supplies for Wounded Knee and to participate in a memorial service for Frank Clearwater. Seven cars made it as far as Valentine, Nebraska. There nineteen people were arrested. Four of the cars eluded the roadblock.[70] The group was led by Douglas Phelps, social activist, Harvard Law dropout, and former student body president at Colorado State. Charges were dropped when a federal grand jury refused to return indictments against them.[71]

Aaron DeSersa, who just a month before had said he would have nothing to do with AIM, took a quick tour of Florida on April 27, 28, and 29 to gain support for Wounded Knee. He appeared on television in Miami and garnered an estimated $1,161 from a liberal group.[72] DeSersa encountered a much cooler reception the next day from the Seminole Indians. Seminole leaders refused to render any support. They insisted they wanted no connection with Wounded Knee because they were satisfied with their current situation in Florida.[73] DeSersa said he would be in New York City that weekend with travel support provided by Doris Duke, the well known tobacco heiress.[74]

Two other AIM leaders, Mike Haney and Clyde Bellecourt, remained active in other parts of the country. Bellecourt arrived at Newark, New Jersey, on May 1 and spoke at Trenton State College. He spoke at Princeton University on May 2 before also proceeding to New York City. Mike Haney spoke for AIM in Austin, Texas, on May 3. Haney talked about breaking into armories to obtain rifles and ammunition and claimed one such break-in had already succeeded. Haney indicated an urgent need for gas masks because AIM believed the government would use gas on them on May 5. Haney said AIM would receive another air drop on either May 4 or May 5.[76]

Frizzell met with Dennis Banks and Leonard Crow Dog in the demilitarized zone on April 28 to arrange a final settlement and discuss the burials of Clearwater and Lamont. The three sat on a gorgeous Indian blanket that Banks had brought along. While smoking a peace pipe, the three engaged in a wide-ranging discussion, exchanging philosophies on many things, but especially the future of the American Indian. For Frizzell it was "one of the most poignant moments he experienced while at Wounded Knee." He indicated, however, that the idyllic encounter was not without humor. The group was alerted to a smoldering blaze in the beautiful blanket that left a two-inch hole. "Some squaw is going to be pissed at you for ruining her blanket," Frizzell told Banks. "Squaw, hell! It's mine and I am pissed," retorted Banks, who proceeded to give Crow Dog a tongue lashing for burning his blanket.[77]

A firm ceasefire was arranged. Colburn notified all federal positions to fire only if fired upon or if AIM attempted to move forward. Both sides agreed to notify the other if they detected firing from third parties. Banks also requested that a meeting be arranged "with fifty traditional headmen and chiefs of the Oglala Sioux" in an obvious effort to preserve the idea of local Indian involvement. Frizzell agreed to six "traditional" Sioux. The government planned a two-track approach to negotiations with Frizzell of Interior negotiating the substantive social issues and Colburn and Hellstern of Justice arranging the disarmament procedures.[78] Frizzell told Crow Dog and Banks that he was almost the only remaining government official still urging restraint and "time is running short." He further refused restoration of telephone service or access to attorneys because he thought the breakdown of the April 5 agreement had been caused at least in part by such outside influence.[79]

Frizzell met with a number of Oglala elders at Frank Fools Crow's home on April 29. Fools Crow was considered an AIM supporter, but in his biography he denied he supported either side. "I wanted no confrontation of any kind at Wounded Knee, so I talked with representatives of both sides: the AIM movement, and the Federal Marshals," said Fools Crow.[80] He added, however, "... most if not all of the problems could have been avoided if they (government) and the news people had just stayed away."[81] In his role as an Oglala medicine man, Fools Crow said, "My vow, given in thanksgiving to Wakan-Tanka, is to assist anyone who sincerely wants my help."[82] Like most traditional tribal leaders, Fools Crow wanted to go back to the 1868 Treaty, so AIM wanted his help and Wilson did not.

At the meeting Frizzell warned that if this round of negotiations failed, "hard choices" would have to be made. He told the elders that the occupants were currently about half white and half Indian and only the most hard core were still there. The government feared the coming summer vacation might bring more students to Wounded Knee. An attack using gas was imminent, but the occupiers could rest assured no attack would occur without prior warning so those who wished to surrender could do so.[83]

That evening, the Wounded Knee Trading Post burned to the ground. The Indians reported that the fire started when a girl accidentally dropped a kerosene lantern in the building. Those who had heard repeated threats that it would be burned were not convinced it was an accident. Federal monitors suggested AIM probably lost a considerable amount of ammunition in the fire because a number of explosions occurred. Also, there was speculation that much of the occupier's food supply may have burned as well.[84]

The following morning, the traditional chiefs: Frank Fools Crow, Tom Bad Cob, George Gap, and Kills Enemy, accompanied by interpreter Matthew King, Fools Crow's cousin, entered Wounded Knee to negotiate. They promised AIM that the 1868 Treaty would be an important part of the bargaining with the government, scheduled for May. The tribal chiefs told Banks the government would not wait much longer before attacking and requested that the protesters disarm themselves not later than May 4.[85] That evening Nixon dumped Haldeman, Ehrlichman, Kleindienst, and Dean.

That time was drawing short for a negotiated settlement was underlined by a New York Times report on April 30. It spelled out the Justice Department's phased plan to take the village by force. First, leaflets urging all noncombatants to leave Wounded Knee would be dropped several hours before the attack. Then, if an attack still seemed necessary, an armored helicopter would spread nauseous gas and smoke over the area. Marshals wearing flack jackets would follow, some walking and some in APCs.[86] The FBI found out about the strategy they had requested earlier by reading the New York Times. Bates in a memo to Gebhardt said, "Repeated attempts have been made by Supervisor John C. Gordon, a representative of FBI headquarters, to obtain a copy of this battle plan from the Deputy Attorney General (Sneed) on a need to know basis, requests denied." Bates lamented, "The information which we in the FBI sought officially now appears in the national media." [87] The government imposed a news blackout on Wounded Knee as of May 1.

Burial of Clearwater and Lamont was becoming a major issue between the tribal government and AIM. On April 28, the tribal council served a restraining order on Clearwater's wife to prevent her from bringing his body to Wounded Knee for burial on the grounds he was not an Oglala Sioux. AIM leaders threatened to defy the tribal order. Frizzell then worked out a compromise with Wilson which would allow Clearwater to be taken to Fools Crow's home near Kyle on May 1 for a twenty-four hour wake. Final rites were scheduled for Leonard Crow Dog's property on the Rosebud Reservation.[88]

Frizzell's agreement did not include immunity from the law, as those in the caravan bearing Clearwater's body learned the next morning. BIA police, assisted by the FBI, stopped the twelve-car caravan, searched it for weapons and ammunition, and arrested four persons for illegal possession of arms and ammunition. Everyone who was not a member of the family or not a resident of the reservation was turned back. The mourners then took the casket to a white tipi at Fools Crow's where about fifty grievers participated in a traditional ceremony. That afternoon, BIA police escorted a caravan consisting of one hearse and four other cars off the Pine Ridge Reservation. When the caravan entered the Rosebud Reservation, it was halted by Rosebud BIA police. A tribal order, signed by tribal chairman Webster Two Hawk, forbade burial of Clearwater on the Rosebud Reservation. When the driver of the hearse refused to proceed further, the Indians took control of the vehicle, dropping the driver out. The hearse, now driven by Vernon Bellecourt, proceeded to Crow Dog's Paradise where Clearwater was buried.

To facilitate the dual-negotiating approach, two school buses were parked inside the demilitarized zone on May 1. Dennis Banks and four members of the AIM security force met with Colburn, Hellstern, and Hall to talk over dispossession. AIM insisted the disarmament would be a simple process if the government agreed to their political considerations which focused on the 1868 Treaty. Civil rights negotiations were led by Leonard Crow Dog, Gladys Bissonette, and six other Oglalas, who met with Frizzell, FBI agent Noel Castleman, and Dennis Ickes, an attorney from the Civil Rights Division of the Justice Department. The Oglala's bargaining strategy followed that of the April 5 aborted agreement. Frizzell insisted, however, that no preliminary meetings with White House officials could occur before disarmament was complete.[89] Colburn and Hellstern told AIM leaders they would not discuss dispossession further until progress was made with Frizzell. Another meeting was set for May 3.[90]

The chiefs were allowed back into Wounded Knee to assist with a settlement. They, along with Buddy Lamont's mother, Agnes, and sister, Lou Beane, discussed Lamont's funeral arrangements as well. The government wanted a small ceremony with just eight or ten close members of the family present. The Lamonts and AIM wanted it to be a major occasion, with a large gathering and the traditional Sioux feast. Frizzell insisted this could only happen if the Wounded Knee occupiers agreed to lay down their arms before the burial. On May 2, Frizzell reached an accord with the insurgents on five points: (1) A letter from the White House to affirm the points agreed on would be presented to AIM leaders by 7:00 p.m., May 3. (2) Disarmament negotiations sessions were scheduled for 10:00 a.m., May 3. Tentative arrangements called for the Indians to lay down arms when Frizzell presented them with the White House letter. (3) Burial of Lamont was scheduled for May 5 at Wounded Knee and would be open to the public. (4) Seventy hours after Lamont's funeral, arrest warrants for AIM would be presented to Fools Crow, whereupon subjects of warrants would surrender. (5) During the third week of May, preliminary treaty commission meetings would be held at Fools Crow's residence, after which negotiation sessions would be held at Washington, D. C.[91] The next evening, May 4, the day of the citizens's committee deadline, the insurgents agreed to a compromise offer which basically agreed to the April 5 terms if they were to receive a letter from the White House assuring that treaty meetings would be held. The Lamont funeral would not be open to everyone, and roadblocks would not go down. All relatives, however, could attend by entering and leaving through government check points.

Government security remained tight and increasingly effective. Hellstern authorized the arrest of five employees of CBS News as they were exiting Wounded Knee because they had no permission to enter. All exposed film was confiscated, and the newsmen were turned over to BIA police who jailed them temporarily.[92] Later the film was returned to CBS on order of new FBI Acting Director William D. Ruckelshaus. Further pressure was exerted by the FBI when they proceeded with authorized federal search warrants to conduct a search of the Community Center Building in Rapid City, which had been leased to AIM sympathizers. An estimated two-and-one-half tons of food, medical supplies, bedding, and other equipment was seized. Authorities considered this raid all but guaranteed a settlement.[93]

Disagreement within AIM, which the government and others suggest had always been a factor in the confrontation, surfaced again as the meetings ground down to what now appeared to be an inevitable conclusion. John Mackey, an assistant professor of sociology at the University of South Dakota and an enrolled member of the Santee Sioux, told the FBI that AIM leaders Ron Petite and Herb Powless had contacted him by telephone for assistance. Both asked him to serve as an intermediary with the Justice Department and AIM leaders outside and inside Wounded Knee. Petite and Powless told Mackey a total lack of communications existed among the AIM factions. They asked Mackey to arrange a meeting in Rapid City or Sioux City with AIM leaders presently in Wounded Knee and AIM leaders on the outside in order to resolve their differences. Mackey, who was not an AIM member and not especially sympathetic to them, expressed a willingness to serve as a spokesman or intermediary and flew to Washington for conferences.[94]

According to FBI sources, Stan Holder and Carter Camp were at odds with other AIM leaders because no bail and defense money had been raised in their behalf and on the behalf of all the secondary type AIM members who were part of the siege. Holder, who was out on bail, was arrested in possession of a .357 magnum while attempting to re-enter Wounded Knee.[95] During a negotiating session in Wounded Knee, Dennis Banks made a personal request for federal protection by the FBI for one year after his surrender. It was denied.[96]

About fifty persons attended a Roman Catholic funeral for Buddy Lamont at Porcupine, May 4. Burial was scheduled for Wounded Knee on May 5, but the caravan did not leave Porcupine until mid afternoon that day, so the ceremony was moved up to May 6. Lamont was buried right next to the 1890 memorial in his army uniform with ten Indians firing salutes of ten rounds each of blank ammunition.[97] About 135 relatives and friends participated in the emotional service featuring a trenchant address by Dennis Banks. He sneaked out of Wounded Knee almost immediately afterward. Expenses for the fairly elaborate casket and tomb were covered by the National Council of Churches as were those for Frank Clearwater.

On May 5, Hank Adams carried an agreement signed by Leonard Garment, special counsel to the President, to Frank Fools Crow for delivery to Wounded Knee. Adams still was banned from the reservation, so the delivery took place over a barbed wire fence on the Pine Ridge Reservation boundary. Fools Crow appeared fully dressed as a traditional chief in buckskins and warbonnett. The government then flew him over the badlands in a small airplane while they read and interpreted the letter. Fools Crow said he was not happy with it because it promised little of consequence, but he liked its tone, so he agreed to present the proposal to the Indians at Wounded Knee.[98] The letter promised that "five or more White House representatives will meet with the headsmen and chiefs of the Teton Sioux during the third week in May for the purpose of examining the problems concerning the 1868 Treaty." The offer also said no meeting would be held until dispossession had been accomplished at Wounded Knee.[99]

Ramon Roubideaux, accompanied by seven tribal leaders, entered Wounded Knee that afternoon to discuss the offer. On the way in, Roubideaux told the press there was a ninety-five percent chance of signing. Frizzell said there was only about a fifty-five percent chance the agreement would be signed. Roubideaux proved right. Late that afternoon, the accord was signed by Frizzell, Colburn, and Hellstern for the government and Leonard Crow Dog, Frank Fools Crow, and others for AIM, the traditional Oglala leaders, and the occupants of Wounded Knee. The government agreed to pull back from their positions and the occupiers would abandon theirs, with dispossession to begin May 9 at 7:00 a.m. All activist weapons, ammunition, and explosives were to be turned over to representatives of the CRS. All persons would then identify themselves and leave. Those with outstanding warrants would be arrested and taken to Rapid City. Wounded Knee residents with no charges would be escorted back to their community. All others would be taken to Pine Ridge. Then the government would search the area, destroy all bunkers, and withdraw, leaving a force behind to prevent further incidents and to protect the militants from reprisals.[100] Not everyone complied with the agreement. Neither Carter Camp nor Dennis Banks elected to sign it. Banks, who departed the next day, left behind a message with Roubideaux:

> Ramon: I have reviewed the agreement which has been arrived at, and find that the document falls outside the protection of the U. S. Constitution and its amendments. I will however submit to the arms laydown because the chiefs and headsman have agreed that unless otherwise it might hamper the Washington meeting, also I agree that Aim's job is done here. It must be understood that AIM was called on to aid these Oglalas in their struggle against repressive govt forces. It was tragic that we lost 2 Brothers however against those same forces. I repeat—AIM will leave by Wed. Please have bail ready for our bond. (Carter-Crowdog- Myself others) Dennis J. Banks (s)[101]

Camp and Crow Dog turned themselves in on May 7 and were released on $70,000 and $35,000 bond respectively. Charges included assault on federal officers, obstructing federal officers, larceny, breaking and entering, and arson. Authorities detained a number of persons leaving Wounded Knee, but quite a few, including Banks, got out. An FBI source advised that the Venceremos and Vietnam Veterans Against the War were involved in removing weapons from Wounded Knee and were concealing them at an unknown site near Porcupine.[102]

Those remaining in Wounded Knee could see no advantage in waiting until May 9 to give up. On May 7, they requested that the final resolution should take place on Monday, May 8. The government agreed to Monday at 7:00 a.m. Two more buildings burned down that evening. CRS personnel entered Wounded Knee at 7:00 a.m. and signaled that the standdown could begin. All APCs were then removed from the roadblocks and a series of helicopter sweeps were made over the bunker areas to determine if the bunkers were clear. One Indian headsman then was flown by helicopter to each bunker to serve as an observer. At about 8:00 a.m., CRS representatives brought out fifteen old guns that represented the weapons remaining inside Wounded Knee. Like

Colonel Forsyth in 1890, Hellstern was not amused, "These guns are a lot of crap," he said, "the arms dispossession part of the agreement has been violated." Processing was delayed for almost an hour when AIM supporter Al Cooper from New Mexico locked himself and a companion in a CRS car upon learning WKLDOC attorneys were barred from the roadblocks. The stalemate ended when lawyers were allowed to witness the surrender and provide advice to their clients which they correctly claimed was a part of the May 5 agreement. It stated, "Processing will be accomplished pursuant to the terms of paragraphs 2(a) and 2(b) of the April 5, 1973, Agreement."[103] The effective part of the April 5 Agreement was 2(b) which said, "If those approached for interviews ask to consult with an attorney prior to consenting to such interview, the Government will, of course, honor that request."[104]

A total of 129 people were processed. Thirty-three were identified as residents of Wounded Knee. About 110 of the 129 were Indian. Only fifteen were arrested, which brought the total FBI arrests for the encounter up to 237. Also detained was the persistent four-man CBS news team. They were waiting for the Marshals when they entered the center of the village. The television newsmen were taken before U. S. Magistrate James Wilson in Rapid City. He declined to issue a complaint against them.[105]

The Marshals moved into Wounded Knee on foot at 9:50 a.m., and were followed by FBI search teams about a half hour later. They found seven rifles, five shotguns, and several rifle barrels and receivers along with about 2,700 rounds of ammunition. Stanley Hollowhorn, the CBS news team, and a goat were also there to greet them. What remained of Wounded Knee was a scene of almost unbearable stench as the day warmed. Many AK-47 shell casings and lots of amphetamines of all kinds were located. The Episcopal church was especially severely damaged. The interior of the church was covered with broken glass and empty cartridge cases. The altar and a heavy brass crucifix had apparently been used as a target for large caliber weapons. Trenches and underground bunkers, cleverly constructed for protection in case of a gas attack, surrounded it. One trench extended to an opening in the floor of the church.[106]

Other damage was noted as well. The night before, the home of the Lansburys was burned to the ground. The Lansburys had been missionaries for most of their lives and had spent a good deal of that time in Chile. Some Wounded Knee residents criticized their fairly high style of living which included a new station wagon, color television, and comfortable furniture. All of that was destroyed. Their tipi-style church was also heavily damaged.[107] After viewing the vandalization of church buildings at Wounded Knee, Father Richard Steinmetz said, "There is a hatred of Christianity involved here, obviously."[108]

Referring to the village as a whole, Hellstern said, "It's as close to a pig sty as I have ever seen." Vernon Bellecourt responded, "We were in an all-out war—there was little time for housekeeping." From Sioux Falls, Russell Means claimed, "The United States government delayed the return of the original residents by twenty-four hours in order for their forces to vandalize and steal from the original residents of Wounded Knee in order to make it appear that the occupiers had done these terrible acts to their own people, thereby creating further division among our people."[109] In spite of the AIM disclaimers, the evidence points to the occupiers as the primary source of vandalism, destruction, and thievery.[110]

When the dispute ended, both those who were leaving the hamlet and those who were returning required assistance. No telephones, electricity, or water could be obtained. Much of the home furnishings were missing. Lyman estimated the direct cost for damages at around $500,000. He indicated, nonetheless, that there were no plans to seek disaster area designation. "We have had enough unfavorable publicity already," he said. The situation could be handled locally through sufficient tribal funding and other allocations, Lyman concluded.[111] Local officials complained that they found it difficult to relate to the federal authorities, even after the confrontation ended. Information simply was not shared. Even superintendent Lyman was forced to attend federal press conferences to obtain information about what was happening.[112] Dick Wilson announced fifteen used trailers were already on site for the dispossessed and forty additional mobile homes would be set up in Pine Ridge while the clean-up of Wounded Knee progressed. NCC funds were also used to help repair and winterize homes and to replace furniture and other household goods lost during the siege. Eighty Mennonite Disaster Service volunteers worked for two months assisting around twenty-five families.[113] Those who stayed at Wounded Knee during the occupation were afraid to come to Pine Ridge because they were afraid of abuse. The people from Wounded Knee who moved into trailers at Pine Ridge in turn feared returning for the same reason. Silas Grant, who had been elected "fifth member" of the tribal council from Wounded Knee, showed great concern for the community and worked diligently to bring it back together, but he died of a heart attack shortly after the dispute was settled.[114]

The estimated one hundred occupiers who were not returning also needed assistance. The NCC provided food and lodging for them at a Rapid City motel and also arranged for purchase of auto parts, chartered buses for larger groups, and ran a traveler's aid for individuals.[115] A considerable amount was contributed to a Pine Ridge Crisis Fund by various denominations throughout the country.[116]

For almost two weeks, the FBI scoured the Wounded Knee area to gather evidence, recover weapons and supplies, and restore property. They even brought in horses to negotiate the gullies, ravines, and draws—especially those that led to Porcupine, but few weapons and supplies were found. A considerable amount of property was redeemed, though. The total value was set at $206,000. Additionally, several thousand dollars worth of professional sound motion picture equipment was discovered.[117] Authorities received reports concerning six to eight fresh graves containing unreported Wounded Knee casualties. After searching the area thoroughly by jeep, horseback, and foot patrol, the only fresh burial site identified was Lawrence Lamont's.[118]

After the dust had settled, the question of the effectiveness of government policy had to be addressed. Was it the best performance that could be expected under the circumstances as Colburn claimed afterward?[119] Did the government confront a very difficult situation and handle it in a proper manner as Sneed maintained?[120] Or was Wounded Knee a "new low" for the government as Judge Fred J. Nichol described it when he dismissed the AIM leadership trial at St. Paul? Most certainly it was not the best the government could do. Nor was it the worst, considering events such as Watergate, Attica, Chicago, and Kent State. Although two were killed and one was severely wounded at Wounded Knee, the toll could have been disastrously more considering the circumstances. If the April settlement had been culminated when anticipated, in fact, no one would have perished.

Speaking as a private citizen, Dennis Ickes of the Justice Department addressed the Gordon Chamber of Commerce, May 22, 1973, concerning his eight-week effort to help mediate the takeover. Ickes said the government took into consideration the legitimate grievances of the reservation Indian. The government's latitude to act was hampered, said Ickes, because there were a series of hostages. First, there were eleven residents who were held in Wounded Knee during the early days of the takeover. Then there was the press, which was there voluntarily and because AIM wanted them for protection and publicity. Last, there were many women and children, who although they were there voluntarily, too, could be victimized by a police assault. The activists really had no place to go and posed no serious threat to the general public well being. Rather than lose lives on both sides, the decision was to lay siege and negotiate instead of using force. Morale within the village would decline as food, facilities, and publicity dwindled. Bickering among the leadership could be expected, similar to what occurred at Alcatraz, Ickes concluded.[121] Surely, with these considerations, authorities would not risk the massacre of Indian women and children at the hands of the government at any place, let alone historic Wounded Knee.[122]

Although the government could have ended the confrontation by force at any time, the Indians knew they could dictate the time of settlement because of the political considerations involved. All evidence indicates the defenders would not have backed down in case of an attack. They were well armed in heavily fortified positions with a cadre of combat veterans leading the defense. The key to the length of the occupation hinged on what the advantages of continuing on were in relationship to those of quitting. In fact, the government had little to offer the occupiers, other than the promise of meetings to discuss grievances and arrest warrants. No official guarantees of amnesty, elimination of the existing tribal government, or reversion to the 1868 Treaty were forthcoming. By holding out, grievances could be aired, national attention could be held, and the embattled government could be further embarrassed. As long as the issue remained in the public eye, speakers such as Means, Banks, the Bellecourts, and others commanded high fees on college campuses and elsewhere. Other funds from churches, colleges, New Left organizations and so on could be collected to provide bail and cover costs. Also, AIM enjoyed excellent legal advisors who thrived on confrontation. Possibly, the strategy of holding tough as long as possible backfired, though, to the extent that credibility with the press and the public plummeted during the last month of the occupation. That loss of approval may have proven more costly than AIM had anticipated.

After the accord, a continuing series of articles in well known and highly regarded periodicals questioned the authenticity of the events at Wounded Knee. Quite thorough was Neil Hickey's "Was the Truth Buried at Wounded Knee?" (TV Guide, four part series, December, 1973). Perhaps most damaging was Terri Schultz's "Bamboozle Me Not at Wounded Knee" (Harpers, June, 1973). Schultz, who covered Wounded Knee for the Chicago Daily News and Harpers, wrote, "In truth, Wounded Knee II was largely a pseudo-event to which the world press responded with all the cautiousness of sharks scenting blood." [123] If AIM had created a new hope for the American Indian at Wounded Knee as it claimed, it had also created a backlash against itself by over-extending the occupation. AIM's time was 1968-1973. Its ascendancy peaked at Wounded Knee but could not be sustained.

Over
the Brink

A IM leadership was decimated by the incapacitating influence of numerous federal and state charges. They led to detention, hearings, high bonds for bail, and restrictive bail conditions. AIM spokesmen maintained the allegations and costs were deliberately exaggerated in order to disintegrate the organization. It never was that cohesive from the beginning anyway. Based upon the number of convictions that eventuated, the question of whether the government's restrictive actions were legitimate or not seemed to have some basis in fact. Yet it appeared as if there were cogent reasons to prosecute, if one accepts the philosophy that breaking the law is not a subjective issue even when legitimate political grievances are involved, as the government obviously did.

After the Wounded Knee accord, key AIM leaders faced a variety of charges and bond conditions. Means was held in jail until June 4 when he posted $75,000 bond. He had to leave almost immediately for arraignment in Phoenix, where he and Herb Powless faced illegal gun-running charges. Carter Camp posted $25,000 bond in Rapid City on May 5 and was restricted to the state of Oklahoma. On May 30, he appeared in Scottsbluff, Nebraska, for arraignment on charges stemming from the January confrontation there. Camp advised local news media (erroneously) that an AIM convention would be held there about July 1. Stanley Holder who had been freed on $25,000 bond, appeared there on June 11. Eventually, all of the Scottsbluff AIM cases were dismissed.

Leonard Crow Dog and Pedro Bissonette were freed on $35,000 and $25,000 bond respectively. Clyde Bellecourt and Ronald Petite were out on cash bond, also.[1] Vernon Bellecourt was arrested on July 23 in Chicago after returning from a European fund raising tour. He had been indicted on two counts of crossing state lines to incite a riot during the siege of Wounded Knee. His bail was set at $10,000.[2] Banks remained a federal fugitive from justice until June 24, when he surrendered in Rapid City. Bail was set at $105,000. Three days later, he managed to raise the money and was released with no bond restrictions. The Iowa Methodist Church provided $85,000. The other $20,000 in United States Treasury notes was deposited by Frank Braggiotti of Phoenix. Banks went to Eagle Butte, South Dakota, to attend the Calf Pipe Ceremony. A significant religious event featuring fasting and a prayer, the ceremony focused around the sacred peace pipe; it was led by Frank Fools Crow. "Anyone who expects to be someone of importance, especially in the contemporary Indian Movement should be there," the FBI reported.[3]

Other than religion, which AIM leaders seemed to be turning to with what some critics viewed as pragmatic urgency, undoubtedly a focus of discussion was the two meetings with the federal government concerning the Wounded Knee accord. At the first meeting on May 17, 18, and 19, emissaries from the President met to discuss treaties with Indian leaders from Pine Ridge Reservation at the home of Frank Fools Crow. The second series of meetings, chaired by Senator Abourezk, was conducted by the United States Senate Subcommittee on Indian Affairs at Pine Ridge and Kyle on June 16 and 17, respectively.

Under an arbor constructed of pine boughs supported by ash logs at Frank Fools Crow's place four White House representatives met with several hundred Indians to discuss treaty rights. Wilson tried to prevent non-reservation Indians from attending by enforcing a ban on non-tribal visitors. He was frustrated by a federal restraining order which allowed many emissaries from other tribes along with an assortment of AIM supporters. Noticeably lacking in rank, the White House delegation was headed by Bradley Patterson, executive assistant to Leonard Garment, who was acting counsel to the President. Patterson was assisted by Crage Becker, a claims specialist with the Interior Department; Leslie Gay, assistant director of tribal operations of the BIA; Charles Soller, legal advisor with Interior, and Barbara Kolberg, special consultant to the White House on Indian Affairs. After spending the morning in conference with Dick Wilson and other elected leaders, the envoys proceeded by two helicopters to Fools Crow's ranch. Wilson told the press he had been assured by Patterson that duly elected officials were the majority representatives of the reservation.[4]

When the government representatives arrived at Fools Crow's, all but Patterson were requested to remain in the helicopter. Before negotiations began, Fools Crow wanted a yes or no answer from Patterson to the question of whether the Sioux could be reinstated to the 1868 Treaty. Patterson explained that the 1871 law had eliminated the right of the President to negotiate treaties with Indian tribes as sovereign bodies, so any changes in the present tribal relationship with the government would have to be made by Congress. He insisted that his colleagues be allowed in to discuss the other concerns expressed in the April 5 agreement. They finally were allowed to disembark the helicopters and present their information.

The focus of attention shifted to the Oglala petition signed by 1,400 members calling for a referendum on a new form of government for Pine Ridge. Gay explained Frizzell's rejection of the petition, which appeared to be legal on the basis that such a referendum would have to have one-third of the eligible voters rather than those registered to vote. In 1969, the BIA determined there were 3,104 members of the tribe entitled to vote. Now Frizzell claimed the rule had been changed from those registered to vote to those entitled to vote which meant the total was now swollen to 9,518, including eighteen-year-olds, thus disallowing the petition.[5] AIM supporters continued to press for a Presidential Commission to review the 1868 Treaty, promising there would be more Wounded Knees if their demands were not met. "I could not speak to you honestly from the White House if I were to tell you that the President would look on the prospect of more Wounded Knees with any equanimity," Patterson warned as the meeting ended.[6]

The White House delegation proceeded to Pierre, South Dakota, to meet with the nine tribal council chairmen who formed the United Sioux tribes of South Dakota. Central to the discussion was the 1968 Indian civil Rights Act which allowed full citizenship rights to reservation Indians. During the meetings, Patterson publicly recognized the tribal councils as the legally elected governing bodies of the various Sioux tribes. He indicated, too, that tribal chiefs and headsmen had no legal status but had some legitimate grievances which should be taken into consideration by the tribal councils.[7]

On May 30, a United States Marshal delivered a letter from Leonard Garment to treaty council chairman Matthew King. In regard to the key issue at hand, the establishment of a Treaty Commission, Garment wrote, "The days of treaty-making with the American Indians ended in 1871, 102 years ago. Only Congress can make changes. Congress is in effect a treaty commission." Garment further indicated that expressions of opinion would be welcomed, civil rights violations were being investigated, and an audit of tribal finances was being conducted by Touche, Ross, and Company. If a second meeting were to occur, Garment advised that comments would have to be put in writing first and "only named chiefs and headsmen and counsel Mr. Roubideaux could attend. "Instigation of further civil disturbances and violations of local or federal law will only bring grief to Indian people themselves," the letter concluded.[8]

Fools Crow and his group were not overawed by the White House pronouncements. "We are not asking for the negotiation of new treaties. We are merely asking for the treaties that already exist to be enforced. . . We ask that you advise your representatives to leave in Washington their preconceived ideas of Indians and to come to the next meeting with open minds. . . ," they responded. The Indians also promised more violence: "Our fathers died protecting this land, and we would be cowards if we continue to allow the federal, state, and local governments to continue racial and cultural genocide against us and our Indian brothers and sisters across this continent."[9] Their warning would prove prophetic beyond most reasonable estimates, especially on Pine Ridge Reservation, which became locked in a violent, deadly struggle between pro-AIM and pro-Wilson factions for the next three years.

Senator Abourezk, representing the Subcommittee on Indian Affairs of the Committee on Interior and Insular Affairs, chaired the hearings at Pine Ridge and Kyle on June 16 and 17 respectively. Known to be sympathetic to the Indians and critical of the BIA, Abourezk allowed everyone a voice and was not adverse to expressing dismay at the policies of government bureaucrats. For example, he grilled area BIA director Wyman Babby and Pine Ridge Superintendent Lyman at length about the peculiar distinctions made concerning the number of votes required on the petition for a referendum on tribal government. ". . . the Bureau of Indian Affairs in this case has become a law unto itself," Abourezk grumbled.[10] During the hearings, Abourezk admitted he had attempted to have Lyman removed earlier but found he did not have the power to do it. Policy, rather than personalities, now seemed the problem. He offered the opinion that a new superintendent would still be bound to Bureau policy. "I don't think that removing the superintendent without changing overall policy would do any good at all," Abourezk said.[11] His assessment was accepted by most informed observers.

Russell Means's testimony at Kyle on June 17 proved one of the high points of the hearings. Means was well prepared and aired his grievances against the tribal government, the BIA, and other authorities in an able manner. Abourezk asked Means what type of society he would foresee if the Oglalas were granted sovereignty. Means replied that it would be based on spirituality with no separation of church and state and a community concept of tribal government, rather than a reservation concept. Abourezk was not taken by Means's idea to allow the minority group to move away and form their own majority if they so desired. The Senator indicated the situation of Indian people fighting Indian people represented one of the most tragic situations he could remember: ". . . I am talking about shooting at each other, beating each other up, whatever happens. I don't think that is right, and I don't think the government ought to approve of that policy, and factionalizing and dividing Indian people so that results." Means retorted that crime prevailed throughout the whole country. Abourezk countered, ". . . in other words you want to be as barbaric as some white men are when they shoot each other and beat each other up, yet you denounce that kind of society at other times."[12]

Some positive action by the government, which could be attributed in part to AIM militancy, was forthcoming during the summer. On July 17, Senator Abourezk introduced Senate Joint Resolution 133 to establish an American Indian Policy Review Commission through which Congress would "undertake a comprehensive review of the historical and legal developments underlying the Indian's unique relationship with the Federal Government to support the formulation of more positive and effective national Indian policies and programs." The resolution was approved as Public Law 93-580 on January 2, 1975, with a funding of $2,500,000. The American Indian Policy Review Commission created largely as its sponsors, Abourezk and Congressman Lloyd Meeds, had envisioned it, consisted of three members from the Senate, three from the House, five members of Indian tribes, and thirty-three task force members. It had until August, 1976, to report its findings.[13]

During the summer of 1973, most of the AIM leaders headquartered in Rapid City and continued to press for more confrontations. Russell Means, especially, promised more Wounded Knees and touted the achievements of AIM. Claiming leadership, not only among Indians but of the radical left as well, Means said, "AIM represents the only true liberation group, a sovereign people with a land base backed by treaties with the federal government."[14] Never cordial, Banks's relationship with Means deteriorated even more because Banks was convinced that Means's fiery statements were hurting AIM.

On the evening of July 3, 1973, the Sacred Heart Catholic Church burned to the ground. AIM blamed the government, saying they were covering up evidence of illegal machine gun bullets that had ripped up the building. Wilson's group suggested that it was AIM who wanted to cover up the senseless damage to the interior of the church which was reating a negative image for them with the many tourists. According to informed sources, the truth was more mundane. Children had been observed playing with matches near the building on several occasions prior to the fire, and they had been seen in the area the evening of the fire.

As summer advanced, AIM busily engaged in a number of confrontations and a series of meetings to organize future activities and plan legal defenses. All the AIM hierarchy assembled at White Oak in Northeastern Oklahoma for the national convention, July 30 through August 3. Mike Haney, Sioux-Seminole director of the Oklahoma City AIM, was charged with arranging for food. He claimed the state had originally promised 15,000 pounds of commodities, but "the state of Oklahoma has put every stumbling block in our paths, including the governor, who promised us support and then withdrew it."[15] Convention leaders issued a statement saying, "No more Wounded Knee confrontations are planned, but we will never back away from a confrontation, and the Indian People know that."[16] Many conservative Indians acknowledged that in AIM they now had an alternative to turn to for assistance.

The major topic of concern at White Oawas how to enlarge AIM into an international Indian movement that would include North and South America. AIM announced it was seeking support from "Arab oil money" and already had received aid from private groups in France, Belgium, England, Switzerland, and Italy. "We have gained a hell of a lot of support throughout Europe," claimed Vernon Bellecourt.[17] His assertion, in fact, remains essentially true.[18] AIM experienced great difficulty, however, in their attempts to become a truly national organization. The vast majority of reservation Indians rejected them, although many admired their militant stance. At White Oak, Carter Camp and John Trudell were elected national co-chairmen.

Controversy marred the group's return to South Dakota. The AIM caravan returned to the Crow Dog ranch to attend the Sun Dance Ceremony. From there AIM originally planned a caravan to the Black Hills to visit the Crazy Horse Monument and then continue to the grand jury proceedings at Custer. The original plan for the Sun Dance had been to hold it on June 25 at the site of the Crazy Horse Monument. Those plans were stopped when the FBI, the governor, and other state officials convinced sculptor Korozak Ziolkowski and Fools Crow to cancel because Indians were bringing guns, dynamite, and explosives into the Crazy Horse area.[19]

On August 7, AIM attorneys attempted a citizen's arrest of four FBI agents in Rapid City, whom they claimed had been violating the civil rights of the WKLDOC by illegal surveillance and harassment. All complaints against the agents were dismissed. The Custer Grand Jury convened on August 8 to start hearing testimony on charges against Banks and Means concerning the February 6 disorder. A few days later, Pottinger announced for the Justice Department the formation of the Office of Indian Rights to protect and foster civil rights of Indians.[20] WKLDOC lawyers said that at least part of the reason for formation of the new office emanated from South Dakota authorities's hostility to out-of-state attorneys such as Mark Lane.[21]

Attention was diverted away from South Dakota to Des Moines, Iowa, on August 22 when a group of armed AIM members led by Harvey Major, Douglass Durham, and Ron Petite took over a state office building near the capitol. The AIM leaders then called Banks and Means who were standing by at a telephone. A list of twelve demands for prison reform was presented. and the three-hour occupation ended peacefully. The media gave the takeover full coast-to-coast coverage. Upon receiving the call, Banks rushed to Des Moines to arrange a meeting with Governor Ray to settle the dispute. Durham, an FBI informant, later claimed Banks's purpose was to establish himself as the peace-bringing mediator who would solve problems like this, if needed, in any future situations.[22]

An event that AIM had neither planned nor anticipated severely damaged its attempt to create a moderate image and maintain internal unity. On August 27, Carter Camp, the new national co-chairman, shot Clyde Bellecourt at Crow Dog's Paradise. Camp, a Ponca from Oklahoma who had spent a good deal of time in California, was somewhat of an unknown quantity to the other AIM leaders, who were primarily Chippewa and knew each other well, but not necessarily as friends. Well-grounded suspicions that the organization had been infiltrated by informers were running rampant and Camp seemed a likely suspect, at least to Bellecourt. Also, the AIM camp was split over who would receive bail money and who would not. Camp had a habit of pulling a gun at the slightest provocation and had done so on a customer at a service station on August 24. When he was charged with assault, his bond was violated by the U. S. District Court, and a warrant for his arrest was issued on August 25. The next day, Camp and Bellecourt, not noted for his even temperament, got into a serious dispute, apparently at least in part over a disagreement Means and Bellecourt had had with Camp's younger brother, Craig, and Bellecourt threw him out of the house. Camp returned the next morning with Craig and Leroy Casados and asked Bellecourt to come outside. The bullet struck above Bellecourt's navel and entered the liver area.[23] Bellecourt was saved by a four-hour operation at Winner, South Dakota.[24]

Means claimed the government had set up the shooting to discredit AIM. Ron Petite sent out a press release from Des Moines urging Indians across the nation to take up arms "to protect ourselves and our families." Petite denied that Camp did the shooting and blamed the incident on "outside sources" such as the federal government or the Pine Ridge tribal council. He said Banks had authorized him to speak for Indians and announce the call to arms.[25] The turmoil in South Dakota ended any chance of a successful government meeting with the nine tribal council chairmen of the United Sioux tribes, scheduled for September 5. Garment cancelled it on August 31.

Camp was arrested and charged with assault with a deadly weapon. But Bellecourt, who had spent some fourteen years in prison, refused to press charges. The National Council of Churches requested that the $25,000 bond on Camp be withdrawn. Bond was reset at $70,000, a figure Camp could not meet. His bond was reduced in December, however, and he again was free on bail. Soon Camp and Bellecourt were sitting together and working together in court.[26] In October AIM Executive Director Banks, who had returned from temporary exile in Canada, announced that John Trudell, a Santee Sioux, would assume Camp's position as national chairman of AIM.

On August 28, arrest warrants for the AIM leaders of the Custer riot were delivered. Russell Means and Vernon Bellecourt were apprehended at the Winner hospital where they were holding a vigil to prevent a second assassination attempt on Clyde Bellecourt. Means demanded his $15,000 bail be reduced. After extensive debate, it was reduced to $10,000 and he was freed on bail.[27]

The slaying of Pedro Bissonette at the hands of BIA police in October evoked more controversy. He was charged by Nebraska authorities on September 26 with possession of a deadly weapon based on evidence that he discharged a gun in a White Clay, Nebraska, bar. His bond was revoked and Bissonette became a fugitive from justice. On October 17, BIA police attempted to arrest him but were forced to retreat when he fired a rifle at them. Later the same day his car was stopped near Pine Ridge and he was ordered to surrender. Instead, according to the BIA police, he came out brandishing a 30.06 rifle, and he was killed by one shot from a twelve gauge shotgun loaded with buckshot. In spite of protests from AIM that they wanted to have their own pathologist examine the body, it was flown to Scottsbluff. Pathologist W. O. Brown indicated, "I found seven pellets. They were buckshot, not rifle or pistol bullets. Seven pellets is the normal load for that type of cartridge."[28] Federal authorities concluded the shooting was justified under the circumstances and closed the case.

The WKLDOC claimed the slaying of Bissonette represented a deliberate murder to silence one of AIM's star witnesses in the forthcoming trials. He was eliminated because he had refused government overtures to testify for them against AIM, said the WKLDOC. Mark Lane concluded Bissonnette had been held down and had seven pistol shots fired into his chest.[29] Lane alleged that Bissonette's court appointed attorney had attempted to force Pedro to make a deal to testify for the FBI. Bissonette's subsequent request to name his own attorneys was denied by the government, according to Lane.[30] The government version indicated Bissonette had contacted the FBI on August 20 indicating a willingness to cooperate with federal authorities if he were paid up to $1,000. FBI headquarters instructed that "no payments were to be made to Bissonette under any circumstances without prior Bureau authority."[31]

One of the mitigating factors in the slaying that created suspicion among Pine Ridge residents involved the relationship to Bissonette of BIA police officer Joe Clifford, who was identified as the one who shot him. Clifford's sister was Pedro's commonlaw wife and the ex-Golden Gloves boxer was known to beat her severely on occasion. At least once she was battered so severely she was hospitalized.[32] The WKLDOC announced Pine Ridge residents were holding hearings at the Jumping Bull place to accumulate information and statements for a Senate investigation of law and order on the Pine Ridge Reservation. The actions of the BIA police and their chief, Del Eastman, would be of particular concern.[33]

Bissonette's parents preferred a quiet, church funeral for Pedro, but AIM insisted that it should be a well-publicized media event. An estimated four hundred and fifty people attended the church ceremony held at the Holy Rosary Mission at Pine Ridge. After the funeral, about seventy-five people gathered at the Bissonette home. Eight guards were stationed in a bunker, and the entrance was blocked with a truck.[34] The government had sought a court order to prevent AIM leaders from attending the funeral, but a federal judge denied the request to ban Pine Ridge residents. Nonresidents, including Banks, were prohibited. The funeral procession detoured to the edge of the reservation so he could view Pedro's body and bid farewell.[35]

Less than a week after Bissonette's death, two BIA policemen suffered arm and shoulder wounds when they tried to detain a carload of youths. Eastman said, "I strongly suspect those who did the shooting were AIM militants because of numerous threats we have received from national leaders of AIM." Means called the charge completely false and distorted.[36] The car the youths were driving was registered to Leonard Peltier, an AIM bodyguard. Violence, followed by charges and countercharges, would follow a graphic and monotonous pattern on the Pine Ridge Reservation for the next three years.

The hearings for the trials of the Wounded Knee defendants finally began in November with many serious issues to resolve. In a speech given at the University of South Dakota, Clyde Bellecourt said the Wounded Knee litigation "will probably be the major conspiracy trial of the century and when it is over, Richard Nixon and his cohorts will be found guilty of conspiracy against the Indian people." Bellecourt said defense lawyers hoped to prove the defendants could not receive a fair trial anywhere in the United States. He claimed the Committee to Reelect the President gave the protesters the

$66,500 to leave the BIA headquarters in Washington, and that gift was illegal and "things like that will be brought out in the trial."[37]

Pre-trial hearings for all of the 116 remaining Wounded Knee defendants took place at Sioux Falls, November 26-30. Defense attorneys, led by William Kunstler and Mark Lane, moved for dismissal, claiming several of the statutes involved were unconstitutional, others were noncriminal, and alleging bad faith and selective prosecution of participants on the part of the prosecution.[38] It was determined that Means and Banks would be tried together in the "leadership cases" under Judge Nichol with a change of venue to St. Paul. The remaining cases would be under Judge Bogue, probably in Sioux Falls. Although the charges varied somewhat, they all tended to involve interstate transporting and use of firearms, impeding a federal officer in the performance of his duties during a civil disorder, and burglary and larceny of the trading post.

Reverend Paul Boe was one of the over-thirty witnesses subpoenaed for the grand jury proceedings. He refused to answer certain questions, saying that in doing so a relationship of trusts would be breached. The prosecution maintained that, under South Dakota law, privileged communication applied only to a clergyman and a member of his church. The jurors voted 16-6 against Boe. When he persisted in invoking the confidentiality privilege, he was cited for contempt. Boe was sentenced to fourteen months in prison in December.[39] On January 14, 1974, sentence was suspended, but Boe was ordered to be available for further call and subsequent testimony.[40]

Meanwhile, AIM leaders attempted to establish their legitimacy as spokesmen for the broad cross-section of Indian people. They displayed great interest in traditional culture and religion and negotiated with more established Indian organizations in an attempt to form a national coalition to press for Indian rights. The two bodies AIM approached most seriously were the National Tribal Chairman's Association and the National Congress of American Indians. Although neither of the two showed any great enthusiasm for an open alliance with their militant would-be allies, spokesmen from both groups showed appreciation for the new dimension AIM brought to Indian affairs. "Now we have a last resort, we can turn to AIM," said one tribal leader.[41] On November 25, 1973, the Senate passed a bill to provide expanded health care programs for American Indians over a five-year period at a cost of $1.6 billion.

Banks also tested the international waters during this period. He made an unsuccessful trip to Latin America to explore possibilities of Native American solidarity. There was even some talk that Banks might become the new Che Guevara. George Roberts, a Los Angeles businessman engaged in an import-export enterprise, accompanied Banks as his "press secretary" to Mexico City for a conference on Indian problems. Possibly, Banks was also exploring the feasibility of fleeing to Mexico or Cuba if convicted for his role at Wounded Knee. The Mexican government promptly detained them in Mexico City for interfering in Mexican internal affairs; they were placed on a Los Angeles bound plane on December 8.[42]

In late December, AIM and a number of supporters including Marlon Brando, Burt Reynolds, William Kunstler, Mark Lane, and others, sponsored a concert in Atlanta to raise funds for the upcoming trials. Singer Paul Ortega and a seven-man rock group called XIT were expected to lure an estimated 15,000 people. Instead, less than 1,000 bought tickets, making the function a financial failure. The press ran a story called "Bury

My Heart at a South-Side Motel" which, among other things, discussed the AIM use of stolen credit cards to bring supporters to the concert.[43]

As the contending groups gathered in St. Paul in early January government officials who badly wanted a conviction to salvage at least a portion of their image, realized the task was strewn with difficulties. It was certain that the formidable defense team would attempt to create a political trial with a format similar to that pursued in earlier trials such as the Chicago Seven. The government had fared poorly in this kind of trial. Also, Judge Fred Nichol's background revealed potential difficulties for the prosecution. Nichol, a former sportswriter and broadcaster, had been active in Democratic politics, serving in the South Dakota legislature for two terms and as a delegate to a Democratic national convention. He had received his appointment as a Federal Judge in 1965 from President Johnson on the recommendation of Senator McGovern. Watergate particularly concerned Nichol, who had been critical of Nixon throughout the period. Nixon's problems would mount until his dramatic resignation on August 8 during the height of the St. Paul trial. Nichol previously had dropped assault charges against an AIM member who had been accused in the 1972 takeover of the Twin City Naval Air Station.[44] Nichol's wife, moreover, was an unabashed civil rights activist, and her sympathy for AIM was well known.[45]

The defense had begun preparations almost a year in advance. Sophisticated techniques such as running profile polls on would-be jurors that included a sociological profile of the community, incourt scrutiny of potential jurors and a field investigation of their backgrounds were employed. This was the same scientific approach pioneered in the Angela Davis murder trial. Thirty volunteers spent five weeks phone interviewing 576 people selected at random in the Twin Cities area. Over one thousand pages of computer printouts were analyzed. Ten observers, including an Indian psychologist and a body language expert, were scattered around the courtroom. The profile polls alone normally would cost $20,000. Sociologist Jay Schulman, fired from Cornell University and City College of New York because of political activism, assisted by psychologist Richard Christi, coordinated the effort.[46]

Pitted against this formidable team was R. W. Hurd, 33, Assistant United States Attorney. Hurd enjoyed a reputation good enough to net him one of the two Outstanding Assistant U. S. Attorney awards in the country in 1973, but he was hardly ready for the likes of the dreaded Kunstler. When the trial ended, William Sumner of Ridder News Service observed, "Hurd, frankly, was as to Kunstler to law and technique as Slippery Rock Teachers would be to Ohio State in football."[47]

Hurd and his defense team were further handicapped by lack of knowledge and misinformation concerning the government's role during the confrontation. Lack of cooperation and communication with Hurd by the FBI and U. S. Marshals Service undermined the federal cause. Nichol had signed an order the previous October that the defense should be provided with pertinent materials in the case. Not only was it revealed that the defense had not received pertinent information, but Hurd also had been denied relevant information by both the FBI and the Marshals. First, Hurd turned over to the defense a log of radio transmissions in and out of Wounded Knee kept by the Marshals after Colburn had told him no log had been kept. Then, as the question of FBI wiretapping was explored during the evidentiary hearing, Hurd admitted that the Justice Department had withheld data on informers from the prosecution. That prompted Nichol to sign an order telling the Justice Department to open its files on Wounded Knee to its own prosecutor. Nichol specifically alerted Hurd to look for data relating to electronic or telephonic interpretations.

When the FBI documents were inspected, Trimbach's denial of an FBI wiretap was shattered by a request he had signed on March 7.[48] Assistant Attorney General Henry Petersen had refused to sign the request because he thought the FBI had made the request based on information obtained from an illegal wiretap. Then the FBI sent in another request, using two informants as the basis for the request. That, too, was turned down. The Justice Department took the position, based on the 1972 Keith decision that warrantless surveillance could not be used against domestic organizations unless there was "substantial financing, control by, or active collaboration with a foreign government and agencies thereof in unlawful activities directed against the Government of the United States." Attorney General Richardson said in 1973 that "before electronic surveillance power is used against groups composed of citizens, a rather clear showing of possible law violation must be shown."[49] The FBI maintained they had demonstrated that unlawful activities were taking place within Wounded Knee. But they had no authorization for the wiretap from the Justice Department. Ironically, the government had to pay the $2,550.34 phone bill for the calls made out of Wounded Knee.

The defense maintained the intensive military involvement in the confrontation violated the Posse Comitatus Act. It forbids the use of United States Armed Forces on American soil against American citizens without a Congressional declaration. The Army replied they had not been in violation because their role was confined to that of observers and logistics coordinators.[50] In this matter, Judge Nichol sided strongly with the defense.

Nichol, who seemed preoccupied by the Watergate controversy, even to the extent of referring to it during the trial, allowed the trial process to drag on interminably. It took twenty-two days to seat the jury, half of whom were under thirty. Hearing the twenty-five government witnesses consumed another month. Then the jury was dismissed for a month while the court held an evidentiary hearing concerning the alleged illegal government wiretap. Yet another month was consumed by Nichol's unsuccessful attempt to subpoena White House tapes relating to Wounded Knee. The prosecution finally rested on June 24, but the defense did not begin its case until August 13. In the meantime, well over two-dozen motions for dismissal were considered and denied. More dramatic than the testimony was the open sarcasm and bitterness between the two sides. February 12, Nichol ejected Kunstler, Lane, and Tilsen from the courtroom for contempt but allowed them back, saying he had made a mistake. On July 18, Means gave Hurd a hard bump with his shoulder while leaving the courtroom. During the cross-examination of Louis Moves Camp, a government witness, Nichol and Kunstler got into such a heated argument that Nichol ordered Kunstler and Lane arrested. The media reported Nichol punched Kunstler in the stomach during the disagreement, but this was later disproved. Kunstler and Lane were released and allowed to continue with the trial.

In a surprise move, the defense took only three days and presented only five witnesses. Dee Brown opened the testimony on August 16 and was followed by Vine Deloria, Jr. Both stressed the long history of violations of Indian treaty rights as did Frank Kills Enemy, 80, whose grandfather, Red War Bonnet, had signed the 1868 Treaty. Gladys Bissonette, on leave with pay from her job at the Oglala Community School cafeteria, testified concerning the inequities of life on the Pine Ridge Reservation, especially under the Wilson administration. Agnes Lamont, dressed in black, supported Bissonette and, of course, proved exceptionally effective from a psychological standpoint. Both Lamont and Bissonette broke into tears on the stand and many spectators cried, too. Although Judge Nichol had earlier insisted the 1868 Treaty should have no bearing on the outcome of the trial, the defense was allowed to enter it as an exhibit of evidence.

Louis Moves Camp, an AIM defector who was disgruntled because he had been ejected from the AIM camp for drinking and other misbehavior, served as Hurd's key rebuttal witness. Unfortunately, Moves Camp's appearance turned into a disaster for the prosecution. Moves Camp claimed he had been in Wounded Knee throughout the occupation and linked Means and Banks with every charge that was brought against them. Kunstler and Lane demonstrated that Moves Camp could not possibly have been at Wounded Knee during the time period he claimed. Irrefutable evidence in the form of television tapes, pictures, and eyewitnesses proved Moves Camp had spent a good deal of his time in California during the Wounded Knee occupation. Two other factors were even more damaging in the opinion of many. First, the defense revealed that Moves Camp had been paid over $2,000 in witness expenses by the FBI. Also, the FBI allegedly covered up a rape charge against him for an incident that occurred while they were sequestered at a plush resort in River Falls. Wisconsin, awaiting his trial appearance. FBI agents Ronald Williams and David Price had accompanied Moves Camp. On August 15, the threesome went bar-hopping in River Falls. Moves Camp encountered and eighteen year old he wanted to take back to the resort. Williams and Price denied the request but said Moves Camp could pursue his good fortune on his own, elsewhere. The next morning, Moves Camp was picked up by police while he was wandering the streets saying he had spent the night with a local school teacher. The girl complained to local authorities that Moves Camp had raped her. No charges were filed. Mark Lane rushed to River Falls to investigate. He insisted the FBI used its influence to hush the case up.[52] Nichol permitted a full discussion of the rape allegations against Moves Camp, much to the discomfiture of the prosecution.

In his final summation Hurd accused Banks and Means of leading a criminal conspiracy in which innocent residents of Wounded Knee were intimidated, terrorized, and driven from their homes. "I don't care and I submit to you it doesn't make any difference if conditions on the Pine Ridge Indian Reservation are good or bad," said Hurd. Hurd asked the jury not to decide whether the takeover of Wounded Knee was right or wrong morally, but whether crimes were committed. [52]

Kunstler eloquently summed up the case for the defense on September 12. He said, "If you can reduce a social movement down to the question of whether its leaders are thieves, then you can discredit a social movement." In regard to the conspiracy charge, Kunstler said it was commonly used to suppress emerging groups who are seeking a higher and more powerful status in society. Concerning Hurd's theme that the trial should be considered only as a criminal trial, Kunstler referred to the trials of Socrates, John Peter Zendt, and Jesus, saying they were all criminal trials. Kunstler denied the action was a constituted revolt and found its genesis in victimization. "It was an attempt to secure some reason for remaining alive—some reason so that Indian children wouldn't have the highest suicide rate in the nation," said Kunstler. He brought back

memories of the 1890 massacre by reciting fellow Yale poet Stephen Vincent Benet's
<u>American Names,</u> which ends with "Bury my heart at Wounded Knee." The impas-
sioned Kunstler also quoted Black Elk and Daniel Berrigan. With tears streaming down
his face he finished, "These men are in your hands. Take good care of them—they are
my brothers."[53]

The jury never ruled on the case. They accepted it on September 12; the next day
they quickly decided 12-0 not to convict on the conspiracy charge. But they were locked
in an 8-4 vote for acquittal on the larceny count when Theresa Cherrier, 53, suffered a
small stroke and was hospitalized. An eleven-man jury could still rule on the case, but
this procedure had to meet with the approval of both sides. Normally, the defense tends
to refuse if a refusal is made. Hurd, however, was convinced that the best chance for the
government in this case rested with another trial. He reasoned incorrectly that Mrs.
Cherrier was one who would be most likely to support the prosecution. Accordingly, he
refused to accept an eleven-man jury.[54]

Nichol then had to decide whether to dismiss the charges or declare a mistrial, which
would allow the government to reopen the case in front of another jury. The veteran judge
had no intention of allowing the government another chance. "It's only fair to say I am
now over the brink," said the angry judge as he announced the dismissal of all charges."
I'm rather ashamed that the government was not represented better in this case," said
Nichol during the course of an hour-long denunciation of the prosecution. "I feel there's
been government misconduct in this case," Nichol opined. He also alluded to the
Watergate scandal as he had throughout the trial, concluding, "I guess this has been a bad
year for justice."[55]

"I think today was a blow for freedom for everyone. If this isn't a clear warning that
someone must begin the cleansing process in America then I don't know what a clear
warning is," proclaimed Kunstler.[56] Not only had the judge spoken; the majority of jurors
expressed their agreement with his decision. Seven jurors and three alternates, Mrs.
Cherrier among them, signed a letter sent to Attorney General William Saxbe requesting
that the government not appeal the case and discontinue prosecution of the other
Wounded Knee cases.[58]

Government officials, who had needed a conviction to prop up their sagging public
image, were enraged with what they believed was Judge Nichol's obvious bias against
them. Chief prosecutor Hurd filed a strongly worded motion of prejudice against Nichol
in early March 1975. It asked him to disqualify himself from the remaining Wounded
Knee trials involving Stanley Holder, Carter Camp, Leonard Crow Dog, and Clyde
Bellecourt "because he has personal bias or prejudice against the plaintiff" (the
government). The affidavits claimed Nichol often expressed respect for the people
involved in the Wounded Knee takeover and sympathy for what they were trying to
accomplish. They alleged that at a luncheon during the time of the trial in St. Paul, Nichol
led a standing ovation for Kunstler and later commented he "didn't give a damn what
people said" about it. Nichol, according to the affidavits, made no secret he thought the
FBI had greatly deteriorated in recent years and singled out Joseph Trimbach as "a liar"
and "that goddamned Trimbach." At one point in April, 1974, the affidavit swore, Nichol
said if the government did not dismiss the charges against Banks and Means, "the FBI
is going to be bloodied all over the courtroom." At another point Nichol said the Justice
Department was more interested in conviction than it was in justice, the affidavits

claimed.[58] On March 14, 1975, Nichol removed himself from further Wounded Knee cases, charging that Hurd and Trimbach had deceived him, especially in regard to Douglass Durham, an FBI informant who had infiltrated AIM and was in charge of AIM security during the St. Paul Trial. The Justice Department's appeal of the acquittal of Means and Banks was dismissed by Federal Court in St. Louis in April, 1975, on the grounds that a retrial would represent double jeopardy for the defendants.

When Saxbe learned of the setback, he called FBI Associate Director Thomas Jenkins and Assistant Attorney General Henry Petersen into a meeting on September 17. Saxbe said he was upset about the results and wanted to know who "blew the case." He instructed Petersen to obtain all possible information concerning the handling of the litigation from Hurd. The FBI was ordered to gather everything they had concerning the case, especially pertaining to the charges against Louis Moves Camp.[59]

In April, 1975, the FBI issued a comprehensive report concerning its role at Wounded Knee entitled, "The Use of Special Agents of the FBI in a Paramilitary Law Enforcement Operation in the Indian Country." The statement said the FBI had been instructed to conduct extremist and criminal investigations reports on AIM by the Justice Department in late 1972. After Wounded Knee was occupied, decisions were made by the Attorney General after consulting with White House representatives. The FBI maintained that the five different government negotiators created a lack of continuity that was exacerbated by the presence of Colonel Volney Warner. On March 4, after consulting with Warner, Erickson issued orders that the use of deadly force could only be employed in self-defense—contradictory to FBI policy. The FBI was not consulted. Because the FBI's request for troops was denied by Warner, the FBI had to operate in a paramilitary role which they were not logistically prepared to do. All military logistics had to be cleared through the Attorney General and Colonel Jack Potter.

SACs Held, Hoxie, DeBruler, and Trimbach claimed complete confusion reigned. Justice Department Officials and Chief Marshal Colburn, for example, would fly back to Washington, presumably for conferences, and would return with a new policy of which FBI headquarters was not aware. "The military did not realize in many cases that they were there to assist and not direct the FBI," the report said. SAC Held advised FBI headquarters at the time that to have any success at Wounded Knee it would be necessary to withdraw "the political types" and make it an FBI operation under FBI direction and leadership. Held recommended that if it should happen again it should be understood clearly that the FBI "is in control." "It is the consensus of opinion among the headquarters supervisors that no government official who is not a trained law enforcement officer be permitted to direct a law enforcement operation the magnitude of Wounded Knee," the report continued.

Director Kelley met with Saxbe and Petersen to brief them on Wounded Knee. He informed them that should a future incident similar to Wounded Knee occur the FBI "will insist upon taking charge from the outset and will not countenance any interference on an operational basis with respect to our actions."[60] As a direct result of Wounded Knee, the FBI immediately organized an effective Special Weapons and Tactics (SWAT) team to deal with future uprisings they might have to handle. Prior to Wounded Knee, no such force existed within the FBI. No confrontation the length and magnitude of Wounded Knee has transpired in the United States since.

A Caldron
of Violence

D uring the long course of the trial at St. Paul, Banks, Means, and other AIM leaders and members participated in a multiplicity of activities with varying degrees of success. Paramount to AIM's interest was the keenly anticipated showdown between Russell Means and Dick Wilson for Pine Ridge Reservation tribal council president. When Means won the primary by more than a hundred votes over second-runner Wilson and almost a dozen others, many thought he would win the February finals. On January 7, 1974, the day before the St. Paul trials began, Means issued a press statement announcing his resignation and "total withdrawal" from all AIM activities "to devote my full undivided efforts to my Oglala people."

Both sides waged a vigorous and at times vicious campaign. Means's promises included: stop all liquor from coming onto the reservation, move the tribal offices to Wounded Knee, establish a free health clinic in each district, secure sixteen mini-buses for public transportation, establish a tribal slaughter house and meat packing plant along with all Oglala farming co-ops, and to gather support from foreign countries.[1] Wilson liked to picture himself as a strong leader who knew what he was doing, got things done, and held everything together like Mayor Daley of Chicago.[2] Wilson claimed if Means was elected and carried out his promise to do away with the Tribal Council, the BIA, and the Public Health Service, the Indian's social and economic base would be devastated and it would lead to state jurisdiction and termination.[3] The lines of division established during the Wounded Knee confrontation continued—to many younger Oglalas Means continued to represent a symbol of change; to many traditionals he represented a return to the old ways. Naturally those with a stake in preserving the existing system supported Wilson. Violence and intimidation became commonplace, with both sides blaming the other.

Wilson's 1709 to 1530 election victory on February 7 triggered an avalanche of protest and violence. When a reporter asked Wilson at the victory party if he had changed his thoughts about Means, Wilson said, "No, I'd still like to challenge him to a fist fight."[5] He gave AIM ten days to get off the reservation "or else." Means, who had publicly complained earlier that it would be impossible to win the election because of corrupt election practices, immediately protested that he had been robbed. He cogently maintained that, even though the election had been stolen from him, the point that 1,500 Oglala people voted for him proved that AIM was not merely a group of outsiders with no support on the reservation. Means answered Wilson's expulsion declaration by saying, "I accept the challenge 'or else,'" and called for all AIM supporters to meet at Wounded Knee on February 27, 1974, the first anniversary of the takeover.[6]

On February 11, Means filed a written complaint with the United States Commission on Civil Rights that alleged many irregularities in the balloting. A formal contest of the election, protesting its conduct and results, was filed with the Oglala Sioux Election Board on February 15. A civil suit seeking to overturn Wilson's victory was also filed by Means and others in the Federal District Court for South Dakota. The hearing was held in July and on September 23, Judge Bogue dismissed the appeal, ruling that it was not a proper suit for Federal Court. An aide to Bogue said the plaintiffs had failed to demonstrate that remedies under tribal law had been exhausted.

So the results stood in spite of a withering report from the U. S. Commission on Civil Rights, whose representatives had spent two weeks on the reservation investigating. They recommended the tribal council conduct a new election. The report said, "In all about one-third of all the votes cast appear to have been in some manner improper. . . ." It went on to say, "The most striking and significant abuse during the election was the failure of the tribal election officials to enforce the tribe's voting eligibility requirements."[7] Although the allegations were never disproven, one should bear in mind that historically Oglala tribal elections have been riddled with fraud charges. Wilson, for example, claimed the Means faction brought in carloads of ineligible voters from Rapid City. Most firsthand observers of the 1974 contest indicate that both sides engaged in underhanded tactics.

After Means's defeat, AIM was associated with the celebrated Patty Hearst kidnap case that took place February 4, 1974. Shana Alexander, Patty's biographer, wrote, "The SLA had shown how easy it is today to stage a media coup d'etat all you need is a single, dramatic situation, preferably in an enclosed space—a lone hijacker—or something more elaborate, such as Wounded Knee."[8] AIM was one of five organizations named by the Symbionese Liberation Army to distribute food as part of the ransom paid by William Randolph Hearst for the release of his daughter. Newspapers throughout the country carried a picture of Dennis Banks assisting the Reverend Cecil Williams of Glide Memorial Methodist Church in San Francisco as a spokesman for the coalition.[9] An increasing number of Indians who had been basically sympathetic to AIM began to question its leaders proclivity to be seen with assorted New Left personalities. Rupert Costo, writing in his San Francisco based newspaper, Wassaja, under the headline, "Which Way the American Indian Movement" said, "Therefore, brothers (and sisters) you can have all the black, brown, Communist, Panther coalition and so-on support you can get. But you won't get anyplace in Indian affairs unless and until you win Indian support."[10]

In early April, AIM directed its attention to the Church of Jesus Christ of Latter Day Saints (Mormons) in Salt Lake City. Utah AIM Director David Hill called for a three-day conference there April 4-7 to "gain assistance from the Church of Jesus Christ of Latter-Day Saints for Indian people throughout the country." A substantial AIM-led demonstration occurred in front of the Temple Square in Salt Lake City. The demonstrators sought changes in social services, missionary work, treaty obligations and "the general paternalistic attitude" of the Mormons toward all Indian people. They requested a grant of $1,000,000 from the church for self-help programs.[11] No money or significant concessions were obtained.

From Salt Lake City, AIM moved on to Sioux Falls. There the trials for the Custer Incident were scheduled to begin in late April under conservative Judge Joseph Bottum of Rapid City. David Hill and Sarah Bad Heart Bull were among the twenty-two defendants in the case. When the defense refused to go on with the trial because of an appeal involving the number of preemptory challenges allowed, Bottum suspended the two out-of-state attorneys and found Ramon Roubideaux in contempt of court. Roubideaux claimed the Indian defendants were being railroaded in ways reminiscent of Mississippi justice against blacks.[12] When spectators did not rise for Bottum on April 26, he ordered the courtroom cleared of onlookers. The defense appeal on the limit of ten challenges was turned down the same day, but Bottum reinstated the two suspended attorneys.

When court convened on April 30, a number of observers were present including two representatives of the League of Women Voters; fifteen clergymen of the American Lutheran Church, including four Bishops, and three press representatives. Only male Indians came as spectators. They again refused to stand for Bottum. He again ordered the courtroom cleared and retired to his chambers. A series of conferences ensued with no resolution of the stalemate. When an officer of the court once more ordered the court cleared and no one left, a tactical squad of twenty-six specially trained and equipped police moved in to remove the Indians. During the vicious fight that followed, the courtroom was left a shambles and many were injured. The Bishops reported that excessive force was employed.[13] Hill was struck on the head and injured severely enough to require hospitalization. Bishop Matteson said Bottum said later, "They were asking for it, so I let them have it."[14] Russell Means was among those arrested for riot and assault.

AIM immediately issued a press release declaring South Dakota a war zone. It said, "Because of the recent hostile activities of white settlers in South Dakota against resident Indians while attending court which resulted in many Indians being brutalized and requiring medical attention, AIM hereby declares the State of South Dakota as being a zone of war." The release warned all Indian people who planned to travel to or through South Dakota to carry gas masks, first aid kits, and self-defense equipment. All non-Indians planning to "visit Wounded Knee, Mt. Rushmore, Black Hills or Richard Wilson" were advised that all Indian hospitals would not accept white settlers for medical treatment. AIM further warned all tourists that if they traveled to South Dakota "Indians will assume they are either there to kill Indians or to help Indians." all non Indians who wished to help Indians on a volunteer basis as clerks, nurses, doctors, x-ray technicians, ambulance drivers, mechanics, or typists were urged to call for further advice.[15]

After a short delay, the Sioux Falls trial continued without the injured Hill. Sarah Bad Heart Bull, Richard High Eagle, and Kenneth Dahl (a white friend of the Bad Heart Bull family) were found guilty. High Eagle and Dahl were sentenced to 5-7 years in prison and Bad Heart Bull received 1-3 years. None were allowed to go free on bond pending appeal, which AIM attorneys claimed was unduly harsh. Herb Rittenbaugh, a white who had testified for the three Custer defendants, was found dead in Hot Springs in August. Police called the death suicide and ruled out foul play. Rittenbaugh was a close friend of Dahl and had been indicted for perjury for his testimony.[16] A Free Sarah Bad Heart Bull campaign gained considerable support. On November 1, 1974, Marlon Brando, Paul Boe, Dennis Banks, Russell Means, Clyde and Vern Bellecourt, and others led a rally at Pierre for Bad Heart Bull's release.[17] She was released on parole on November 15, 1974.

Following the Sioux Falls trial, AIM sponsored the International Treaty Council, June 8-16, 1974, hosted by the Standing Rock Reservation. Government prosecutors at St. Paul later intimated the conference served as a "summit meeting" between AIM leaders and Communist block representatives who offered them assistance. According to AIM sources, 2,590 Indians from ninety-four different tribes registered as participants. Camp rules, including no alcohol or drugs and a midnight curfew, were enforced by AIM security forces. At the outset the camp was threatened by a severe outbreak of hepatitis, but serum was flown in at the expense of the U. S. Public Health Service in time to check the problem. The little town of Mobridge (population 4,391) adopted a siege mentality during the convention. Everything closed at 6:00 p.m. Merchants in grocery stores complained that Indians created disturbances in one part of the store and took items from other sections. Others accused the visitors of using stolen credit cards for gasoline.[18]

Several authorities on international relations were invited to speak and offer advice. The conference agenda purposed "to move outside the U. S. Constitution" to seek Indian national status and recognition from and through international bodies and other nations. Among the guests was Joel Carlson, a lawyer exiled from the Union of South Africa. He had aided black and Indian people fight for their rights there. Carlson was a member of the executive board of Amnesty International, a human rights organization with headquarters in London, England. Richard Falk, Milbank Professor of International Law at Princeton and vice president of the American Society of International Law, also spoke. He suggested Indians might receive international support in their fight for sovereignty and treaty rights.[19]

If St. Paul represented a triumph for AIM, Sioux Falls had not gone well. Many of their difficulties were caused by the skill and dogged determination of William Janklow, Assistant Attorney General of South Dakota, who served as chief prosecutor. Janklow, a Republican, announced his candidacy for State Attorney General against young Democratic incumbent Kermit Sande on a "get tough with AIM" platform. Janklow allegedly said all AIM militants belonged "either in jail or under a jail." A large man with an aggressive, exuberant personality, Janklow, 35, brought an unusual breadth and depth of experience. He was born in Chicago and lived at Fort Bragg, North Carolina, during World War II. At the end of the war, Janklow moved to Germany where his father, a career military man, was a prosecutor at the Nuremberg war crime trials. When Janklow was fourteen, his father died, leaving a wife and six children. She returned to her home town of Flandreau, South Dakota, to raise her family. Janklow dropped out of high school at age sixteen to join the marines. After a successful military tour, he earned degrees in business administration and law from the University of South Dakota. Janklow served six years as a Legal Aid lawyer on the Rosebud Reservation before becoming assistant attorney general.[20] During the course of his stay on the Rosebud, he became closely acquainted with Russell Means, who also worked there at the time, and with future United States Senator James Abourezk, whose family owned a store at Mission.

The entire Republican slate at the state level in South Dakota made a crackdown on AIM a key campaign issue. U. S. Senate candidate Leo Thorness urged that AIM be banned from South Dakota. McGovern, Thorness's foe, said he deplored AIM violence but would not go as far as Thorness. John Olson, opposing incumbent Richard Kneip for governor, said, "These militants must not be allowed to continue to ransack the state with their violence and malicious tactics." On August 22, Kneip telegrammed President Ford asking for federal cooperation to control the "serious threat to public order and legal processes" posed by the legal restraints imposed by federal law and federal court decisions.[21]

Janklow became the target of one of the worst mudslinging contests in the history of the state. Sande claimed that he had to fire Janklow for malfeasance in office and charged that Janklow had a criminal record. Janklow replied that he had quit his position and his only slip-up had been as a juvenile when at sixteen he was involved in an assault on a seventeen year old girl, but it was not rape. Janklow also charged Sande with illegally revealing a confidential juvenile record.[22]

On October 16, AIM made a calculated move to discredit Janklow by publicizing a rape charge against him that allegedly occurred while he was working on the Rosebud Reservation. Dennis Banks, who had been admitted to practice law before the Rosebud Tribal Court, filed a petition for the disbarment of Janklow. He had not resigned from the Tribal Court to which he had been admitted as head of the OEO sponsored legal services agency. Banks's charges included rape, perjury, obstruction of justice, dereliction of duty, conflict of interest, and unprofessional conduct. Tribal Judge Mario Gonzales issued notice of hearing for Janklow to show cause why such action should not be taken. Janklow did not appear and was disbarred by Gonzales, who also found sufficient evidence to warrant a trial on rape and morals charges. A warrant was issued for Janklow's arrest if he appeared on the Rosebud Reservation. The rape trial never happened, though, contrary to a number of popular accounts.

Gonzales said that the rape of fifteen year old Jancita Eagle Deer in 1969 (a number of sources indicate 1967) by Janklow had been covered up by the government. Eagle Dear claimed the attack took place as Janklow was returning her home after a babysitting job. Both the BIA and the FBI investigated the case but no charges were filed. Janklow cooperated fully, even to the extent of submitting to a lie detector test, which he passed. Janklow charged his accuser failed the same test when it was secretly administered to her in Minneapolis.[23]

When President Ford nominated Janklow to head the Federal Legal Services Corporation in May, 1975, Indian groups testified against him before the Senate Labor Committee. After a full investigation, Presidential counsel Philip Buchen sent a letter to the committee saying the rape charges were unfounded. Democrat Cranston, a committee member, added that a separate investigation by the Senate Labor Committee uncovered "absolutely no substantiation" for the charges.[24] "Moreover, we share the hope of the White House that this official investigation process will put these charges to rest once and for all," said Cranston.[25]

When Janklow was elected attorney general by an almost two-to-one margin, Banks said the election was an outrage and would increase tensions in South Dakota. NBC's

<u>Tomorrow</u> show granted Janklow time to present his side after the election. Mark Lane and Russell Means had appeared in October to give the AIM version of South Dakota. Means spoke of racism and genocide and branded South Dakota "the Mississippi of the North for Indians." Lane said four white men attacked Wesley Bad Heart Bull at Buffalo Gap and insisted that Sarah Bad Heart Bull had been victimized by South Dakota injustice to Indians.[26] Janklow requested equal time to tell America "the truth about AIM and its misleaders."

Janklow defended the justice system of South Dakota, holding that in every instance authorities had attempted to be impartial. The sentence for Sarah Bad Heart Bull was justified, explained Janklow, because she was out on probation for another serious offense when she became involved in the protest at Custer over her son's death. She and two others had been convicted of using a tire iron on another Indian. They broke his leg in eleven places and also his cheekbone and nose. Because it was her first conviction and she had a number of dependent children, Sarah had been given probation in that case.[27]

Jancita Eagle Deer dropped out of school after the alleged rape and moved to Des Moines, Iowa, where she became an alcoholic drifter. AIM security director Douglass Durham found her there and brought her to St. Paul. After she made her charges against Janklow on a Sioux Falls television station in October, 1974, Jancita returned to St Paul with Durham and then accompanied him to Phoenix. Her troubled life ended on an interstate highway in Nebraska on April 4, 1975, when she was struck by a car while wandering aimlessly on a dark night.[28] No charges were filed against the driver of the vehicle that hit her. The following December Jancita's stepmother, Delphine Eagle Deer, who was Leonard Crow Dog's sister, was found beaten to death in a field. AIM blamed Durham for Jancita's death and the BIA police for Delphine's, but no serious evidence in either case has ever been uncovered, as all-too-frequently has been the case in such incidents.

The increased rate of violence attributed to AIM members, on the other hand, stretched the organization's credibility and created internal friction and distrust. AIM leaders were convinced they were being undermined by the FBI's counterintelligence program and the CIA's operation CHAOS—both designed to infiltrate, undermine, and discredit "subversive" organizations. From 1956 until 1971, the FBI's program was called COINTELPRO, but Hoover broke it up after the successful theft of COINTELPRO documents from a depository at Media, Pennsylvania, in March, 1971. By no means had the FBI forsaken undercover counterintelligence activities, though.[29]

AIM's prestige in California sustained a severe setback when a taxicab driver was brutally murdered at their encampment in Box Canyon near Los Angeles. At the time of the incident it was called AIM Camp 13. Just north of the camp was the area used by the Charles Manson family as a hideout after the Tate-LaBianca murders. In 1958, a real Indian guru and some of his followers had been blown up there by a disenchanted follower. AIM leased the camp prior to the Wounded Knee encounter and named it Redwind. During the summer of 1973, it became the West Coast focus for AIM. Many South Dakota members spent the summer there. By the summer of 1974, however, it had become a haven for drifters with drug and alcohol problems and was virtually abandoned by AIM. Two second echelon leaders, Paul Skyhorse (Durant) and Richard Mohawk (Billings), were assigned to the camp to straighten it out. Skyhorse had problems with alcohol and instability and was known to feign insanity to avoid jail. He had been active in the direction of the Indian House in Brooklyn, New York, as coordinator for the New York City American Indian Cultural Workshop and was one of the original founders of the Chicago AIM. Mohawk, from Niagara Falls, New York, also helped organize the Chicago AIM and had worked in Arizona on the legal defense of Wounded Knee. After several weeks at Camp 13 the two reported the situation could not be salvaged but stayed and became part of the problem rather than help resolve it. On October 8, two youths from Camp 13 robbed and tortured a neighboring resident. On October 10, a white taxi driver was brutally murdered at the camp. Mohawk and Skyhorse were charged with the crime.

Their case dragged on until they were finally acquitted on May 24, 1978, after spending three years and five months in jail. During the long process of justice, proof of FBI infiltration of AIM was unveiled. One of the key prosecution witnesses was Los Angeles AIM treasurer "Blue Dove" or Virginia Deluce, who revealed herself as a paid FBI informant from early 1973 through January 1976. Born in San Francisco, Virginia had scored some minor successes in Hollywood movies, sometimes as an Indian in westerns. In recent years she had donned a black wig and posed as an Indian. Virginia was known as "Blue Dove" when she showed up at Alcatraz in 1969. On the day of the murder, she had taken Mohawk and Skyhorse to a nonexistent "free Sarah Bad Heart Bull" meeting in Los Angeles and driven them back to Camp 13.[30] AIM security director, Douglass Durham, an FBI informant, investigated the case and concluded that the two were guilty, and they were expelled from AIM. But as AIM grew convinced the case was set up by the government to discredit the organization, they renewed support and helped win acquittal for Mohawk and Skyhorse.[31]

Adverse publicity, generated by the sensational murder, drastically cut back AIM support in California. It was thought to be significant in Marlon Brando's cancellation of plans to make a movie based upon the events of Wounded Knee. Brando gave title to forty acres in Box Canyon on December 31, 1974, to the Survival of American Indian Association headed by Hank Adams. The property was valued at over $300,000. Brando vowed he would stop owning real estate and give it back to the Indians as an example.[32]

Violence continued at an alarming rate in South Dakota. Pine Ridge residents still question the "suicide" death of off-duty police officer Jess Trueblood. He allegedly shot himself after opening fire on the home of the Chester Stone family on November 17, 1974.[33] Supposedly Trueblood, who had problems with his bad temper, had argued with Louis Tyon, an AIM supporter who lived at the Stone house, all of whom were known as AIM supporters. Trueblood was at his sister's home, working on his car when he received a phone call. After the call he proceeded to the Stone residence in his car. Witnesses said Trueblood drove up to the house and began firing with a shotgun, and then left when pistol shots were fired toward him. Stone, his wife, their stepdaughter, Debbie Richards Mousseau Camp (Carter Camp's wife), and Louis Tyon were superficially wounded. Debbie Camp's young son was flown to Denver with a shattered arm. Trueblood was found with a bullet wound in his head.[34]

In spite of the fact both Jess and his brother had congenital afflictions in their arms, which allegedly prevented them from raising their arms properly, and the bullet wound entered from the rear, the death was ruled a suicide by the FBI. Trueblood's car. the key to the investigation disappeared for several days after the shooting. When it was recovered all prints had been carefully removed. Based upon a petition by the Oglala Sioux Tribe in 1977, the Justice Department ordered a review of the case but concluded "the medical and ballistic evidence thus point clearly toward a suicide." Among several studies polygraph tests of those with possible motives to harm Trueblood were negative.[35]

In spite of the Justice Department disclaimers, several experts remain dubious. Pathologist Garry Peterson, a highly regarded leader in his field, wrote a letter in March, 1978, that said, "The wound position is fairly typical for a homicidal wound of the 'executive' type."[36] He said if he had access to more evidence it might be possible for him to completely exclude suicide.[37] Other experts, including Jim Gilbert, author of a nationally known text on criminal investigation, doubt it was suicide.[38] Reservation police officials suggest Trueblood had an accomplice and he shot Trueblood in the back of the head when an argument resulted after they quit shooting at the house.

Violence also erupted at the Sioux sovereignty hearings at Lincoln, Nebraska, in December. The special hearings were important because they were called as an aftermath of Wounded Knee to determine if the Sioux Nation had sovereignty based on the 1868 Treaty.[39] John Moore, 20, a Penobscot Indian, was found on December 3, 1974, with a hunting knife thrust almost completely through his neck. He was staying at an old Lincoln Air Base barracks provided for those who wanted to attend. His death was ruled a suicide. Two authorities questioned the suicide conclusion. Dr. Richard McWilliams, a forensic anthropologist at the University of Nebraska, said a suicide finding was "totally incomprehensible and indefensible."[40]

Although Moore's death cast a chill on the proceedings, the sovereignty issue remained central. Federal Judge Urbom conducted the hearings with dignity and sensitivity. Some fifty-one witnesses ably portrayed the long history of betrayal and frustration endured by the original Americans. When Urbom released his opinion on January 18, 1975, however, he could only conclude that despite an ugly history that included treaties "pocked by duplicity on the part of the United States Government," neither the Sioux nor any other American Indian nation had full sovereignty. Judge Urbom said that he was following an unbroken line of decisions of the U. S. Supreme Court which had consistently held that Indian treaties were superseded by law made by the government. Indians were subject to the legislative powers of that government and therefore did not enjoy full sovereignty.[41] Had Urbom decided otherwise the impact could have been enormous, although the government undoubtedly would have appealed such a decision.[42]

During 1975, AIM participated in a number of confrontations. They included: the seizure of the Fairchild Electronic Plant at Shiprock, New Mexico; the takeover of the Wagner meat packing facility at Wagner, South Dakota; and the seizure of the abandoned Alexian Brothers Monastery near Gresham, Wisconsin. The thirty-four day occupation of the monastery by armed Menominee Indians and their supporters, January 2 through February 14, was by far the most significant of the three. It paralleled the Wounded Knee occupation in some respects. But there were many differences—the most notable was that the monastery was located on private property on the edge of the Menominee Reservation. This allowed governor Patrick Lucey to promptly cordon the area off with several hundred well equipped national guardsmen assisted by other state and federal law enforcement officials.

Founded as a novitiate by the Alexian Brothers, who decided to move to Chicago in 1968 for a more central location, the substantial premises were offered for sale for $1 million. Because of high maintenance costs and the out-of-the-way location, it had gone unsold for five years. With substantial assistance from out-of-state AIM members, a group of Menominees occupied the facility on January 2, 1975, saying they wanted it to serve the tribe for health and educational purposes. Menominee tribal leadership specifically disclaimed support of the takeover.[44]

After the seizure, Lucey replaced the local sheriff's force with National Guard troops from outside the immediate area to lessen hostility and tighten security. Armored vehicles were strategically stationed around the abbey, mainly to protect the occupiers from a large group of armed, angry whites from the area who wanted to settle the matter with vigilante justice.[45] Willis Merriman, Executive Secretary of the Wisconsin Council of Churches, commented, "I don't condone the takeover of the abbey but I don't think those of us who are Monday-morning quarterbacks should begin to evaluate the rightness or the wrongness of the situation. We have to weigh the takeover against the fact that a building as plush as that one had been allowed to stand vacant for five years in the midst of great poverty and need. . . ."[46] Clergy served as observers and helped raise bail money for those arrested when the siege ended. Marlon Brando and Father James Groppi of Milwaukee also were present to show support when it ended.

To bring an end to the tense situation and prevent bloodshed, the Alexian Brothers agreed to give the monastery to the Menominee tribe when the occupation was settled. They promised to maintain the $3,000-a-month cost of upkeep until the tribe could fully assume responsibility. After considering the cost of upkeep and the cost of converting the facility into a medical, vocational or child care center, as had been proposed, tribal leaders backed away from the deal and called it a white elephant. This decision caused sharp divisiveness, especially among young AIM supporters. In July, the Alexian Brothers cancelled their offer when they determined no positive use was being made of it.[47] On October 12, 1975, the novitiate house in the monastery complex was severely damaged by fire.

Bloodshed stemmed from the incident when AIM leaders John Waubanascum and Arlin Pamanet were killed in a gun battle with Menominee County Sheriff Kenneth Paddo Fish and his deputies early in 1976. Waubanascum was a decorated Vietnam marine who had received a bad conduct discharge. He had served with AIM in Chicago and helped set up AIM in Green Bay and also had been at Wounded Knee. Pamanet was his brother-in-law. Fish swore John's wife had come to the police department and told the dispatcher her husband had a gun and was going to shoot her. The officers testified that they were fired upon when they got to the house and had to fire back to protect themselves.

Shortly after the end of the Gresham occupation, AIM substantiated its claim of unconstitutional FBI infiltration of their organization. They proved that Douglass Durham, AIM's national security chief, was employed by the FBI to furnish regular reports on the plans and activities of AIM and its leadership.[49] At St. Paul, prosecutor Hurd and SAC Trimbach swore there was no "confidential source material in the FBI documents on Wounded Knee that revealed evidence of an invasion of the defense legal camp." But AIM leaders and attorneys were quite sure it was happening, and uncovered documents that proved Durham's relationship with the FBI. Durham was confronted with the official documents by Dennis Banks and Vernon Bellecourt at Des Moines, March 7, 1975. The meeting was witnessed by reverend John Adams, the United Methodist official who served at Wounded Knee. Durham admitted he was an under-cover agent when confronted with the evidence and disclosed he had been paid an average of $1,000 a month for two years by the FBI to deliver regular reports on AIM.[50]

Durham, a non-Indian who looked remarkably like one, grew up in Omaha but made his home in Des Moines. He had served in various aspects of law enforcement before becoming involved with the FBI and AIM. The FBI cleared his way into Wounded Knee on March 20, 1973, as a photographer for Pax Today, a now extinct underground newspaper. When Durham returned to Des Moines, he turned over the complete set of pictures he had taken within AIM's defense perimeter to the FBI and gave detailed reports of activities he had observed. The FBI suggested that he take the pictures to Harvey Major, the AIM chairman for Des Moines, and that Durham try to get close to the Des Moines AIM.[51] Within a month Durham was vice chairman of Des Moines AIM. Within ten months he was national chief of security for AIM and coordinator of the Wounded Knee Legal Defense/Offense office in St. Paul. Durham claimed, "If you wanted to see Dennis or Russell, you had to see me first. If you wanted to work as a volunteer in the offices of AIM or the Legal Defense/Offense Committee, it had to be cleared with me. If you wanted money, I controlled that also." At the time of his denouncement Durham commented favorably on AIM, "I saw AIM as a social protest organization that is not illegal and does not do anything wrong, and in fact. . . is morally right. The only thing I saw wrong about AIM was that it was infiltrated," he said. Durham also praised Dennis Banks for whom he had served as a private pilot and personal bodyguard, portraying him as a sincere leader who placed the interests of Indian people above personal self-interest.[52]

Durham changed his opinion of AIM. He became a regular on the John Birch Society lecture circuit where he consistently denounced AIM as a Communist front organization. As the sole witness before a closed session of the U. S. Senate Internal Security subcommittee in April, 1976, Durham pictured AIM as a terrorist, Communist-inspired-and-run group that "is dedicated to the overthrow of our Government." Mississippi Senator James Eastland, the committee head, said AIM's main activity was running an "underground railroad" to smuggle weapons and "warriors" between Canada and the United States. "They are in cooperation with Communist groups within the United States, Canada, Puerto Rico, and Cuba," Eastland maintained. Durham testified that the seizure of Anishinabe Park in Kenora, Ontario, Canada, during the summer of 1974 was planned by Dennis Banks who then flew in with Durham to arrange a peaceful settlement. In essence, Durham asserted, AIM was negotiating with AIM so Banks could build an image of a man of moderation and an effective peace maker.[53]

Jill and Harry Schafer, III, were also identified as FBI infiltrators of AIM. They got their start with AIM by organizing a demonstration in front of the FBI's New Orleans office to raise money during the Wounded Knee occupation. As a consequence, they were invited to Rapid City to set up an alternative fund raising operation for AIM. The Schafers clandestinely diverted the funds they received away from AIM. Late in the takeover, Schafer accepted an assignment to parachute food and supplies into Wounded Knee. He purposely delayed the flight until the confrontation ended. Schafer was with Pedro Bissonette when Bissonette was arrested by the FBI in Rapid City in April 1973.[54]

Pine Ridge Reservation experienced an increase in violence in 1973 and 1974,, but it did not compare to the epidemic of shootings and assaults during the first half of 1975. An officially reported six people were killed and sixty-seven assaulted through the first four months of the year.[55] Young Indian men on the reservation reported tremendous pressure to the point of physical intimidation was exerted upon those who did not support AIM. "Either you were for them or against them," confided a young Sioux Vietnam veteran. Actually, most Oglalas were neutral and mainly hoped for a restoration of law and order. Although Wilson's "goons" were not blameless, most impartial reservation Indians credit AIM with initiating much of the violence. Jim Lomax, who was then superintendent of schools in Pine Ridge, said anyone from the village of Pine Ridge who perpetrated any crime was assumed to be a goon whether he had anything to do with Wilson or not.[56] Private individuals, a number of whom were outsiders with lawless backgrounds, took advantage of the conflict between Wilson and AIM, using Wilson's goons as a convenient scapegoat.

Russell Means became involved in one fracas after another during this period. The murder of Martin Montileaux at a bar at Scenic, South Dakota, March 1, 1975, highlighted his misadventures. Montileaux, 28, accompanied by Marion Poor Bear and another couple, had spent the afternoon and evening in the bar. Means and about five followers arrived around midnight. Montileaux, who was known to be sympathetic toward AIM, at least during its early stages on the reservation, got into an argument with Means and his companion, Richard Marshall, one of the founders of the Oglala Sioux Civil Rights Organization. Whether the dispute concerned serious issues, such as the recent violent death of one of Montileaux's friends, or whether it merely represented a barroom disagreement involving individuals with too much to drink has not been determined. Montileaux, Means, and Marshall retired to the men's room and a loud thump followed by a shot was heard. Montileaux was found with a bullet wound in his neck and Marshall and Means were identified as the persons present. After they were arrested in a high speed chase, both were later charged with first degree murder. Montileaux died on March 7 but swore on his deathbed that Means did not shoot him.[57]

Marshall was convicted of the crime in April, 1976, and given a life sentence. His attorneys say the key to his conviction was the controversial testimony of Myrtle Poor Bear, who claimed she was Marshall's girlfriend and had heard him admit the shooting on at least two separate occasions. Myrtle Poor Bear signed an affidavit repudiating her testimony in May, 1977. In 1978, nevertheless, the South Dakota Supreme Court confirmed Marshall's conviction. An appeal based on post-conviction relief was also denied. The same court ruled against him in 1981 on the basis of this appeal.[58] The court ruled surprise witness Poor Bear's testimony was "not significant" and the jury had been given "overwhelming evidence" on which to base a conviction without her testimony.[59]

During 1975, unabated violence increased to the point of almost open warfare on the troubled reservation. A popular misconception prevails that almost all of the Oglalas were involved on one side or the other. Most still sustained neutrality and continued to prefer law and order. That desire would not be realized for at least another year. On March 9, William Steele, 58, a Wilson supporter, was shot and killed by gunfire from a passing vehicle. On March 20, Jerry Bear Shield was arrested, charged in the shooting, and released on bond. He was shot in the throat while he and his friend Stacey Cottier were walking at night. Cottier was found dead the next morning with several gunshot wounds in the back.[60] On March 25, Roger Pfersick charged Leonard Crow Dog with assault and battery with a chain saw blade and claimed he was otherwise brutalized at Crow Dog's residence. Two white women testified against Crow Dog. Prosecutor R. D. Hurd claimed Pfersick was beaten because they thought he was an informer. Crow Dog later was found guilty of the charges.[61]

By April, violence on the reservation had increased to such an intensity that April 20-26 was designated Law and Order Week. Jeannette Bissonette, Pedro's sister-in-law, was killed in her car parked on property belonging to Dick Wilson's brother, Jim, by an unknown sniper firing a high-powered rifle on March 25. The shooting took place near the village of Oglala—rapidly becoming an AIM stronghold.[62] On April 14, Louis Moves Camp, who had testified against AIM at St. Paul, was critically wounded by a rifle shot at Wanblee. That same night a parent-child center in Porcupine burned. New York Times reporter Grace Lichtensten wrote a front page report called, "Legacy of Wounded Knee: Hatred, Violence and Fear," on April 22. She referred to the reservation as "a caldron of violence." Unfortunately, it had not reached its boiling point yet.

AIM suffered another blow to its prestige when the Navajo Tribal Council, representing the nation's largest and most powerful tribe, declined to allow AIM's annual convention on their reservation. Instead, AIM met at Farmington, New Mexico, June 6-18, to face the problem of declining membership and support. It would represent the last national convention where most of the leaders and a large following would gather. The theme of the Farmington meeting involved objection to the sale of alcohol and drugs on reservations.[63] AIM also asked for a year's boycott of tourism on Indian reservations during the bicentennial with special emphasis on South Dakota.[64] Banks and several of his supporters returned to the Pine Ridge Reservation where he had rented a small log house and a campsite on the Fred Jumping Bull Place, three miles east of Oglala. There, he prepared to face trial at Custer, South Dakota, beginning June 23.

Russell Means, who had shunned the Farmington meeting, was shot in the stomach by BIA police on the Standing Rock Reservation in North Dakota on June 7, 1975. The police report said Means and some companions were involved in an incident at a bar in Fort Yates. Two white men were assaulted and police were called. When they tried to arrest one of Means's group, an altercation broke out and Means was shot in the stomach. He was hospitalized in good condition. The next day, a fire heavily damaged a small liquor store in Cannonball, North Dakota. The store was owned by the wife of the policeman who shot Means. A fourteen year old boy was killed in the fire, which was reportedly caused by arson. Federal charges were filed against Means for resisting and interfering with a Federal Officer and a separate complaint charged Means with assault in the bar incident.[65]

Leonard Crow Dog, Carter Camp, and Stan Holder were tried at Cedar Rapids, Iowa, during this same period. Prosecutor Hurd decided to keep the case simple and as non-political as possible by lodging one specific charge against the three—the illegal harassment and detention of postal inspectors at Wounded Knee, March, 1973. They were found guilty. Banks called for as large a support group as possible to be at Cedar Rapids for sentencing on June 27.[66]

Three shooting deaths involving AIM and the FBI on June 26 catapulted the Pine Ridge Reservation back into the national headlines. This violent confrontation capped the series of shootings, burnings, and robberies that had plagued the reservation.

Informed sources acknowledge no one group held a monopoly on antisocial activity, but much of it stemmed from three well known AIM centers: Crow Dog's Paradise on the Rosebud Reservation, Selo Black Crow's spiritual camp near Wanblee, and Dennis Banks's "West Coast" AIM encampment near Oglala. Of the three, law enforcement officials considered the Banks group the most dangerous.[67] The FBI regarded the Oglala camp as an advanced field training base for young AIM "dog soldiers." Antagonism toward the FBI had been mounting daily. Of the various law enforcement agencies at Pine Ridge, the FBI easily was the most despised and feared by most reservation inhabitants. Some believed the FBI was spoiling for revenge after their embarrassment at Wounded Knee, something akin to the Seventh Cavalry in 1890. This suspicion remains unconvincing. An objective observer would have to consider the bitter atmosphere of fear, hatred, and intimidation on the reservation that was provoked by individuals and groups other than the much disliked FBI. In reality, the FBI represented the last resort for protection of lives and property at Pine Ridge, rather than the AIM groups who maintained they were dedicated to that purpose and the government posed the principal threat. Whether the FBI always used sound judgment in carrying out their responsibilities might well be questioned, though.

The tragedy at Oglala was precipitated on June 23 by an incident at the Orville Schwarting ranch near Batesland on Pine Ridge Reservation. The Schwartings needed some help to brand cattle. Orville's son, Jerry, an agriculture student at the University of Nebraska, contacted Hobart Horse, a young Oglala who had worked for them so often he was considered almost part of the family. Horse said he could enlist three others to help. Schwarting and Robert Dunsmore, 14, the son of a woman married to a hired hand, were taken captive at gun point by Horse and his associates—Herman Thunder Hawk, Teddy Pourier, and Jimmy Eagle, Gladys Bissonette's grandson, after the two had taken them back to the home of Pourier. They were held overnight and were robbed, threatened, and beaten. Dunsmore was undressed and kept away from Schwarting. Pourier slashed Schwarting on the arm with a pocket knife and both Dunsmore and Schwarting had a gun fired over their heads repeatedly. When the two were released, Schwarting's sister reported the incident to authorities in Pine Ridge.[68] It was not a case of an overnight drinking session among old friends that got out of hand and resulted in the theft of a pair of cowboy boots, as AIM advocates suggest.[69] Authorities believe it was a deliberate ploy to lure reservation law enforcement into a confrontation.

Warrants for the arrest of the four involved in the kidnapping were issued by the FBI. Pourier was arrested on June 25 on charges of assault with a deadly weapon. That afternoon, FBI agents Ronald Williams, 27, and Jack Coler, 28, accompanied by BIA police officers Robert Ecoffey and Glen Little Bird, searched the White Clay area for the other suspects, especially Jimmy Eagle. Their investigation led them to the Jumping Bull area and the home of AIM supporter Wallace "June" Little, less than a quarter of a mile from the Jumping Bull residence. They were told none of the suspects were there and a search of the house proved negative. The officers said they planned to continue the investigation in the Oglala area the next day—a bad mistake. On the way back to Pine Ridge they apprehended three youths on the road from Oglala to the AIM camp and took them back to Pine Ridge. None of them were among the wanted suspects and they were released that evening.[70]

Ecoffey, a Pine Ridge native, was scheduled to accompany Coler and Williams the next day. They had promised to return to the Jumping Bull area, and sensing their impatience, the young Oglala reminded them that the Jumping Bull place was a known AIM stronghold and should be approached with extreme caution and security. Williams had been stationed in Rapid City for two years, so he should have been fairly well acquainted with the situation, although Ecoffey suggests Williams spent most of his time in Rapid City and was not as familiar with the reservation as one might assume. A bachelor of medium build and clean-cut good looks, Williams was universally liked and respected by those with whom he worked. Several have commented that he seemed destined for a top leadership role in the FBI. Coler, SWAT trained and aggressive, had been assigned to Rapid City from Colorado Springs on a sixty-day assignment just the month before. He had left his wife and two small children in Colorado. Both agents grew up in the Los Angeles area.

Williams showed up at Pine Ridge, but Coler must have proceeded directly to Oglala and began investigating. Ecoffey and his partner proceeded to Batesland to gather evidence there. Williams must have joined forces with Coler in the Oglala area. They presumably pursued a van which they thought contained Jimmy Eagle and/or Leonard Peltier, who was on the FBI's wanted list. Coler led the way and Williams backed him. According to Ecoffey, the occupants of the van were radioing ahead to the camp to alert them that they were being pursued. Williams was the only voice heard over the FBI frequency as they approached the camp. Coler apparently did not make a transmission during the last half hour of his life, possibly because he thought his calls would be monitored by the fugitives or their allies.

When the van stopped at a Y fork just south of the Jumping Bull residence at approximately 11:50 a.m., Coler began to receive fire from the high ground to the east and from the occupants of the van.[71] Frantic messages from Williams requesting immediate help were received by the FBI and BIA police in the area. "It looks like they're going to shoot at us," Williams reported, followed by, "We have been hit," and, "hurry and give us some help with fire cover or we will be killed."[72] Upon receiving fire, Coler apparently got out of his car, took his rifle out of the trunk, and crouched behind it. Caught in a crossfire, Coler suffered a bullet wound that all but tore off his right arm at the elbow. Williams, wounded in his foot and his left side, ran over to Coler, stripped off his shirt and attempted to fix a tourniquet on his dying companion. During this process, the Indians must have closed in around the two wounded agents. According to the FBI, Williams threw down his gun and told the Indians Coler needed medical help immediately.

When it became apparent that they planned to shoot him, Williams begged for mercy, but was shot in the head at very close range with an AR-15 rifle. The bullet first went through his hand, which he was apparently using to ward off the weapon.[73] Coler also was shot in the head. Rather than being riddled by bullets as early media reports indicated, both agents received only three bullet wounds; but their damage was so extensive it would be easy to assume there were more.[74]

Soon a large force consisting of FBI, Marshals, BIA tribal police, and South Dakota State Patrol surrounded the area and engaged the defenders in a five-hour shootout. Immediately, an intense dispute over jurisdictional rights broke out between the BIA forces, led by Superintendent Kendall Cumming, and the FBI. The BIA police were ready to assault the Jumping Bull encampment and were frustrated almost to the point of physically confronting the FBI agents who stopped them.[75] More than likely few, if any, of the defenders would have survived an onslaught by the BIA police. A frontal assault in relatively open country against a well armed force who had already demonstrated deadly shooting expertise, on the other hand, would have proven costly to the attackers as well. BIA police officer Duane Brewer, who was located on high ground above the Jumping Bull place reported their group spotted thirteen defenders through field glasses when they successfully broke out.

In spite of the murder of two colleagues, again the FBI showed professional restraint and successfully avoided a much bloodier incident that might have rivaled Wounded Knee 1890. How all but one of the occupants of the camp could escape cleanly in broad daylight without some deliberate police negligence remains a nagging question. Attorney General Janklow, who was on the scene, charged that Cumming's men deliberately allowed the AIM force to slip away into the surrounding hills after an ultimatum was given that the authorities would attack by 5:00 p.m. BIA police report that one of their leaders, who resigned shortly after the shootout, was responsible.[77]

Joseph Bedell Stuntz, 23, originally Joe George of the Lapwai Agency near Coeur d'Alene, Idaho, did not escape. Wearing Coler's fatigue jacket, which he had taken from the dead agent's car trunk, Stuntz was shot and killed around 2:30 p.m. He was just outside the door of the green tarpaper shack located beside the Jumping Bull residence. The elderly Jumping Bulls were away selling their cattle at Gordon. Stuntz was one of three Indian children adopted by Dr. and Mrs. E. C. Stuntz of Monticello, Indiana. Stuntz a psychiatrist, had later separated from his wife. Joe Stuntz graduated from the Onarga Military School, Onarga, Illinois, and attended the Institute of American Indian Art at Santa Fe, New Mexico. He married Ida Charles of Port Angeles, Washington, a friend of Peltier's. She had returned to the Seattle area with their two children.[78]

Stuntz was charged with assault and battery and malicious destruction of property in Gordon on October 25, 1974. He was sentenced to two concurrent thirty-day terms in the Sheridan County jail and two years probation in January, 1975. One of the seven terms of probation was "the defendant will possess and use no firearms."[79] Stuntz was serving as Banks's chauffeur and bodyguard at Oglala and was with the group in the van pursued by Coler and Williams.[80] Dennis King, Sheridan County Prosecuting Attorney in 1975, said he was surprised to learn Stuntz had been killed because he had impressed King as a "nice, well-spoken young man." Stuntz had confided to King that he was eager to return to the West Coast in order to avoid further trouble.[81]

AIM leader John Trudell issued a statement that the FBI agents "attempt to play cowboys and Indians backfired and they got what they had coming." Public opinion, however, generally condemned the militants.[82] Methodist Bishop James Armstrong, bishop of the Dakotas area, who had been sympathetic toward AIM in 1973, issued a statement saying the killing of the two FBI agents could not be viewed as anything other than murder, despite "just grievances American Indians have against the United States government." Both Indians and whites, said the bishop, "must distinguish between legitimate expression of social protest and violent terrorism."[83] The violence at Oglala and other incidents of like nature precipitated a severe backlash of public opinion against AIM and Indian activism in general.

The FBI's attitude definitely changed after the two murders. They were not about to overlook the death of two of their own. Although their quarry had temporarily eluded them, it was common knowledge on the reservation that the Jumping Bull group was still in the area. Over 150 specially equipped agents, dressed in military fatigues, and carrying M-16 rifles, employed helicopters, jeeps, dogs, and armored personnel carriers to pursue the suspects. Many Pine Ridge residents complained the FBI certainly did not react like that when Indians were being murdered on an almost weekly basis.

In spite of complaints from reservation inhabitants that their civil rights were being violated and a critical report from an investigator from the U. S. Commission on Civil Rights, the FBI bored ahead.[84] Their efforts were rewarded by a commando-type raid at the Al Running place near Crow Dog's Paradise on September 5. one of the prime suspects, Darelle "Dino" Butler, a Los Angeles based AIM leader and a convicted felon, was arrested while brandishing a revolver. His Eskimo wife, Nilock, also known as Kelly Jean McCormick, at one time an aspiring Hollywood actress, was detained, too. In addition to several others, Anna Mae Aquash, the most visible woman in the AIM organization, was apprehended emerging from a tent that contained an M-1 carbine with the serial number obliterated, three hand grenades, and bundles of dynamite.[85]

Four others who had been at the shootout at Oglala—Bob Robideau, Mike Anderson, Norman Charles, and Jean Bordeaux—and Kamook Banks were arrested when their station wagon, containing dynamite and grenades, exploded on the Kansas Turnpike on September 10. Among the badly damaged ruins were Coler's .308 rifle and an AR-15 rifle the government claimed was the weapon used in the murder of Coler and Williams.[86] Robideau, a friend of Butler's and a cousin of Leonard Peltier; Butler; Jimmy Eagle; and Peltier were indicted by a Federal Grand Jury in Rapid City in November 1975.[87]

Robideau and Butler were tried together in Cedar Rapids, Iowa, for "aiding and abetting" in the two murders. The FBI produced documents from the Rapid City grand jury which they said proved that Peltier had actually shot the agents. Although the prosecution presented numerous witnesses and much circumstantial evidence, the large and proficient defense team, headed by Kunstler, won a jury acquittal on July 16, 1976. The jury deliberated for five days and twice reported they were deadlocked before the decision was announced. The entire defense team burst into tears and embraced each other when the verdict was rendered.[88] Given the defeat at Cedar Rapids, the Justice Department dropped its case against Jimmy Eagle and concentrated on Peltier.

Based upon eyewitness testimony, ballistics reports, and circumstantial evidence, the government was convinced Peltier pulled the trigger on Coler and Williams.[89] Part Chippewa and part Sioux, Peltier was born September 12, 1944, on the Turtle Mountain Reservation in North Dakota. He experienced a difficult childhood in North Dakota and Montana, featuring numerous scrapes with the law, before moving to Oakland, California, in the late 1950s. By 1965, Peltier moved to Seattle, where he was part owner of an auto body repair shop and helped counsel Indian alcoholics. Peltier became active in the Washington State fishing rights struggles and participated in the occupation of Fort Lawton near Seattle. He moved to Milwaukee and helped lead the Trail of Broken Treaties and the Alexian Novitiate takeover. Peltier did not participate in the Wounded Knee occupation because he was in a Milwaukee jail awaiting trial for placing a revolver to the head of an off-duty police officer in a Milwaukee bar and pulling the trigger. The weapon failed, but Peltier was charged with attempted murder. He was later declared innocent because he swore he knew the gun would not work. Instead of reporting for his pre-trial hearing on the attempted murder charge, Peltier went underground in July, 1973, and headed for South Dakota.[90] Peltier became one of Banks's bodyguards and developed a reputation as the AIM "enforcer" on the reservation.[91]

Based upon FBI informant information, it was reported that Banks and Peltier reunited after the Oglala shootout and Banks's flight from his conviction at Custer. They were thought to be travelling through Oregon in November in a motor home owned by Marlon Brando. Oregon State Patrolmen stopped this vehicle and a station wagon travelling east near Ontario, Oregon, the night of November 4, 1975. They arrested the two men in the station wagon, Kenneth Loudhawk and Russell Rednor. Kamook Banks and Anna Mae Aquash, who were in the van, also surrendered. Unexpectedly, the van sped off. A man said to be Peltier, who had also been arrested, ran off, firing at the patrolmen as he fled. The van was found a short distance down the road, but the driver, allegedly Dennis Banks, had escaped. The vehicles were reported to have contained seven boxes of dynamite, detonation equipment, nine hand grenades, and fourteen firearms, including Coler's service revolver in a brown paper bag carrying Peltier's thumbprint.[92]

Again, based upon informants's tips, the FBI soon located Peltier and Banks. Peltier fled to Canada and was arrested at Smallboy's spiritual camp near Hinton, Alberta, in February 1976. Frank Black Horse, another AIM fugitive, was also arrested. Black Horse, said by some AIM insiders to really be an Italian from Cleveland, was wanted in connection with the shooting of agent Fitzgerald during the Wounded Knee siege.[93] Canadian officials held Peltier in solitary confinement in British Columbia while furtive extradition negotiations between the Unites States and Canada transpired. Two affidavits signed by Myrtle Poor Bear in February and March were involved in the proceedings. Poor Bear claimed she had been living with Peltier on the Jumping Bull ranch since late May, 1975. She said she heard plans to kill FBI or BIA officers and saw Peltier shoot the agents.[94] Peltier said he had never heard of Myrtle Poor Bear and she later refuted her charges against him. In spite of the significance placed upon the Poor Bear affidavits by Peltier's defenders, it is crucial to understand that the Canadian Minister of Justice had evidence of the falsity of those documents before him when he upheld the Peltier extradition order.[95] Peltier's extradition evoked a storm of protest in Canada, nevertheless, and many Canadians remain convinced it was wrong.[97]

Peltier was found guilty on two counts of first degree murder by a jury at Fargo, North Dakota, on April 18, 1977. In spite of the importance of the case, the jury took only ten hours to reach a verdict. The government entered some fifty exhibits of evidence against Peltier that overrode Poor Bear's complete turn around.[98] She testified for the defense and claimed on the witness stand she had been intimidated by the FBI, had not witnessed any wrongdoing by Peltier, and had never seen him until the trial. She swore the FBI had used the death of AIM activist Anna Mae Aquash to intimidate her into testifying against Peltier. On at least three occasions Poor Bear's testimony was interrupted by mental disturbances. Judge Paul Benson, a Nixon appointee who had replaced Judge Nichol when he disqualified himself from the case, finally ruled her testimony irrelevant because she was obviously afraid and disturbed.[99]

Perhaps the most damning testimony was presented by Mike Anderson, a young Navajo. He testified that he observed the FBI chase of Peltier's van on to the Jumping Bull property; saw Peltier, Stuntz, and Norman Charles emerge from the van; saw Peltier in possession of an AR-15 rifle and heard shooting.[100] Thomas Naguchi, the well-known Los Angeles pathologist, was brought in to explain the victims's wounds and to match up a .223 shell casing, supposed to have been recovered from the trunk of Coler's car, with the weapon Peltier allegedly used.[101] The prosecution also introduced statements from four inmates in the Pennington County jail in Rapid City. They testified they heard Jimmy Eagle describe the killings when he was incarcerated with them. They said Eagle bragged he was an eyewitness. Eagle's version was that the agents were ambushed and one was hit. The other threw down his gun and pleaded for his life but was shot by Peltier at close range.[102] Eagle insisted the FBI fabricated this story and one of the four informants later recanted.

Other controversies abound. An FBI agent testified he spotted Peltier at the crime scene at seven hundred yards through the seven power telescopic sight on his rifle. The defense swore they had run tests proving it was physically impossible to verify an identification at that distance with that telescopic sight. The FBI also falsified ballistic information concerning shell casings found on the site according to the defense.[103] Many inside the Peltier defense camp urged that Anderson should be brought back to the stand as a defense witness. Elliott Taikeff, the New York lawyer who served as chief defense attorney in the absence of Kunstler, declined to bring Anderson back, suggesting he could ruin the case for Peltier. Anderson died in an automobile accident in New Mexico a year later.

Witnesses irrefutably identified as witnesses at the scene refused to testify for the government. Their reluctance may have stemmed from intimidation or a desire to protect Indians from the law or both. Two Indian women thought to have witnessed those present at the scene of the murder preferred prison terms in lieu of cooperating with authorities. Legal aide worker Joanna LeDeaux, a friend of Peltier's, was sent in to negotiate and apparently observed Butler, Robideau, and Peltier at the cars where the dead agents were found. Rather than testify, LeDeaux spent eight months in federal prison, giving birth to a child during her stay. The Jumping Bull's granddaughter, Angie Long Visitor, who was living in the green tar-paper shack at the time of the shootout, testified at the grand jury trial only after spending three months in jail. She then refused to cooperate at the trial of Robideau and Butler in Cedar Rapids. Long Visitor was arrested in January, 1977, as a material witness in the Peltier trial. Myrtle Poor Bear did not appear as a prosecution witness in either trial.

Peltier received two consecutive life sentences. The Eighth Circuit Court of Appeals refused to grant an appeal on April 12, 1978. On March 5, 1979, the United States Supreme Court declined to accept the Peltier case for review. He remains in a federal penitentiary, where he will stay at least until the year 2015 when he first will become eligible for parole.

Peltier's conviction remains somewhat of a cause celebre with AIM and its liberal supporters as exemplified by Peter Matthiessen's attempt to vindicate him in his book, In the Spirit of Crazy Horse. Matthiessen, New York blueblood, Yale graduate, cofounder of the Paris Review, and highly regarded author of some fourteen other fiction and non-fiction works, wrote a tremendously detailed book based upon court records,

FBI files, and personal interviews in an attempt to demonstrate Peltier's innocence. Qualified reviewers were not convinced. Reviewing the book in the <u>New York Times Book Review</u> magazine, Alan Dershowitz, respected professor of criminal law at Harvard Law School, said, "He is utterly unconvincing—indeed embarrassingly sophomoric—when he pleads the legal innocence of individual Indian Criminals. . . Mr Matthiessen not only fails to convince; he inadvertently makes a strong case for Mr. Peltier's guilt."[104] Tim Giago, editor of Pine Ridge's <u>Lakota Times</u>, wrote a critical review beginning, "Matthiessen's limited knowledge of the Pine Ridge Reservation and its residents is apparent throughout the book."[105] On May 13, 1983, Governor Janklow filed a libel suit against Matthiessen and his publisher, Viking Press, for repeating allegations concerning the rape of Jancita Eagle Deer and other criticisms. "There comes a time when you don't have to take this even if you're a public official," said Janklow.[106] His suit was later denied.

Dennis Banks was the source of many charges against Janklow. As attorney general, Janklow personally led the prosecution of Banks at Custer in August 1975. Although he had lawyers available, Banks chose to act as his own attorney much of the time. He said the Custer confrontation constituted a police riot caused by police provocateurs. But Janklow presented strong evidence to the contrary, including pictures made by both regular media representatives and amateur photographers at the scene. Banks was speedily convicted on arson and riot charges.[107] Because he owned a prior criminal record, his conviction meant a mandatory prison sentence in South Dakota. He fled the state as a "political exile" before sentence could be pronounced. His attorney said there was "every possibility that Banks would be killed in prison."[108] Banks was arrested January, 1976, on an informant's tip. He was at the home of Lehman Brightman, Director of the Native American Program at Contra Costa Junior College.

Yet another murder, which closely followed Banks's apprehension, contributed to the rapid disintegration of AIM. Conceded by all to be a heavily male dominated group, AIM saw one woman, Anna Mae Aquash, emerge as a significant leader. Her tragic demise remains unresolved and casts a pall upon both AIM and the FBI. Born Anna Mae Pictou at Shubenacadie on the Micmac Reserve in Nova Scotia in 1945. She moved to Boston in 1963 and became a teacher's aide. After her first marriage ended in 1968, Anna Mae linked up with Nogeeshik Aquash, an activist Chippewa artist from Ontario, Canada.[109] She became involved with the Boston Indian Center and helped plan and participated in the demonstration at <u>Mayflower II</u> on Thanksgiving Day, 1970. There she met Russell Means and assorted AIM leaders. Anna Mae and others from the Boston Indian Council joined the occupation of the BIA building in Washington. When Wounded Knee erupted, she left her two children with her sister and departed with Nogeeshik for South Dakota. They were married in a traditional Sioux ceremony at Wounded Knee.

During the Wounded Knee trials at St. Paul, Anna Mae entered into an intimate relationship with Dennis Banks. She hoped to emerge as Banks's top lieutenant and worked diligently and effectively for AIM, especially in organizational and fund raising efforts in the Los Angeles area.[110] Anna Mae developed a reputation as Banks's "West Coast Woman." She told friends in Canada if Banks were convicted at St. Paul, he might exile himself, and she was hoping to accompany him if it happened. Spring, 1975, Banks informed Anna Mae that their relationship was over. He was married to an Oglala Sioux, and did not want to sever that important political tie to the reservation which provided the strongest support for AIM. Anna Mae had also worked closely with Douglass Durham at St. Paul, Los Angeles, and during the Menominee takeover. Possibly the same documents that revealed Durham's identity as an FBI informant also unveiled damaging evidence against Anna Mae. No proof exists, but she seemed to suddenly lose her status in AIM after Durham's exposure. Anna Mae returned to Pine Ridge and lived in a small trailer house near the Jumping Bull camp. She was one the first ones questioned in the March, 1975, shooting death of Jeannette Bissonette, casting suspicion she was cooperating with the government. At the AIM convention at Farmington Anna Mae was rumored to be an FBI informer and shunned. She left the convention "confused and mixed up."

Although discredited by many, Anna Mae continued her work with AIM at Pine Ridge. She was attending the trial of Camp, Crow Dog, and Holder when the shootout happened.[111] She returned to Pine Ridge and attended the Sun Dance ceremony in late July at Crow Dog's Paradise. There she again was accused of being an informer by Crow Dog and her friend Peltier and was ordered to leave.[112] After her arrest at the Al Running place in September she was taken to Pierre, South Dakota, where she underwent intensive interrogation concerning the murder of the two FBI agents and the whereabouts of Peltier, Robideau, Black Horse, and Banks. Because it was her first offense, she was released on $500 bail, which seemed suspiciously light to AIM observers. She said the FBI had threatened her life if she did not cooperate.

On November 14, Anna Mae and Kamook Banks were detained in the Ontario, Oregon, van incident. She was extradited to South Dakota to face charges stemming from the September arrest. Again, seemingly too easily, she fled her motel room and became a fugitive, further fueling rumors she was an informant. Apparently someone at the Washington State encampment where the motor home started its trip must have informed the FBI. Many suspected Anna Mae had been allowed to escape because she would lead the FBI to Peltier and Banks. In early December, Anna Mae was taken from Denver to Rapid City for intensive questioning by AIM leaders. She was released and went to the West Coast where she continued to work for AIM. On December 20, she called her friend Paula Giese in Minneapolis and said she would be there by January. She also told Giese she had information about events on the West Coast that would interest her. When Banks was arrested at the home of Lehman Brightman on an informer's tip, the FBI did not press charges against Brightman in order to cover the source of their information. In the Oregon van arrests, moreover, the FBI released a document showing there were two informants in the case but destroyed the confiscated dynamite before the trial in order to protect them.[113] All charges were dismissed on May 20, 1983, on the grounds of prejudicial delay by the government.[114]

Anna Mae never made it to St. Paul. Her partially decomposed body was found February 24, 1976, at the bottom of a steep embankment by Roger Amiotte on his ranch near Wanblee. The ten law enforcement officials who investigated the scene could find no identification but determined she had been thrown down the embankment. Her clothing was intact and there were no apparent signs of foul play. Dr. W. O. Brown conducted the autopsy and concluded she had died of exposure. His tests revealed that the woman had engaged in sexual intercourse shortly before death, but there was no indication she had been attacked. Because no one could identify the body, Brown cut off the hands at the wrists and turned them over to the FBI for identification. Later, critics would make much ado over nothing concerning the severed hands. Brown's "heinous" act represented standard procedure in such cases according to knowledgeable law enforcement experts.[115] With neither a death certificate nor a burial permit, the body was buried in a pauper's grave near Pine Ridge.

On March 3, the FBI received positive identification that the corpse was Anna Mae Pictou Aquash and filed a request to exhume the body for a second autopsy. Their intention was to take X-rays since Brown had not done so. On March 11, Judge Bogue ordered the exhumation and autopsy. Dr. Garry Peterson, an expert pathologist from Minneapolis, was brought in by the WKLDOC. Peterson soon determined that death was caused by a .38 caliber bullet wound in the head. Signs of powder burns on her neck indicated close range. Peterson further said the condition of the body indicated she probably had been dead three weeks or more before she was found. Brown's contract was cancelled.[116]

The details of Aquash's death loosed a storm of rumors and accusations about who pulled the trigger on her. WKLDOC lawyers charged the FBI was perpetrating a cover-up either to hide its own involvement or to protect the murderer. Some of Aquash's friends, including Frank Star, a tribal official, claimed she was killed by one of the reservation goon squad because of her AIM affiliation. Her death did occur close to the violent weekend of January 31. A clash assumed to be between Wilson forces and AIM supporters centered around Wanblee, an anti-Wilson stronghold, led to the shooting death of Byron DeSersa, the son of AIM's press secretary during the early stages of the Wounded Knee occupation.[117]

Anna Mae Tanequodle, a friend of Aquash's, alleged in Oklahoma City that Aquash was eliminated by AIM because she was an FBI informer.[118] Norman Zigrossi, FBI, Rapid City, denied Tanequodle's formal charge.[119] Protection of informants has always been standard procedure with the FBI. A dead informant does not encourage others to cooperate, and, like it or not, informants play a crucial role in law enforcement at all levels. Tanequodle later denied she made the accusation. Zigrossi became SAC of the San Diego office and was honored as 1982 law enforcement officer of the year by the Association of Federal Investigators. In an interview on that occasion, Zigrossi said his three-year investigation of the slaying of Coler and Williams haunted him. "It's a part of my life I try to black out," he said. A popular theory on Pine Ridge, though never proven, was that Aquash was being groomed by the FBI to play the role as a key witness against the killers of Coler and Williams. Bob Ecoffey, the BIA police officer in charge of the case at the time, however, insists Anna Mae was not an FBI informant.[120]

Because it was commonly acknowledged that AIM leadership had openly denounced Anna Mae as an informant on a number of occasions, her death proved awkward for them to explain. During the trial of Butler and Robideau, John Trudell revealed that in California Dennis Banks told him on February 24 or 25, 1976, that Anna Mae was the woman who had been shot in South Dakota. Banks later insisted the dates were confused. But Trudell remained equally sure his statement came "two or three days" after her discovery.

None of the AIM leaders showed up for the wake and funeral following her identification. Vernon Bellecourt phoned from Minneapolis, indicating he would come but did not. The Means and their supporters declined to participate though they were nearby on the reservation. Banks, in California fighting extradition to South Dakota, delayed several days before he declared the day of Anna Mae's funeral a national Indian day of mourning. Reportedly, he had initiated an investigation and called it off, fearing AIM involvement might surface.[122] AIM's later investigation concluded, "It wasn't our people who killed her."[123] Undoubtedly AIM lost a great deal of credibility because of the Aquash murder, whether they were responsible or not. Indian women, who were uneasy with AIM's chauvinistic approach from the outset, especially questioned this latest act of violence. "Anna Mae's death did not destroy AIM. What it did was show that AIM was dead," said Paula Giese.[124] AIM supporters disagree with Giese because the organization continued to function. Its time, however, had come and gone. Like a cut flower, the group's vitality had ended.

The only AIM backer called to give testimony before the grand jury investigating the Aquash shooting was Selo Black Crow. A spiritual leader from Wanblee, he had housed a number of outsiders at his camp, including young Charles Abourezk, the Senator's son. Black Crow had had his share of difficulties with the FBI since the death of Coler and Williams, including a commando-type raid on his camp.[125] The government's theory on Black Crow is that he did not actually pull the trigger, but he may well know who did.[126] Suspicion of Black Crow was increased because his Caucasian wife had called Wanblee authorities on February 17, 1976, from Rapid City telling them of a hit-and-run accident that occurred where Anna Mae's body was finally discovered on February 24. Some claim that Anna Mae's executors were becoming worried that the body would not be found and no example would be set for other potential informers. This theory holds that the FBI, on the other hand, buried her before identification for the opposite reason. Black Crow was not charged and the case is still under investigation. An intelligent young Oglala student remarked recently that it is always a mystery to reservation residents how they seem to know all about local crimes, but law enforcement officials hardly ever are capable of resolving them.

Heroes or
Freebooters?

A fter the traumatic experiences of 1975, AIM as an organization evolved into a more sectional entity. Arrests, trials, convictions, and internal dissent posed problems. But AIM also began to suffer a noticeable white backlash because of its growing reputation for violence and anarchy. Banks continued to speak from California as if he were representing the national group, much to the irritation of the other AIM leaders. Means stayed in South Dakota and organized a separate group called Dakota AIM. The Bellecourts, the only two top leaders not entangled with the law in one way or another for any length of time after Wounded Knee, were content to build a power base in Minnesota.

Whether AIM's ventures into confrontation politics had brought substantial benefits for the American Indian remained controversial. A leading college history textbook summarized AIM's decline after Wounded Knee, "Such episodes alienated the Nixon Administration, which abandoned the reform effort begun so promisingly in 1970. Random AIM terrorism also antagonized many Indians, not only tribal leaders whose position was threatened by the militants, but men like Vine Deloria, Jr. , who wrote, 'When the media collide with a social movement its chief contribution seems to be the simplification of issues and creation of instant personalities. '"[1] The text concluded that by 1975 AIM's urban orientation and violent tactics had failed to win the support of reservation Indians and was in decline.[2] AIM spokesmen, in an effort to make the movement more palliative, announced that the main goal of AIM was now the spiritual reawakening of the Indian people, stressing the return to the Sacred Pipe.[3]

Pine Ridge Reservation proved an effective operational base for Means. He had a number of close relatives and other supporters there. They were willing to back him in the continuing struggle against the Wilson administration. The Sioux had also been involved in a long treaty rights struggle over the Black Hills and were in a strategic location to participate in the growing debate over the exploitation of mineral resources, both on and off the reservation, that had been accentuated by the world energy crisis. Means needed to stay in South Dakota, too, to clear a lengthy list of criminal charges.

Means's trials and tribulations mounted in an almost unbelievable manner during the post-Wounded Knee period. He was shot twice, stabbed once, and suffered serious injuries on several other occasions.[4] Means received thirty days in prison in November, 1975, for his part in a brawl at the Mission, South Dakota Country Club, June 22, 1974[5] After the brawl Means and his followers retreated to the Rosebud Reservation and refused to surrender, claiming they were protected by reservation tribal sovereignty. An FBI command post was set up by Trimbach at Mission, but no aggressive action was taken because of the volatile situation. When a federal judge ruled against the sovereignty claim, Means surrendered. Because of head injuries from being struck by a pool cue Means missed the 1974 Sun Dance. After the Scenic bar death of Martin Montileaux, Means was wounded at Fort Yates. In late July, 1975, a bullet or a thrown bottle shattered the window of a car in which Means was riding, but Means escaped with minor cuts.

On January 1, 1976, Means was handed a four-year prison sentence for his role in the courthouse battle at Sioux Falls in 1974. The sentence was appealed and Means was released on bail with some nine different conditions, including no direct participation in AIM activities. Means and a companion were deliberately but superficially wounded at the Yankton Sioux Reservation on May 5, 1976. They were shot by two of the Yankton Seven, a group of activists charged in the 1975 occupation of the Wagner pork plant.[6]

Means recovered enough to enable him to lead the AIM protest over the centennial celebration of the Battle of the Little Big Horn. He objected to the way the government was portraying the Indian role and insisted upon a Sioux celebration of the battle, planned and controlled by Indians only. The Indians were allowed to celebrate their version of the battle on June 26.[7]

Most of the rest of Means's summer was taken up by trials. A jury acquitted Means on the Montileaux murder charge in August. Taking Banks's fate into account, Means decided to avoid trial on the Custer riot charges and plea bargained. In return for a guilty plea to a misdemeanor assault charge, the state dismissed all other pending allegations against him. Means was sentenced to thirty days in jail and a $100 fine.

After his release, Means continued his activist leadership role in South Dakota AIM, which prompted Attorney General Janklow to request his bail on the Sioux Falls case be revoked.[8] In September, 1977, the South Dakota Supreme Court revoked Means's bail, but he was released to await a decision on his appeal of the Sioux Falls charges. That appeal was denied and Means was ordered to begin his four-year sentence at the South Dakota State Penitentiary in August.

During the interim, Means participated in the Logest Walk, a demonstration march conceived by the exiled Dennis Banks. When the group arrived in Washington, it was reported that they kept Vice President Mondale waiting for an hour for a scheduled meeting. They also distributed a leaflet that charged their erstwhile supporter, Senator Edward Kennedy, with sponsoring a bill that would deprive Indians of their treaty rights. Means and Kennedy got into a heated debate. Means charged that Kennedy's bill would turn reservations into "state parks or national parks."[9] Wilcomb Washburn of the Smithsonian Institute called the Longest Walk an Indian media play by a radical minority that was attempting to usurp the power of duly elected tribal governments. Washburn said it was the radicals who had undermined tribal sovereignty.[10]

Imprisonment provided a new publicity vehicle for Means. He immediately embarked upon a thirty-six day spiritual fast intended to expose the racism and injustice of the South Dakota judicial system. On September 16, just before a rally for Means was supposed to get underway in Sioux Falls, he was superficially stabbed in the chest by another inmate. Early that afternoon, he was well enough to hold a press conference with Marlon Brando. No charges were filed against his assailant. Two months later, Senator Abourezk provided a work release position for Means. After serving a total of a year, he was released on parole in July, 1979.

Means resumed his role as an advocate for Native American rights and became especially involved in the mutual concern of whites and Indians in South Dakota for environmental protection.[11] A combination of Indians and whites formed the Black Hills Alliance to defend the region against the dangers to the environment of irresponsible mining, manufacturing, water use, and other exploitation. A Dakota AIM auxiliary group called Women of all Red Nations (WARN), dominated by Means's female relatives, was especially vocal about the danger from multi-national energy corporations.[12] Lorelie Means, wife of Ted Means, charged in March, 1980, that contaminated water from uranium mining was causing cancer, miscarriages, and birth defects on the Pine Ridge Reservation.[13] She requested that the government declare the reservation a disaster area. Subsequent investigation has not substantiated her charges. The Black Hills Alliance held a massive meeting near Rapid City during the summer of 1980 to alert citizens of the region to the dangers of environmental exploitation.[14]

The Sioux claim to the Black Hills regained its paramount position in April, 1981. About one hundred Pine Ridge residents took over a campsite in Victoria Canyon, about twelve miles southwest of Rapid City. Their claim was based on the Fort Laramie Treaty of 1868, the American Indian Freedom of Religion wilderness sites for schools and churches. On April 6, they filed a claim with the United States Forest Service and announced their intention to stay indefinitely.[15] The camp was named Yellow Thunder in honor of the Oglala killed at Gordon in 1972. Lake Victoria, on the site, was re-named Lake Lamont in honor of Buddy Lamont. The camp was sustained by a variety of private contributors, especially church groups. Means moved his permanent residence from Kyle to Yellow Thunder Camp in 1982 and served as its principal spokesman. The Oglala Sioux tribal council, which went on record as not supporting Yellow Thunder Camp, attempted a short-lived camp of their own near Wind Cave in the Black Hills during the summer of 1981.

Another highly publicized death resulted from the Yellow Thunder confrontation. Clarence Tollefson, a retired air force officer, was shot and killed on a hill overlooking the camp on July 21, 1982. Two escapees from the Colorado State Penitentiary were charged. The judge became so disturbed with the prosecutor's opening statements at the trial that he ruled gross negligence and threw the case out with prejudice.

Means and his supporters continued waging a legal struggle in Federal District Court. Their attempt to retain Camp Yellow Thunder was based mainly on the idea that the Black Hills have always been a sacred place of worship to the Lakota Indians. Also it was a test of whether they had the right to be there. Historian James Hanson, coordinator of the Native American Program at the Smithsonian Institute from 1976-1980, testified that the Black Hills had never been considered a holy area by the Lakotas and should not be returned to Indian ownership on those grounds. Acting as a lay lawyer, Means told the court, ". . . This is the fantasized, genocidal line of the Smithsonian Institute. It's the stereotypical, racist interpretation. It's insulting."[17] James Mathers, supervisor of the Black Hills National Forest, testified, "It seemed at almost every juncture. . . there was broad media coverage and an attempt at intimidation of the Forest

Service... and the public."[18] Yellow Thunder Camp was quietly abandoned in 1986 after Senator Bill Bradley introduced a bill to return a good portion of the Black Hills to the Sioux.

On February 27, 1983, the tenth anniversary of the Wounded Knee takeover, Means's brother Dale presided over the grand opening of radio station KILI near Porcupine. Tied into the Corporation for Public Broadcasting, KILI got its start from a $93,000 federal grant and managed to raise over $300,000 in grant support before opening. Managed by Dale Means, KILI broadcasts in English and Lakota. KILI bills itself as independent, but it appears strongly AIM oriented.[19] Its history has been marked with constant controversy. Also on the day of the tenth anniversary of Wounded Knee, Russell Means announced his candidacy for the Oglala Sioux tribal chairmanship. He was ruled out of the race because felons are not eligible. Neither he nor Dennis Banks have ever been elected to a leadership position by reservation Indians.

Banks appeared to have established himself in California until conservative Republican George Deukmejian won the governorship in November 1982. After Banks's arrest in San Francisco in January 1976, South Dakota governor Richard Kneip asked for his extradition. It looked as if California would comply with the request as a routine matter. Then governor Jerry Brown seemed to suddenly change his mind. Apparently his turnaround was influenced by a huge "save Dennis Banks" petition drive headed by William Kunstler and the strong lobbying of Hollywood liberals such as Marlon Brando and Jane Fonda.[20]

Brown's extradition secretary said, "The decision was premised on the history of Indian/white relations in South Dakota and the activities of Dennis Banks, which angered a lot of people, and the personal animosity of Janklow towards Banks." She concluded, "When you balance that against the relatively light conviction, the danger to his life seems significant enough to refuse the extradition request."[21] Many South Dakotans charged that the real reason for the denial rested with the hard political fact that Brown could afford their wrath much more readily than that of California's liberals. When Brown granted asylum, a practice incidentally not that unusual—Ronald Reagan made twenty-seven such concessions when he was governor—Janklow initiated a lawsuit in California to reverse the decision. The Third District Court of Appeals ruled Brown had to send Banks back, but Brown appealed that decision to the California Supreme Court, which contained several of his appointees. That body ruled in April, 1977, that only the governor had the power to decide and the decision rested with Brown—not the courts. Two days later, Brown notified South Dakota that he was denying extradition.

Banks resigned his position as AIM executive director when he accepted asylum in 1977. This came partly because other AIM leaders resented his press statements indicating he still spoke for the national organization. Finally, AIM national chairman John Trudell abolished all AIM national offices in 1979, thus acknowledging the fractionalization of the organization which had been a reality for several years.[22]

Banks became somewhat of a celebrity on the liberal lecture tour in California. His base of operations was at Mexican-Indian Deganawidah-Quetzalcoatl University at Davis. Here, he first served as professor of Indian law and culture and later became chancellor. During his six-year sanctuary, Banks adopted some of the trappings of a middle class California suburbanite. His wife, Kamook, was able to transfer her federal probation from South Dakota to Davis. The 643 acre D-Q University site consisted of an old army communications center abandoned by the army in 1968 and designated to go to the University of California as a research facility. A group of Indians seized it for and Indian cultural center in 1970. It was transformed into a two year "university" especially oriented toward minority studies. From its inception, it came under constant government attack because of low enrollments and questionable academic standards.

Janklow, a popular choice for governor of South Dakota in 1978 and 1982, continued to fight for Banks's extradition. He said Banks was content to let others serve jail sentences for deeds Banks had perpetrated. "One of the key things people like Dennis Banks complain about is the dual standards of justice in this country," said Janklow. In 1982, Janklow announced he had sent ninety-three convicted felons to California in lieu of prison terms in South Dakota because the Golden State seemed to welcome South Dakota law breakers.[23] Brown's legal affairs director offered to jail Banks in California for up to fifteen years to resolve the conflict, but Janklow refused. When it became apparent Brown would not run again and a conservative might well become governor, Banks and his supporters busily negotiated behind the scenes for his continued refuge status. In January, 1982, Banks and Means met in San Francisco for the first time in five years in an attempt to revive AIM as a national organization. Supposedly the much-publicized split between the two was resolved amicably. It was agreed Banks could resume an AIM national leadership office.[24] Little evolved from this new strategy, however.

When Deukmejian, a former law and order oriented California attorney general, was elected governor in 1982, he announced he would comply to an extradition request against Banks if such request were made. Banks's supporters launched a massive effort to change his mind. In December, the Davis City Council unanimously approved a resolution urging Deukmejian to consider Banks's contributions to Davis and California and rule in his favor.[25] The influential Los Angeles Times in an editorial entitled, "Dennis Banks Shouldn't Be Extradited," said, "The circumstances that led to Brown's decision do not appear to have changed enough to justify a reversal. Many people in California and South Dakota who are familiar with the case agree with Indian leader Russell Means that 'Dennis Banks's life won't be worth a nickel if he is returned for sentencing.'"[26] The Times repeated the canard against Janklow regarding the alleged rape of Jancita Eagle Deer and claimed incorrectly, "Janklow was found guilty by the Tribal Court of assault with intent to commit rape and carnal knowledge of a female under the age of 16. . . ." No such trial was ever held and Deukmejian had been fully informed.

Banks was notified in December that Deukmejian had received the new extradition request from Janklow and he would honor it on January 2. The Banks group decided that New York, under newly elected governor Mario Cuomo, would be the most likely state to grant sanctuary. As New York Secretary of State, Cuomo had been quite cooperative with the Mohawks during the highly publicized Moss Lake takeover. Cuomo was severely criticized for his role in the negotiations by state senator James Donovan, in whose district the occupation occurred. Donovan said, "Cuomo's so-called negotiation with a small group of Canadian renegades that took over the state's $800,000 Moss Lake property consisted of giving them everything they wanted to get them out."[27] Besides the prospect of favorable consideration from Cuomo, Banks would also be close to Kunstler and his associates for legal assistance and favorable public relations work.

Banks's longtime Mohawk ally, Oren Lyons, was contacted and Banks's brother, Mark, flew to New York to make arrangements.[28] Sometime in late December, Banks and his family left California by car for New York. Reverend Charles Leute reported Banks spoke at the wake of his wife's grandmother, Mrs. Agnes Lamont, at Pine Ridge.[29] On January 13, 1983, Leon Shenandoah, one of the fourteen chiefs of the 7,300 acre Onondaga nation announced Banks had been on the reservation for two or three weeks. Shenandoah said Banks came uninvited, at least to his knowledge. Although a federal warrant had been issued for Banks's arrest , the FBI said it was in contact with high New York state officials because the reservation was owned by the state and not by the federal government.[30]

Cuomo did not live up to expectations in the sanctuary issue. On January 16, Syracuse lawyer Joseph Heath told reporters he and Kunstler were representing Banks. Heath distributed a packet of information about Banks that contained several letters of character reference, including one from Senator Edward Kennedy. Kunstler claimed that chances of Banks receiving sanctuary in New York looked good. "Banks is a very urbane guy with a lot of friends who wants to start a new life in New York as a college professor," said Kunstler.[31] Kunstler said Banks would stay on the reservation if necessary to avoid extradition.[32] "The FBI has assured me that it has no intention of going on any reservation in order to effect Dennis's arrest," he said later, "but experience has taught me that the bureau's word is generally worthless and that it frequently has no hesitation in provoking violence by its actions."[33]

In an obvious effort to avoid the sanctuary question, Cuomo announced he would allow Banks to serve time in a New York prison if that was acceptable to Janklow. Janklow did not comment.[34] Cuomo had informed Banks and his attorneys that he was not granting sanctuary. So Banks his wife, and three children were granted sanctuary "under the wing of the Onondaga Nation with the full support" of the Six Nation Iroquois Confederacy. Chief Oren Lyons said, "Dennis Banks and his family now sit under the Long Leaves of the Great Tree of Peace planted at Onondaga long before your people came to our shores and our lands."[35]

Banks grew restless on the tiny reservation and returned to South Dakota in the mid-1980s to voluntarily surrender. After serving his prison term, Banks returned to Pine Ridge as a school counselor. Since then Banks has emphasized activism in business ventures and kept a low political profile. He unsuccessfully attempted to establish an ongoing electronics components assembly operation for the Honeywell Corporation. Then he established a limousine service.

Vern and Clyde Bellecourt, Banks's early Chippewa allies, possibly fared the best among AIM leaders after Wounded Knee. The brothers were among the few top leaders not convicted on serious criminal charges as a result of Wounded Knee and the events that surrounded it. Part of the explanation of their good fortune was that both were under severe parole restrictions during the entire episode and were fairly careful not be directly involved in activities that would clearly violate parole stipulations. "No way I wanted to go back to prison," said Clyde, "That's why you didn't see me running around at Wounded Knee with a gun."[36] For a time he helped run a housing complex, an education program for prisoners, and a new housing development program in Minneapolis. Many considered him the most influential Indian in Minnesota until he was convicted of drug dealing in the late 1980s and returned to prison.[37] He has since been released.

Vern returned to the White Earth Reservation and won election to the tribal council, serving as Secretary/Treasurer for four years. He holds the distinction of being the only nationally known AIM leader to hold elected office on a reservation. Vern ran for tribal council chairman twice, but was defeated. Since his defeats at White Earth Bellecourt's focus has been the International Treaty Council. This association has led him to visit Libya at least seven times, Nicaragua three times, and attend assorted other international gatherings concerned with racism and racial discrimination.[38]

Looking back at Wounded Knee II from the perspective of ten years, Tim Giago, editor of the Lakota Times, saw some positive outcomes. According to Giago, the confrontation focused national attention upon the ineptitude of the BIA and the Interior Department. "It caused the Indian people themselves to demand changes within these bureaucratic structures and put entrenched bureaucrats on notice. We learn from history and this has truly been a lesson in history."[39] Giago also said the encounter made reservation inhabitants more aware of whom they selected to fill elected office. Since that time all tribal council presidents of the Pine Ridge Reservation after Wilson have been at least acceptable to all factions.

Of course, the confrontations and the militant rhetoric only represented a highly visible form of lobbying, designed to influence the real changes that were transpiring in the legislative halls, courtrooms, and executive board rooms. Undoubtedly AIM exerted a measure of pressure on these policy decisions. Just how much impact they generated remains incalculable and varies enormously according to the assessor. AIM supporters surely would assume some credit for such favorable developments as the Indian Self-Determination Act of 1975, the Indian freedom of Religion Act of 1978, more generous federal funding, and various courtroom victories. The claim that AIM's militant defense of Native Americans brought a new pride and meaning to the lives of many cannot be ignored, either.

Sovereignty for individual Indian reservations was the key objective of the Wounded Knee takeover. It represented much of AIM's appeal to Indian traditionals. If the recommendations of the American Indian Policy Review Commission had been legislated, many Indians would agree that the cost of AIM violence and destruction was a small price to pay. Submitted to Congress in May, 1977, the report provided a glimmer of hope for those advocating complete tribal sovereignty. It recommended a fundamental concept: "Indian tribes are sovereign bodies, having the power to determine their own membership and power to enact laws and enforce them within the boundaries of their reservations."[40] Vice Chairman Lloyd Meeds, from northwest Washington State, issued a vigorous one hundred page dissent, terming the report "one-sided advocacy" seeking to "convert a romantic political notion into a legal doctrine."[41] Commission chairman Abourezk replied that Meeds was dissenting to things which the report did not say. Abourezk charged Meeds with a lack of objectiveness in making recommendations where "the ultimate consequences would be the virtual assimilation of Native Americans into the dominant culture, destroying the last vestiges of a distinctively proud and independent way of life."[42] Neither Abourezk nor Meeds remained in the Congress and the Commission report's recommendations were never ratified.

Shortly after the report was submitted, the landmark Oliphant decision again affirmed the limited sovereignty of Indian nations with the United States. The case involved two white youths who were arrested for speeding on the Suquamish Reservation in Washington. The question of jurisdiction was taken to the U. S. Supreme Court which ruled "Indian tribal courts do not have the inherent jurisdiction to try to punish non Indians, and hence may not assume such jurisdiction unless specifically authorized to do so by Congress."[43] The verdict also said, "Indian tribes are proscribed from exorcism both those powers of autonomous states that are expressly terminated by Congress and those powers inconsistent with their status." Again the Court explained why Indian nations do not have complete sovereignty, ". . . upon incorporation into the territory of the United States the Indian tribes thereby come under the territorial sovereignty of the United States and their exercise of separate power is constrained so as not to conflict with the interests of the overriding sovereignty."[44] Although the sovereignty debate continues, it appears, based upon consistent Supreme Court decisions, that pure sovereignty in the international sense will not be granted Indian tribes by the United States.

The Supreme Court, however, has ruled favorably on a number of Indian claims not involving complete sovereignty On June 30, 1980, it ended the longest running claim in United States history by ruling that the Black Hills had been illegally taken from the Lakota people. It upheld the U. S. Court of Claims ruling that the Sioux nation should be awarded $17. 5 million for the land at 1877 prices plus $105 million simple interest for over 103 years at five percent.[45] The decision called for a cash settlement and said nothing about the return of the Black Hills to the Sioux. Spread over the estimated 60,000 members of the seven Lakota nations, this payment would hardly end poverty for them. The suit helped prevent poverty among the members of the Washington law firm of Fried, Frank, Shriver, Kanpelman, Smosky and Payne—represented by Arthur Lazarus, though. They requested and received a maximum $10,595,943 fee that was deducted from an Indian trust fund held by the Interior Department.[46] In spite of some pressure from various individuals and groups to accept the cash payment, six of the seven tribes in the Great Sioux Nation have refused to consider payment and have demanded a property settlement. In November, 1982, the Oglala Tribal Council voted to forbid the interior Department from holding any hearings on their reservation about distributing the money.

The tribal council further voted in February, 1983, to give a steering committee $20,000 to begin lobbying in Washington. The Sioux sent around five hundred letters to President Reagan saying "the legal right to the title of the Black Hills has never been extinguished or sold by the Lakota, the 1868 Fort Laramie is still in effect.[47] In 1985, Senator Bradley introduced a bill to return over one million acres of federally held land to the Sioux. It has not made substantial headway, however, and the cash award continues to draw interest.[48]

Although Dakota AIM strives to maintain a posture in the controversy, they are, in reality, outside of the Sioux power structure and given little accord by the legally established tribal governments. From the start of his administration, moreover, Reagan and his representatives in the Interior Department let it be known they wanted to work only with the elected tribal officials and expressed their weariness of contending with various tribal factions bent on tearing down the creditability and influence of one another. On January 14, 1983, Reagan announced a new National Indian Policy. The President said he would deal with Indian tribes on a government-to-government basis because Indian tribal governments retained all of their original sovereignty not otherwise given up or taken away by Congress. This new policy gave the tribes the power to tax and encouraged their sovereignty and economic development. It specifically repudiated "a lingering threat of termination."[49] Reagan's new policy provoked a letter to him signed by sixty-seven United States Congressmen praising him for the new policy but protesting, ". . . the budgets you have submitted to Congress do not reflect commitment to this policy." The letter also noted "a striking omission" of the approximately 700,000 Indians who live off the reservation.

South Dakota reservations suffered an economic decline during the Reagan-Bush era. A 1982 census report placed four of the ten poorest counties in the nation in South Dakota. All four were primarily Indian reservations. Shannon County, dominated by the Pine Ridge Reservation, had the lowest per capita income, $2,627, in the United States.[50] Since that census report, income in Shannon County dropped even lower. Because of the Reagan cutbacks in CETA and other programs, unemployment on the Pine Ridge Reservation has held at over eighty percent.[51]

The village of Wounded Knee remains burned out and abandoned. Senate Resolution Number 378 provided for payments "to the innocent victims of the occupation of Wounded Knee. . . ." After extensive pre-trial proceedings, a federal trial commissioner conducted a lengthy trial, first in Deadwood, September 18-23, 1978, and later in Washington, May 6-20, 1980. The government filed a motion requesting that the review panel adopt the trial commissioner's findings of fact and opinion as the basis for the panel's recommendation to the Senate in November, 1981. It affirmed that the government had acted as well as could be expected under the circumstances and ". . . although many of the plaintiffs sustained verifiable damages as a result of the occupation of Wounded Knee, none of the plaintiffs has either a legal or an equitable claim against the United States because of such damages, and any money payments to the plaintiffs because of such damages would constitute gratuities."[52] The report justified its decision by saying in part, "The innocent victims of the occupation of Wounded Knee are in the same category as thousands of other persons in this country who each year, unfortunately and sometimes tragically, suffer personal injuries or property damages as the result of the criminal activities of lawless persons.[53] It now appears that all 115 cases filed against the government are closed.

Because they owned more property than the other claimants, the Gildersleeves and the Czywczynskis were especially hurt. Like most of the others, they had no insurance on their holdings. The Gildersleeves lived on a small social security pension at nearby Rushville, Nebraska, before joining family in Maryland. They did not blame reservation Indians for their plight but claimed "educated outside Indians" were responsible.[54] Both are now deceased. AIM leaders maintain that the loss of a relatively small amount of property, although unfortunate, was justified because it was needed to achieve much greater objectives for Indian people.

Considering the bleak employment situation at Pine Ridge Reservation plus the cost in lives, property, and social disruption, it would seem that the second encounter at Wounded Knee served the interests and concerns of outside Indians and whites better than it did those of the Oglalas. An airing of Native American grievances was long overdue, though. What more appropriate site could be selected than the land of Red Cloud, Crazy Horse, Wounded Knee, Custer, and all the other reminders of an inglorious history of governmental malfeasance? The unfortunate aspect of Wounded Knee II emanated from the propensity of the media, polemicists, and militants to promote the old cowboys and Indians syndrome that flourished in the nineteenth century. By the middle of the twentieth century, that approach seemingly had long been outmoded by the realities of contemporary Indian-white relationships. If the revival of the confrontational approach improved the lot of the majority of Native Americans, nonetheless, it may have been the most effective strategy for the time. Whether it did poses the pivotal issue.

Barring a dramatic turnaround, it would appear that AIM does not loom as a significant force in contemporary American Indian affairs. More of a movement than an organization, it seemed to possess the quality of being the right group in the right place at the right time during the Wounded Knee II era. Politics and public opinion have shifted to a far more conservative stance and AIM appears to be irreparably fragmented as a national organization. The verdict on AIM's contribution to Native American advancement, therefore, must be based upon the evidence that has already accumulated. Whether they are "the heroes of contemporary history" or if they fit the critical assessment, "freebooters of racism," depends upon one's perspective. It has been argued that the Native American would have received better treatment whether AIM and Wounded Knee had happened or not. The evidence seems to indicate, however, that positive change was spurred by the radical activists.

Bibliography

Adams, John H. "AIM, the Church and the FBI: The Douglass Durham Case." Christian Century. 489-495, May 14, 1975.

Adams, John. At the Heart of the Whirlwind. New York: Harper and Row, 1976.

Akwesasne Notes (newspaper). Mohawk Nation. Rooseveltown, New York.

Anderson, Robert, Joanna Brown, Jonny Lerner, and Barbara Lou Shafer, Eds., Voices From Wounded Knee. Rooseveltown, N. Y.: Akwesasne Notes, 1974.

Bellecount, Clyde. American Indian Social Activism. Pacifica Tape Library: Los Angeles, 1968.

Berkofer, Robert F., Jr. "The Political Context of a New Indian History." Pacific Historical Review, 40: 357-382, August, 1971.

Bonney, Rashel A. "The Role of AIM Leaders in Indian Nationalism." American Indian Quarterly. 209 224, Autumn 1977.

Brand, Johanna The Life and Death of Anna Mae Aquash. Toronto: James Lorimer, 1978.

Brown, Dee. Bury My Heart at Wounded Knee: An Indian History of the American West. New York: Bantam, 1972.

Brown, Dee. "The Ghost Dance and the Battle of Wounded Knee." American History Illustrated. 1:4-17, December, 1966.

Bumette, Robert and John Koster. The Road to Wounded Knee. New York: Bantam, 1974.

Calio, Jim. "Murderer, Mantyr Or Both? The Tangled Case of the Sioux 'Enforcer,' "Leonard Peltier." People. 111-114, April 20, 1981.

Church, Frank. Final Report of the Select Committee to Study Governmental Operations with Respect to Intelligence Activities. Report No. 94-755, United States Senate, April 23, 1976.

Cohen, Fay G. The Indian Patrol in Minneapolis: Social Control and Social Changes in an Urban Context. Unpublished Ph. D. Dissertation. University of Minnesota, 1973.

Collier, Peter. "Only good Indian. . . "Ramparts. 36-37+, December,1972.

____. "The Red Man's Burden," Ramparts. 26-38, February, 1970.

____. "Wounded Knee: the new Indian War." Ramparts. 25-29+, June, 1973.

Cummings, Jean. Alias the Buffalo Doctor. Athens, Ohio: Swallow Press, 1980.

Decker, Doug. An Analysis of the 'Bradley Bill' Proposing to Return the Black Hills to the Great Sioux Nation. South Dakota Legislative Research Council Issue Memorandum 87-4. May 14, 1987.

Deloria, Vine, Jr., Behind the Trail of Broken Treaties. New York: Dill, 1974.

____. We Talk. You Listen: New Tribes, New Turf. New York: Macmillan, 1970.

DeMallie, Raymond J. "Pine Ridge Economy: Cultural and Historical Perspective" in American Indian Economic Development, edited by Sam Stanely, 237-312. The Hague: Mouton Publishers, 1978.

Dewing, Rolland. "South Dakota Newspaper Coverage of the 1973 Occupation of Wounded Knee." South Dakota History 12, no. 1:48-64, 1982.

____. Editor. The FBI Files on the American Indian Movement and Wounded Knee (26 reels with printed guide). Frederick, MD: University Publications, 1987.

Dilley, R. "Standoff at Wounded Knee." Christian Century. 527-528, May 9, 1973.

Dollar, Clyde D. "The Second Tragedy at Wounded Knee: A 1970's Confrontation and Its Historical Roots." The American West. 6-9, January, 1974.

Donner, Frank. "The Confessions of an FBI Informer." Harper. 245-54-8+, December, 1972.

Doyle, B. "Bury My Tithe at Wounded Knee." Christianity Today. 40-41, June 8, 1973.

Elliff, John T. The Reform of FBI Intelligence Operations. Princeton University Press, 1979.

Feaver, George. "Wounded Knee and the New Tribalism." Encounter. 28-37, February, 1975.

Hanlon, W. T. "Whose Ox Was Gored at Wounded Knee?" America. 190-192, March 16, 1974.

Hertzberg, Hazel W. The Search for an American Indian Identity: Modern Pan-Indian Movements. Syracuse University Press, 1971.

Hickey, Neil. "Was the Truth Buried at Wounded Knee?" TV Guide. (four-part series) December 1, 8, 15, 22, 1973.

Hoover, Herbert T. The Sioux: A Critical Bibliography. Indiana University Press, 1979.

House Committee on Interior and Insular Affairs, Subcommittee on Indian Affairs. Seizure of Bureau of Indian Affairs Headquarters. 92nd Congress, 1st Session, 83-105, 1972.

Huck, Susan M. "Renegades: The Second Battle of Wounded Knee." American Opinion. 1-14, April 12, 1973.

Hunter, Wesley C. Wounded Knee Revisited, 1973: The Second Confrontation. Richland Center, Wisconsin, 1990.

Hyde, George E. Red Cloud's Folk. University of Oklahoma Press, 1937

____. Spotted Tail's Folk: A History of the Brule Sioux. University Oklahoma Press, 1969.

Jacobs, Wilbur. "The Indian and the Frontier in American History: A Need for Revision." Western Historical Quarterly. 43-56, January, 1973.

Jensen, Richard E. , R. Eli Paul, and John E. Carter. Eye Witness at Wounded Knee. University of Nebraska Press, 1991.

Johansen, Bruce. "Indians for Sovereignty: The Reservation Offensive" Nation. 204-207, February 25, 1978.

Josephy, Alvin M. , Jr. Now That The Buffalo's Gone: A Study of Today's American Indians. New York: Alfred A. Knopf, 1982.

Kanter, Elliot. "The FBI Takes Aim at AIM." American Indian Journal. 14-18, August, 1977.

Kaufman, Donald L. "The Indian as Media Hand-Me-Down." Colorado Quarterly. 489-504, Spring, 1975.

Kickingbird, Kirke. "The American Indian Policy Review Commission: A Prospect for Future Change in Federal Indian Policy." American Indian Law Review. 3:243-253, Nov. 2, 1975.

Koster, John. "American Indians and the Media." Cross Currents. 164-171, Summer, 1976.

Lazarus, Edward. Black Hills White Justice: the Sioux Nation Versus United States: 1775 to the Present. New York: Harper Collins, 1991.

Lounber, Dan. "The Face of the American Indian Movement." Crisis. 463-466, December, 1977.

Lyman, Stanley. Wounded Knee 1973: A Personal Account. University of Nebraska Press, 1991.

Matthiessen, Peter. In the Spirit of Crazy Horse. New York: Viking Press, 1983.

Maynard, Eileen and Gayla Twiss. That These People May Live: Conditions Among the Oglala Sioux of the Pine Ridge Reservation. DHEW Publication N. 72-508, 1970.

Meriam, Lewis. The Problem of Indian Administration. Baltimore: The Johns Hopkins Press, 1928.

Messerschmidt, Jim. The Trial of Leonard Peltier. Raritan, N. J. : South End Press, 1984.

Mooney, James. The Ghost-Dance Religion and the Sioux Outbreak of 1890. Glorieta, NM: Rio Grande Press, 1973.

Olson, James. Red Cloud and the Sioux Problem. University of Nebraska Press, 1965.

Ortiz, Roxanne Dunbar. "Wounded Knee 1890 to Wounded Knee 1973: A Study in United States Colonialism." Journal of Ethnic Studies 1-15, Summer, 1980.

Parman, Donald L. American Indians and the Bicentennial. 261-273, In The American Indian Past and Present Second Edition Roger L. Nichols, Editor, New York: John Wiley and Sons, 1981.

Peroff, Nicholas C. Menominee Drums: Tribal Termination and Restoration, 1954-1974. University of Oklahoma Press, 1982.

Pierce, Margaret Hunter. "The Work of the Indian Claims Commission." American Bar Association Journal. 227-232, February, 1977.

Proto, Brian L. The Policy Process in American Indian Affairs: Patterns of Interaction between American Indian Interest Groups, the BIA, and the Indian Affairs Committees of the Congress. Ph. D. dissertation, Miami University, 1979.

Prucha, Francis P. U. S. Indian Policy: A Critical Bibliography. Indiana University Press, 1977.

"A Report from the Pine Ridge, Conditions on Oglala Sioux Reservation." Civil Rights Digest. 28-38, Summer, 1975.

Robinson, Doane. A History of the Dakota or Sioux Indians. Minneapolis: Ross and Haines, 1956.

Roos, Philip D. , and others. "The Impact of the American Indian Movement on the Pine Ridge Indian Reservation." Phylon, 41:1:89-99, 1980.

Sherrill, Robert G. "Lagoon of Excrement, Pine Ridge an Impoverished Indian Reservation in South Dakota" Nation. 209-500, November 10, 1969.

Taylor, Graham D. The New Deal and American Indian Tribalism: The Administration of the Indian Reorganization Act? 1934-45. University of Nebraska Press, 1980.

Rosenthal, Harvey D. Their Day in Court: A History of the Indian Claims Commision Ph. D. dissertation, Kent State University, 1976,

Schultz, T. "Bamboozle Me Not at Wounded Knee." Harper's. 46-48, June, 1973.

___. "Continuing Massacre at Wounded Knee: Election for Presidency of the Tribal Council." Harper's. 30, June, 1974.

Sievers, Michael A. "The Historiography of 'The Bloody Field. . . That Kept Everlasting Word': Wounded Knee." South Dakota History. 33-54, Winter, 1975.

Smith, D. "Wounded Knee: The Media coup d'etat." Nation. 806-809, June 25, 1973.

South Dakota Oral History Project. University of South Dakota. Herbert Hoover, Director.

Stang, Alan. "American Indian Movement—Red Indians." American Opinion. 1-22, September 1975.

A Symposium on American Indians: Policy, Paradigms and Prognosis. The Social Science Journal. July, 1982.

Trexle, E. R. "Lutheran and American Indians: a Confrontation." Christian Century. 1103-5, September 16, 1970.

Truscott, Lucian K. "Vietnam Veterans Against the War." Saturday Review. 557-8+, October 7, 1972.

Ungar, Sanford J. FBI. Boston: Little Brown, 1975.

U. S. Congress. Senate. Committee on Interior and Insular Affairs. Subcommittee on Indian Affairs. Occupation of Wounded Knee: Hearings before the Subcommittee on Indian Affairs. 93rd Congress, 1st session, June 16, 1973, Pine Ridge, South Dakota; June 17, 1973, Kyle, South Dakota.

Utley, Robert M. The Last Days of the Sioux Nation. New Haven. Yale University Press, 1963.

Vaughan, Alden T. "From White Man to Redskin: Changing Anglo-American Perception of the American Indian." The American Historical Review. 917-953, October, 1982.

Vizenor, Gerald. Tribal Scenes and Ceremonies. New York: Crowell-Collier Press, 1972.

Walker, James R. Lakota Society. University of Nebraska Press, 1982.

Washburn, Wilcom. "The Writing of American Indian History" Pacific Historical Review. 40: 261-281, 1971.

Wassaja (Newspaper). San Francisco, California.

Weisman, Joel D. "About that Ambush at Wounded Knee." Columbia Journalism Review. , 28-31, September-October, 1976.

Weyler, Rex. Blood on the Land: The Government and Corporate War against the American Indian Movement. New York: Everest House, 1982.

Witt, Shirley Hill. "The Brave Hearted Women: The Struggle at Wounded Knee." Civil Rights Digest. 39-45, Summer, 1976.

Zimmerman, Bill. Airlift to Wounded Knee. Chicago: The Swallow Press, 1976.

Notes

AMERICA'S MOST NEGLECTED MINORITY

1. Hazel Hertzberg, The Search for an American Identity: Modern Pan-Indian Movements (Syracuse University, 1971), pp. 2-12.
2. Vine Deloria, Jr., Behind the Trail of Broken Treaties: An Indian Declaration of Independence (New York: Delacorte Press, 1974), pp. 11-20.
3. George E. Hyde, Spotted Tail's Folk: A History of the Brule Sioux (Norman: University of Oklahoma Press, 1976), p. 3.
4. Forrest W. Seymour, Sitanka: The Full Story of Wounded Knee (West Hanover, Massachusetts: The Christopher Publishing House, 1981).
5. George E. Hyde, Red Cloud's Folk (Norman: University of Oklahoma Press, 1976), pp. 8-9.
6. Raymond De Mallie, "Pine Ridge Economy: Cultural and Historic Perspectives," American Indian Economic Development, Ed. Sam Stanley (The Hague: Mouton, 1978), pp. 239-247.
7. Hyde, Red Cloud's Folk, pp. 53-55.
8. De Mallie "Pine Ridge Economy," pp. 240-241.
9. Clark Wissler, Indians of the United States (New York: Doubleday, 1966), pp. 173-201.
10. Willoughby M. Babcock, Jr., "Radiograms of Minnesota History: Sioux Versus Chippewa," Minnesota History Bulletin, 6:1 (March, 1925), 41-45.
11. Hyde, Red Cloud's Folk, pp. 3-19.
12. Ray Billington, Westward Expansion: A History of the American Frontier (New York: Macmillan Publishing Co., 1974), pp. 564-565.
13. Charles M. Oehler, The Great Sioux Uprising, (New York: Oxford U. Press, 1959).
14. Wilcomb Washburn, ed., The American Indian and the United States: A Documentary History (New York: Random House, 1973), 1:134-162.
15. Billington, Westward Expansion, p. 570.
16. James C. Olson, Red Cloud and the Sioux Problem (Lincoln: University of Nebraska Press, 1965), pp. 69-82.
17. Washburn, The American Indian and the United States, 4:2517-2526.
18. Robert M. Utley, "The Celebrated Peace Policy of General Grant," North Dakota History (July 1953), pp. 121-142; Loring Priest, Uncle Sam's Stepchildren (New York: Octagon Books, 1969), pp. 28-41.
19. Robert Mardock, The Reformers and the American Indian (Columbia: University of Missouri Press, 1971), pp. 50-56.
20. Ibid., pp. 28-41.
21. Oliver Knight, Following the Indian Wars: The Story of the Newspaper Correspondents Among the Indian Campaigners (Norman: U. of Oklahoma Press, 1960), p. 21.
22. Utley, "The Celebrated Peace Policy of General Grant," p. 2.
23. Knight, Following the Indian Wars, p. 21.
24. Stanley Vestal, Sitting Bull: Champion of the Sioux (Boston: Houghton-Mifflin, 1932), pp. 140-149; Alexander B. Adams, Sitting Bull: A Biography (New York: Capricorn, 1973), pp. 285-308; Washburn, The American Indian and the United States, 1:197-214.
25. Stan Haig, The Battle of the Washita: The Sheridan-Custer Indian Campaign of 1867-69 (New York: Doubleday, 1976).
26. Knight, Following the Indian Wars, p. 11.

27. Ibid., p. 218.
28. Robert M. Utley, Frontier Regulars: The United States Army and the Indian, 1886-1891
    (New York: Macmillan, 1974), pp. 275-299; Jerome A. Green, Slim Buttes 1876: An Episode
    of the Great Sioux War (Norman: U. of Okla. Press, 1982).
29. James R. Walker, Lakota Belief and Ritual, Eds. Raymond J. De Mallie and Elaine A. Jahner
    (Lincoln: University of Nebraska Press, 1980).
30. Hyde, Red Cloud's People, pp. 275-276.
31. De Mallie, "Pine Ridge Economy," pp. 252-254.
32. Hyde, Spotted Tail's Folk, pp. 280-286.
33. Ibid., pp. 299-300.
34. Priest, Uncle Sam's Stepchildren, pp. 227-241; Helen Hunt Jackson, A Century of Dishonor
    (New York: Harper Torchbacks, 1965), Originally published in 1881.
35. Mardock, The Reformers and the American Indian, pp. 216-223.
36. Olson, Red Cloud and the Sioux Problem, pp. 309-319.
37. Vestal, Sitting Bull, pp. 264-266.
38. James Mooney, The Ghost Dance Religion (Glorieta, New Mexico: Rio Grande Press, 1973),
    pp. 771-791.   The classic study, originally published in 1896.
39. Paul Bailey, Wovoka: The Indian Messiah (Los Angeles: Western Lore Press, 1957); Elaine
    G. Eastman, "The Ghost Dance and the Wounded Knee Massacre of 1890-91," Nebraska
    History, 26 (1945), pp. 26-42.
40. S. L. A. Marshall, The Crimsoned Prairie (New York: Charles Scribner's Sons, 1972), p.
    233.
41. Vestal, Sitting Bull, pp. 279-280; Doane Robinson, History of the Sioux (Minneapolis: Ross
    and Haines, 1956), pp. 459-469.
42. Mooney, The Ghost Dance Religion, p. 848.
43. Robert M. Utley, The Last Days of the Sioux Nation (New Haven: Yale University Press,
    1963) pp. 103-104.
44. Mooney, The Ghost Dance Religion, p. 850.
45. Elmo S. Watson, "The Last Indian War, 1899-91— A Study of Newspaper Jingoism,"
    Journalism Quarterly (1943), pp. 205-219; "Saddles to Satellites," Historical booklet,
    Sheridan County Diamond Jubilee, Rushville, Nebraska, 1960.
46. Virginia Johnson, The Unregimented General (Boston: Houghton-Mifflin, 1962), pp. 29-31.
47. Vestal, Sitting Bull, pp. 300-315.
48. Barbara Bonham, The Battle of Wounded Knee: The Ghost Dance Uprising (Chicago: Reilly
    and Lee Books, 1970), pp. 112-134.
49. Utley, Last Days of the Sioux Nation, pp. 200-230.
50. Knight, Following the Indian Wars, p. 11.
51. Mooney, The Ghost Dance Religion, p. 868.
52. Ibid., pp. 868-869.
53. Donald F. Kander, "The Wounded Knee Interviews of Eli S. Ricker," Nebraska History,
    Summer 1981, pp. 151-243.
54. Mooney, The Ghost Dance Religion, p. 871.
55. Ibid.
56. Dee Brown, Bury My Heart at Wounded Knee (New York: Bantam Books, 1972), p. 418.
57. Elaine G. Eastmen, "The Ghost Dance Wounded Knee Massacre of 1890-91," p. 38.
58. Jan C. Kuxhausen, "The Ghost Dance Uprising: The Wounded Knee Massacre" (Master's
    paper, Chadron State College, 1973), p. 66.
59. Alistair Cooke, America (New York: Alfred A. Knopf, 1970), p. 242.
60. Utley, The Last Days of the Sioux Nation, pp. 245-248.
61. Johnson, The Unregimented General, p. 289.
62. Chadron Democrat, January 8, 1891.

63. Eastman, "The Ghost Dance and the Wounded Knee Massacre of 1890-91," p. 39.
64. Utley, Frontier Regulars, pp. 416-418.
65. Utley, Last Days of the Sioux Nation, p. 249.
66. L. G. Moses, "Jack Wilson and the Indian Service: The Response of the BIA to the Ghost Dance Prophet," American Indian Quarterly (November 1979), p. 312.
67. Michael A. Sievers, "The Historiography of 'The Bloody Field...that Kept the Secret of the Everlasting War': Wounded Knee," South Dakota History (Winter 1975), pp. 35-44.
68. Ibid.
69. D. Alexander Brown, "The Ghost Dance and the Battle of Wounded Knee," American History Illustrated (December 1966), p. 17.
70. Patrick J. Buchanan, "Big Foot Had It Coming," Tulsa World, January 16, 1975.
71. Mooney, The Ghost Dance Religion, p. 889-890.
72. Utley, Last Days of the Sioux Nation, p. 274.
73. Wilcomb, Washburn, The Indian in America, pp. 246-247; Laurance F. Schmeckebier, The Office of Indian Affairs: Its History, Activities and Organization (Baltimore, 1927).
74. Ibid.
75. Vivian One Feather, "Agricultural Development and Resources on the Pine Ridge Reservation," (Unpublished paper, Pine Ridge Reservation, 1976), p. 14.
76. Ibid., p. 13.
77. Monroe Price, Heirship, Law and the American Indian (Indian-apolis : Bobbs-Merrill), pp. 646-672.
78. Randolph C. Downes, "A Crusade for Indian Reform, 1922-1934," Mississippi Valley Historical Review (December 1945), pp. 331-354.
79. Michael T. Smith, "The History of Indian Citizenship," Great Plains Journal (Fall 1970), pp. 25-35.
80. Angie Debo, A History of the Indians of the United States (Norman: U. of Okla. Press, 1970), p. 288.
81. Kenneth R. Philip, John Collier's Crusade for Indian Reform, 1920-1954 (Tucson: University of Arizona Press, 1977).
82. Randolph C. Downes, "A Crusade for Indian Reform," pp. 331-354; Graham D. Taylor, The New Deal and American Indian Tribalism (Lincoln: University of Nebraska Press, 1980).
83. Ibid.
84. De Mallie, "Pine Ridge Economy," pp. 257-258.
85. Ibid., p. 258.
86. U. S., Congress, Senate, Committee on Interior and Insular Affairs, The Causes and Aftermath of the Wounded Knee Takeover, Hearings before a subcommittee on Indian Affairs, 93rd session, 1st session, 1973, pp. 4-5.
87. Rapid City Journal, March 8, 1973.
88. Taylor, The New Deal and American Indian Tribalism, p. 115.
89. Ibid.
90. Ibid., p. 116.
91. De Mallie, "Pine Ridge Economy," pp. 259-263.
92. Margaret Hunter Pierce, "The Work of the Indian Claims Commission," American Bar Association Journal (February 1977), pp. 227-231; United States Indian Claims Commission, August 13, 1946-September 30, 1978: Final Report (Washington: Government Printing Office, 1979).
93. Debra R. Boender, "Termination and the Administration of Glenn L. Emmons as Commissioner of Indian Affairs, 1953-1961," New Mexico Historical Review (October 1979), pp. 287-304.

94. Nicholas C. Peroff, <u>Menominee Drums: Tribal Termination and Restoration, 1954-1974</u> (Norman: U. of Okla. Press, 1982).
95. Debo, <u>A History of the Indians of the United States</u>, p. 311.
96. Donald L. Parman, "American Indians and the Bicentennial," <u>New Mexico Historical Review</u> (July 1976), pp. 233-246.
97. Bayard Rustin, "Black Power's Legacy," <u>Newsweek</u> (November 13, 1972), pp. 18-19.
98. George Feaver, Wounded Knee and the New Tribalism," <u>Encounter</u> (February 1975), pp. 28-37.
99. Ibid.
100. Donald L. Kaufman, "The Indian as Media Hand-Me-Down," <u>Colorado Quarterly</u> (Spring 1975), pp. 489-504,
101. Alvin Josephy, Jr., <u>Red Power</u> (New York: McGraw-Hill, 1971), pp. 49-52.
102. Deloria, Jr., <u>Behind the Trail of Broken Treaties</u>, pp. 25-26.
103. For SNCC background see Clayborne Carson, <u>In Struggle: SNCC and the Black Awakening of the 1960s</u> (Cambridge: Harvard U. Press, 1981).
104. Stan Steiner, <u>The New Indians</u> (New York: Harper & Row, 1968), pp. 66-72.
105. Ralph Nader, "Lo the Poor Indian," <u>New Republic</u> (March 30, 1968), pp. 14-15; Robert G. Sherrill, "Lagoon of Excrement, Pine Ridge an Impoverished Indian Reservation in South Dakota," <u>Nation</u> (November 10, 1979), pp. 209+.
106. Debo, <u>A History of the Indian of the United States</u>, pp. 347-348.
107. <u>New York Times</u>, August 24, 1969.
108. U.S. Congress, Senate, Committee on Interior and Insular Affairs, <u>The Impact of Public Law 280 Upon the Administration of Justice on Indian Reservation, Hearings before a Subcommittee on Indian Affairs on the Indian Law Enforcement Act of 1975</u>, 95th session, 1st session, 1975, pp. 185-205.
109. Frances Svensson, <u>The Ethnics in American Politics: American Indians</u> (Minneapolis: Burgess Publishing Company, 1973), p. 44.
110. Peter Collier, "Wounded Knee: The New Indian War," <u>Ramparts</u> (June 1973), p. 26.
111. <u>Senate Hearings on the Impact of Public Law 280</u>, pp. 200-201.
112. Collier, "Wounded Knee: The New Indian War," p. 26.
113. Alvin M. Josephy, Jr., "Wounded Knee and All That—What the Indians Want," <u>New York Times Magazine</u> (March 18, 1973).
114. Wilcomb Washburn, "Red Power," <u>The American West</u> (January 1969), pp. 52-53.
115. Francis P. Prucha, <u>American Historical Review</u> (April 1972), pp- 589-590.
116. Feaver, "Wounded Knee and the New Tribalism," pp. 28-37.
117. Svensson, <u>The Ethnics in American Politics: American Indians</u>, pp. 40-41.
118. Steiner, <u>The New Indians</u>, pp. 90-94.
119. Gerald Vizenor, <u>Tribal Scenes and Ceremonies</u> (Minneapolis: The Nodin Press, 1976), pp. 120-121.
120. Ibid., p. 121.
121. Ibid., p. 122.

RED POWER

1. Letter from Douglas Hall to the author, January 18, 1983.
2. Fay G. Cohen, "The Indian Patrol in Minneapolis: Social Control and Social Change in an Urban Context," Ph.D. dissertation, University of Minnesota, 1973, pp. 45-46.
3. Ibid., p. 48.

4. Vizenor, <u>Tribal Scenes and Ceremonies,</u> p. 137.

5. Cohen, "The Indian Patrol...," p. 52.

6. Ibid., pp. 55-60, 226-227.

7. <u>Minneapolis Morning Tribune</u>, March 10, 1973.

8. Vizenor, <u>Tribal Scenes and Ceremonies</u>, p. 137.

9. Ibid.

10. Rachel A. Bonney, "The Role of AIM Leaders in Indian Nationalism," <u>American Indian Quarterly</u> (Autumn 1977), p. 213.

11. Svensson, <u>The Ethnics in American Politics: The American Indians</u>, p. 41; Vizenor, <u>Tribal Scenes and Ceremonies</u>, pp. 70-71.

12. Vine Deloria, Jr., <u>Custer Died for Your Sins:</u> An Indian Manifesto (New York: Avon Books, 1969), pp. 249-251.

13. Vine Deloria, Jr., <u>God Is Red</u> (New York: Delta, 1973), p. 58.

14. Report from Walt Weber, Director of Lutheran Social Services of South Dakota, April 1973.

15. <u>Rapid City Journal</u>, April 17, 1973; <u>Detroit News</u>, March 25, 1973.

16. Interview with Dr. Paul Boe, Chadron, Nebraska, Spring 1975.

17. Interview with Bishop E O. Gilbertson, American Lutheran Church, Sioux Falls, South Dakota, April 1, 1977.

18. Ibid.

19. <u>Detroit News</u> March 25, 1973.

20. Ibid.

21. Ibid.

22. Daniel Moynihan, <u>Maximum Feasible Misunderstanding</u> (New York. The Free Press, 1969), p. 140.

23. AIM statement signed by Vernon Long and Eddie Whitewolf, August 16, 1973.

24. Undated newspaper clipping from Fargo-Moorhead newspaper, received from Dr. Ed Pluth, St. Cloud State University, St. Cloud, Minnesota: Interview with Stig Ericson, Swedish writer and publisher Chadron, Nebraska, May 18, 1983.

25. Robert Burnette and John Koster, <u>The Road to Wounded Knee</u> (New York: Bantam Books, 1974), pp. 259-264.

26. Interview with Dennis Banks, Chadron, Nebraska, May 1975.

27. Bill Zimmerman, <u>Airlift to Wounded Knee</u> (Chicago: The Swallow Press, Inc., 1976)P, pp. 110-128.

28. <u>Minneapolis Tribune</u>, November 16, 1979.

29. Interview with Vernon Bellecourt, Fort Robinson, Nebraska, September 1972; Bill Lawrence, Interview: Vernon Bellecourt," <u>Penthouse</u>, February 1983.   pp. 34-38; "Vernon Bellecourt," <u>Penthouse</u>, April 1973.

30. "Interview with Russell Means," <u>Black Hills State College Today</u>, October 26, 1982.

31. "Russell Means Interview," <u>Penthouse</u>, April 1981, pp. 136-138+.

32. Interview with Russell Means, Fort Robinson, Nebraska, September 1972 and Chadron, Nebraska, January 27, 1983.

33. Burnette and Koster, <u>The Road to Wounded Knee,</u> pp. 196-197.

34. <u>New York Times</u>, January 16, 1972.

35. Peter Collier, "The Red Man's Burden," <u>Ramparts</u> (February 1970), pp. 26-38.

36. "New Flag over Alcatraz," <u>Time</u>, April 12, 1971, p. 21.

37. <u>New Republic</u>, January 17, 1970, pp. 10-11.

38. <u>New York Times</u>, November 28, 1969.

39. W. Mormon, "Anomie at Alcatraz," <u>Time</u>, April 12, 1971, p. 21.

40. E. R. Trexle, "Lutherans and American Indians: A Confrontation," <u>Christian Century</u> (September 6 1970), pp. 1103-1105.

41. Interview with Jorgen Thompson, Vice President for Student Affairs, Augustana College, April 1, 1977.
42. Sioux Falls Argus Leader, August 7, 1970.
43. New York Times, December 17, 1970.
44. Minneapolis Tribune, October 16, 1971.
45. Ibid.
46. Ibid.
47. Interview with Reginald Cedarface, Executive Director, Black Hills Sioux National Council, December 8, 1982.
48. Letter from John M. Lane, Title III Coordinator, Cheyenne River Community College, Eagle Butte, South Dakota, February 25, 1981; Rachel Bonney, "The Role of AIM Leaders in Indian Nationalism," pp. 209-211, 220-222.
49. Vizenor, Tribal Scenes and Ceremonies, pp. 70-71 139.
50. Interview with Mike Smith, then Sheridan County Attorney, Gordon, Nebraska, December 21, 1982; Interview with Joanne Jones, juror in Bayliss trial, Chadron, Nebraska, March 15, 1977.
51. Report of Maynard Jensen, Commander Nebraska American Legion, Rushville News Star, March 23, 1972.
52. Smith Interview.
53. Hugh Bunnell, Managing Editor, The Alliance Times. "The Yellow Thunder Case," (Unpublished trial report).
54. Ibid., p. 12.
55. Ibid., p. 13.
56. Ibid. , p. 18.
57. Ibid.
58. Gordon Journal, March 8, 1972.
59. Interview with Jo Matula, Rushville, Nebraska, March 4, 1983.
60. Smith Interview.
61. Gordon Journal, March 15, 1972.
62. Rapid City Journal, January 26, 1973.
63. Peter Matthiessen, In the Spirit of Crazy Horse (New York: The Viking Press, 1983), p. 60.
64. Alvin M. Josephy, Jr., Now That the Buffalo's Gone (New York: Alfred A. Knopf, 1982), p. 237.
65. Interview with Clive and Agnes Gildersleeve, Rushville, Nebraska, December 22, 1982.
66. New York Times, March 10, 1972.
67. Burnette and Koster, The Road to Wounded Knee, p. 197.
68. Minneapolis Morning Tribune, March 10, 1973.
69. Bunnell, "The Yellow Thunder Case," pp. 1-2.
70. Alliance Times Herald, May 24, 1972.
71. Ibid., May 27 , 1972.
72. Muriel Waukazoo, Oral History Tape #853, South Dakota Oral History Project, University of South Dakota, Vermillion, South Dakota, July 13, 1972.
73. Deloria , Jr., Behind the Trail of Broken Treaties, pp. 46-47.
74. Peter Collier, "Only good Indian... ," Ramparts (December 1972), pp. 36-37+.
75. Interview with Vance Nelson, Curator, Fort Robinson Museum, Chadron, Nebraska, March 2, 1976.
76. Burnette and Koster, The Road to Wounded Knee, pp. 195-219.
77. Deloria, Jr., God Is Red, pp. 325-364.
78. Ibid.; Deloria, Jr., Behind the Trail of Broken Treaties, pp. 49-53.
79. Burnette and Koster, The Road to Wounded Knee, pp. 203-209.

80. Washington Evening Star, November 12, 1972.
81. George Feaver, Wounded Knee and the New Tribalism," Encounter (March 1975, p. 23.
82. The Innocent Victims of the Occupation of Wounded Knee South Dakota v. The United States, Report to the United States Senate, Congressional Reference Case No. 4-76, Filed June 10, 1981, pp 13-14.
83. Washington Evening Star, November 12, 1972.
84. Burnette and Koster, The Road to Wounded Knee, p. 217.

THE NEW INDIAN WARS

1. Senate Hearings, The Causes and Aftermath of the Wounded Knee Takeover, pp. 30-31.
2. Ibid., pp. 12-13.
3. Interview with Gerald One Feather, Former tribal council president and director of public safety, Pine Ridge, South Dakota, April 20, 1977.
4. Rapid City Journal, February 28, 1973.
5. Ibid.
6. Ibid.
7. Interview with Father Paul Steinmetz, Chadron Nebraska, March 26, 1983.
8. Deloria, Jr., Custer Died for Your Sins, p. 29.
9. Interview with David Varmette, Pine Ridge BIA, December 22, 1972.
10. Eileen Maynard and Gayla Twiss, That These People May Live: Conditions Among the Oglala Sioux of the Pine Ridge Reservation, Washington, D.C., Government Printing Office, 1970, p. 25.
11. Ibid., p. 29.
12. Ibid., p. 31.
13. Interview with Gladys Bissonette, Pine Ridge, South Dakota, October 16, 1976; Interview with Birgil Kills Straight, Pine Ridge, South Dakota, October 16, 1976.
14. Deloria, Jr., Behind the Trail of Broken Treaties, p. 73.
15. Deloria, Jr., God is Red, p. 257.
16. Scottsbluff Star Herald, January 18, 1973.
17. Ibid.
18. Ibid., January 17, 1973.
19. Ibid., January 21, 1973.
20. Ibid., January 25, 1973.
21. District Court Records, Scotts Bluff County, Gering, Nebraska, Cases 22895, 22661, 22663, 22664, 22893.
22. Rolland Dewing, "South Dakota Newspaper Coverage of the 1973 Occupation of Wounded Knee," South Dakota History (Spring 1972), pp. 60-63.
23. Interview with Jim Snow, Former probation officer, Fall River County, Chadron, Nebraska, August 4, 1982; Aberdeen American News, February 11, 1973.
24. South Dakota v. Darld Schmitz (7th Circ. 1973) Court Proceedings File, Pennington County Court House, Rapid City, South Dakota.
25. Ibid.
26. Ibid.; Jim Snow Interview.
27. South Dakota v. Darld Schmitz.
28. Ibid.
29. Ibid.; Interview with Darld Schmitz, Custer, South Dakota, October 27, 1977; Aberdeen American News, February 11, 1973.

30. Ibid.
31. Ibid.
32. Taped Interview with Sheriff Ernie Peppin and County Attorney Robert Gates, Spring, 1980. This interview was conducted by Neal Sieger, High School History Teacher at Custer High School, Custer, South Dakota.
33. Ibid.
34. Custer Chronicle, February 1, 1973.
35. Criminal Investigators from the United States Justice Department.
36. Mayor Gene Reese, Oral History Tape #681, South Dakota Oral History Project, University of South Dakota, Vermillion, South Dakota, July 25, 1973; Custer Chronicle, February 8, 1973.
37. Interview with Mrs. Jessie Sundstrom, Editor and Publisher, Custer Chronicle, November 10, 1976.
38. Peppin and Gates Tape.
39. Rapid City Journal, February 6, 1973.
40. Interview with Lyn Townsend, Reporter, Rapid City Journal, November 10, 1976; Interview with Jim Likens, Reporter, Gordon Journal, November 16, 1976.
41. Peppin and Gates Tape.
42. The February 6, 1973, confrontation at the Custer County Court House was tape-recorded live on the scene and Gates made the recording available to me through Neal Sieger.
43. Peppin and Gates Tape.
44. Sioux Falls Argus Leader, February 8, 1973.
45. Custer Chronicle, February 8, 1973.
46. Peppin and Gates Tape.
47. Custer Chronicle, February 8, 1973.
48. Ibid., February 15 , 1973.
49. Joan Hathaway, Nurse at Custer Hospital, Oral History Tape #806, South Dakota History Project, July 25, 1973.
50. Custer Chronicle, February 8, 1973.
51. Ibid.
52. Ibid.
53. Minneapolis Star, February 7, 1973.
54. Scottsbluff Star Herald, February 9, 1973.
55. Custer Chronicle, February 15, 1973.
56. Letter to Ramon A. Roubideaux from Hobart Gates, March 2, 1973.
57. Custer Chronicle, February 15, 1973.
58. Letter to Hobart Gates from Ramon Roubideaux, April 26, 1973.
59. Letter to Ramon Roubideaux from Hobart Gates, March 23, 1973.
60. Interview with Ramon Roubideaux, Chadron, Nebraska, March 8, 1978; Vizenor, Tribal Scenes and Ceremonies, p. 57.
61. Interview with Darld Schmitz, Custer, South Dakota, October 27, 1977.
62. Ibid.
63. Custer Chronicle, May 10, 1973.
64. Ibid.
65. Bennett County Booster, March 15, 1973.
66. Dewing, "South Dakota Newspaper Coverage... ," pp. 48-64.
67. Clyde Bellecourt, "American Indian Social Activism," Pacifica Tape Library, Los Angeles, California, March 1974; Clyde Bellecourt, Oral History Tape #955, South Dakota Oral History Project.

68. Robert D. Williams, Member of Racial Conciliation Board, Oral History Tape #1030, August 14, 1973.
69. Rapid City Journal, February 11, 1973.
70. Ibid., February 13, 1973.
71. Sturgis Tribune, February 14, 1973.
72. Hot Springs Star, February 15, 1973.
73. Ibid.
74. Jim Snow Interview. He was in the courthouse during the entire incident.
75. Sturgis Tribune, February 21, 1973.
76. FBI Form 302 Interview with BIA Supt. Stanley D. Lyman, March 7, 1973, Section 3, p. 9.
77. FBI, Chronology of Events, Section 11, p. 9.
78. Birgil Kills Straight Interview.
79. Interview with Fred Two Bulls, Pine Ridge Chief of Police, May 22, 1979.
80. FBI, Chronology of Events, Section 11, p. 10.
81. Interview with Lieutenant James L. Fields, Rapid City Police Department, May 25, 1983. Fields participated in the Imperial 400 Motel eviction. He thinks this is one of the few times AIM was caught off-guard in Rapid City.
82. Rapid City Journal, February 24, 1973.
83. Zimmerman, Airlift to Wounded Knee, p. 79.
84. Deloria, Jr., God Is Red, p. 257.
85. FBI, Section 6, Interview with Edgar Red Cloud, Pine Ridge, March 10, 1973, p. 28.
86. FBI, Section 3, March 8, 1973, p. 309; FBI, Section 3, March 8, 1973, p. 318.
87. Interview with Professor George R. Morgan corroborated by his wife Mary Walker Morgan, October 14, 1982.   Both are members of the Native American Church on Pine Ridge Reservation. Mrs. Morgan is an enrolled member of the Oglala Sioux Tribe.
88. Ibid.
89. Jim Likens Interview.
90. Interview with Clive and Agnes Gildersleeve, Rushville, Nebraska, December 21, 1982.
91. Minneapolis Tribune, March 1, 1973.
92. FBI, Section 2, March 3, 1973.
93. Ibid.

Return to Wounded Knee

1. Rapid City Journal, March 1, 1973.
2. Telephone Interview with Kent Frizzell, March 17, 1983.
3. FBI, Section 22, May 10, 1973, p. 160.
4. FBI, Section 2, kMarch 10, 1973.
5. Gildersleeve Interview.
6. Ibid.
7. FBI, Section 3, March 13, 1973.
8. Ibid.
9. FBI, Section 3, March 10, 1973.
10. FBI, Section 3, March 6, 1973.
11. Ibid.
12. Ibid.; Birgil Kills Straight Interview.
13. Rapid City Journal, February 28, 1973.

14. "Wounded Knee Just a Prelude?" U. S. News and World Report, March 26, 1973, p. 57.

15. Ted Elbert, "Wounded Knee: A Struggle for Self Determination," Christian Century (March 28, 1973), pp. 356-357; Rapid City Journal, March 18, 1973.

16. Pierre Daily Capital Journal, March 21, 1973.

17. Neil Hickey, "Was the Truth Buried at Wounded Knee?: An Inquest Into a Political Confrontation in Which Television Was the Primary Weapon," TV Guide, December 1973; Stephen Lesher, Media Unbound: The Impact of Television Journalism on the Public (New York: Houghton Mifflin Co., 1983); Dewing, "South Dakota Newspaper Coverage... ," pp. 48-64.

18. Ibid., Part II, p. 34; Rex Weyler, Blood on the Land: The Government and Corporate War Against the American Indian Movement (New York: Everest House, 1982), pp. 176-180.

19. Dan Rather, The Camera Never Blinks (New York: William Morrow and Co., 1977).

20. FBI, Section 1, Gebhardt to Felt, February 28 1973.

21. FBI, Section 3, Herington to Kinley, March 1, 1973.

22. Ibid.

23. FBI, Section 3, Gallagher to Gebhardt, March 2, 1973.

24. FBI, Section 3, Trimbach to Acting Director, March 1, 1973.

25. Western Outlook (Ogallala, Nebraska), May-March 1973.

26. Laurence French, Ed., Indians and Criminal Justice (Totowa, New Jersey: Allenheld, Osmun Publishers, 1982), pp. 10-15.

27. New York Times, August 6, 1973.

28. Martin Garbus, "General Haig at Wounded Knee," Nation, November 9, 1974, pp. 454-455.

29. FBI, Section 11, Chronology, p. 14.

30. FBI, Section 3, Gehhardt to Felt, March 2, 1973.

31. FBI. Section 11, Updated Chronology, March 2, 1973, n. 13.

32. FBI, Section 3, Gebhardt to R. E. Bates, March 3, 1973.

33. Alliance Times Herald, April 2, 1973.

34. New York Times, December 2, 1975.

35. "Garden Plot—'Flowers of Evil'," Akwesasne Notes, Early Summer 1974, p. 6.

36. Ibid.

37. Jack Anderson and Less Whitten, "Wounded Knee Massacre Nearly Replayed," Washington Merry-Go Round, October 3, 1975.

38. Ibid.

39. Ibid.

40. Sanford J. Ungar, FBI (Boston: Brown and Company, 1975), p. 25.

41. Frizzell Interview.

42. FBI, Section 3, Gebhardt to R. E. Bates, March 3, 1973.

43. Ibid.

44. FBI, Section 3, Gebhardt to Felt, March 9, 1973.

45. Robert Anderson, Joanna Brown, Jonny Lerner, and Barbara Lou Shafer, Eds., Voices From Wounded Knee: The People Are Standing Up (Rooseveltown, New York: Akwesasne Notes, 1974), pp. 34-35.

46. Ibid., p. 36.

47. FBI, Section 3, Gebhardt to Felt, February 28, 1973.

48. Rapid City Journal, March 1, 1973.

49. New York Times, March 1, 1973.

50. FBI, Section 3, Trimbach to Gray, March 5, 1973, pp. 177-178.

51. Ibid.

52. Ibid., p. 180.

53. FBI, Section 9, Chronology, p. 14.

54. Rapid City Journal, March 2, 1973.
55. FBI, Section 9, March 24, 1973, p. 14.
56. Gildersleeve Interview.
57. FBI, Section 11, Updated Chronology, p. 15.
58. FBI, Section 6, March 6, 1973, p. 34.
59. Lucian K. Truscott, "Vietnam Veterans Against the War," Saturday Review, October 7, 1972, pp. 557558+.
60. New York Times, March 3, 1973.
61. Charles McCarry, "A Few Soft Words for the Rabble Rousers," Esquire, July 1969, pp. 107-108+; "Four for the Show," Newsweek, November 10, 1969, p. 41; Joseph Bishop, Jr., "Will Mr. William Kunstler Please Step Down?" Esquire, April 1971, pp. 115+.
62. Cynthia R. Fadool, Ed., Contemporary Authors (Detroit: Gale Research Co., 1976), Vol. 61-64, pp. 115+.
63. FBI, Section 20, SAC Los Angeles to Acting Director, May 8, 1973; FBI, Section 21, SAC Trimbach to Acting Director, May 21, 1973; VVAW Newsletter Number Four, March 25, 1973, Chicago, Illinois.
64. Burnette and Koster, The Road to Wounded Knee, p. 240.
65. FBI, Section 3, March 8, 1973, p. 322.
66. FBI, Section 3, March 7, 1983, p. 293.
67. FBI, Section 3, March 8, 1973, p. 252.
68. FBI, Section 6, March 9, 1973.
69. FBI, Section 6, March 10, 1973, p. 322.
70. Anderson, Voices from Wounded Knee, p. 101.
71. FBI, Section 3, March 3, 1973, p. 119.
72. Zimmerman, Airlift to Wounded Knee, p. 163.
73. Interview with Russell Means, Chadron, Nebraska, January 27, 1983; Frank Donner, "The Confessions of an FBI Informer," Harpers, December 1972, pp. 245-254.
74. FBI, Section 3, March 7, 1973, p. 294.
75. FBI, Section 1, R. F. Bates to Gebhardt, March 4, 1873.
76. FBI, Section 2, R. F. Bates to Gebhardt, March 4, 1973.
77. FBI, Section 3, March 5, 1973, p. 203.
78. FBI, Section 3, Gebhardt to R. F. Bates, March 3, 1973.
79. FBI, Section 9, March 22, 1973.
80. John Kifner, "It's A Very Serious Thing They're Asking For," New York Times, March 6, 1973.
81. FBI, Section 2, R. F. Bates to Gebhardt, March 5, 1973.
82. Anderson, Voices from Wounded Knee, p. 45.
83. FBI, Section 1, R. F. Bates to Gebhardt, March 5, 1973.
84. Anderson, Voices from Wounded Knee, p. 46.
85. Ibid., p. 47.
86. Pierre Daily Capital Journal, March 6, 1973.
87. FBI, Section 11, p. 18.
88. FBI, Section 3, March 7, 1973, p. 387.
89. FBI, Section 3, March 7, 1973, p. 395. See Jean Cummings, Alias the Buffalo Doctor (Athens, Ohio: Swallow Press, 1980).
90. FBI, Section 3, March 8, 1973, p. 40G.
91. Cummings, Alias the Buffalo Doctor.
92. FBI, Section 3, March 7, 1973, p. 250.
93. Kim C. Rogal, "Indians and Ranchers: Bad Days on the Reservation," Nation, November 20, 1976, pp. 525-530.

94. Ralph Erickson, Press Release, Washington, D.C., March 10, 1973.
95. FBI, Section 2, Gebhardt to Felt, March 7, 1973.
96. New York Times, March 8, 1973.
97. Ibid.
98. Erickson Press Release.
99. FBI, Section 3, March 11, 1973.
100. Lincoln (Nebraska) Journal, March 8, 1973.
101. Rapid City Journal, March 8, 1970.
102. Picture can be seen in Anderson, Voices from Wounded Knee, p. 51.
103. FBI, Section 2, R.J. Gallagher to Gebhardt, March 8, 1973.
104. Ibid.
105. FBI, Section 2, March 8, 1973.
106. FBI, Section 2, Trimbach to Gray, March 8, 1973.
107. Burnette and Koster, The Road to Wounded Knee, p. 233.
108. Aberdeen American News, March 9, 1973.
109. Pierre Daily Capital Journal, March 8, 1973.
110. FBI, Section 3, March 8, 1973, p. 47, 228.
111. FBI, Section 2, Trimbach to Gray, March 8, 1973.
112. Pierre Daily Capital Journal, March 9, 1973.
113. St. Cloud (Minnesota) Daily Times, March 8, 1973.
114. FBI, Section 2, Trimbach to Gray, March 8, 1973.
115. Mary A. Kellogg, "The Siege of Wounded Knee," Newsweek, Narch 19, 1973, p. 23.
116. Ken Huff, "A Suspenseful Show of Red Power," Time, March 19, 1973, pp. 16-18.
117. FBI, Section 2, Trimbach to Gray, March 9, 1973.
118. Huff, "A Suspenseful Show of Red Power," p. 17.
119. John Adams, At the Heart of the Whirlwind (New York: Harper and Row, 1976), pp. 100-110.
120. Ibid.
121. Interview with Robert and Mary Tice, Methodist Lay Leaders, Chadron, Nebraska, November 1982: Kent Frizzell described Adams as "a thorn in the side - a true detriment to negotiations." Frizzell Interview, March 17, 1983.
122. Adams, At the Heart of the Whirlwind, p. 102.
123. Ibid.
124. FBI, Section 11, Chronology, p. 20.
125. FBI, Section 4, Trimbach to Gray, March 10, 1973.
126. Minneapolis Tribune, March 11, 1973.
127. FBI, Section 30, December 5, 1973.
128. Minneapolis Tribune, March 11, 1973.
129. "Twin Stalemates," Time, March 19, 1973, p. 16.
130. Ibid.
131. Minneapolis Tribune, March 11, 1973.
132. "A Suspenseful Show of Red Power," Time, March 19, 1973, p. 16.
133. Denver Post, March 12, 1973.
134. Columbus (Nebraska) Telegram, March 13, 1973.
135. FBI, Section 6, Trimbach to Gray, March 11, 1973, p. 15.
136. FBI, Section 4, Trimbach to Gray, March 11, 1973; FBI, Section 6, March 11, 1973, pp. 241-242; FBI, Section 15, p. 199.
137. See Documentary Photo Aids Series, Mount Dora, Florida, Wounded Knee #7.
138. Anderson, Voices from Wounded Knee, p. 58.
139. FBI, Section 15, March 11, 1973, pp. 161-163.

140. FBI, Section 6, pp. 16-17.
141. FBI, Section 4, Trimbach to Gray, March 11, 1973.
142. FBI, Section 4, Gebharlt to Felt, March 12, 1973.
143. New York Times, March 12, 1973.
144. FBI, File 4, Gebhardt to Felt, March 12, 1973.
145. "The Siege of Wounded Knee," Newsweek, March 19, 1973, pp. 22-23.
146. For an anti law enforcement view see Weyler, Blood on the Land, pp. 57-96.

AN IMPASSE UPON AN IMPASSE

1. Ungar, FBI, p. 413.
2. Ibid.
3. FBI, Section 5, R. J. Gallagher to Gebhardt, March 14, 1973.
4. New York Times, March 10, 1973.
5. Rapid City Journal, March 11, 1973.
6. New York Times, March 12, 1973.
7. Anderson, Voices from Wounded Knee, p. 55.
8. Rapid City Journal, March 12, 1973.
9. FBI, Section 5, Report prepared by Joseph T. Sneed, Deputy Attorney General and Robert G. Dixon, Jr., Assistant Attorney General, Office of Legal Counsel, Concerning legal implications of "Declaration of Sovereignty," March 14, 1973.
10. FBI, Section 31, March 15, 1973; "Twin Stalemates," Time, March 26, 1973, p. 32.
11. "Chronology of Events," Pacifica Tape Library, Los Angeles, Calif., March 29, 1974.
12. Pierre Daily Capital Journal, March 12, 1973.
13. Alan Stang, "American Indian Movement - Red Indians," American Opinion, Belmont, Mass., September 1975, p. 3.
14. FBI, Section 5, SAC Los Angeles to Trimbach, March 14, 1973.
15. Yakima (Washington) Herald Republic, March 12, 1972; Seattle Times, March 12, 1973; Lincoln Journal, March 13, 1974.
16. John Adams, "The FBI at Wounded Knee," Minnesota Public Radio Program #A-120, St. Paul, Minnesota, March 26, 1974.
17. "Chronology of Events," Pacifica Tape Library, Los Angeles, KPFA Berkeley, March 29, 1973.
18. FBI, Section 11, Updated Chronology, p. 23.
19. FBI, Section 5, Trimbach to Gray, March 14, 1973.
20. FBI, Section 5, Gallagher to Gebhardt, March 14, 1973.
21. Ibid.
22. FBI, Section 5, W. B. Campbell to Felt, March 16, 1973.
23. FBI, Section 5, Trimbach to Gray, March 16, 1973.
24. Court Order dated March 16, 1973, obtained from Les Marella, a Chadron State College student who was arrested under this order on April 16, 1973.
25. Tice Interview.
26. Dick Wilson, #918, South Dakota Oral History Project, July 17, 1973.
27. Minnesota Star, March 17, 1973.
28. John Adams, At the Heart of the Whirlwind, p. 126.
29. Fremont (Nebraska) Tribune, March 12, 1973.
30. FBI, Section 13, March 28, 1973, p. 12.

31. Ibid.
32. Valentine Newspaper, March 22, 1973.
33. New York Times, March 14, 1973.
34. Congressional Record, H 1738-39, March 14, 1973.
35. Ibid.
36. Aberdeen American Nevs, March 14, 1973.
37. New York Times, March 17, 1973.
38. FBI, Section 7, March 19, 1973.
39. Rapid City Journal, March 20, 1973.
40. FBI, Section 7, Trimbach to Gray, March 17, 1973.
41. Rapid City Journal, March 16, 1973.
42. FBI, Section 7, Trimbach to Gray, March 17, 1973.
43. New York Times, March 18, 1973.
44. Anderson, Voices from Wounded Knee, pp. 114-115.
45. FBI, Section 5, Bates to Gebhardt, March 16, 1973.
46. Anderson, Voices from Wounded Knee, pp. 94-97.
47. FBI, Section 7, Trimbach to Gray, March 19, 1973.
48. Joseph Cash, Tape #935, Interview with Nathen Little Soldier, Fort Bethold, No. Dak., August 9, 1973, South Dakota Oral History Project.
49. New York Times, March 20, 1973.
50. New York Times, March 24, 1973.
51. FBI, Section 9, March 21, 1973.
52. FBI, Section 7, Trimbach to Gray, March 20, 1973.
53. Ibid.
54. FBI, Section 8, Answer to Senator Henry Jackson, March 22, 1973.
55. FBI, Section 7, SAC San Francisco to Gray, March 21, 1973.
56. San Mateo Times, March 22, 1973.
57. FBI, Section 8, SAC San Francisco to Trimbach, March 23, 1973.
58. Ibid., March 22, 1973.
59. FBI, Section 9, March 20, 1973.
60. Aberdeen Anerican News, March 20, 1973, p. 6.
61. FBI, Section 8, SAC Albuquerque to Trimbach, March 22, 1973.
62. FBI, Section 7, March 25, 1973.
63. FBI, Section 8, Charlotte SAC to Trimbach, March 23 and 24, 1973.
64. Minnesota Star, March 20 and 21, 1973.
65. Pierre Daily Capital Journal, March 20, 1973.
66. FBI, Section 7, Trimbach to Gray, March 18, 1973.
67. Ibid., March 19, 1973.
68. FBI, Section 8, Trimbach to Gray, March 22,1973; Anderson, Voices from Wounded Knee, p. 124.
69. FBI, File 11, March 23, 1973.
70. FBI, File 3, Trimbach to Gray, March 22, 1973.
71. FBI, Section 8, Summary, March 23, 1973.
72. FBI, Section 8, Trimbach to Gray, March 23, 1973.
73. FBI, Section 8, Summary, March 26, 1973.
74. FBI, Section 11, Chronology, p. 29.
75. Vine Deloria, Jr., "The Most Important Indian," Akwesasne Notes, Early Winter 1974.
76. Frizzell Interview.
77. Gladys Bissonette Interview; Bessie Cornelius, Oral History Tape #917, South Dakota Oral History Project, July 17, 1973; Reginald Cedarface Interview.

78. Anderson, Voices from Wounded Knee, pp. 124-125.
79. FBI, Section 11, Eugene White Hawk v. Stanley Lyman, etc., U. S. District Court.
80. FBI, Section 11, March 25, 1973.
81. FBI, Section 10; Interview with Duane Brewer, Chadron, Nebraska, May 20, 1983.
82. Ibid.; Alan Stang, "American Indian Movement—Red Indians," pp. 1-22; Terrie Schultz, "The Continuing Massacre at Wounded Knee: Election for Presidency of the Tribal Council," Harpers, June 1974, p. 30.
83. FBI, Section 13, March 26, 1973.
84. Pierre Daily Capital Journal, March 28, 1973.
85. Duane Brewer Interview; Schultz, "The Continuing Massacre at Wounded Knee," p. 30.
86. Akwesasne Notes, Early Summer 1973, p. 13.
87. FBI, Section 10, Trimbach to Gray, March 27, 1973.
88. Richard Wilson, Oral History Tape #918, South Dakota Oral History Project, July 17, 1973.
89. Reginald Cedarface Interview, Wilson blockade member.
90. FBI, Section 11, W. M. Felt to Gray, March 26, 1973.
91. FBI, Section 10, Trimbach to Gray, March 25, 1973.
92. Ibid.
93. Chadron Record, March 29, 1973.
94. Anderson, Voices from Wounded Knee, p. 130.
95. Frizzell Interview.
96. FBI, Section 10, March 26, 1973.
97. Anderson, Voices From Wounded Knee, p. 129.
98. FBI, Section 10, Bates to Gebhardt, lMarch 26, 1973.
99. New York Times, March 28, 1973.
100. Ibid.
101. Minnesota Star, March 28, 1973.
102. Ibid.
103. George Feaver, "An Indian Melodrama," Encounter, May 1975, p. 31.
104. Minnesota Star, March 29, 1973; Minneapolis Tribune, March 29, 1973: FBI, Sect ion 10, Trimbach to Gray, March 28, 1973.
105. "Guerilla Theater," Newsweek, April 9, 1973, p. 38.
106. Chadron Record, March 29, 1973.
107. Minneapolis Tribune, March 29, l973.
108. Ibid.
109. U.S., Congress, Senate, Committee on the Judiciary, Revolutionary Activities Within the United States: The American Indian Movement. Hearings before the subcommittee to investigate the administration of the Internal Security Act and other internal security laws. 94th Congress, 2nd session, April 6, 1976, p. 93.   (Eastland Hearings).
110. Columbus Telegram, March 29, 1973; W.G. Buckley, "Brando at Wounded Knee," National Review, April 27, 1973, pp. 486-487.
111. Feaver, "An Indian Melodrama," p. 30.
112. New York Times, March 28, 1973.
113. Denver Post, March 25, 1973.
114. New York Times, March 24, 1973.
115. "Twin Stalement; Sioux Protest," Time, p. 32.
116. "Birth of a Nation," Newsweek, March 26, 1973, p. 22.
117. Anderson, Voices from Wounded Knee, p. 136.
118. Lincoln (Nebraska) Journal, March 19, 1973.
119. Ibid., March 27, 1973.
120. New York Times, March 15, 1973.

121. Lincoln (Nebraska) Star, March 29, 1973.
122. Rapid City Journal, April 11, 1973.
123. New York Times, March 26, 1973.
124. FBI, Section 11, Trimbach to Gray, March 30, 1973.
125. Pierre Daily Capital Journal, March 30, 1973.
126. Rapid City Journal, April 21, 1973.
127. Ibid., March 28, 1973.
128. Ibid., April 5, 1973.
129. Sturgis Tribune, April 18, 1973.
130. Mike Smith Interview.
131. Courtney R. Sheldon, "Saga of Wounded Knee: Nixon Gets into the Act," Christian Science Monitor, March 28, 1973.
132. Ibid.
133. FBI, Section 11, R. F. Bates to Gebhardt, March 29, 1973.
134. New York Times, March 30, 1973.
135. Sioux Falls Argus Leader, April 1, 1973.
136. FBI, Section 11, Trimbach to Gray, March 30, 1973.
137. Ibid.
138. FBI, Section 13, April 1, 1973; Anderson, Voices from Wounded Knee, pp. 134-152.
139. Ibid.
140. New York Times, April 1, 1973.
141. Reginald Cedarface Interview; Interview with Les Marella, Chadron, Nebraska, August, 1981.
142. FBI, Section 13, Summary Report, April 3, 1973.
143. Congressional Record, S 6277, April 2, 1973.
144.
      Ibid.
145. Minneapolis Star, April 4, 1973.
146. Congressional Record, E 2117, April 4, 1973.
147. New York Times, April 5, 1973.
148. FBI, Section 15, April 5, 1973.
149. FBI, Section 12, Trimbach to Gray, April 3, 1973.
150. Occupation of Wounded Knee Hearings, pp. 262.
151. Rapid City Journal, April 22, 1973.
152. Anderson, Voices from Wounded Knee, pp. 145-148.
153. FBI, Section 12, Portland SAC to Gray, April 6, 1973.
154. FBI, Section 12, Trimbach to Gray, April 6, 1973.
155. Ibid.
156. FBI, Section 12, Trimbach to Gray, April 7, 1973.
157. FBI, Section 12, Bissonette Letter, April 6, 1973.
158. Akwesasne Notes, Early Summer 1973, p. 11.
159. FBI, Section 14, Washington Field Representatives to Gray, April 19, 1973.
160. New York Times, April 11, 1973.
161. FBI, Section 30, Wounded Knee White Paper, p. 34.

REACHING AN ACC0RD

1. "Guerrilla Theater," Newweek, p. 38.
2. Minneapolis Tribune, April 10, 1973.

3. Pierre Daily Capital Journal, April 12, 1973; Minneapolis Tribune, April 10, 1973.
4. FBI, Section 15, Kleindienst to Gray and Colburn, April 13, 1973.
5. FBI, Section 30, White Paper, p. 36.
6. Chadron Record, April 9, 1973.
7. Rushville News Star, April 12, 1973.
8. Crawford Tribune, April 12, 1973.
9. Rushville News Star, April 12, 1973.
10. Interview with William Quigley, Valentine, Nebraska, March 30, 1977.
11. Pierre Daily Capital Journal, April 12, 1973.
12. New York Times, April 17, 1973.
13. Gladys Bissonette Interview.
14. FBI, Section 15, Trimbach to Gray, April 16, 1973.
15. Burnette and Koster, The Road to Wounded Knee, p. 264.
16. New York Times, April 13, 1973.
17. FBI, Section 15, Trimbach to Gray, April 13, 1973.
18. Anderson, Voices from Wounded Knee, pp. 171-174.
19. Sioux Falls Argus Leader, April 16, 1973.
20. see Bill Zimmerman, Airlift to Wounded Knee.
21. FBI, Section 16, Trimbach to Gray, April 17, 1973.
22. FBI, Section 16, Trimbach to Gray, April 19, 1973.
23. see Bill Zimmerman, Airlift to Wounded Knee.
24. Ibid., p. 305.
25. FBI, Section 16, Trimbach to Gray. April 19, 1973.
26. New York Times, April 19, 1973.
27. Anderson, Voices from Wounded Knee, p. 186.
28. Chadron Record, April 23, 1973.
29. FBI, Section 30, Wounded Knee White Paper, p.39.
30. FBI, Section 16, Felt to Gray, April 19, 1973.
31. For an exactly opposite point of view read Edith Lee, Forked Tongues and Wounded Knees. Northwood, North Dakota, 1973, available in Sheridan County Historical Museum, Rushville, Nebraska.
32. Rapid City Journal, April 22, 1973.
33. FBI, Section 17, SAC Oklahoma City to Trimbach, April 21, 1973.
34. Sioux Falls Argus Leader, April 25, 1973.
35. Hot Springs Star, April 26, 1973.
36. FBI, Section 17, Dick Hellstern to Kleindienst and Sneed, April 22, 1973.
37. FBI, Section 17, Trimbach to Gray, April 22, 1973.
38. FBI, Section 13, Trimbach to Gray, April 25, 1973.
39. New York Times, April 27, 1973.
40. Anderson, Voices From Wounded Knee, pp. 164-165.
41. FBI, Section 18, Trimbach to Gray, April 24, 1973; FBI Section 18, SAC Pine Ridge to Trimbach, April 23, 1973.
42. New York Times, April 24, 1973.
43. FBI, Section 18, Felt to Gebhardt, April 24, 1973.
44. New York Times, April 25, 1973; FBI, Section 17, Trimbach to Gray, April 24,1973.
45. FBI, Section 18, Felt to Gebhardt, April 24, 1973.
46. Ibid.
47. New York Times, April 26, 1973.
48. Frizzell Interview.
49. New York Times, April 27, 1973.

50. Alliance Times Herald, May 5, 1973.
51. Anderson, Voices from Wounded Knee, p. 202.
52. FBI, Section 18, SAC Omaha to Acting Director, Apirl 26, 1973.
53. FBI, Section 18, Bates to Gebhardt, April 26, 1973.
54. Denver Post, April 27, 1973.
55. New York Times, April 29, 1973.
56. Chadron Record, April 26, 1973.
57. FBI, File 18, Bates to Gebhardt, April 27, 1973.
58. Mrs. Agnes Lamont, #A123, Minnesota Public Radio, August 30, 1974.
59. Burnette and Koster, The Road to Wounded Knee, p. 247.
60. Ibid., p. 248.
61. Zimmerman, Airlift to Wounded Knee, p. 321.
62. Akwesasne Notes, Early Summer 1973, p. 22.
63. Ibid., Early Autumn 1974, p. 13.
64. Lincoln Journal, April 27, 1973.
65. "FBI Chief Resigns," Alliance Times Herald, April 27, 1973; "A Saddened Witness," New York Times, August 6, 1973.
66. Aberdeen American News, April 27, 1973.
67. FBI, Section 24, SAC Los Angeles to Ruckelshaus, June 14, 1973.
68. FBI, Section 18, Trimbach to Gray, April 27, 1973.
69. Akwesasne Notes, Early Summer 1973, p. 26.
70. Valentine Newspaper, May 3, 1973.
71. Akwesasne Notes, Early Winter 1973, p. 8.
72. FBI, Section 19, U. S. Department of Justice Report, May 3, 1973.
73. Fort Lauderdale News, April 29, 1973.
74. Ibid.
75. FBI, Section 19, Trimbach to Acting Director, May 2, 1973.
76. FBI, Section 19, SAC San Antonio to Acting Director, May 4, 1973.
77. Frizzell Interview.
78. FBI, Section 18, Trimbach to Gray, April 29, 1973.
79. Anderson, Voices from Wounded Knee, p. 222.
80. Thomas E. Mails, Fools Crow (Garden City, New York: Doubleday, 1979), p. 191.
81. Ibid., p. 192.
82. Ibid., p. 190.
83. FBI, Section 30, Wounded Knee White Paper, p. 41.
84. FBI, Section 19, Trimbach to Acting Director, April 30, 1973; Anderson, Voices from Wounded Knee, p 222.
85. FBI, Section 19, Trimbach to Acting Director, May 2, 1973.
86. New York Times, April 30, 1973.
87. FBI, Section 19, Bates to Gebhardt, April 30, 1973.
88. FBI, Section 30, FBI White Paper, p. 43.
89. Anderson, Voices from Wounded Knee, p. 224.
90. FBI, Section 19, Trimbach to Acting Director.
91. FBI, Section 19, Trimbach to Ruckelshaus, 1973, May 5, 1973.
92. Ibid., May 4, 1973.
93. FBI, Section 20, Trimbach to Ruckelshaus, May 5, 1973.
94. FBI, Section 19, SAC Omaha to Ruckelshaus, May 3, 1973.
95. FBI, Section 21, SAC Omaha to Ruckelshaus, May 9, 1973.
96. FBI, Section 19, Trimbach to Ruckelshaus,.May 3, 1973.

97. Interview with Gayla Twiss, Pine Ridge, South Dakota, May 22, 1979. She attended the funeral.
98. Mails, Fools Crow, p. 192.
99. FBI, Section 30, FBI White Paper, p. 42.
100. Ibid., pp. 45-46.
101. Document provided by Ramon Roubideaux in author's possession.
102. FBI, Section 20, SAC Los Angeles to Ruckelshaus, May 8, 1973.
103. FBI, Section 20, May 5 Agreement.
104. FBI, Section 12, April 5 Agreement.
105. FBI, Section 21, Trimbach to Ruckelshaus, May 8 and 9, 1973.
106. FBI, Section 22, May 9, 1973; Gordon Journal, May 16, 1973.
107. Ibid.
108. Rapid City Journal, May 11, 1973.
109. Akwesasne Notes, Early Summer 1973, p. 32.
110. Gildersleeve Interviews; Gordon Journal, May 16, 1974; New York Times, May 10, 1973; Jere Brennan, Welfare worker in charge of reconstruction, Tape #916, South Dakota Oral History Project, July 18, 1973.
111. Gordon Journal, May 16, 1973.
112. Ibid.
113. John Adams, At the Heart of the Whirlwind, p. 132.
114. Jere Brennan, #916, South Dakota Oral History Project.
115. Adams, At the Heart of the Whirlwind, p. 132.
116. Rapid City Journal, May 11, 1973.
117. FBI, Section 21, May 18, 1973; FBI, Section 21, Trimbach to Ruckelshaus, May 12, 1973.
118. FBI, Section 23, Trimbach to Ruckelshaus, June 7, 1973.
119. Rapid City Journal, May 10, 1973.
120. Letter from Joseph T. Sneed to author, November 23, 1982.
121. Gordon Journal, May 23, 1973.
122. FBI, Section 30, FBI White Paper, pp. 50-51.
123. Schultⁿ, "Bamboozle Me Not at Wounded Knee," p. 46.

OVER THE BRINK

1. FBI, Section 24, Trimbach to Ruckelshaus, June 7, 1973.
2. New York Times, July 23, 1973.
3. FBI, Section 25, General Investigative Division to Ruckelshaus, June 22, 1973.
4. Rapid City Journal, May 18, 1973.
5. Occupation of Wounded Knee Hearings, pp. 92-97.
6. FBI, Section 2, Trimbach to Ruckelshaus, May 21, 1973.
7. Ibid.
8. FBI, Section 14, Letter from Leonard Garment, May 29, 1973.
9. The entire fourteen page letter to Garment is in Occupation of Wounded knee Hearings, pp. 150-163.
10. Ibid., p. 95.
11. Ibid., pp. 115-133.
12. Ibid., pp. 171-172.
13. Kirk Kickingbird, "The American Indian Policy Review Commission: A Prospect for Future Change in Federal Indian Policy," American Indian Law Review, 3 (1975): 243-253.

14. Undated Fact Sheet on AIM distributed by the American Indian Defense Committee, Philadelphia, PA.
15. Wassaja, September 1973.
16. Ibid.
17. New York Times, July 26, 1973.
18. Interview with Stig Ericson, Swedish author and publisher, Chadron,.Nebraska, May 17, 1983; Interview with Hans Smith, Sr., Dutch businessman, Amsterdam, The Netherlands, August 5, 1981.
19. Russell Means, "Native American Spiritual Values," Minnesota Radio, #A-116, April 4, 1974.
20. New York Times, August 14, 1973.
21. Mark Lane, "On Wounded Knee," Pacifica Tape Library, Los Angeles, CA., 1973.
22. Eastland Committee Hearings on the American Indian Movement, pp. 30-37, 106-107.
23. FBI, Section 27, Trimbach to Kelley, August 30, 1973.
24. Burnette and Koster, The Road to Wounded Knee, pp. 259-262.
25. Des Moines Tribune, August 28, 1973.
26. FBI, Section 28, Trimbach to Kelley, October 13, 1973.
27. Burnette and Koster, The Road to Wounded Knee, p. 261.
28. Joseph Cash, Field Notes, South Dakota Oral History Project, Tape #940, October 19, 1973.
29. "Wounded Knee goes On," North Country Anvil, January 1974, p. 50.
30. Ibid.
31. FBI, Section 27, R. F. Bates to Gebhardt, August 21, 1973.
32. Joseph Cash, Field Notes, #940.
33. Rapid City Journal, October 29, 1973.
34. FBI, Section 28 Trimbach to Kelley, October 25, 1973.
35. Schultz, "The Continuing Massacre at Wounded Knee: Election for Presidency of the Tribal Council," p. 30.
36. New York Times, October 23, 1973.
37. Clyde Bellecourt, South Dakota Oral History Project, Tape #955, November 9, 1973.
38. Rapid City Journal, November 19, 1973.
39. New York Times, December 16, 1973.
40. Dean M. Kelley, "The Clergy's 'Confidentiality' Dilemma," Christian Century, January 30, 1974 pp. 90-92+.
41. New York Times, November 1, 1973.
42. Ibid., December 8, 1973.
43. Eastland Committee Hearings on the American Indian Movement, pp. 60-61, 145.
44. Judge Fred J. Nichol, Minnesota Public Radio Interview, Tape #A-121, March 18, 1973.
45. Eastland Committee Hearings, pp. 54-55.
46. "Judging Jurors," Time, January 28, 1974, p. 60.
47. Akwesasne Notes, Early Autumn 1974, pp. 4-6.
48. FBI, Section 5, March 7, 1973.
49. John T. Elliff, The Reform of FBI Intelligence Operations (Princeton: Princeton U. Press, 1979), p. 65.
50. FBI, Section 31, Letter from Department of the Army to Laurence H. Silbenman, Deputy Attorney General.
51. Paula Giese, "Rape Cover-Up in River Falls," North Country Anvil, August-September 1975, pp. 58-69.
52. Akwesasne Notes, Early Autumn 1974, pp. 9-11.
53. Ibid.
54. Ibid.

55. "Over the Brink," Time, September 30, 1974, p. 32; "Verdict at Wounded Knee," Newsweek, September 30, 1974, pp. 54-55.
56. New York Times, September 17, 1974.
57. Akwesasne Notes, Early Autumn 1974, pp. 4-6.
58. St. Paul Pioneer Press, March 4, 1975.
69. FBI, Section 31, Gordon to Bates, September 20, 1974.
60. FBI, Section 32, J. E. O'Connell to Gebhardt, April 24, 1975.

A CALDRON OF VIOLENCE

1. Schultz, "The Continuing Massacre at Wounded Knee," p. 10.
2. Ibid.
3. Undated Wilson campaign flyer.
4. Schultz, "The Continuing Massacre at Wounded Knee," p. 10+.
5. Ibid.
6. Speech by Russell Means, St. Paul, Minnesota, February 11, 1974.
7. U. S. Commission on Civil Rights, Report of Investigation Oglala Sioux Tribe, General Election 1974, to Rogers Morton, Secretary of the Interior, July 1974.
8. Shana Alexander, Anyone's Daughter: The Times and Trials of Patty Hearst (New York: The Viking Press. 1979) p. 310.
9. Alliance Times Herald, February 21, 1974.
10. Wassaja, March-April 1974.
11. AIM release, May 13, 1974.
12. Akwesasne Notes, Summer 1974, pp. 13-15.
13. Interview with Bishop E. O. Gilbertson, April 1., 1977.
14. WKLDOC Newsletter, Vol. II No. 15, July 1, 1974.
15. AIM Press Release, May 6, 1974.
16. WKLDOC Release, Sioux Falls, South Dakota, August 1974.
17. Paula Giese, "Free Sarah Bad Heart Bull," North Country Anvil, October-November 1974, pp. 64-71.
18. Interview, Couple from Mobridge, South Dakota, Rapid City, January 8, 1983.
19. AIM Press Release No. 4, International Treaty Conference, Mobridge, South Dakota, June 1974.
20. Rapid City Journal, October 17, 1982.
21. Akwesasne Notes, Early Autumn 1974, p. 19.
22. Ibid., Early Winter 1974, p. 28.
23. William Janklow vs. Newsweek, United States District Court for the District of South Dakota, February 24, 1983, p. 4.
24. Ibid.
25. Ibid.
26. Akwesasne Notes, Early Winter 1974, p. 28.
27. William Janklow, Tape #1037, South Dakota Oral History Project, June 16, 1977.
28. Paula Giese, "Secret Agent Douglass Durham and the Death of Jancita Eagle Deer," March-April 1976, North Country Anvil, p. 36.
29. U. S., Congress, Senate, Final Report of the Select Committee to Study Governmental Operations with Respect to Intelligence Activities, 94th Congress, 2nd session, Five Vol., Cril Payne, Deep Cover (New York: Newsweek Books, 1979).
30. Elliot Kanter, "The FBI Takes Aim at AIM The American Indian Journal, August 1977, pp. 14-18.

31. Ibid.; Dan Blackburn, "Skyhorse and Mohawk: More Than a Murder Trial," Nation, December 24, 1977 pp. 682-686.
32. New York Times, December 31, 1974.
33. Interview with Duane Brewer, Wilson BIA police officer, Chadron, Nebraska, May 20, 1983.
34. Rapid City Journal, November 21, 1974.
35. Letter to Congressman James Abdnor from Benjamin R. Civiletti, Assistant Attorney General, September 22, 1977; Donna Giago (Ludwick), then with KEVN Television, Rapid City, made her complete file on the case available to me.
36. Letter to Lindy M. Trueblood from Garry Peterson, M.D., March 10, 1978.
37. Ibid.
38. Interview with Jim Gilbert, Assistant Professor of Criminal Justice, Chadron, Nebraska, March 29, 1983; James Gilbert, Criminal Investigation (Columbus, Ohio: Charles E. Merrill Publishing, 1980), pp. 216-253.
39. Roxanne Dunbar Ortiz, Ed., The Great Sioux Nation: Sitting in Judgment on America (Berkeley, California: Moon Books, 1977).
40. Omaha World Herald, December 10, 1982.
41. Roxanne Dunbar Ortiz, Ed., The Great Sioux Nation.
42. "The New Indian-Treaty Wars," Newsweek,.January 13, 1975, pp 58-59.
43. For information about the Wagner takeover see: Reverend Robert McBride, Tape #1032, South Dakota Oral History Project, May 26, 1975.
44. John P. Adams, "Why the Alexians Gave the Abbey to the Indians," Christian Century, March 5, 1975, pp. 223-228.
45. Jean Caffey Lyles, "Gresham Occupation and Aftermath," Christian Century, February 19, 1975, pp. 155-157.
46. Ibid.
47. Ibid.
48. Akwesasne Notes, Early Spring 1976, pp. 16-18.
49. John Adams, "AIM and the FBI," Christian Century, April 2, 1975, pp 325-326; John Adams, "AIM, the Church and the FBI: The Douglass Durham Case," Christian Century, May 14, 1975, pp. 489-493.
50. Ibid.
51. Eastland Hearings, p. 11.
52. Akwesasne Notes, Late Autumn 1976, p. 4, and Early Spring 1975, p. 31.
53. Eastland Hearings, pp. 65-67.
54. New York Times, March 23, 1975.
55. Ibid., April 22, 1975.
56. Interview with Jim Lomax, at that time Superintendent of Oglala Community schools, Chadron, Nebraska, December, December 3, 1982.
57. Interview with Francis Montileaux, Martin's brother, January 3, 1981, Rapid City, South Dakota.
58. Amnesty International, A Proposal for a Commission of Inquiry into the Effect of Domestic Intelligence Activities on Criminal Trials in the United States of America (London: Amnesty International, 1981), pp. 39-40. (Hereafter referred to as "Amnesty International.").
59. Ibid., pp. 46-49.
60. Akwesasne Notes, Early Summer 1975, p. 9.
61. Ibid., Early Springs 1976, p. 12.
62. Duane Brewer Interview.
63. Rex Weyler, Blood on the Land, pp. 132-136.
64. Akwesasne Notes, Later Summer 1975.
65. New York Times, June 9 and 10, 1975.

66. "Conviction at Cedar Rapids," Program B-241, Minnesota Public Radio Program, St. Paul, Minnesota, 1974.
67. Duane Brewer Interview.
68. Interview and written statement, Lavon Schwarting (Jerry's mother), Chadron, Nebraska, May 26, 1983; Interview with Robert Ecoffey, BIA Police Officer, June 8, 1981; New York Times, June 29, 1975.
69. Matthiessen, In the Spirit of Crazy Horse, pp. 212-213; Weyler, Blood of the Land, p. 178; "Annie Mae: Brave Hearted Woman," (film), Brown Bird Productions, Los Angeles, California.
70. Robert Ecoffey Interview.
71. Duane Brewer Interview.
72. Akwesasne Notes, Late Summer 1975, p. 7.
73. Matthiessen, In the Spirit of Crazy Horse, pp. 464-471.
74. Duane Brewer Interview (He was on the scene); Joel Weisman, "About That 'Ambush' at Wounded Knee," Columbia Journalism Review (September-October 1975), pp. 28-31.
75. Robert Ecoffey Interview and other sources.
76. Duane Brewer Interview.
77. Ibid.
78. Letter to author from Attorney Dennis D. King, Gordon, Nebraska, April 15, 1983.
79. The State of Nebraska vs. Joseph George, Case No. C1363, January 1975.
80. Robert Ecoffey Interview.
81. Conversation with Dennis King, April 6, 1983.
82. "The Struggle for Native American Sovereighty," Pacifica Tape Library, Los Angeles, California, 1975.
83. Christian Century, August 6-13, 1975, p. 704.
84. "A Report from Pine Ridge, Conditions on the Oglala Sioux Reservation," Civil Rights Digest, Summer 1975, pp. 28-38.
85. Rapid City Journal, March 11, 1976; "FBI Abuses," Minnesota Public Radio (Part I, March 1, 1977; Part II, March 2, 1977; Part III, March 3, 1977).
86. Matthiessen, In the Spirt of Crazy Horse, pp. 238-240.
87. New York Times, November 26, 1975.
88. Timothy Fay, "Indian Brothers Innocent," North Country Anvil, July-August, 1976 pp. 10-11.
89. Robert Ecoffey Interview; Duane Brewer Interview.
90. Matthiessen, In the Spirit of Crazy Horse, pp. 41-58; Jim Calio, "Murderer, Martyr—of Both? The Tangled Case of the Sioux 'Enforcer,' Leonard Peltier," People, April 20, 1981, pp. 110-114.
91. Ibid.
92. Ibid.; Weyler, Blood on the Land, pp. 190-191.
93. New York Times, February 7, 1976.
94. Amnesty International, p. 41.
95. Ibid., p. 43.
96. Ibid.
97. Discussion with J. S. Milloy, Assistant Professor of History, The University of Winnepeg, Winnepeg, Canada, October 1979.
98. Robert Ecoffey Interview, (He was a trial witness for the prosecution).
99. Fargo Forum, April 14, 1977.
100. Matthiessen, In the Spirit of Crazy Horse, pp. 331-333.
101. Robert Ecoffey Interview.
102. Fargo Forum, April 12, 1977.

103. "An Indian Leader's Fight Goes On,' Newsweek, July 19, 1982, pp. 8-9.
104. New York Times Book Review, March 7, 1988.
105. The Lakota Times May 12, 1983.
106. Rapid City Journal, May 14, 1988.
107. Interview with Jessie Sundstrom, Editor, Custer Chronicle, November 1977.
108. Akwesasne Notes, Early Winter 1975, p. 18.
109. Johanna Brand, The Life and Death of Anna Mae Aquash (Toronto: James Lorimer & Co., 1978), pp. 46-65.
110. Ibid., pp. 114-119.
111. Shirley Hill Witt, "The Brave-Hearted Women: The Struggle at Wounded Knee," Civil Rights Digest, Summer 1976, pp. 38-45.
112. Brand, The Life and Death of Anna Mae Aquash, pp. 129.
113. Ibid., pp. 136-138.
114. Rapid City Journal, May 21, 1983.
115. Jim Gilbert Interview.
116. Brand, The Life and Death of Anna Mae Aquash, p. 19-22.
117. Telephone Interview with Judy Cornelius, May 11, 1983; Duane Brewer Interview.
118. Rapid City Journal, March 11, 1976.
119. Ibid.
120. Telephone Interview with Bob Ecoffev, March 19, 1983.
121. Matthiessen, In the Spirit of Crazy Horse, p. 306.
122. Brand, The Life and Death of Anna Mae Aquash, p. 143.
123. Ibid., p. 145.
124. Ibid., p. 143.
125. Selo Black Crow, Minnesota Public Radio Program B-276, September 29, 1975, St. Paul, Minnesota; Interview with Father Paul Steinmetz, December 20, 1982.
126. Matthiessen, In the Spirit of Crazy Horse, pp. 469-470.

HEROES OR FREEBOOTERS?

1. John S. Blum, et. al., The National Experience (New York: Harcourt Brace and Jovanovich, 1977), pp. 838-839.
2. Ibid.
3. Dan Lounberg, "The New Face of the American Indian Movement," Crisis, December 1977, pp. 463-466.
4. Paula Giese, "The Trials of Russell Means," North Country Anvil, October-November 1975.
5. FBI, Section 31, Bates to Gebhardt, July 1, 1974.
6. Akwesasne Notes, Early Summer 1976, p. 13.
7. New York Times,.June 25, 26, 1976.
8. Annesty International, pp. 66-70.
9. New York Times, July 19, 1978.
10. Ibid., July 21, 1978.
11. Daniel Pedersen, "From 1890 to 1980: Conflict Is Way of Life for Wounded Knee," Des Moines Register, December 28, 1980.
12. Bruce Johansen, "Uranium Rush in Black Hills, S.D.," Nation, April 14, 1979, pp. 393-396.
13. New York Times, March 6, 1980.
14. Weyler, Blood on the Land, pp. 230-231.
15. Rapid City Journal, April 5-30, 1981.

16. "Yellow Thunder Camp," Treaty Council News, 77 United Nations Plaza, New York, N.Y., April 1983, p. 6.
17. Chadron Record, December 4, 1982.
18. Rapid City Journal, December 2, 1982.
19. Ibid., February 27, 1983 and October 24, 1982.
20. "Dennis Banks's Last Stand," Newsweek, March 21, 1983, p. 28.
21. Los Angeles Times, January 4, 1983.
22. Rapid City Journal, February 27, 1983.
23. "Dennis Banks's Last Stand." p. 28.
24. Rapid City Journal, February 27, 1983.
25. Sacramento Bee, January 7, 1983.
26. Los Angeles Times, January 4, 1983.
27. Akwesasne Notes, Summer 1978, p. 29.
28. Ibid., Late Winter 1983, pp. 4-8.
29. Rapid City Journal, January 6, 1983.
30. Ibid., January 14, 1983.
31. Ibid., January 17, 1983.
32. Ibid.
33. Ibid., February 5, 1983.
34. Los Angeles Times, February 27, 1983.
35. "Banks Asks Onondagas for Sanctuary," Wassaja, January-February 1983.
36. "Dennis Banks at the Six Nations," Pacifica Tape Library, Los Angeles, California, 1983.
37. "Dennis Banks's Last Stand," Newsweek, February 21, 1983, p. 28.
38. William Janklow vs. Newsweek, p. 28.
39. Ibid., p. 4.
40. Ibid., pp. 4-5.
41. "Bellecourt: Central Figure among Indian Leaders," Minneapolis Tribune, November 16, 1979.
42. Ibid.
43. Bill Lawrence, "Interview: Vernon Bellecourt," Hustler, pp. 34-38+.
44. Ibid.
45. Denver Post, February 27, 1983.
46. Lakota Times, January 13, 1983.
47. David Sink, "Making the Indian Child Welfare Act Work: Missing Social and Governmental Links," Phylon, December 1982, pp. 360-367; David Salisbury, "Indian Tribes Decry Reagan Budget Cuts," Christian Science Monitor, June 23, 1981.
48. Shirley Hill Witt, "Pressure Points in Growing Up Indian," Messenger, Fall-Winter, 1981, pp. 5-9.
49. Letter from U. S. Senator Janes Abdnor to author, May 21, 1982.
50. The Innocent Victims of the Occupation of Wounded Knee, South Dakota v. the United States, Report to the United States Senate, December 14, 1981, p. 3.
51. Ibid., p. 5.
52. Opinion of Trial Commissioner, June 10, 1981, p. 7.
53. Agnes and Clive Gildersleeve Interview.
54. American Indian Policy Review Commission, Final Report, May 17, 1977, Vol. I, p. 4.
55. Ibid., pp. 571-612.
56. Ibid. pp. 615-617.
57. New York Times, August 7, 1977.
58. Akwesasne Notes, Late Spring 1978, p. 16.
59. Ibid.

60. "Backlash Stalks the Indian," <u>Business Week</u>, September 11, 1978, pp. 153-156.
61. <u>Akwsasne Notes, Early Summer 1981, p. 23.</u>
62. <u>New York Times</u>, May 27, 1981.
63. <u>Lakota Times,</u> December 30, 1983.
64. <u>Rapid City Journal</u>, February 12, 1983.
65. Read Letters to the Editor, <u>Lakota Times,</u> Pine Ridge, South Dakota.
66. <u>Rapid City Journal,</u> January 30, 1983; For sharp criticism of Reagan's Indian policy see Hazel W. Hertzberg, "Reaganomics on the Reservation," <u>The New Republic</u>, November 22, 1982, pp. 15-18.
67. Melinda Beck, "Watt's Latest Stand," <u>Newsweek</u>, January 31, 1983, p. 26.
68. Ibid.
69. <u>U. S. News and World Report,</u> October 18, 1982, p. 18.
70. <u>Lakota Times</u>, December 23, 1982.

Index